PHILOSOPHICAL RO

Philosophical Romanticism is one of the first books to address the relationship between philosophy and romanticism, an area which is currently undergoing a major revival. This collection of specially written articles by world-class philosophers renews the tradition of 'philosophical romanticism' by exploring and enlarging its contribution to topics such as freedom, autonomy and subjectivity; the normativity of the new; philosophy's relation to its own time; memory and imagination; art and ethics; skepticism and irony; and cosmology and technology.

While the roots of romanticism are to be found in Kant, German romanticism and German idealism, *Philosophical Romanticism* shows that it is not a purely European phenomenon: the development of romanticism can be traced through to North American philosophy in the era of Thoreau, Emerson and Dewey, and up to the current work of Stanley Cavell, Charles Taylor and Richard Rorty. The articles in this collection suggest that philosophical romanticism offers a compelling alternative to both the reductionist tendencies of naturalism dominating current "analytic" philosophy, and the skeptical tendencies dominating current "continental" philosophy.

This outstanding collection will be of interest to those studying philosophy, literature and nineteenth- and twentieth-century thought.

Contributors: Frederick Beiser, J. M. Bernstein, Albert Borgmann, Stanley Cavell, Hubert Dreyfus, Richard Eldridge, Jane Kneller, David Kolb, Nikolas Kompridis, Jeff Malpas, Robert Pippin, Fred Rush, Martin Seel, Charles Spinosa.

Nikolas Kompridis is currently Assistant Professor of Philosophy at York University, and author of *Critique and Disclosure: Critical Theory Between Past and Future*.

PHILOSOPHICAL ROMANTICISM

Edited by Nikolas Kompridis

LONDON AND NEW YORK

First published 2006
by Routledge
2 Park Square, Milton Park, Abingdon, Oxon OX14 4RN

Simultaneously published in the USA and Canada
by Routledge
270 Madison Ave, New York, NY, 10016

Routledge is an imprint of the Taylor & Francis Group, an informa business

© 2006 Nikolas Kompridis for selection and editorial matter; individual
contributors for their contributions

Typeset in Goudy by
Taylor & Francis Books
Printed and bound in Great Britain by
TJ International Ltd, Padstow, Cornwall

British Library Cataloguing in Publication Data
A catalogue record for this book is available from the British Library

Library of Congress Cataloging in Publication Data
A catalog record for this book has been requested

ISBN10 0–415–25643–7 ISBN13 978–0–415–25643–8 (hbk)
ISBN10 0–415–25644–5 ISBN13 978–0–415–25644– 5 (pbk)
ISBN10 0–203–50737–1 ISBN13 978–0–203–50737–7 (ebk)

FOR KAELEN

Each individual that comes into the world is a new beginning; the universe itself is, as it were, taking a fresh start in him and trying to do something, even if on a small scale, that it has never done before.

(John Dewey, "Construction and Criticism," *Later Works, Volume 5*)

CONTENTS

ACKNOWLEDGMENTS

Before all, I would like to express my thanks and gratitude to all the contributors to this volume, first, for their splendid contributions, and second, for their enthusiastic support and cooperation.

The volume possesses an uncanny unity that is owed entirely to their contributions and the deep attunement to the volume's overall goals with which they were written. Perhaps, this uncanny unity across differences in approach and in topics is itself a persuasive indication of the contemporary actuality of "philosophical romanticism."

I want also to thank Tony Bruce at Routledge for taking a keen interest in this project from the very beginning, and for his support and patience throughout.

The volume is dedicated to my son Kaelen, from whom I have learned that the success of any new beginning, no matter how well begun, rests on a generous act of self-transformation. His new beginning was mine as well. For that, and *so much more*, I am deeply thankful.

Finally, I should say a word or two about my choice of cover image for the volume, Francisco Goya's 'The Dog', one of his very last paintings. Why *this* image, one might ask? It is surely very poignant, and just as surely very ambiguous. Is the dog in a state of wonder or displacement? Is it meant to suggest hope or despair? Is that sun rising or setting (for him, for us)? Is it mourning an irrecoverable loss, perhaps, the loss of its voice, or awaiting some new possibility, a second chance, a new beginning? What of the future that lies ahead (or hovers above) – is it welcoming or indifferent? What blocks our view? What must we overcome to open our view of things, to open the horizon again? Since these are some of the central questions of romanticism, questions that we cannot and should not evade even if we can't come up with definitive answers, I cannot think of a better cover image to represent this volume than this ordinary-looking dog set in what looks like an 'extraordinary' situation.

CONTRIBUTORS

Frederick Beiser is Professor of Philosophy at Syracuse University. He is the author of *The Fate of Reason* (1987); *Enlightenment, Revolution and Romanticism* (1992); *German Idealism* (2002); and *The Romantic Imperative* (2003).

J. M. Bernstein is University Distinguished Professor of Philosophy at the New School for Social Research, New York. Among his works are: *Against Voluptuous Bodies: Late Modernism and the Idea of Painting* (2005); *Adorno: Disenchantment and Ethics* (2001); and *The Fate of Art* (1992). He edited and introduced the volume on *Classical and Romantic German Aesthetics* (2002) in the Cambridge History of Philosophy series.

Albert Borgmann is Regents Professor of Philosophy at the University of Montana, Missoula, where he has taught since 1970. His special area is the philosophy of society and culture. Among his publications are *Technology and the Character of Contemporary Life* (1987); *Crossing the Postmodern Divide* (1992); *Holding On to Reality: The Nature of Information at the Turn of the Millennium* (1999); and *Power Failure: Christianity in the Culture of Technology* (2003).

Stanley Cavell is Walter M. Cabot Professor Emeritus of Aesthetics and the General Theory of Value, at Harvard University. He is the author of *Must We Mean What We Say? A Book of Essays* (1969, reprinted 1976); *The Claim of Reason: Wittgenstein, Skepticism, Morality and Tragedy* (1979); *In Quest of the Ordinary: Lines of Skepticism and Romanticism* (1988); *This New yet Unapproachable America: Lectures after Emerson after Wittgenstein* (1989); *Conditions Handsome and Unhandsome* (1990); *A Pitch of Philosophy* (Harvard, 1994); *Emerson's Transcendental Etudes* (2003); *Cities of Words: Pedagogical Letters on a Register of the Moral Life* (2004); and *The Day After Tomorrow* (2005).

Hubert Dreyfus is Professor of Philosophy in the Graduate School at the University of California at Berkeley. His publications include *On the Internet* (2001); *What Computers (Still) Can't Do* (3rd edn, 1992); *Being-in-the-World: A Commentary on Division I of Heidegger's Being and Time* (1991); and *Mind over Machine: The Power of Human Intuition and Expertise in the Era of the Computer* (with Stuart Dreyfus, 1987).

Richard Eldridge is Charles and Harriett Cox McDowell Professor of Philosophy and Religion at Swarthmore College. He is the author of *Leading A Human Life: Wittgenstein, Intentionality, and Romanticism; The Persistence of Romanticism* (2001); and *An Introduction to the Philosophy of Art* (2003); and the editor of *Stanley Cavell* (2003).

Jane Kneller is Professor of Philosophy at Colorado State University. She has published in the area of Kantian aesthetics, Kantian social theory, early German romanticism, and Novalis. Her translated edition of Novalis' *Fichte Studies* was published in 2003 (Cambridge University Press) and she is currently working on a book, *Kant and the Power of the Imagination*.

David Kolb is presently the Charles A. Dana Professor of Philosophy at Bates College. His writings concern the history of philosophy and issues around the intersection of modernity and tradition. His books include *The Critique of Pure Modernity: Hegel, Heidegger, and After* (1987); *Postmodern Sophistications: Philosophy, Architecture, and Tradition* (1990); *Socrates in the Labyrinth: Hypertext, Argument, Philosophy* (a hypertext essay collection, 1994). His current work includes discussions of Hegel, of new modes of unity for "places" today, and new modes of scholarly communication.

Nikolas Kompridis is currently Assistant Professor of Philosophy at York University in Toronto. He is the author of *Critique and Disclosure: Critical Theory between Past and Future* (2006), and several papers on various topics in aesthetics, political philosophy, epistemology, and critical theory. He is currently working on a pair of new books: *Educating Subjectivity: Music, Ethics, Politics*; and *The Idea of Freedom as a New Beginning*.

Jeff Malpas is Professor of Philosophy at the University of Tasmania. He is the author of *Place and Experience* (Cambridge, 1999), among other works, and has written extensively on topics within both the "analytic" and the "continental" traditions.

Robert Pippin is the Raymond W. and Martha Hilpert Gruner Distinguished Service Professor in the Committee on Social Thought, the Department of Philosophy, and the College at the University of Chicago. He is the author of several books on German idealism, including *Kant's Theory of Form* (1982); *Hegel's Idealism: The Satisfactions of Self-Consciousness* (1989); and *Modernism as a Philosophical Problem: Henry James and Modern Moral Life* (2001); *The Persistence of Subjectivity* (2005); and *Nietzshe Moraliste Français* (2006).

Fred Rush is Assistant Professor of Philosophy at the University of Notre Dame. He has written several articles on Kant, Hegel, critical theory, and aesthetics. He is completing a book on the philosophical significance of early German romanticism and its relation to Kant and Kierkegaard. He is the editor of *The Cambridge Companion to Critical Theory* (2004).

Martin Seel is Professor of Philosophy at Justus-Liebig-Universität Gießen. He is the author of *Die Kunst der Entzweiung. Zum Begriff der ästhetischen Rationalität* (1985); *Eine Ästhetik der Natur* (1991); *Versuch über die Form des*

Glücks (1995); *Adornos Philosophie der Kontemplation* (2004); and *Aesthetics of Appearing* (2005).

Charles Spinosa is currently an executive vice-president at VISION Consulting, in which role he writes on strategy and marketing. He remains active in philosophy; he is co-author of *Disclosing New Worlds* (MIT Press, 1997), and has published on Heidegger and Derrida in Theodore Schatzki (ed.) *The Practice Turn of Contemporary Theory* (2001); on "Heidegger and Greek Gods," in Jeff Malpas and Mark Wrathall (eds) *Heidegger, Coping, and Cognitive Science* (MIT Press, 2000); and with Hubert Dreyfus on Heidegger and realism in "Coping with Things-in-Themselves," in *Inquiry* (1999).

INTRODUCTION

Re-inheriting romanticism

Nikolas Kompridis

What is philosophical romanticism? Why now?

One does not have to be particularly attentive to notice that a good deal of what goes on in philosophy these days cannot be neatly categorized either as "analytic" or as "continental." Thanks especially to the path-breaking work of Charles Taylor, Richard Rorty, Stanley Cavell, Hubert Dreyfus, Robert Pippin and others, all the crossing and recrossing in recent years between Anglo-American and European philosophical traditions has opened up a depoliticized philosophical space between "analytic" and "continental" philosophy. As a result questions and issues are being approached from a much wider and much more illuminating range of perspectives. And this makes possible previously unthinkable conversations across considerable historical, cultural, and philosophical distance.

For many of us it is a welcome sign that the categories "analytic" and "continental" have lost some of their ideological power to shape philosophical outlooks. While they still play an institutional role as *political* categories, as *philosophical* categories they are becoming increasingly irrelevant. That doesn't mean, however, that they are going to disappear anytime soon as an unstoppable wave of toleration and cooperation spreads throughout the academic philosophical world; but their ideological power has weakened enough to allow us to see the real philosophical divisions that run through it more perspicuously.

The deepest and most decisive of these is the line dividing naturalistic from non-naturalistic views of agency, intentionality, reason, and normativity. Of course, this dividing line runs through the whole culture of modernity, and not just through philosophy. Philosophy merely articulates this division, providing us with one of the most salient expressions of it.[1] For this reason, it is highly unlikely that "strictly philosophical" arguments (or empirical evidence) will ever determine which side is right, or which view, ultimately, "triumphs." That outcome will be determined by the kind of society we choose to become, the kind of future we want for ourselves, the kind of being we think a human being should be.

A second dividing line, almost as decisive, but not as extensive or deep since it runs only through philosophy, intersects the line dividing naturalism from non-naturalism. On one side of this second line is a philosophical orientation and self-image derived from the natural sciences; on the other a philosophical orientation and self-image derived from the humanities. If scientism threatens philosophy from too close an identification with the sciences, then syncretism threatens it from too close an identification with the humanities. In both cases, it is a loss of identity that is threatened, either through a process of assimilation or through a process of hybridization. Neither of these threats can be eliminated; they are part of the existential condition of philosophy. That condition defines philosophy as that form of intellectual inquiry which cannot settle the question of its own identity: its identity will always be a question for it.

What is gained by looking at the divisions in philosophy in this way? First of all, it provides a far more complex and telling picture of the tensions and divisions in philosophy. On which side of these divisions one stands says a lot more about one's philosophical identity and orientation than can be said by using "analytic" and "continental" as terms of self-description. Second, it allows for finer discrimination and classification of the various positions and movements in philosophy, at once more precise and more elastic. It allows for more heterogeneity, and makes visible unexpected alignments and points of difference, creating more capacious and distinctive standpoints from which to reconstruct the history of philosophy. Third, and most important, it helps us see with far greater clarity what is at stake in the ongoing struggle over what it is philosophy is about, what it should be doing, and what cultural role it should play.

The essays collected in this volume represent a distinctive tradition of philosophy that originates in, and continues to be informed by, German romanticism and German idealism. But it is broader and more heterogeneous than either of these, encompassing a wider range of concerns and positions, the nature of which makes it difficult to keep questions of political philosophy, aesthetics, ethics, language and epistemology from becoming entangled with one another. It is a strain of philosophy that is essentially non-naturalistic and that identifies closely with the arts and the humanities. I call it "philosophical romanticism." By "philosophical romanticism" I do not mean to name an explicit philosophical position or a particular historical period. What I am referring to shows up, in whole or in part, in the work of various thinkers, historical and contemporary, some of whom would not wish to be associated with anything called "romanticism."[2] This is understandable, given what romanticism has come to stand for. Unfortunately, it is too often simply taken for granted that "romanticism" reduces to an anti-rationalist aestheticism; that it promotes communitarian anti-individualism; that it involves exaggerated, highly inflated conceptions of difference and particularity; and, that it is informed by impulses, and that it espouses ideals, incompatible with democratic forms of life.[3]

I think of the essays collected here as enacting a re-inheritance of romanticism, which re-inheritance, to borrow a metaphor of Goethe's discussed in Albert Borgmann's chapter, requires a growing backwards towards the past that is inherited. Thus, I want to think of contemporary philosophical romanticism

2

as not simply continuing in various ways and with varying degrees of awareness the philosophical projects of German romanticism and German idealism, but as reaching back to them, reclaiming and renaming a living romanticism for our time, and for a time that will follow our own.

A skeptical reader – and I expect that there will be more than a few – might justifiably ask: "So if it is not anything like what it is commonly assumed to be, then what *is* 'philosophical romanticism?' And why is there a need to make a big deal about it now? Surely, the academic world has an overabundance of philosophical "isms" of various kinds. Adding unnecessarily to the ever-growing and ever-more fragmented number of philosophical specializations and sub-specializations would not be wise. It is already too hard to keep up with all the stuff already out there. If this is going to be more than just one more well-marketed product looking for its own little niche in the academic marketplace, shouldn't it have to prove that it is really worthy of our attention, that it is something that lets us see things in a new way, and so represents a real alternative to what is already available?"

I think the essays in this volume will easily answer the second question ("why now?"), each in their own way. As for the first question, I can begin to answer it by briefly outlining the defining concerns and preoccupations of philosophical romanticism:

(1) Most obviously, philosophical romanticism is a critical response to the Enlightenment interpretation of modernity, not just by making that interpretation problematic, but also by making modernity itself a central, if not *the* central, philosophical problem of the age. This means looking at "philosophical" problems as both responding to the problems of modernity and as implicated in them – as responding to and implicated in living modernity's form of life. Under what conditions, and in what form, can the modern ideals of autonomy, reason, critique, and expressive subjectivity be lived successfully – lived, that is, without reproducing the standard list of self-defeating consequences (e.g. fragmentation, anomie, the leveling of meaning, loss of freedom, self-crippling forms of skepticism, etc.)?

(2) In so far as it understands itself as responding to the conditions of modernity, philosophical romanticism takes the question of what philosophy is or what it should be as a question defined and shaped by those very conditions. So the metaphilosophical question of what philosophy is or should be is inseparable from what it means to be modern, from the question of what constitutes philosophy's own modernity. In being responsive to the conditions of modernity, philosophy is seeking to make sense of the conditions of its own possibility. To make sense of those conditions is to make sense of its own calling, and so the obligation to make sense of its own time is internal to the possibility of philosophy.

(3) As a protean form of life, open to abrupt, incessant and apparently uncontrollable processes of change, modernity is also a very disorienting form of life. The more responsive philosophy is to the conditions of its own modernity, the more unsettled its identity will be. The more unsettled its identity, the more

pressing the question of the *form* in and through which philosophy should express itself. Questions about the nature, sources and limits of its expressivity, of how it can "speak" in a voice of its own, become another one of its central preoccupations. The preoccupation (some might say, obsession) with the problem of its own expressivity draws philosophical romanticism ever closer to the humanities, sharing one of its own defining concerns with those of modern art and literature.

(4) To identify with the humanities rather than with the sciences means to become concerned with the fate of the humanities, with the fate of the "human" as such, particularly now that "the whole humanistic enterprise of trying to understand ourselves" is in danger of becoming "unnecessary and archaic, something that is best preserved as part of the heritage industry."[4] As it comes to recognize that philosophy's fate is bound up with the fate of the culture to which it belongs, philosophical romanticism engages in a normative critique of culture that is continuous with a normative critique of philosophy.

(5) Once the search for a voice of its own is regarded as internal to the activity of philosophy, and once philosophy identifies principally with the humanities than with the sciences, it becomes both more difficult and less necessary to defend some pure form of philosophical argument as the proper (and only) "voice" of philosophy. So the line between "narrative" and "apodictic" forms of argument will be happily and necessarily blurred, allowing the emergence of non-standard and pluralistic forms of arguments. Transcendental, dialectical, hermeneutic, deconstructive, genealogical, and narrative forms of argument all take the form they do because what needs saying or showing can't be said or shown any other way.[5] Ultimately, the purpose of such arguments is to get us to see things in a different light, and that light can shine only when a new perspective is made available to us.

(6) Thus, for philosophical romanticism, the primary task of philosophy is to help enlarge the cultural conditions of intelligibility and possibility, and thereby open the horizon of the future. Since it is especially sensitive to the tendency of the life forms of modernity to become rigid and inflexible, to become unresponsive to the need for new ways of thinking and acting, philosophical romanticism thinks philosophy can play a role, albeit a necessarily modest role, in facilitating normative and cultural change. In this sense, to "romanticize" the world, is to make room for the new, to make room for new possibilities.

(7) The emphasis on the new might make philosophical romanticism indistinguishable from artistic modernism, but that impression gets altered once we see the normative primacy that philosophical romanticism assigns to receptivity. The new is not something we will, something we can make happen; it is something that we "let" happen. As Stanley Cavell, summarizing the view of philosophical romantics like Emerson and Heidegger, puts it, "what happens in the world . . . is always happening."[6] Receptivity is essential to "making" the new possible – receptivity to the present, to the difference between today and yesterday, receptivity to as yet undisclosed possibilities.

(8) For philosophical romantics, thinking about receptivity in this way also invites a reconsideration of our inherited conceptions of agency. The more we emphasize the positive role of receptivity, the more we stress the embodied nature of human agency, and its historical and cultural dependencies, the less likely are we to make mistake mastery for agency. We will come to see agency as a matter of what we let ourselves be affected by rather than a matter of exercising control over what we encounter. This redirection of our inherited notions of agency from mastery to receptivity is what Emerson is up to when he inverts the usual Kantian image of agency as spontaneous activity by making spontaneous receptivity primary. "All I know is reception; I am and I have: but I do not get, and when I have fancied that I have gotten anything, I found I did not."[7]

(9) Contrary to a popular but erroneous view, philosophical romanticism does not take flight from the everyday into some extraordinary dimension; it seeks to reclaim the everyday as the site where the ordinary and extraordinary are at home together, where they animate one another. Philosophical romanticism has a special interest in the everyday, not just as it now is, but as it might one day be. Since the everyday is where all that has gone wrong with modernity is most deeply felt, and where its effects are most devastating, the everyday is where the recovery must begin.

(10) As with early romanticism, philosophical romanticism continues to be preoccupied with the problem of how to recover nature as a source of meaning and orientation. That romantic idea, more than any other perhaps, seems to be completely out of place in a disenchanted universe. Acutely aware that that we are inclined immediately to dismiss this "romantic" idea, Albert Borgmann writes in his contribution to this volume:

> Yet it remains that no one has been able to answer the romantic complaint that there is more to the world than a mechanical universe and a mercenary world and that we cannot be fully human beings until the missing regions of reality have been recovered by an appropriate ontology and appropriated by vigorous practices.

Such a recovery would also require the redemption of the world of things with which we are daily in contact. As Cavell, commenting on Heidegger's essay "The Thing," writes:

> rather than saying [as Kant did] that in order for there to be a world of objects of knowledge for us, a thing must satisfy the conditions . . . of human knowledge, Heidegger is saying that in order for us to recognize ourselves as mortals . . . we must satisfy the conditions of there being things of the world. . . . And this apparently means: The redemption of the things of the world is the redemption of human nature, and chiefly from its destructiveness of its own conditions of existence.[8]

(11) While all of these concerns help to individuate philosophical romanticism, there is one over-arching concern that distinguishes this "tradition" from all other traditions of modern philosophy, and that is the concern with realizing a form of *freedom* that conditions of modernity make possible and thwart at the same time. Reducible neither to negative or positive freedom, it is a non-individualistic form of freedom which aspires to a state in which one is able to recognize one's words and actions as one's own, as *spontaneously* originating from oneself. A lot hangs on how we understand "one's own" and "spontaneously originating from oneself," which is why so much of this philosophical tradition is equally preoccupied with the corresponding and complementary relations of dependence which would make it possible to recognize one's words and actions as one's own (relations of dependence to which the normative ideal of receptivity is closely tied). What kinds of social and political relationships, call them positive dependencies, allow one to recognize one's words and actions as one's own? Can we lead lives that are "self-determining" without being "self-alienating?"[9] But since this form of freedom must also be spontaneous, capable of initiating a self-determining new beginning, the need for which will be inelimminable, philosophical romanticism is just as much preoccupied with the question of what it means to begin anew. In what sense can a new beginning be an expression of freedom and agency? Since the freedom of new beginnings will always be in productive tension with the social relations, cultural practices, and political institutions from which we derive our identities and sense of ourselves as agents, the degree to which we are able to recognize our words and actions as our own will be provisional at best, and the forms of recognition upon which we rely permanently subject to new normative challenges.

Overview

The chapters in this volume touch on all the outlined concerns in multiple, provocative ways. I have organized them into five thematic areas: (I) Beginning anew; (II) Self-determination and self-expression; (III) Art and irony; (IV) The living force of things; and (V) Returning to the everyday.

Beginning anew

The chapters in this section by Stanley Cavell, Nikolas Kompridis, and David Kolb are all concerned with the problem of the new, of how to begin anew, and of how to make sense of a new beginning in relation to the past from which it departs. They are also concerned with the role philosophy ought to play in initiating a new beginning, and why philosophy might be enjoined to play such a role. Stanley Cavell's "The Future of Possibility" was written in response to the "counter-romantic mood" of the times, a mood marked by a pervasive sense of social and cultural exhaustion. For Cavell, this counter-romantic mood provokes the romantic question of the availability of a human future, of whether there can be new possibilities for us. What can human beings say or do to open up the future, to make it responsive to our unmet needs? What are we now saying and doing that prevents the future from opening up to us? What if "the step to the future is closed not through depletion but through fixation?" The worry Cavell expresses here is not that we have lost the power to imagine other possibilities for ourselves, but that we have become so fixated upon our current possibilities that we find unintelligible the possibility of other possibilities, the possibility of other futures.

As a philosophical romantic, Cavell believes that it is philosophy's job to keep the future open – "philosophy as such is thinking for the future." The question of the future of human possibility is also the question of "whether philosophy has a future." That future has to be voiced, somehow, in some new way, making it approachable, responsive. It is philosophy's "peculiar task," claims Cavell, to "think anew," from "a new stance," "after thinking has come to a dead end, or, say, has become exhausted." To think anew in this sense is to think in a *romantic* mood, and to do that is unavoidably to risk melancholy and depression, the classic romantic diseases, and, thereby, to risk "disexpressiveness," the classic romantic fear, the fear that one will lose one's voice or be forced to speak in a voice not one's own. Why take that risk? What could philosophy possibly say, anyway? Maybe, it would be "peculiar" for anyone to take on such a task, but perhaps it would be most "peculiar" for philosophy to take it on. Yet, Cavell is convinced that part of philosophy's peculiarity is that it must struggle for or over its own voice. To regard its peculiar task as giving voice to possibility is to see that task as continuous with philosophy's search for voice, the voice with which to respond to its own time, with which it can respond as philosophy and at the same time open up its time to the future.

In "The Idea of a New Beginning: A Romantic Source of Normativity and Freedom," I explore the complex and ambiguous normativity of the new, showing its internal relation to the modern idea of freedom as a self-determining beginning. The normativity in question is of a kind that cannot be converted into rule-governed or law-like form. Although Kant was the first to articulate the idea of freedom as the capacity to initiate a new beginning, he could not accept a form of normativity that could not be converted into rule-governed or law-like form so he ended up obscuring rather than elucidating its normativity. As Cavell points out in the previous chapter, our hesitation before the new is due to the fact that we are dealing with something that is both unfamiliar and uncontrollable; hence, we are reluctant to regard it as a source of (accountable) normativity. However, our relation to the new is constitutive of our modernity; modernity defines itself by its openness to the new, and by a relation to time, to the present, which makes attunement to the new obligatory. For us, it is not a question of *whether* to be open to the new; but of *how* to be open to it. And, as it turns out, a question of *what* we are open to when we are open to the new. I explore these questions (and their implications for philosophy's relation to the new) in connection with Adorno's critique of the new

7

and William Gibson's novel, *Pattern Recognition*. With help from the films *The Eternal Sunshine of the Spotless Mind* and *The Awful Truth*, I then turn to the question of what it means to begin anew, and how it is that we can begin anew without denying or distorting our relation to the past or to our past selves.

The question of how we can begin anew and "yet remain authentic to what we have been" is at the centre of David Kolb's own reflections on the problem of the new, "Authenticity with Teeth: Positing Process." But how can we remain "authentic to what we have been" if by authenticity we do *not* mean remaining true to some "fixed patrimony?" If this is what we mean by authenticity, then any change affecting the content of that patrimony will be seen as external to it. Drawing first on Hegel, and then on Deleuze (an odd couple if there ever was one, but that's philosophical romanticism for you), Kolb redescribes authenticity as a certain kind of attunement or normative relation to the *process* of change. And that process is understood as a real possibility present in any social or normative formation.

> We come to self-presence within systems of thought and practices of politics and culture that are already underway trying to accomplish their own explicit goals, but which are stages of processes that turn out to have fuller goals, though those goals are graspable within the current formation.

These formations are themselves "inclining toward change." Change does not have to be imposed or dictated from outside. It is a "self-manifesting" process, "positing its own motions and moments." These show up as "inadequacies" or "breakdowns" of some kind, pointing to some other way of continuing the practice, or some other way of going on. "The goal is to develop institutions that show in their operation the process that creates and sustains them." If institutions can do that, opening up the process by which they themselves change in response to tensions and posited "moments" constitutive of the institutions they are, then we can say that this process is "authentic."

Self-determination and self-expression

In "Letting Oneself Be Determined: A Revised Concept of Self-Determination," Martin Seel proposes to rethink and rehabilitate the "passive" or "receptive" aspect of self-determination – the part which consists in our *letting* ourselves be determined. Seel wants to show that there is agency in the letting, and that getting human agency right means recovering the "unity of doing and letting-be-done" (what Dewey called the unity of "doing and undergoing"). Surveying various construals of self-determination, those of Hume, Kant, Hegel, Nietzsche and Heidegger, Seel argues that they all failed to recognize or to unify both aspects of self-determination. "To be able to determine (actively), we must be capable of letting ourselves be determined." For example,

8

we let ourselves be determined in the future as a consequence of decisions we make or of projects we undertake. We also let ourselves be determined by what we let ourselves be open and receptive to – "by our positive and negative affinity to the circumstances of the world." Taking his bearings from Harry Frankfurt, Seel claims that it is what we care about, what comes to matter for us, not the "conscious or reasoned choice of this or that goal which seems to us worth achieving" that determines what we do with our lives. "If we want to be self-determining, we must in the end let ourselves be determined." This view of self-determination comes very close to David Kolb's Hegelian rendering of authenticity as involving a certain kind of attunement, a being-true-to, the process of self-determination, or self-change.

> To *let* oneself be determined as one lets oneself be *determined* – this is the most propitious position. We can thus speak of successful self-determination only insofar as we grant the subjects of these determinations the capacity to enter into the relations in which they are already embedded in their own way.

In their chapters, both Richard Eldridge and Robert Pippin extend and test the possibilities of leading a life that aspires to independent self-determination and self-expression but under inescapable conditions of dependence. In "Romantic Subjectivity in Goethe and Wittgenstein," Eldridge asks the question of what it is to be a human subject, and looks at how romantic literature and philosophy have often responded to this question by figuring the ordinary and the extraordinary, the beautiful and the sublime, and conventionality and originality as irreconcilably opposed.

> Either nature in the aspect of the sublime conspires with inwardness to resist the sways of ordinary life and conventionality, thus setting up the image of the chthonic genius as the exemplar of moral achievement, as in Nietzsche, or nature in the aspect of the beautiful conspires with ordinary life and conventionality, thus setting up an image of pastoralized domesticity as the exemplar of moral achievement, as in certain moments in Rousseau. Each image then stands in immediate criticism of the other, and no stable image of moral achievement persists.

What is interesting to note is that both the rapprochement with the everyday and militant opposition to it can be, and have been, viewed as quintessentially romantic. Both "wild excess" and "pastoralized domesticity" represent romantic moral images. Eldridge puts it this way: "In the grip of such a desire, impossibly seeking original selfhood both against the grain of all conventionality and yet blended with social identity, no one knows what to do." Can these images be reconciled? Can one achieve "autonomous selfhood and continuing sociality?" A look at Goethe's *Werther*, the quintessentially tragic romantic hero, shows how the aspiration to reconcile them can fail completely. A look at Wittgenstein's *Philosophical Investigations*, which Eldridge approaches as an equally romantic text, shows that even if this aspiration cannot be fully satisfied, it can be lived in non-destructive and surprisingly satisfying ways.

Robert Pippin's "On 'Becoming Who One Is' (and Failing): Proust's Problematic Selves" takes up the problem identified by Richard Eldridge and restates it as the problem of negotiating the complicated relations between dependence and social independence, a change of approach that also involves showing that not all dependencies are alike. This appears to be one of the lessons learned by the protagonist/narrator of Proust's famous novel, *Remembrance of Things Past*. And that lesson seems to be connected to another, that in seeking authentic self-determination and self-expression we can fail to achieve it:

> being the subject of one's life, a subject who can lead a life rather than merely suffer what happens, who can recognize her own agency, the exercise of her subjectivity, in the deeds she produces, also means *being able to fail to be one*.

(Perhaps it is this acknowledgment of possible (and likely) failure that explains why Proust's novel does not end up as a "novel of horrible disillusionment" the way that Goethe's *Werther* does.) As Pippin shows, Proust has a much more relaxed, a much more positive view of passivity and receptivity, prepared to let our success as agents hinge on chance and on letting ourselves be determined. That leads to the counter-intuitive idea that agency should not be understood as mastery: "We can only become who we are when, in a way, we cease to be so 'in control.'" Since failure is internal to any attempt to become who one really is, one must continually contend with and make sense of the provisional and often ephemeral nature of what one has been. "In this context, the question of whether there can ever be any end to this provisionality, re-formulation and re-engagement is obviously a pressing one." But how does one "test" one's success or failure in becoming who one is? Can there be a reliable test? For Proust, as we know, that "test" must be conducted in the dimension of time. The problem of recovering "lost time," the problem of Proust's novel, becomes continuous with the problem of "establishing" or "verifying" that one has indeed become who one is – or, "who one 'really' was."

Art and irony

One of the questions at issue in all of the chapters in this section, particularly in discussing the "claims of art" and of "aesthetic reason," is to what extent these claims contradict or confirm Hegel's assertion that "art has ceased to be the highest need of spirit." Put another way: Does the kind of reflection our encounter with art initiates have any "public" as opposed to merely "private" implications for how we live? Another question concerns the proper relation of philosophy to art. It seems that art is able to express philosophical concerns or problems not accessible to or expressible by philosophy independently of art; and that there is something art can say about the kind of writing philosophy is or philosophy requires. Just how close can philosophy get to the concerns of art without losing its own identity? Can art do for philosophy what philosophy can't do for itself? Or can philosophy do for art what art can't do for itself? The history of philosophy's relation to art is not just of philosophy's so-called disenfranchisement of art; it is a long and complicated history of art making demands on philosophy that philosophy can't meet, and of philosophy making demands on art that art can't meet.

In "Poesy and the Arbitrariness of the Sign: Notes for a Critique of Jena Romanticism," J. M. Bernstein identifies romanticism as a complex response to "a profound crisis of reason" arising from the disenchantment and dematerial-izing of nature and the deworlding of freedom and subjectivity. That response explains why romanticism privileges "aesthetic reason."

> If art works are going to be a response to the crisis, to project or insin-uate or promise or exemplify a resolution, then they must suspend the dematerialization of nature and the delegitimation of its voice, and, simultaneously, reveal the possibility of human meaningfulness becoming incarnated, materially saturated and embodied. Hence the core of art's rationality potentiality relates to the role and status of artistic mediums.

To work in a medium is to work with

> a material that is conceived of as a potential for sense-making in a manner that is material specific. Hence in art the medium is not a neutral vehicle for the expression of an otherwise immaterial meaning, but rather the very condition for sense-making.

These first two steps of Bernstein's argument lead to a third step in which the materiality and medium-dependence of art works allows the reconnection of reason to nature as a source of meaning and normativity:

> Since art is that kind of sense-making that is medium dependent, and mediums are aspects of nature conceived of as potentials for sense making, then art, its reason, is minimally the reason of nature as a potential for sense-making at a certain time. . . . The idea of an artistic medium is perhaps the last idea of material nature as possessing poten-tialities for meaning.

However, these connections among art, reason and nature, are broken by Jena romanticism, argues Bernstein. He claims that Schlegel's view of literature as medium-independent (based on the doctrine of the arbitrariness of the

11

linguistic sign), leads to a view of the freedom of the imagination as materially unconstrained, which thereby severs the medium of art from its essential link to nature. It also leads to a kind of skepticism about meaning and a kind of hyper-reflexivity about works of art exemplified in the influential writings of Maurice Blanchot and Paul de Man, and ultimately to the metaphysically motivated substitution of "the fragile aesthetic object" with a "special" kind of philosophical knowing – "the knowing of non-knowledge."

In more ways than one, Bernstein's chapter revisits and updates Hegel's critique of Schlegel and Fichtean romanticism. The chapter by Fred Rush, "Irony and Romantic Subjectivity," offers a defense of romantic irony and subjectivity that tries to blunt the Hegel/Bernstein critique of romanticism by bringing out the essential Kantian modesty, pluralistic openness, and anti-foundationalism of Schlegel and Novalis. By stressing these features of Schlegel's and Novalis's thought, Rush is able to separate them from Fichte's foundationalist views of subjectivity and philosophical reflection, and show that it is Kant, not Fichte, who is the philosophical source of Jena romanticism. Both Schlegel and Novalis thought of modern art as already philosophical, philosophical in a way that philosophy couldn't be independently of art. This is particularly clear in Schlegel's view of irony as the condition in which modern art exists as art – the condition of having to reflect on its own conditions of possibility. For a work of art to be in that condition requires that it be capable of taking two distinct but interlocking stances towards itself: affirmation of the work's own perspective and at the same time reflective distance from the limitations of its perspective. As Rush puts it, "irony is the acknowledgement that works [of art] are 'partial,' in two senses of the word – one who shares the affirmation they contain is partial to them, and one recognizes they are but partial representations of the world." Rush's defense of Schlegel thus consists in showing, contra Hegel, that romantic irony does not collapse affirmation (or commitment) into distance. They are co-equals, and they make it a requirement of modern sensibility to see "experience as lying on a continuum between identification and distance that typifies irony, along with the commitment to constant self-criticism that it entails."

In her chapter, "Novalis's Other Way," Jane Kneller also emphasizes the Kantian sources of philosophical romanticism, and along the way, Kant's own romanticism. Like Rush, she points that those associated with Jena romanticism had a deepy anti-metaphysical and anti-foundationalist orientation, which at the same time was deeply utopian, aiming at the transfiguration of the empirical world. It was an orientation that combined a Kantian respect for the limits of human knowledge with a faith in the capacity we human beings have to get "outside ourselves." Through the exercise of that capacity, we gain access to a non-foundationalist, non-discursive form of knowledge. That access is made possible by art and poetry, not philosophy, and it is an access that is both concrete and highly mediated, reconnecting art to nature, and bridging the Kantian divide between freedom and nature.

It is the most arbitrary prejudice that it is denied to human beings to be able to be outside themselves, to have consciousness beyond the senses. Humans may at any moment be supersensible beings. Without this ability they could not be citizens of the world, they would be animals.

On Novalis's view art does for philosophy what philosophy cannot do for itself, opening up the range of philosophical reflection by opening up philosophy to a form of non-discursive knowledge that has the power to enlarge the field of experience, the logical space of possibility.

The living force of things

The chapters by Frederic Beiser and Albert Borgmann offer quite different accounts of the romantic response to naturalism, and of the romantic idea that there can be a non-naturalistic understanding of nature that can serve as a source of meaning and orientation and that is somehow complementary to but distinct from the naturalistic understanding of nature as the realm of law. Beiser's chapter, "The Paradox of Romantic Metaphysics," goes against the grain of current *Romantikforschung*, inspired by the work of Dieter Henrich and Manfred Frank, the influence of which appears in the chapters by Fred Rush and Jane Kneller (as well as in the writings of Richard Eldridge, Charles Larmore, and others).[10] Beiser argues that Jena romanticism consists in the failed, and bound to fail, attempt to fuse Fichtean idealism and Spinozist realism – i.e. a non-naturalistic view of human freedom and a form of naturalism that places everything within nature as the realm of law. The problem with Fichtean idealism, as Hölderlin put it, was that it made the self everything and the world nothing.[11]

It was the need to explain the reality of the external world, to do justice to the sheer otherness of the non-ego, that eventually forced the romantics to abandon the one-sidedness of Fichte's idealism and to complement it with the "higher realism" of Spinoza.

And that required appeal to a concept of nature as an organic whole, the most important implication of which is that "there is no distinction *of kind*, but only one *of degree*, between the mental and physical." That lets us see, as Schelling put it, "nature as visible spirit" and "spirit as invisible nature." But this apparent reconciliation of nature and freedom is merely notional, hides the fact, argues Beiser, that the organic concept of nature logically requires the rejection of the Kantian/Fichtean conception of freedom as spontaneity: "Once the self finally grasps its identity with nature, it then regards determination by nature as another form of self-determination." Thus, for Beiser, romantic metaphysics failed to avoid the Spinozist trap also identified by Hölderlin, making the world everything and the self nothing.

In some ways, Albert Borgmann's chapter, "Broken Symmetries: The Romantic Search for a Moral Cosmology," can be read as one more romantic attempt to redeem the life of things silenced by the scientific and ethical disenchantment of the world. However, Borgmann is also interested in showing how it is possible to render complementary and interdependent the scientific conception of nature and the poetic or aesthetic conception of nature, which would make room for a "moral cosmology." Borgmann treats Schelling's philosophy of nature as an unsuccessful but promising attempt to combine Kantian lawfulness with Goethean presence. Already in his *Critique of Pure Reason* and in *The Metaphysical Foundations of Natural Science*, Kant expressed the worry that the mechanistic account of nature could not "capture the living force of things." But Kant could not bring himself "to give scientific standing to truly living forces." Goethe, on the other hand, was able as a novelist to capture the "force of contingency and presence." Borgmann's fascinating analysis of Goethe's *Elective Affinities* (that has its own affinities with Eldridge's analysis of Goethe's *Werther* and Pippin's analysis of Proust) sets up an account of how Schelling's critique of the mechanistic view of nature culminates in an attempt to "mark out a realm of agency and life" and thereby "recover the contours of a moral cosmology."[12]

> The interdependent complement of a law of nature is the instance that constrains the law to yield the description and explanation of a state of affairs or an event. Newton's laws of motion merely outline a possible space. They describe an actual world when we insert the values of, e.g., the solar system in place of the variables for mass, acceleration, distance, etc. Among the greatest of instantiations are works of art. They are the most eminent complements to laws. They are instances of high contingency – unpredictable and unprocurable and, in that sense, free. So are the nuisances of life and the results of throwing dice. But these are part of the low contingency of everyday reality. Works of art rise above and lend orientation to the plains of normalcy.

Borgmann thus suggests a solution to Schelling's problem of how to bring together Kantian lawfulness with Goethean presence. Bringing them together conceptually is one thing; fostering the the cultural conditions of receptivity which would make room for the requisite moral cosmology another.

Returning the everyday

The final chapters of the collection are also concerned with the presence of things in our lives, this time primarily from the perspective of how they come to presence in a technological world, as in the chapter by Hubert Dreyfus and Charles Spinosa, and, as in the chapter by Jeff Malpas, how philosophy comes into being in its encounter with how things come to presence for us in the experience of "wonder." In "Further Reflections on Heidegger, Technology, and the Everyday," Dreyfus and Spinosa ask the question of how we can gain a free relation to things, and so continue the line of inquiry opened up by Borgmann. Taking up Heidegger's reflections on technology, they argue that gaining a free relation to technology involves getting right what is most significant about human beings and the everyday things in our midst. They argue on behalf of Heidegger's claim that what is most significant about human beings is not that they are knowers and doers, but that they are "world disclosers" – beings who are capable of opening up "coherent, distinct contexts or worlds in which we perceive, feel, act, and think." The question of what it is to be human is particularly urgent in our historical epoch, the epoch dominated by what Heidegger calls "the technological understanding of being." Heidegger understood that modern technology is completely different and new, but had to struggle with the problem of how to formulate what was new and different about it, and the danger it represents.

> The real danger . . . is not the destruction of nature or culture nor a self-indulgent consumerism, but a new totalizing style of practices that would restrict our openness to people and things by driving out all other styles of practice that enable us to be receptive to reality. This threat is not a problem for which we must find a solution, but an ontological condition that requires a transformation of our understanding of being.

That transformation involves seeing that "our understanding of being" is not something over which we dispose or directly control: it is something we *receive*. It also involves the realization that everyday resistance to the modern technological style requires resisting its "tendency toward one unified world" that impedes "the gathering of local worlds." Living that form of resistance requires learning to dwell in plural worlds, between which we need to move freely, openly. This romantic image of dwelling in plural worlds nicely captures the contemporary talk of living with multiplicity and difference without forgetting the need for gathering and sustaining local worlds.

There is no better way to close this volume on philosophical romanticism than with Jeff Malpas's concentrated and provocative chapter, "Beginning in Wonder: Placing the Origin of Thinking." It could have been titled less modestly, but just as appropriately, "The Origin of the Work of Philosophy." From what impulse does philosophy originate? Is it curiosity or wonder? How is wonder distinct from curiosity? "But what then is wonder, such that it may be the origin of philosophy? And what is philosophy, if wonder is its origin?" To be in a state of wonder, the state out of which philosophy can be said to originate, is to be captured by something "that can enthrall and enrapture," which makes it sound as though one has to be smitten by the things of the world in order to philosophize, and smitten in such a way as to experience the fusion and interplay of the ordinary in

15

the sudden *presencing* of things in a particular taste, a touch, a sound, a movement. What is at issue here is not only wonder at light and sight, but wonder as a response to the often sudden and striking *encounter* with things.

The kind of wonder out of which philosophy arises reveals our prior belonging to the world, our "being already *with* things, already given over to them and them to us." Thus wonder brings into view something both ordinary and strange, trivial and illuminating, something Malpas calls the "event of intelligibility." What implications does philosophy's beginning in wonder have for how philosophy is supposed to understand its own activity?

> Philosophy may thus begin in wonder, but inasmuch as the demand for explanation constitutes a demand for illumination and transparency, so it can also come to constitute a blindness to the interdependence between transparency and opacity, and so also a blindness to the prior belonging to the world that first drives the demand for explanation as such. In this respect, philosophy begins in wonder, but it often ends in alienation – alienation from self, from others, and from ordinary things, as well as the extraordinary. Such alienation is not just a matter of the experience of philosophical difficulty in understanding or explaining how there can be knowledge of the external world or of other minds or of one's own "mental states," but also of how philosophical activity can connect up with the fundamental and everyday experiences of human life, with the things that drive us, that affect us, that matter to us.

Notes

1 It goes without saying that naturalism is hegemonic in philosophy and in the culture of modernity. Of course neither naturalism nor non-naturalism consist of homogeneous positions; there is considerable variety on both sides, and the closer one gets to the borderline, more subtle differences and more hedging, too.
2 For various reasons, "romanticism" is not capitalized in this text. Depending on the context in which it appears the term can refer to the historical period or genre of art, literature, and philosophy, to a specific philosophical tradition, as in the case of "philosophical romanticism", or, more generally, to a philosophical ethos or attitude.
3 For an excellent detailed overview of various misconceptions about philosophical romanticism, see Richard Eldridge's introduction to *The Persistence of Romanticism* (Cambridge: Cambridge University Press, 2003) pp. 1–30.
4 Bernard Williams, "Philosophy as a Humanistic Discipline," *The Threepenny Review*, Spring 2001.
5 For example, the kinds of arguments marshaled by Heidegger and later Wittgenstein.
6 Stanley Cavell, *Conditions Handsome and Unhandsome. The Constitution of Emersonian Perfectionism* (Chicago: University of Chicago Press, 1990) p. 20.
7 Ralph Waldo Emerson, *Essays*, p. 261. For analysis and interpretation of this passage of Emerson's, see Stanley Cavell, *This New Yet Unapproachable America. Lectures after Emerson and Wittgenstein* (Albuquerque NM: Living Batch Press, 1989); and Nikolas

Kompridis, *Critique and Disclosure: Critical Theory Between Past and Future* (Cambridge MA: MIT Press, 2006).

8   Stanley Cavell, *In Quest of the Ordinary. Lines of Skepticism and Romanticism* (Chicago: University of Chicago Press, 1988) p. 66.

9   Robert Pippin, "Hegel, Ethical Reasons, Kantian Rejoinders," in *Idealism as Modernism*, pp. 98–9. See also Richard Eldridge, *The Persistence of Romanticism*, pp. 20–1.

10 See Dieter Henrich, *The Course of Remembrance and Other Essays on Hölderlin*, ed. Eckart Förster (Stanford: Stanford University Press, 1997), and Manfred Frank, *The Philosophical Foundations of Early German Romanticism*, trans. Elizabeth Millan-Zaibert (Albany: SUNY Press, 2004).

11 Friedrich Hölderlin, *Sämtliche Werke, Grosser Stuttgarter Ausgabe*, vol. 3, ed. Friedrich Beissner (Stuttgart: Cotta, 1945–85) p. 236.

12 In contrast to Beiser's reading of Schelling, Borgmann emphasizes Schelling's insistence on the "freedom and contingency" in nature just as much as necessity and law. However, as Beiser would concur, Borgmann points out that in his Jena years

> Schelling's comments on the natural sciences became more impatient and peremptory. A dialectical monism of mind and matter began to eclipse and cover up the dilemma Schelling had uncovered in the *World Soul*. Eventually, art (and later religion) took the place of nature as the great datum philosophy had to acknowledge and understand.

17

Part I

BEGINNING ANEW

1

THE FUTURE OF POSSIBILITY

Stanley Cavell

In 1994, invitations to the Sixth *Le Monde* Forum held at Le Mans, with the title "The Future Today," posed to its participants an introductory statement for discussion that contained the following passage: "Everything is worn out: revolutions, profits, miracles. The planet itself shows signs of fatigue and breakdown, from the ozone layer to the temperature of the oceans." The disappointed or counter-romantic mood of this passage produced the following intervention from me, one that has distinctly affected my work since that time.

Keep in mind that I come from that part of the world for which the question of old and new – call it the question of a human future – is, or was, logically speaking, a matter of life and death: if the new world is not new then America does not exist, it is merely one more outpost of old oppressions. Americans like Thoreau (and if Thoreau then Emerson and Walt Whitman, to say no more) seem to have lived so intensely or intently within the thought of a possible, and possibly closed, future that a passage like the one I just cited would be bound to have struck them as setting, that is putting on view and enforcing, an old mood. Compare with that passage a sentence from the opening chapter of Thoreau's *Walden*: "Undoubtedly the very tedium and ennui which presume to have exhausted the variety and the joys of life are [themselves] as old as Adam."[1] This is, I think we might say, a compounding or transcendentalizing of the sense of the worn out, showing that concept of our relation to the past to be itself nearly worn out. And this recognition provides Thoreau not with compounded tedium and ennui but with an outburst of indignant energy. He continues: "But man's capacities have never been measured; nor are we to judge of what he can do by any precedents, so little has been tried."[2] This is why he can say, when he appeals to sacred writings and defends them against the sense that they are passé: "We might as well omit to study Nature because she is old." As if to say: Beware of the idea of The Future Today – that is, of Today's Future; it may be a function of Yesterday's Today, and you will discover that Today was always already Tomorrow, that there is no time for origination. Yet Thoreau's idea is that time has not touched the thoughts and texts he deals in. What chance is there for us to share his faith today, now? When is now?

An intricate intersection of old and new is also the burden of Emerson's great essay "Experience." Indeed, it should not be surprising that America found its philosophical voice in thinking, and having to think, about the future – if you grant me the claim that Emerson and Thoreau represent the founding of the American difference in philosophy. Emerson writes in "Experience":

> In liberated moments we know that a new picture of life and duty is already possible. . . . The new statement will comprise the skepticisms as well as the faiths of society, and out of unbeliefs a creed shall be found. . . . The new philosophy must take [these skepticisms] in and make affirmations outside of them, just as much as it must include the oldest beliefs.[3]

This demand for integration sounds like a beginning of that American optimism or Emersonian cheerfulness to which an old European sophistication knows so well how to condescend. But it has never been sure, even where I come from, that Emerson's tone of encouragement is tolerable to listen to for very long – as if it expresses a threat as much as it does a promise. I note that his words about finding a creed out of unbeliefs, unlike those of his familiar followers as well as detractors, contain no word of hope. What occurs to us in liberated moments is that we know. That "we" claims to speak for us, for me and for you, as philosophy in its unavoidable arrogance always claims to do; and moreover claims to speak of what we do not know we know, hence of some thought that we keep rejecting; hence claims to know us better than we know ourselves. I suppose Emerson is claiming to know this, as we do, only in liberated moments. Then presumably his writing the thought was one such moment – as if something about such writing tends to such moments. Does reading such writing provide us with further such moments? If – or when – it does not, how could we fail to find Emerson's claims intolerable?

Let us provisionally surmise just this much from Emerson's passage: if we are to think anew it must be from a new stance, one essentially unfamiliar to us; or, say, from a further perspective that is uncontrollable by us. If we formulate this by saying that to think the future one would have to be in the future, this sounds like a way also of summarizing Nietzsche's *Beyond Good and Evil*, whose subtitle is *Prelude to a Philosophy of the Future*. This is as it should be since that text of Nietzsche's – like so many of Nietzsche's texts, early and, as in this case, late – is pervasively indebted to Emerson's *Essays*, "Experience" pivotally among them. But unlike his reiterated, implicit rebuke to Wagner's *Der Kunstwerk der Zukunft*, Nietzsche's continuous invocation of Emerson is something we will recognize and remember only intermittently, in liberated (vanishing) moments.

Beyond Good and Evil speaks, as Emerson does, of thinking through pessimism to affirmation. Nietzsche specifies pessimism as what is most world-denying; Emerson's name for this, in the passage I cited from "Experience," is skepticism; its opposite Nietzsche specifies as world affirmation, which is precisely what Emerson understands the new world to be awaiting. Nietzsche specifies the world-affirming human being as one who, reconceiving time, achieves the will to eternal recurrence; Emerson specifies this figure as one who finds the knack of liberation in moments. Since Nietzsche's thinking through pessimism in his articulation of nihilism, the philosophical stakes he puts in play are not alone the national existence of the so-called new world, but the continuation of old Western culture, of what it has so far told itself of the human.

Emerson and Nietzsche are variously explicit in saying that philosophy as such is thinking for the future – so that their sense of going beyond philosophy in what they say about the future is at the same time a claim to the stance of philosophy. In *Beyond Good and Evil*:

> More and more it seems to me that the philosopher, being of necessity a man of tomorrow and the day after tomorrow, has always found himself, and had to find himself, in contradiction to his today. . . . By applying the knife vivisectionally to the chest of the very virtues of their time, they betrayed what was their own secret: to know of a new greatness of man, of a new untrodden way to his enhancement.[4]

We might think here of Plato, who is explicit in his *Republic* in staging the moment of philosophy, specifically of philosophy's entrance into the public world, as in some future that is now datable only paradoxically, as when philosophers will become kings; in the meantime we (re)construct our city only with words, as with the text of the *Republic*. Or we may think of Kant, for whom moral sanity depends on a reasonable hope for future justice, and his necessary positing of the good city as a Realm of Ends – where each of us is legislated for in legislating for all. Unlike Plato's *Republic*, Kant's good city is essentially unrepresentable by philosophy: if we could represent it we could claim to know it, but that would leave room neither for genuine faith in our effectiveness toward a future nor for genuine knowledge of the present. (Among the choices we have for dating the modern, one may choose Freud's discovery that anything I think, except negation, I can dream, and anything I dream is a work of representation, hence a guide for myself to what I all but inescapably already know.)

Nietzsche's words about the philosopher as the man of tomorrow and the day after tomorrow, hence as necessarily having to find himself in contradiction to today, and his specifying this as his vivisecting the very virtues of his time, are virtual transcriptions (with a Nietzschean accent) of words of Emerson's. In Emerson's "Self-Reliance" there is a pair of sentences I have previously had occasion variously to cite and interpret: "The virtue in most request is conformity. Self-reliance is its aversion." I will merely assert here that Emerson uses his signature concept of self-reliance, in contradiction to the conforming usage of it, to characterize his writing, hence his thinking; hence to place it, in every word, in aversion to, and as averse to, his conforming society. And assert further that Nietzsche's sense of the philosopher's words as in "contradiction to today" are not only a rewriting of Emerson's "aversion to conformity," but that Emerson's citing of conformity as a virtue, and precisely as epitomizing the virtues of his today, from which in every word he writes his writing recoils ("Every word they say chagrins us" is another formulation in "Self-Reliance"), casts Emerson as the figure most directly captured in Nietzsche's terrible image of the philosopher as vivisectionist. (This is evidently a further shade of intervention than Socrates is colored with, as gadfly or midwife.) That Emerson is supplying words for Nietzsche's description of the philosopher – or himself, of course – comes out again later in the same paragraph, in his speaking of philosophical violence as the philosopher's betraying his own secret of a new greatness of man, which Nietzsche specifies as an untrodden way to man's enhancement.

The picture of philosophizing as taking steps on a path is an ancient one, but Emerson's "Experience" is remarkable for its concentration on the idea of thinking as a new succession, or success: "To finish the moment, to find the journey's end in every step of the road . . . is wisdom."[5] This might strike one as giving up on the future; the possibility will come back. The English translation of Nietzsche's passage rather loses another echo from "Experience" in rendering Nietzsche's philosophical secret of a new greatness of man by speaking of an untrodden way to man's "enhancement." "Enhancement" conceives greatness, which Nietzsche calls *eine Grösse*, as found on a path to his heightening, whereas Nietzsche's characterizing the newness as a *Vergrösserung*, enveloping and intensifying *Grösse*, leaves quite open what form the magnification is to take – "expansiveness" is one characteristic Emersonian term for productive human thinking.

The value of leaving open the proposed idea of human increase or expansiveness is that it is at the end of the section begun by Nietzsche's paragraph concerning the new greatness that he reformulates the question of the future by asking: "Today – is greatness *possible*?"; a question explicitly both about the human capacity to think and the capacity to will. Now Emerson's "Experience" can be taken as an essay on greatness, and greatness precisely as preparing a joyful future – if the human past of grief, with its endless cause for grievance, may be set aside, not so much survived as outlived. As Emerson here measures grief by his response to the death of his young namesake son, he repeatedly figures the possibility of expansiveness, in mood and in thought, as the greatness of pregnancy (English used to speak about "being great with child"). This is how I read Emerson's call for the "soul [to attain] her due sphericity," and his account of "the great and crescive self," perhaps above all his report of insight from "the vicinity of a new . . . region of life," which he conveys as a region of new life giving a sign of itself "as it were in flashes of light." He reports:

> And what a future it opens! I feel a new heart beating with the love of the new beauty. I am ready to die out of nature and be born again into this new yet unapproachable America I have found in the West.[6]

24

What's going on? What number of hearts does Emerson feel beating, one or two? If America opens a joyful future, why is it "unapproachable" – which seems to imply that it is forbidding, or hideous, or otherwise beyond clear grasp?

Put aside the arresting fact that Emerson identifies the writing of this essay with the growth of an embryo, and focus on the underlying Emersonian proposition (not without apparent contradiction elsewhere) that greatness is to be found only in little things. From Emerson's essay "Character":

> Is there any religion but this, to know, that whenever in the wide desert of being, the holy sentiment we cherish has opened into a flower, it blooms for me? If none see it, I see it; I am aware, if I alone, of the greatness of the fact.[7]

This perhaps marks the point of Neitzsche's radical difference with Emerson. In *Beyond Good and Evil* we have heard: "The time for petty [*kleine*] politics is past: the very next century will bring the fight for the dominion of the earth – the *compulsion* to large-scale [*grössen*] politics."[8] This prophecy made in the late eighties of the nineteenth century seems a fairish way of tracking the progress of the twentieth, including a certain prediction of an essential region of Heidegger's reflections on his century. Has the century ended? Was it in 1989? And in Berlin, or in Moscow?

Plotting the reticulation of differences implied in the audiences or possibilities of America and of Europe is still worth some patience; and I would like to sketch here two further encounters between Emerson's *Essays* and Nietzsche's *Beyond Good and Evil* – (1) regarding the specific way time is reconceived; and (2) regarding the appearance of the feminine in characterizing, or protecting, philosophy.

Take time first. In "Circles," perhaps Emerson's most concentrated pages on the concept of the new (pages from which Nietzsche cites explicitly and climatically near the end of his Untimely Meditation with the title *Schopenhauer as Educator*), the first paragraph contains these sentences: "Our life is an apprenticeship to the truth that around every circle another can be drawn."[9] This is, whatever else, a formulation of what an Emersonian essay is, and does; each Emerson essay contains such self-formulations. Emerson goes on at once to gloss the image of the circle by saying that there is "no end in nature, but every end is a beginning," and that "under every deep a lower deep opens," and that "there is always another dawn risen on mid-noon." Thoreau – I suppose Nietzsche's only rival as an interpreter of Emerson – recasts the thought more famously in the concluding two brief sentences of Walden: "There is more day to dawn. The sun is but a morning star."[10] The figuring of "more day" or of "another dawn risen on mid-noon" provides a hint for taking Nietzsche at his characteristic word when he says that the philosopher is the man of "tomorrow and the day after tomorrow."

English and French picture the leap over the day after today as its being "after" (*après*) that after. But German says *Übermorgen*, which plays uncannily into the attention Nietzsche gives to the prefix *über*. I take it we are to understand the relation of *Übermorgen* to *Morgen* on the model of the relation of *Übermensch* to *Mensch* – so that the *Übermensch* precisely is whatever the man of *Übermorgen* is, its discoverer or creator. This singles out the one who has learned (which must mean that he has taught himself) how to think of, and how to live in, a further day, which is to say, in the future – the thing Thoreau calls "more day" and that Emerson calls "another dawn," an after dawn. Such a day is not one assurable from the fact of the past risings of the sun (Hume was right enough about that), but one the course to which is plottable only through an ambitious philosophy, thinking it through, aversively, which is to say, by turning ourselves around, not presuming at once to head into the future. The future – call it America, or call it the world that may be – cannot be approached as in a picture of a boat approaching a shore, not even a magic boat called *Mayflower* (Emerson apparently, if momentarily, fantasizes otherwise in his first defining work, *Nature*); nor, as Nietzsche tried to explain in *Beyond Good and Evil*, can it be taken by the strength we picture as of blood and iron. (Heidegger, accursed, for a time neglected Nietzsche's warning not to take hope from this dangerous, self-prescribed healing.)

It seems that we have to learn to think after thinking has come to a dead end, or, say, has become exhausted. We may express this as philosophy's coming to conceive of itself as taking place in, or as, an aftermath, an aftermath of thought, sometimes now called a closure of philosophy or of history.

Here one should recollect philosophy's tendency to fantasize scenes of its own destruction, as if it becomes burdened with prophecy; I cite, for example, the knowledge Wittgenstein expresses in *Philosophical Investigations* that his thinking is repeatedly taken as merely destructive of everything important. Philosophy evidently has its melancholy side – why else would Emerson so insist, and so gratingly, on finding instants of joy, and Nietzsche on his tincture of laughter? Philosophy's knowledge was always painful, as when Emerson says, at the close of "Experience":

> I know that the world I converse with in the city and in the farms, is not the world I *think*. I observe that difference, and shall observe it. One day I shall know the value and law of this discrepance.[11]

Take this as philosophy's ancient perception of the distance of the world from a reign of justice. (When philosophy refuses any longer to cede this reign to theology's afterlife, as Emerson and Nietzsche write to refuse it, the destruction entailed by justice becomes an event, and the approach of an event, within finitude, an approach the living may represent to themselves, without being able to decipher it.) This distance, or discrepance, is the world's public business, now on a global stage. I hope nothing will stop it from becoming the principal business of the twenty-first century. But it is, on my view, while a task that philosophy must join in together with every serious political and economic and,

26

I would say, therapeutic theory, not now philosophy's peculiar task, as it was in Plato's *Republic*.

Philosophy's peculiar task now – that which will not be taken up if philosophy does not take it up – is, beyond or before that, to prepare us, one by one, for the business of justice; and to train itself for the task of preparation by confronting an obstacle, perhaps the modern obstacle, to that business: I mean a sense of the exhaustion of human possibility, following the exhaustion of divine possibility.

Nietzsche, after Emerson, links the sense of human exhaustion with the sense of the unresponsiveness of the future to human will (how different is that from the sense of the unresponsiveness of God?). As if the grief in witnessing the discrepance from the reign of justice has depended on, and been fixated by, a despair of change. Here we have to think of Emerson's description of the mass of men as in a state of secret melancholy; Thoreau will say "quiet desperation"; Nietzsche sometimes formulates the sense of exhaustion as "boredom"; I note in passing that it is as some intersection of boredom with melancholy that Wordsworth, at the beginning of a different romanticism, takes a general human withdrawal of interest in the world as the condition to which poetry is called to respond, or to teach response. It may be thought of as a state of tragedy not experienced as such – which is, I allow myself to add, a way of characterizing skepticism.

Secret melancholy, Emerson says. Naming a historical phenomenon, this names not an isolated matter of an individual sense of pointlessness in saying anything, but a more general sense of lacking, or failing, the language in which to express what has to be said, as if calling philosophical as well as political attention to a shared aphasia. Editing these remarks for publication to an English-speaking readership, I am moved to confess how swiftly, with how few steps, one can feel out of earshot of one's native company. It is my latecomer's view of Lacan that his emphasis on registers and textures of speech, and its failures (say, its wants), epitomized by his fascination with Roman Jakobson's ordering of the linguist's interest in aphasias, casts all psychoanalytic experience of discrepance as of forms of what might be grasped as (a transfiguration of the concept of) aphasia. This reconstitutes, or re-enacts, Freud's early ("pre-psychoanalytic") interest in the phenomenon of aphasia; one might call it the phenomenon of disexpressiveness.

So philosophy becomes a struggle against melancholy – or, to speak with due banality, against depression. It is here that I conceive the image of woman to enter into the thoughts of Emerson and of Nietzsche, in Emerson briefly and hopefully, in Nietzsche recurrently and scandalously. Those who find Nietzsche an essential voice in today's confusion of tongues will often wish that he had not spoken as he did about "the woman." Without a word of argument now, I simply state my sense that it is still today worth hearing his naming the struggle between the man and the woman as something that cannot without remainder be understood in political terms. (But then for Nietzsche neither can politics be so understood.) Nor does it seem to me that the struggle he names is simply an allegory of an individual condition, though that is no less true for his writing than it is for Plato's in the *Republic*. I would rather begin with the fairly open fact of Nietzsche's fear and need of the woman, seen as functions of his demand for a future, hence for a philosophy of the future. (How could his treatment of the thought of woman be exempt from the confession he makes about the way of his confessions, that they are crooked? The idea of the path to the future as crooked bears placing against Emerson's idea in "Experience" of the path to reality as indirect, or glancing.)

A sense of the image of the woman in *Beyond Good and Evil* could in practice begin by putting in conjunction its following ideas: that steps to the future are aversive, or put otherwise, that philosophy's way to the future is through destruction; that since this is the only source of genuine philosophy, the philosopher essentially risks suffering and melancholy, risks "suffocating from pity"; that woman is "clairvoyant in the realm of suffering," and her character-istic faith is that love, perhaps identified with pity, can achieve everything; and that "every profound thinker is more afraid of being understood than of being misunderstood."[12] What I begin to draw from this conjunction is the sense of woman – I suppose leaving open where that turns out to exist – as Nietzsche's most essential audience, the best and the worst. She is the best, because she understands, through her power of love and of pity, his suffering and (as when he all but identifies his condition with that of Jesus) his insatiable, suicidal desire for love; so understands that in his words his body is on the line. But she is also his worst audience, because her faith cannot compass his terror of love, that it will crucify him, which means, in the terms of this book of his, that it will deny that he is "still unexhausted for [his] greatest possibilities," hence in those terms, since the future is what is new, she would deny him his future. Taking woman as his essential audience, he identifies with her while he differ-entiates from her – as when he characterizes man as "the sterile animal" and when he, too, perceives the philosopher as pregnant.

I think of philosophy's essential difficulty in representing its future in connection with its inability to establish the conditions of philosophy, the look and sound in which, in particular historical contexts, it can have its peculiar effect, take its aversive, unassertive steps. A group of half a dozen texts not always associated with philosophy come to mind here, texts in which the future is presented as a course so puzzled as to call for philosophy. I first encountered these texts during the period of two or three years in which I was searching, not always hopefully, for a way to begin teaching and writing philosophy that I could believe in and make a living from.

I had begun reading Wittgenstein's *Investigations*, perhaps the first philosoph-ical text which successfully for me staked its teaching on showing that we do not know, or make ourselves forget, what reading is. I found its attack on meta-physics – call it the history of philosophy as such – by, in Wittgenstein's formulation, "leading words back from their metaphysical to their everyday

28

use," to be continuously and surprisingly surprising, discovering surprise where you least expect it, in the banal. So that philosophy came to begin for me with the question whether philosophy has a future, which means whether there is an event that has happened to end philosophy, or whether philosophy's ending is an event that happens within philosophy, hence precisely and essentially continues it.

This opening of philosophy for me, synchronized with the opening of philosophical and non-philosophical texts towards one another, was set in motion in the year or two leading into 1960, marked as the years in which three of the texts I name here, three films it happens, were released: Ingmar Bergman's *Smiles of a Summer Night*, Alain Resnais and Marguerite Duras's *Hiroshima, Mon Amour* and Antonioni's *L'Avventura* – each associated with the question about whether something new might happen (Samuel Beckett's *Waiting for Godot* and *Endgame* were still new), shadowed by the question whether love is an exhausted possibility, a question incorporating some residue of a fantasy of marriage. In each case the answer is presented as in the hands of a woman – in Marguerite Duras's woman of Nevers it is one capable, in Duras's words, of giving herself body and soul, which she characterizes as discovering marriage; in Antonioni's Claudia (in the form of Monica Vitti) it is a woman capable of granting a man's terrible wish, as it were, for her to change her love for him into pity; in Bergman's Desirée (Eva Dahlbeck) it is a woman who at the end sits smoking a cigar behind the head of a man who speaks to her with unaccustomed sincerity as he is lying on a couch, and who answers him by saying that she is putting his love into her big pocket, a man in whom she explicitly perceives the child – all a fair parody, in acceptance, of the image of Freud and what he called (around the period in which the film is set) his therapy of love. (One of Freud's debts to old philosophy.) These are works of cinematic art decisive in modifying concepts, as in America, of what were thought of as foreign films and as ordinary movies, hence in modifying concepts of high and low culture, and of what constitutes a medium of thought – ones which, in a word, served to alter the iconography of intellectual conversation.

Those presentations are oddly tied up in my mind with two works from Victorian England that one with my intellectual itinerary could hardly fail to know about but that it happens I had not read until the years in question; neither of them may be counted among the greatest accomplishments of their illustrious authors, but both took on the urgency of the doubts I was harboring then – a familiar story. One is Dickens's *Great Expectations*, an inspired title at once for all the ways human beings try to take the future by storm – by boat or by blood and iron – and, turned ironically, a title for the disappointment or depression that follows the deflation of that inflation. It is Pip who is explicitly said to be a young man "of great expectations," yet he can be said to have had no expectations great or small, but simply to have formed his character on a love quite independent of its fate in the world – on love, in short; a figure, therefore, with some hard things to learn, yet who survives the learning. Miss Havisham's

29

expectation can be said to have been the greatest, measured by the power of her outrage and vengeance when she allowed it to be shattered – call it the expectation of being loved; it was a disappointment, a piece of learning she refused to survive, her body in its rotting bridal gown becoming a private monument of the institution of marriage. I recognize Miss Havisham as Cinderella, of course with a sublimed conclusion – *eternally* awaiting the glass slipper – a realistic conclusion, as it were, given the difficulty of locating and knowing her original away from the dance. I imagine it as Pip's princely understanding of her, from his hallucinating on a wall of her barn the shadow of a hanged woman who is missing one shoe. How far therefore is he imagining that the condition of women is more generally to be understood as laid down by fairy-tales in the early transfiguring enchantments that never achieve their undoing; tales whose ending is not just unhappy but arbitrary, as though an ending is missing, possibilities not exhausted but cursed? But then what assures us that a given narrative is a fairy-tale? Isn't *Great Expectations* more or less a fairy-tale? And while Dickens, significantly, wrote two endings for the novel – one in which Pip and Stella do not have a future together, and one in which they do – does either of them really untie the suffering we have come to know about?

Take Miss Havisham's story to be the projection of a woman's sense of the unapproachability of the future. The other book I adduce from that time and place is John Stuart Mill's *Autobiography*, which contains a man's companion sense of the event of the future, or of its non-event. He characterizes his early state of crisis exactly as a despair over the exhaustion of possibilities – a state in which he broods over the fact that Mozart and Weber had exhausted all the possible combinations of tones that will achieve beautiful melody. This is the form familiar to Nietzsche in assigning to philosophy the task of the future. Miss Havisham shows possibilities not to be everywhere exhausted but everywhere untried, which suggests that the step to the future is closed not through depletion but through fixation, through the withholding or the theft of love; it is the fate Nietzsche's phantasm threatens him with in the face of woman's fanaticism of love. The philosophers of possibility who see us not as sensing depletion or loss but as fixated through a lack of trial or experience are rather Emerson and Thoreau. The philosophers who later take fixation itself as the negation of philosophy, its most intimate opponent, are Heidegger and Wittgenstein. In the later work of both we are invited – or seduced? – to take steps, but without a path. And that is itself to acknowledge a future, the fact of futurity. Shall we say that this opens the future to the human will? It opens the will, like a hand.

Notes

1 Henry David Thoreau, *Walden and Other Writings*, New York: Modern Library, 2000, p. 9.
2 *Ibid.*, pp. 9–10.
3 Ralph Waldo Emerson, *Essays. First and Second Series*, New York: Vintage, 1990, pp. 256–7.

4 Friedrich Nietzsche, *Beyond Good and Evil*, in Walter Kaufmann (ed.) *Basic Writings of Nietzsche*, trans. Walter Kaufmann, New York: Modern Library, 1992, p. 327.
5 Emerson, *Essays*, pp. 248–9.
6 *Ibid.*, p. 255.
7 *Ibid.*, p. 278.
8 Nietzsche, *Beyond Good and Evil*, p. 321.
9 Emerson, *Essays*, p. 173.
10 Thoreau, *Walden*, p. 312.
11 Emerson, *Essays*, pp. 261–2.
12 Nietzsche, *Beyond Good and Evil*, p. 419.

2

THE IDEA OF A NEW BEGINNING

A romantic source of normativity and freedom

Nikolas Kompridis

The very object of praxis is the new.
(Cornelius Castoriadis, *The Imaginary Institution of Society*)

At the beginning of the film, *Buffy the Vampire Slayer*, its heroine-to-be complains rather bitterly about the unfair grade she received from her high school history teacher: "He tells me, 'You have no sense of history.' I have no sense of history?! – He wears a brown tie!" A few seconds later, seeking to revive her spirits by indulging in some power-shopping at the local mall, Buffy is drawn to an attractive leather jacket but decides against buying it the moment one of her chums pronounces it "so five minutes ago." Although an inconsequential part of the film, this little scene does possess a certain significance of its own.

An altogether typical conversation between teenage mallrats offers itself as an unexpected occasion for considering what it means to have a sense of history and to a live a life under conditions in which our freedom (or lack of it) is somehow fatefully connected to how we respond to the new and to our own time. These questions are at the heart of Baudelaire's well known reflections on the experience of "modernity" in *The Painter of Modern Life*, and I will be drawing upon them later in this chapter. They are also questions that are daily confronted in everyday life, in reflective and not so reflective ways. They are daily confronted in everyday life because they are among the unavoidable questions we face in our ongoing efforts to live the life of modernity.

We should not make too much of the significance of this scene. But it is worth understanding the cause of Buffy's indignation. Buffy is not indignant because someone who has no sense of fashion has accused her of having no sense of history; she is indignant because she believes that her teacher is not himself fully aware of what having a sense of history means. The "brown tie" is not just a sign of her teacher's unfashionable style of dress, but of an epistemically faulty grasp of the times in which he lives. How can someone who believes in having a sense of history be so unattuned to his own time? To be thus unattuned is somehow to be in the wrong relation to time; hence unable to see and understand the difference between yesterday and today – the difference between old and new. Her teacher's failure is not so much a failure of knowledge as it is of sensibility.[1]

It is not incidental to the significance of this scene that an originally attractive article of clothing is made instantly undesirable the moment it is pronounced to be "so five minutes ago." An evaluative vocabulary in which something can be "so yesterday" or "so five minutes ago" is certainly attuned to the present, or, more precisely, to the presence of something new. But such an attunement to the new raises the question of whether the attunement to its presence is based on freedom or on compulsion. It raises the question of whether we are attuned in the right way to the new, and, of what it is about the new that calls for, enjoins, our attunement. Just what role does the new play in the life forms of modernity? What sort of normativity (if any) does it possess, and how is it connected to the romantic idea of freedom as a new beginning? And what does all this imply for philosophy? Must philosophy rethink its own relation to its time and to a culture that is seemingly obsessed with the new?

The normativity of the new

We are accustomed to thinking of normativity as law-like or rule-governed in form, and I think it is indisputably the case that normativity is generally law-like or rule-governed. However, I think it is a mistake to assume that all normativity is law-like or rule-governed, or that it must always take such form. That this assumption needs to be put in question becomes evident whenever we encounter a new kind of experience, a new meaning, a new perspective, or a new cultural practice. On such occasions, in so far as we are dealing with something genuinely new, we find that we are typically unable to make sense of its newness by drawing upon (or subsuming it within) our current conceptual and evaluative frameworks: the new poses a challenge, a normative challenge, to our sense-making practices. We construe the new as a *normative* challenge because we feel ourselves answerable to it, answerable both to what makes it new and to why its newness eludes and unsettles our sense-making frameworks. Thus, in coming to terms with the new, we are often compelled to revise or abandon some previous way of thinking and acting in light of some insight the new itself makes possible; we are compelled to go on differently, understanding that we could not go on as before if we are to go on more reflectively.

Since the new does not conform to rules or laws, we cannot formulate *ex ante* normative procedures for responding to it, or rules or methods for dealing with it. What makes the new *new* is that we can only say what's new about it *after* we have recognized and understood the difference it introduces in virtue of what we can think and do. Our old ways of thinking and acting could not have prepared us in advance for the difference the new introduces. There are no empirical or inferential relations that allow us to move from the old to the new without expanding our empirical or logical space: the new introduces empirical and inferential relations that were not already there. Thus, afterwards, we may speak of a moral and epistemic gain in understanding, the test of which is the capacity of our new way of thinking and acting to reorder, reorganize, and redescribe our previous empirical and inferential relations.

If we insist on thinking that normativity necessarily takes rule-governed or law-like form, we will be unable to recognize or explain the normativity of the new. Ultimately, we will be unable to provide an account of normativity itself (at least not in terms irreducible to a naturalistic vocabulary). To preserve some version of the Kantian distinction between freedom and nature or, as McDowell puts it, between the space of reasons and nature as the realm of law, we must appeal, as Kant and his idealist successors did, to some notion of spontaneity. The great innovation of Kant's critical philosophy was to reconceive reason as spontaneously self-determining, or self-legislating, such that reason

> frames for itself with perfect spontaneity an order of its own according to ideas to which it adapts the empirical conditions and according to which it declares actions to be necessary even though they have not taken place and, maybe, never will take place.[2]

The normativity that is implicitly appealed to here is tightly connected to a newly disclosed *possibility* ("ideas"), compelling enough to make certain kinds of actions necessary "even though they have not taken place and, maybe, never will take place."

Of course, one of the immediate concerns provoked by talk of reason's "perfect spontaneity" is the worry that reason's self-determining freedom would be indistinguishable from an arbitrary or random freedom. What kind of normativity can spontaneity possess if it is not something that can be converted into the normativity of rules or laws? If we're going to make room for spontaneity, then it has to be rule-governed. But if spontaneity must always take rule-governed form, will we not lose something normatively essential to it? Certainly, it cannot be said of Kant that the spontaneity he had in mind lacked sufficient constraints. As Robert Pippin points out, "in Kant's actual theory, the spontaneity in question is far less than 'perfect.'"[3] Indeed, for all of Kant's appeal to spontaneity, the normativity upon which it draws is immediately converted into the more familiar and acceptable normativity attributable to rules and laws. Just as the epistemic spontaneity of the understanding (*Verstand*) and reason (*Vernunft*) are constrained by the forms of intuition and the architectonic of reason, so the practical spontaneity of the will is constrained by the moral law. The conversion of spontaneous practical freedom into law – "the law of freedom" – is meant to eliminate all arbitrary and random elements; but this process of elimination requires the exclusive identification of reason's spontaneous freedom with the procedure of universalizable normative justification – i.e. the categorical imperative, and other similar normative procedures of public justification inspired by it (e.g. Habermas's "U" principle and Rawls's "veil of ignorance"). And so the attempt to eliminate randomness and arbitrariness, to quell the various anxieties provoked by Kant's "revolutionary" reconceptualization of reason, ends up obscuring the very feature from which it draws its normativity: the spontaneous freedom of new beginnings, beginnings that are creative responses to intractable problems, irresolvable conflicts, and communication breakdowns.

After all, what is spontaneity if not the mark of freedom, the freedom to initiate a new beginning when our action possibilities appear blocked or restricted? Spontaneity does not just play an epistemological role in our lives, showing that if something is going to count as an x, the rules or criteria by which it counts as an x will have to be settled or determined by the subject itself, not by anything "given" to it. While this new approach is a momentous move in the history of epistemology, there is much more to spontaneity than epistemic spontaneity. Imported into the epistemological domain is a much richer and much more encompassing conception of modern freedom, freedom reconceived as "a new self-determining beginning."[4]

Because rule-governed or law-like normativity is the only form of normativity that Kant could recognize or accept, indeed, the only kind that is generally recognized or accepted, he was unable fully to articulate the normativity of freedom as "a new self-determining beginning." That is why even when he directly confronts the problem of the new in the third critique, Kant remains highly ambivalent about its status as a source of normativity. If we are to understand and explain the normativity of this form of freedom, and put its still unrealized possibilities into practice, we will have to understand and explain the normativity of the new. Otherwise, we will render opaque and inaccessible a source of normativity that is essential to the lives of modern agents, and to the institutions of modern societies. Modernity as a form of life is unthinkable without this often puzzling and certainly ambiguous source of normativity.

Neuzeit: the time of the new

According to the influential view first articulated by Kant, and rearticulated with minor and major modifications ever since, modernity is to be understood as the age that comes into being with the coming of age of reason: the autonomy of reason and the autonomy of modernity reciprocally elucidate and legitimate one another. To assert, as Habermas has, that an autonomous modernity must "create its normativity out of itself"[5] is simply to assert of modernity what Kant asserted of reason, namely, that autonomous reason is "concerned with nothing but itself."[6] Just as reason must determine for itself what can count as a reason (for belief or action), without appealing to or relying upon tradition, external authority, the senses, or the passions, so modernity must create its normativity out of itself, reassuring itself about its own "legitimacy" without appealing to or relying upon any inherited or alien sources of normativity.

In defending this Kantian idea of modernity as autonomy, Habermas, like Kant before him, also helps himself to the idea of modernity as "a new self-determining beginning." The new beginning is not understood merely as some original founding moment, e.g. the Enlightenment, to which succeeding generations of moderns look back as a point of orientation and with which they must constantly realign themselves. Rather, such a new beginning is an ever-present possibility, because modernity is "the epoch that lives for the future, that opens itself up to the novelty of the future."[7] If the idea of modernity as autonomy defines a new relation to normative justification, such that moral or political or cognitive norms must meet a demanding public test of their validity, then the idea of modernity as a new beginning defines a new (exciting and burdensome) relation to time, such that the success of any critical analysis of our social practices and political institutions will require that we be properly responsive to our own time. So if one definitive feature of being modern is getting into the right justificatory relation to our norms, another is getting into the right relation to our time. Already Hegel and Marx were working out as well as presupposing this new normative relation to time:

> It is surely not difficult to see that our time is a birth and transition to a new period. Spirit has broken with what was hitherto the world of its existence and imagination and is about to submerge all this in the past; it is at work giving itself a new form . . . [F]rivolity as well as the boredom that opens up in the establishment and the indeterminate apprehension of something unknown are harbingers of a forthcoming change. This gradual crumbling is interrupted by the break of day that like lightning all at once reveals the edifice of the new world.[8]

> For our part it is our task to drag the old world into the full light of day and to give positive shape to the new one. The more time history allows thinking humanity to reflect and suffering humanity to collect its strength, the more perfect will be the fruit which the present now bears within its womb.[9]

Employing the now standard terms in which this contrast is typically drawn, Hegel characterizes the transition between old and new, between past and future, as involving a dramatic break with the past and a dramatic new beginning. The break, when it comes, is sudden; the new world, arising like a lightning flash (Blitz), is unknowable in advance. In this tensed relation between old and new, the present, the time in which we now live, must become the special focus of our attention. It is not just that it lies at the point between an old world about to fade away and a new one about to emerge. Failure to be receptive to the present, attentively attuned to its hidden significance, would mean failure to get into the right normative relation to our own time. That relation comes with a particular normative expectation: that we are *obligated* in some indeterminate sense to bring about the new beginning, obligated to help give "new form" to our form of life by apprehending the present in which we live as a time of "birth and transition." Meeting that obligation requires that we apprehend precisely those possibilities within the present upon whose realization the new form of the world depends. This stance towards the present supposes a complementary stance of anticipatory openness towards the future, to how things might otherwise be.

There is some obvious ambiguity in both of these passages as to whether the emergence of the new is something we undergo or something we ourselves initiate. For although Marx makes it sound as though *we* are the ones dragging "the old world into the full light of day," he also makes it sound as though the birth of what the "present now bears within its womb" takes place according to a will and logic of its own. This ambiguity may be irremovable, because the new is not something over which we exercise direct control. There is always a contingent aspect to the new, and, moreover, once it emerges, the new can possess a self-instituting and self-verifying quality. Here I want only to emphasize that both Hegel and Marx suppose that we are under some normative obligation to help facilitate the self-determining new beginning now visible to us only as an "indeterminate apprehension of something unknown." For it is through our capacity and willingness to do this that we realize the form of freedom upon which the practices, hopes and aspirations of modernity depend.

Standing alongside the idea of modernity as autonomy, then, is this other idea of modernity as the time of the new, the time of new beginnings. These two ideas of modernity stand in a complex relation to one another: they feed off one another, compete with one another, and put pressure on one another. If it were not for the fact that modernity's self-understanding has been shaped as much by its relation to time as by its relation to normative justification, the idea of modernity as an "unfinished project" (Habermas) would not be as implausible or self-undermining. The "epoch" that is expectantly open to the novelty of the future is not an "epoch" that can bring its idea of itself to completion. It cannot "ground" itself in its claim to autonomy so long as it is open to the new, to unforeseeable new beginnings.

Since the idea of modernity as the time of the new is as constitutive of modernity's self-understanding as the idea of modernity as autonomy, failure to acknowledge the complex interconnections and tensions between these two ideas of modernity can lead to an emphasis upon one at the expense of the other – typically, an emphasis on the idea of modernity as autonomy at the expense of modernity as the time of the new. So long as modernity's idea of itself does not accommodate both its constitutive relation to the new and to normative justification, it will continue to run up against the paradox of "grounding" itself in the ungroundable.

When Habermas proposes to ground modernity's legitimacy in its power to create its own normativity, and so provide it with the requisite "self-reassurance," he unwittingly entangles modernity in the skeptical problems and paradoxes with which we are now only too familiar. A form of life that understands itself as radically unprecedented, self-suffcient and self-creating can never satisfy, only multiply, its need for "self-reassurance." The same kinds of skeptical problems arise in Kant's attempt to render his new conception of reason crisis-proof, exercising its powers in time, but not in any way subject to time. Thus, Kant ascribes to reason the power of spontaneously beginning a new series of events, which power is derived from reason's intelligible character.

> [R]eason . . . is present to all the actions of human beings in all conditions of time, and is one and the same, but it is not itself in time, and never enters into any new state in which it previously was not; in regard to a new state, reason is determining but not determinable.[10]

But if reason is not determinable by time, if it "never enters into any new state in which it previously was not", it cannot learn anything new; it cannot experience *Entzweiuung* – i.e. crisis, breakdown, a conflict between itself and its concept. Hence its putative capacity to initiate a new beginning would be meaningless: only if it were in time, receptive to the conditions of time and history, would the new beginning count as a meaningful response to conflict, crisis and breakdown, would appear as a harbinger of something new, of something better than what we have known.

In living time as the time in which "the new and the unexpected continually happen,"[11] modernity's form of life is decentering and destabilizing, putting into question modernity's own epochal uniqueness and its project of autonomy. Modernity's openness to the novelty of the future renders it open to its own self-dissolution (and not just as a notional possibility).[12] Openness to the novelty of the future keeps perpetually open the possibility of a future different from the past, a possibility that contains the promise of a break with the past, and the promise of a new beginning. But with such an open, expectant stance to the future, we also impose a number of burdens upon ourselves, rendering our form of life crisis-prone. Because the present is where new and old, contested pasts and possible futures, constantly collide with one another, the present is subject to crisis experiences arising from such disorienting collisions. It is an unavoidable consequence of this future-oriented stance: the more open to discontinuity we are, the more we have to wrestle with the problem of continuity.

Employing the concepts "space of experience" and "horizon of expectation" as metahistorical categories, Reinhard Koselleck demonstrates how modernity – *die Neuzeit* – "is first understood as a *neue Zeit* from the time that expectations have distanced themselves ever more from all previous experience."[13] Formerly, getting oriented was a matter of drawing upon inherited experience to open up the horizon of expectation, a matter of connecting what we've known to what may be. But experience must not only have an open relation to the future, it must be able to illuminate the future, to serve as a bridge to what is to come, to what might be. The relation to time distinctive of *Neuzeit*, however, is one in which "the previously existing space of experience is not sufficient for the determination of the horizon of expectation."[14] It can no longer be derived or deduced from previous experience: that is the very condition of being modern, of living *Neuzeit*. This is why the significance of the present moment can appear urgent and obscure, portentous and opaque – why, in other words, normative disorientation is an ever-present possibility, and normative reorientation an ever-arising need. It also indicates why normative reorientation will necessarily require normative reflection on our relation to time, and the disclosure of hidden, unnoticed, or suppressed possibilities lying within our own time. Getting reoriented requires disclosing the significance of the present moment, reconnecting it, if only tentatively and temporarily, to an inscrutable future and a fragmented past. In living *Neuzeit*, we become aware of just how much our sense-making practices, including our critical practices, depend on the disclosure of alternative possibilities, and on our capacity freely to begin anew.

Along with awareness of this dependence, comes an awareness of responsibility to the future. Our openness to the novelty of the future turns the future into a source of pressure, by which we are forced to regard ourselves as responsible for getting right "the proportion of continuity and discontinuity"[15] in the forms of modernity we inherit and pass on. That same pressure is exerted upon our practices and institutions, obligating them to be time-responsive, capable of new beginnings. As Dewey noted in *The Public and its Problems*, to the extent that our existing political institutions and social practices limit our action possibilities, it may not be enough to reform them so that they can meet newly arising needs; we may have to form a new "public," bringing about a change in self-conception and collective sensibility at the same time as we bring about a reform of our political institutions. "To form itself, the [new] public has to break existing political forms. This is hard to do because these forms are themselves the regular means of instituting change."[16] Change at this level requires a change in the means by which change is instituted: it requires new political forms capable of being more time-responsive, responsive to the demands for and of new beginnings. But as yet, we do not really know how to design our political forms and institutions to be time-responsive. That is largely due to the fact that we have not yet learned how to coordinate our normative relation to public justification and our normative relation to the new, to new beginnings.

Dewey's point is a much needed reminder of our dependence on the new as a source of normativity, and as a vehicle of normative change. Of course, the idea that forms of life are subject to breakdowns, and therefore always in need of renewal, is one of the central arguments of Hegel's *Phenomenology*. Going one step further than Kant, Hegel proposed a time-incarnated conception of reason that incorporated normative and conceptual change. That project stalled after the demise of the Young Hegelians. These days we are presented with a choice between some version of instrumental reason (Hobbesian or Humean) or some version of reason as public justification (neo-Kantian or neo-pragmatist). But Hegel had considerably more in mind, and it is very difficult to bring that into view today.[17] It is a fairly constant feature of the "philosophical discourse of modernity" that it has been primarily a disputatious discourse about the idea of modernity as autonomy, and appeal to the new has been generally employed as a skeptical strategy to undermine the claims of autonomy. It has been a one-sided and counter-productive discourse, and will not be revitalized unless both ideas of modernity, as autonomy and as a new beginning, are brought together in a new way.

This is not just a "philosophical" problem; we are in need of a future much more welcoming than the one we now face – a future with a much wider horizon, less bleak, more hopeful. The future, for which so much of the old was sacrificed and so much of the new embraced, once had a much broader horizon of possibility, and a much more welcoming visage. To say that an openness to the novelty of the future, an openness to disruption, discontinuity, and unforeseeable change, is what makes modernity historically distinctive as an epoch and as a form of life is not to say quite enough. For what had until recently made such openness to disruption and discontinuity sustainable, which is to say, what made it livable, endurable, was the expectation that the "novelty" to come would be of a kind that answered our hopes and needs. While massive, jarring, relentless, accelerating change continues apace, our experience of such change has altered. It has altered because our relation to the future has altered – perhaps, for good.

We sense that our possibilities may be exhausted, our utopian energies used up.[18] Our capacity for hope requires a capacity to disclose our possibilities in some new way.

Such possibilities must be capable of reopening the future, rendering it responsive to our hopes and needs. A future no longer open to our hopes and needs reinforces our sense of bewilderment and our sense of cultural exhaustion. Given its relation to time, its openness to the novelty of the future, modernity is an inherently unsettling form of life; perhaps, an unsustainable one. So while it may be true to describe modernity as the epoch that is open to the novelty of the future, this is not normatively informative. Should we be open to any and every manifestation of the new, to any and every novelty the future might bring? Or are there better and worse ways to be open to "novelty" of the future, ways that enlarge rather than contract the horizon of the future?

Open to what, exactly?

"The new statement is always hated by the old, and, to those dwelling in the old, comes like an abyss of skepticism."[19] "What is new . . . is always *evil*, being that which wants to conquer and overthrow the old boundary markers and the old pieties; and only what is old is good."[20] These two nearly identical characterizations of the relation between old and new, the first from Emerson's "Circles," the second, a direct echo, from Nietzsche's *The Gay Science*, together evoke an image of the new that continues to find resonance today. But this image of the new – as a transgressive, unruly, unsettling force in our lives, and as standing in a mutually hostile relation to the old – is not so new anymore. Indeed, it has gotten to be rather old, a commonplace of modern culture.

This now "aging" idea of the new which Emerson and Nietzsche evoke is no longer as easy to imagine or defend today. It was not easy then, either; but for different reasons. Modernity was still new; its future still seemed open, full of possibilities. After the close of a barbaric century, and the beginning of another that already promises more of the same; after seeing what can be done in the name of the new, we are justifiably wary of it. The distance between Emerson's and Nietzsche's time and our own is marked by a deepening ambivalence in our relation to the new, in our openness to the "novelty" of the future. Now that there is nothing solid left to melt into air, and we must evidently learn to adapt to life conditions of fluidity, hybridity, of rapid and relentless change, we are also growing weary of the new. Modernity is an exhausting form of life. Having had to endure the constant enmity between old and new, we are much less sure which to trust; which to regard as "good," and which as "evil." It could very well be that construing the relation between the new and old as necessarily hostile opens up one more abyss of skepticism.

Yet, for all of our ambivalence about the new, we can't but be open to it. The promise it makes, no matter how many times it is broken, is a promise without which we cannot render our circumstances intelligible or bearable. For us it is not a question of *whether* to be open to the new; but of *how* to be open to it. An openness to the new is an openness to possibility, and it would seem to involve some commitment or obligation to enlarging the cultural conditions of possibility. But talk of "openness" sounds pretty empty to most people. Open to what? Are we supposed to be open to anything that comes our way? Could it be that we are not open in the right way? The normative meaning of "being open to the novelty of the future" is ambiguous between being open in a merely passive come-what-may way, and being open in some way that would allow us retrospectively to endorse the future to which we were open. It may well be decisive which way we are open to the new if the novelty that the future brings is to answer our real needs – our sense-making and problem-solving needs.

Unfortunately, the question of whether we are open in the right way to the new and the future is not one we tend to ask. And it is not one we have time to ask, because our relation to time is such that the time for such questions is very scarce: we must "keep going." We must "keep going" – not knowing exactly how or exactly where – under the vertiginous pressure of our modern relation to time. As we are hurled forward into the future at an ever-accelerating speed, there is less and less time and, therefore, more and more pressure to bring into some intelligible pattern the shifting relationships between the past, the present and the future. There is also evidence that as the pressure mounts to make sense of these shifting relationships, so does the pressure to abandon or regard as useless the effort. Perhaps, nothing is more typical of the culture of modernity than the insistent, endlessly repeated exhortation to embrace the new, to embrace the future – a future into which we seem to rush headlong. Whether it is in the name of "globalization," the "new economy," or the "digital age," no matter how familiar, no matter how transparently ideological or strategic, it is an exhortation with an almost irresistible appeal. Because the source of its power is deeply and inseparably anchored in modernity's self-understanding, the appeal to the "new" retains its power to be a highly persuasive – perhaps the most persuasive – rhetorical device of modern culture.

The new is not just seductive; it also arouses fear: the fear of being left behind, rendered out of date, obsolete – and this fear is not the only or primary appeal of the new. The new also contains the promise of something better, a promise that tomorrow might be better than today. It can only be exploited for ideological purposes or for profit *because* it contains the promise of something better than what we have known. It is this promise that also brings the new into proximity with myth. Adorno and Benjamin regarded the recurrent appeal to the "new" as an appeal possessing a "mythical" power, since such change as we are exhorted to embrace is change we are forced to experience as our unavoidable fate rather than as the outcome of our reflectively exercised agency.

In "Late Extra," one of the last entries in *Minima Moralia*, Adorno offers an extremely compressed critique of the new that sheds some light on why we have become both weary and wary of it, and why we nonetheless remain open to it, why it still *appeals* to us, and why we crave it, like addicts. Anticipating a distinction that I'll make explicit a little later, the primary object of Adorno's critique is the *capitalist new*, the new whose function is to sustain the "phantasmagoria of capitalist culture,"[21] the seductive universe of commodities whose apparently inextinguishable allure is newness itself. Once it is instrumentalized by the capitalist enterprise, the new comes into contradiction with itself, and becomes an ever-present, demoralizing reminder of "the fact that there is no longer anything new."[22] The capitalist new seeks to consume the idea of the new, turning the new into that which can be consumed. But the idea of the new cannot be completely instrumentalized or turned into an object of consumption, for the capitalist enterprise must continually draw upon the idea of the new, must keep it "alive" as a possibility; otherwise it could not be turned into its very opposite: a phenomenon of compulsion rather than of freedom. "The layer of spontaneity, freedom from intentions, on which alone intentions flourish. . . . Of it the idea of newness dreams."[23]

The experience of spontaneous freedom of which "newness dreams" is the experience of being open to something whose emergence *as* something new is made possible by our openness to it. To this form of openness to what is new and other to us, Adorno gave the name "mimesis." By contrast, the capitalist new is a medium of "false mimesis": a compulsive, repetitive absorption in the "sensation" of newness, in the "*frisson du nouveau*." Reduced to sensation, the new acts as a stimulant and an intoxicant; the craving for the new displaces "the fulfilled relation of experience to its subject-matter."[24] So from this perspective the defining feature of modern capitalist culture looks to be the perpetual, ultimately unsatisfiable, craving for novelty, exposing the ambiguity in the idea of modernity as the epoch that is open to the "novelty" of the future.

Looking back at the nineteenth century, Adorno singles out as particularly salient inscriptions of the new as sensation Poe's short story "The Maelstrom" and Baudelaire's *Les Fleurs du Mal*. Both Poe and Baudelaire are read as attesting to, while at the same time rebelling against, "the fact that there is no longer anything new." Poe's story presents itself as an allegory of "the novel," the new, and its central image is "that of the breathlessly spinning yet in a sense stationary movement of the helpless boat in the eye of the maelstrom."[25] The narrator of "The Maelstrom" finds that as he is spinning hopelessly towards his doom, his original terror becomes supplanted by an "unnatural curiosity" about the other objects spinning in the maelstrom.

> I now began to watch, with a strange interest, the numerous things that floated in our company. I *must* have been delirious – for I even sought *amusement* in speculating upon the relative velocities of their several descents towards the foam below.[26]

The sensation which Poe's narrator feels as he plunges to his watery doom turns the threat of annihilation into a promise of joy. "The new, a blank space in consciousness, awaited as if with shut eyes, seems the formula by means of which a stimulus is extracted from dread and despair. It makes evil flower."[27] In this case, however, the new is not "evil" because it seeks "to conquer and overthrow the old boundary markers and the old pieties"; it is "evil" because it is a medium of "satanic" compulsion, an addictive sensation. An image from the last poem of *Les Fleurs du Mal*, "Le Voyage," captures the compulsive and addictive character of the new that Adorno regards as definitive of the new as such. It is the image of the world-weary *flâneur* plunging "au fond de l'Inconnu pour trouver le nouveau," thereby seeking an escape from the "oasis d'horreur dans un désert d'ennui" that is life under conditions of capitalist modernity. It does not matter ("qu'importe?") whether the "unknown" into which one plunges is a heaven or hell; all that matters is that one finds something *new*, something that at once comforts and revives the exhausted modern subject. The descent into the "unknown" is of course an escape from or evasion of the everyday, a turning away from the common everyday world we share. To plunge into the "unknown" is to admit that there is no hope – the everyday world cannot be redeemed, which is why the *flâneur*'s search for the new is also the search for the cessation of sensation.[28]

Looking around at the marketized commodity world of today, one could say that Baudelaire's *flâneur* has morphed into a "coolhunter," and found gainful employment, if not meaning, in the advertising agencies of the world. Plunging into the heart of the multitude, the "coolhunter" looks for the next new thing.

William Gibson's novel, *Pattern Recognition*, pays close attention with insights into the yearning for the new, both in its capitalist form and in a form that evades even the subsuming powers of the capitalist imagination.

Gibson updates Baudelaire's reflections on the *flâneur* by looking at the contemporary world's hunger for "cool." His novel's protagonist, Cayce Pollard, is distinguished above all by a capacity to detect the new, to see it coming before everybody else. She can pick out some new thing not yet commodified, and "point a commodifier at it." "[L]iterally, allergic to fashion,"[29] the reverberations of her own body tell her whether a proposed new way of branding products will work. She just knows what works, but very much like Kant's genius, in whom "nature in the subject" gives the rule to art, "[s]he has no way of knowing how she knows."[30]

Although the peculiarities of her embodiment allow her to distinguish between successful and unsuccessful instances of the capitalist new, she is herself yearning for the unconsumably and unsubsumably new. Answering this yearning is a fragment of film footage that is mysteriously uploaded on the web, followed by other fragments whose connection to one another is obvious but at the same time utterly inscrutable. Along with the other members of the small internet discussion group spawned by the footage, she is devoted to this material, to savouring it, and to making sense of it. The fragments consist of two lovers meeting and embracing.

> They are dressed as they have always been dressed, in clothing Cayce has posted on extensively, fascinated by its timelessness, something she knows and understands. The difficulty of that. Hairstyles too.
>
> He might be a sailor, stepping onto a submarine in 1914, or a jazz musician entering a club in 1957. There is a lack of evidence, an absence of stylistic cues, that Cayce understands to be utterly masterful. His black coat is usually read as leather, though it might be dull vinyl, or rubber. He has a way of wearing its collar up.
>
> The girl wears a longer coat, equally dark but seemingly of fabric, its shoulder-padding the subject of hundreds of posts. The architecture of padding in a woman's coat should yield possible periods, particular decades, but there has been no agreement, only controversy.
>
> She is hatless, which has been taken either as the clearest of signs that this is not a period piece, or simply as an indication that she is a free spirit, untrammeled even by the most basic conventions of her day. Her hair has been the subject of similar scrutiny, but nothing has ever been definitively agreed upon.[31]

The newness of the footage makes it uncontextualizable, even by prodigious "coolhunters" like herself; it can't be "placed," resists placement, in existing logical space. It looks like the new in its pure, uncontaminated form, making it a fragile protest against the "the fact that there is no longer anything new," and the expression of a fragile hope that this is not an inescapable circumstance. When watching the fragment Cayce "knows that she knows nothing,"[32] but she also feels as though she is the fortunate witness of a genuinely new beginning. "It is as if she participates in the very birth of cinema, that Lumière moment, the steam locomotive about to emerge from the screen, sending the audience fleeing, out into the Parisian night."[33]

Her relation to this footage is also protective, motivated by an interest in preserving its purity, as if there were some way to walk on newly fallen snow without leaving a mark on it. Given her line of work, and modern culture's hunger for the new, her worry is understandable: keeping the forces of commodification at bay is part of an existential struggle against resigning herself to the "fact that there is no longer anything new." So when the head of an agency whose logo design she has been asked to evaluate probes her knowledge of the fragment, she plays dumb, acting as though she doesn't know what he, the aptly named Hubertus Bigend, is talking about. When it becomes clear that she cannot keep up the pretence, she asks him why he is so interested in the footage. His reply is revealing, for he makes it clear he already understands that they have two quite different, though equally passionate, attitudes to the new: his is thoroughly instrumental, while hers is deeply existential.

> "Am I a true believer? That is your first question. Because you are one yourself. You care passionately about this thing. It's completely evident in your posts. . . . But am I a believer? My passion is marketing, advertising, media strategy, and when I first discovered the footage, that is what responded in me. I saw attention focused daily on a product that may not even exist. You think that wouldn't get my attention? The most brilliant marketing ploy of this very young century. And new. Somehow entirely new."[34]

For Bigend, what makes the footage new is that it audaciously markets "a product *that may not even exist*." Recall for a minute how Kant described the power of reason to create a new normative order, thereby making some actions "necessary even though they have not taken place and, maybe, never will take place." Here we have the potential power of marketing to create a desire for products that do not exist, and may never exist. In other words, the power to create a consuming desire for what is unconsumable – the mere possibility of newness itself. Phantasmagoric, indeed. Cayce Pollard, on the other hand, holds out the hope that an openness to the genuinely new will be transformative and redemptive – the hope (or faith) that our possibilities are not exhausted, that a new beginning is still possible; that there is a kind of new that is not commodifiable, that can't be instrumentalized, but rather, answers real human needs.[35] Not the least of these is the need to interrupt the automatic course of daily life and the flow of historical events, making room for an expression of our freedom to begin something new, to express the agency that is proper to "beginners."[36]

In these exchanges between Pollard and Bigend, our two basic orientations to the new are revealed as both colliding and entangled with one another. There is the new as something to be instrumentalized and consumed, as an exploitable source of ecstatic escape from the everyday. And there is the new as something that by definition can't be instrumentalized and consumed, as that which returns us to the everyday in a new way. The former leads us inevitably to the demoralizing conclusion that "there is no longer anything new," and makes us skeptical about our agency; the latter keeps open "the future of possibility" (Cavell), and so keeps open the possibility of a future that responds to our present needs. Most certainly this latter conception of the new can be, and needs to be, distinguished from, and defended against, contemporary culture's drunken infatuation with the idea of limitless possibility – be it in the form of a consumer-driven reordering of our quotidian life, the cosmetic remaking of our "plastic" bodies,[37] or the various familiar attempts at "ecstatically" escaping the constraints of a life shared with others – diving into the "unknown" with the help of a bungee cord or a drug. We can conceptually distinguish an orientation to the new as a form of compulsion from an orientation to the new as an expression of our agency and freedom; and, we can distinguish the new as a commodity and narcotic from the new as a normative challenge and normative resource. But we have to work very hard to do this because these relationships to the new as "objects" of our needs and desires are often very much entangled with one another, and will need continually to be disentangled from one another so long as we live under the conditions of capitalist modernity. So long as these conditions obtain, it will always be hard to know which kind of "evil" we are dealing with. Adorno's critique of the new as a seductive piece of capitalist ideology is implicitly an argument *for* the new – the new as a normative challenge to our current practices and a normative resource for going beyond them, and so is just as much "a rebellion against the fact that there is no longer anything new." The practice of critique, too, depends on the possibility of a new beginning, and it is part of its normative obligation to disclose that possibility, and thereby prevent the foreclosure of the future.

This orientation to the new, to the affirmation of a future different from the past, is the distinctive mark of the "philosopher of the future." Taking Emerson and Nietzsche as exemplars of this type of "philosopher," Stanley Cavell helps us to identify a little more clearly why it is that an orientation to the new as a source of normativity provokes worry and suspicion. "[I]f we are to think anew it must be from a new stance, one essentially *unfamiliar* to us; or, say, from a further perspective that is *uncontrollable* by us."[38] The value of Cavell's remark lies in the connection it makes between the unfamiliar and the uncontrollable. It is this connection, so I claim, that best explains why the new makes most moral and political philosophers anxious and suspicious. From a purely cognitive standpoint, the new provokes fear and anxiety because it is not something

46

whose effects we can predict and control. We cannot master what we do not know. From a moral and political standpoint, we are understandably suspicious about any stance or perspective that is uncontrollable. Our suspicion here arises from the assumption that a stance that is uncontrollable is a stance that is morally and politically unaccountable. And so it is quite unclear how thinking anew can be thinking responsibly, how it can be anything more than a dubious source of normativity. How can "philosophers of the future" accountably affirm the future they disclose?

If thinking anew from a new stance means thinking unaccountably, then we would most certainly be evading rather than embracing the responsibility we must bear for the proportion of continuity and discontinuity in the forms of modernity we inherit and pass on. But perhaps we can defend the normative orientation to the new distinctive of the "philosopher of the future," by recalling that to think anew from a new stance arises from an objective need. And so it is possible to evaluate the new stance according to the degree to which it illuminates both the past and the present. Thus, to the degree to which it helps make better sense of the problem of how to go on, the new stance can be assessed by how well it answers the need which gives rise to it. The challenge, then, is to see how a stance that is uncontrollable can be made accountable.

The idea of freedom as a new beginning

By attributing to reason a spontaneous power to begin anew, Kant produced a radical vision of reason in which this form of freedom could be exercised in a manner consistent with, at the same time as it was bound by, the moral law. But in making *identical* a free will and a will under moral laws, Kant's conception of reason ends up neutralizing spontaneity, removing in advance the anxiety and threat posed by what is unfamiliar and uncontrollable. Reason as Kant newly conceived it, and as he himself recognized, could not be reduced to a rule-governed faculty of mind. As distinct from the rule-governed activity of the understanding (whose rule-governed spontaneity is internally consistent with its concept), reason is a *possibility-disclosing* activity, proposing ends ("ideas") that go beyond what is already given empirically or normatively. This much Kant already understood, if not fully appreciated, which is why he distinguished the possibility-disclosing activity of reason from the rule-governed acquisition and exercise of knowledge: "as pure self-activity [*Selbsttätigkeit*]" reason "is elevated even above the understanding ... with respect to ideas, reason shows itself to be such a pure spontaneity and that it far transcends anything which sensibility can provide it."[39] If it is to be normatively innovative, making some actions "necessary even though they have not taken place and, maybe, never will take place," reason cannot draw its normativity from the normativity of (already existing) rules. Rules and laws must catch up to the new possibilities that reason discloses, since those possibilities are themselves inarticulable from within the logical space of existing rules and laws. The latter mark the current boundary of the logical space of possibility; they cannot on their own be the source of new possibilities.

Anticipating Dewey, Heidegger and Arendt, Kant appealed to the normativity of possibility – the possibility of a future different from the past, the possibility of transforming our relation to one another and to the world. Because this particular source of normativity is not assimilable to the normativity of rules or laws, it was not good enough for Kant, not good enough as a source of normativity. Here again, we have the ever-reappearing worry that whatever is not rule-conforming or rule-governed – because unfamiliar and uncontrollable – must be inherently unruly; if not irrational, definitely non-rational, and, hence, normatively suspect. Thus, whatever it is taken to be, being unfamiliar and uncontrollable, it cannot serve as the basis of a morally accountable practice. Given these circumstances, the normativity of the new contained within Kant's original conception of spontaneity needs to be recovered and rearticulated in a way that strengthens rather than compromises the idea of freedom as a self-determining new beginning. In my view one of the best ways to do that is to draw on Hannah Arendt's theory of freedom and action, at the centre of which is the human capacity to begin anew.[40] Arendt, unlike Kant, did not worry about or recoil from the contingencies and conditions in which new beginnings were initiated. What matters to Arendt is that the capacity to begin anew is not disembedded from its specific historical conditions. The new beginning has to be understood as an accountable response to those conditions, which, at the same time, could not be logically and empirically derived from them. As Arendt recognized, once new beginnings were set in motion, no matter how arbitrary or random (or "evil") they may have originally seemed, they shed their arbitrariness and randomness as they acquired, or, rather, founded, their own reality. A new way of acting, a new way of speaking, a new stance from which to think, makes possible its own content.[41] That is why we can't set up fixed normative criteria to test the new. In so far as we are dealing with something unfamiliar and uncontrollable, its "scope and limits of application are ascertained *experimentally* in the process of application."[42]

For Arendt, the freedom to initiate a new beginning needs to be understood as an extension of "the freedom to call something into being which did not exist before, which was not given, not even as an object of cognition or imagination, and which therefore, strictly speaking, could not be known."[43] In almost every way, this way of putting it is indebted to Kant, but Arendt, because she treats it as the most basic category of human thought and action, did not wish to make the freedom to initiate a new beginning more palatable by making it subject to fixed normative criteria. For Arendt, the central category of social and political thought is *natality*, the distinctively human capacity to initiate a new beginning, because we ourselves "are new beginnings and hence beginners."[44] On this view of freedom, human beings can experience their freedom as their own only in so far as they can initiate a new beginning for themselves, through which they break free of something oppressive and debilitating in their relationship to one another. Moreover, such new beginnings can constitute a public space of freedom which can be preserved only so long as "new beginnings are constantly injected into the stream of things already initiated."[45] Which, in turn, depends on our ability freely to disclose alternative possibilities, "to call something into being which did not exist before, which was not given, not even as an object of cognition or imagination, and which therefore, strictly speaking, could not be known."

Arendt thus belongs to a group of "romantic" theorists – Emerson, Dewey, Castoriadis, Cavell, Taylor – who recognize that the capacity to begin anew, and so found anew our traditions, practices and institutions, is essential to the success of democratic forms of life. Because they have tried to incorporate modernity's relation to time into the basic concepts of social and political theory, these are theorists who are able to draw upon sources of normativity unavailable to proceduralists and instrumentalists. Without these sources we cannot reopen the future by disclosing alternative possibilities for ourselves; and when we cannot do that, when we must or are willing to accept an already given range of possibilities, we render otiose the idea of critique, and the idea of a kind of individual and collective change that we can attribute to, and through which we express, our own agency.

Arendt's view of freedom does not deny the conditionedness of human action. Historical and cultural conditions both constrain and enable the initiation of new actions, the disclosure of new possibilities. They are not initiated or disclosed in a normative vacuum, but in the context of historically specific normative order. Of course, in contemporary culture there is an awful lot of talk of new beginnings, talk which makes new beginnings simply a matter of will. Any aspect of our lives can be made new again, if we buy the right product or undergo the right kind of treatment or just put our mind to it. This popular, easily consumed image of freedom as a frictionless and painless new beginning denies all historical and cultural embeddedness, all connection to and dependence on others. The fact that it is unlivable does not prevent it from being a bewitching image of freedom. (It is one of the ironies of this image of freedom that it can be lived only outside the conditions of a shared life with others, apart from which conditions it would be unintelligible *as* an image of freedom.)

Of course, it takes more than a cogent argument to release the hold of pictures like this on our intellectual and moral imaginations: it takes a new way of looking at things "forced" upon us by their unlivability (or their "one-sidedness," in more Hegelian jargon). Although consumerist popular culture endlessly recycles the image of freedom as the unconstrained possibility of beginning anew, there are counter-currents in popular culture in which the problem of beginning anew is treated with as much philosophical sophistication and seriousness, and with as much concretion as one could wish for. In the recent film, *The Eternal Sunshine of the Spotless Mind*, written by Charlie Kaufmann, the film's two central characters, Joel and Clementine, have found their life together more than they can bear. To make a fresh start for themselves they choose, in turn, to undergo a procedure that physically removes all memory of their life together. Offered by the memory-erasing firm, Lacuna Inc., it can eliminate all memories of anyone we want forever to forget, literally creating "a blank place in consciousness" out of which something new can emerge. Awaiting the appearance of the new "as if with shut eyes" we no longer need to feel constrained by or answerable to the (painful) past we once shared with others. As Lacuna's founder Dr Howard Mierzwiak reassuringly puts it to Joel: "When you awake in the morning, you'll find yourself in your own bed, a new life awaiting you." Unaware that her own memories of her hopeless relationship with the married Mierzwiak have been erased, his assistant rhapsodizes that this procedure is Mierzwiak's gift to the world because it lets "people begin again. It's beautiful. You look at a baby, and it's so pure, and so free, and so clean. And adults are like this mess of sadness and phobias – and Howard just makes it all go away."

The narrative devices of Charlie Kaufmann's screenplay are almost as complex as the philosophical questions it poses concerning the relations between memory, self-knowledge, and freedom. One reviewer fittingly described it as "*The Awful Truth* turned inside-out by Philip K. Dick," making it a candidate, a very dark candidate, for the film genre Cavell calls "comedies of remarriage." What is of interest to me here is the final scene of the film, when the two mixed-up lovers, Joel and Clementine, find themselves in a situation parallel to the final scene of *The Awful Truth*[46]. In the latter scene, the charming and effervescent characters played by Irene Dunne and Cary Grant find themselves standing with their backs to a past to which they cannot return, facing a future they cannot yet find a way to enter together. Their possibilities look to be exhausted, their chances of finding a way out of a divorce that neither want used up.

What change is possible under such conditions? The struggle to bring about change is almost always under conditions in which the prospect of any real change looks to be improbable if not impossible. For Cavell, whose illuminating meditations on the Hollywood comedy of remarriage are rounded out with *The Awful Truth*, the particular significance of the exchange between Grant and Dunne in the film's final scene is that it thematizes in everyday conversation a highly complex philosophical question: How can something be the same and, yet, somehow, different? How can human lives and human relationships be at once identical and non-identical, continuous and discontinuous, with themselves? The outcome of this philosophical conversation as far as these two particular people are concerned, depends on whether they can actually begin again; whether they believe themselves capable of beginning again. And this possibility turns on the availability of certain kind of trust or faith, not that things won't go wrong again, but that when they do, they will be able to begin anew together. The film leaves us with the thought that they will be able to begin anew, because they (and we) have learned that they are good at it, having learned that the success of any new beginning also depends on being able to recognize and respond to the new normative expectations that make it possible.

Now since all new beginnings are potentially awkward, they are filled with comic potential. Beginning anew can be very humbling. It requires a capacity to be reflective and self-critical, *and* the capacity to bear the comedy of one's bumbling attempts to recommit oneself to something which one had become convinced was unsustainable. All this can be frighteningly comic because it entails a commitment to one's own possible self-transformation. A commitment to self-transformation of this kind raises normative expectations, expectations we have of ourselves, and expectations others have of us. Thus, we render ourselves exposed and vulnerable to failure, and failure in this endeavour can make us look and feel foolish, pathetic, and unworthy: in risking failure, we also risk entering the domain of comedy, where the joke's on us.

The kind of self-transformation we're talking about is not some radical overhaul, making us unrecognizable to ourselves and to others, for we can't but remain the same: *we* are the ones who are answerable, accountable, to ourselves and others. But somehow, we must become different while remaining the same. To become other than we are, we must be held accountable, must hold ourselves accountable, for what we have been.

Lucy (Irene Dunne): Things are just the same as they always were, only you're just the same, too, so I guess things will never be the same again.
Jerry (Cary Grant): Things are different, except in a different way. You're still the same, only I've been a fool. Well, I'm not now. So as long as I'm different, don't you think things could be the same again? Only a little different?

The parallel scene at the close of *The Eternal Sunshine of the Spotless Mind* also tries to work out this same problematic of how to begin anew under conditions that make such new beginnings both improbable and "necessary." Joel and Clementine have done just about everything possible to hurt each other, to the point of impairing their own cognitive and emotional abilities to become intelligible to themselves. Yet, in the midst of bringing to completion the process by which Clementine is permanently erased from his memory and his life (as she has already erased Joel), Joel wants it to stop, and manages, in the end, to stop it. Out of his own memories, Clementine reaches out to him, speaks to him, conspiring with him to abort the procedure, reassuring him that he will not awake to a "blank space in consciousness" where she and he once shared a history. "Joel – you'll remember in the morning, and you'll come to me, and you'll tell me about you, and we'll start all over." Now it is what they make of this new start – to be precise, how they understand what it means and what it demands of them – that distinguishes it from the popular image of freedom as an unconstrained new beginning, disembedded from history and shared human relationships.

51

The decisive exchange takes place after listening to their recorded conversations with Mierzwiak in which they stated rather brutally the reasons why they never want to remember each other again. It is improbable that two human beings can say such hurtful and disrespectful things about each other and remain in any way interested or motivated to "go on" together. The improbable new beginning once again hinges not so much on whether they can begin again now, but whether they will be capable of beginning again after they once again encounter the inevitable breakdowns, disappointments and claustrophobia to which all human relationships, romantic and otherwise, are perpetually heir.

Clementine: I'm not a concept, Joel. I'm just a fucked-up girl who is looking for my own peace of mind. I'm not perfect.

Joel: I can't think of anything I don't like about you right now.

Clementine: But you will. You will think of things. And I'll get bored with you and feel trapped because that's what happens with me.

Joel: Okay.

Clementine: Okay. (Pause). Okay. (Smiling and laughing)

Joel: Okay. (Smiling and laughing together)

They cannot undo the past, nor take back what they have said. Their problem is how to affirm their new beginning without denying their past. It is the problem of how to integrate old and new, without distorting or neutralizing either the old or the new. And it requires making of their new stance a position from which they can restate their possibilities, including what they owe one another, without failing to acknowledge the skepticism that led to their breakdown and the skepticism which accompanies each new beginning. Emerson had precisely this in mind when reflecting on how the new can make a certain kind of peace with the old, how the "evil" and "skepticism" which attaches to them both can be turned into the material, the very complex material, of a new affirmation, exceeding the logical space of possibility of any "written record," the already inscribed normative rules and laws governing our shared form of life.[47]

Philosophy's relation to the new

As that which is unfamiliar and uncontrollable, the new exceeds our conceptual grasp and evades our intellectual mastery. And because it does not already occupy a recognizable and stable position in our logical space, its significance can be easily missed or just as easily dismissed. Given its troublesome status and persistent presence, philosophy tends to view the new as occupying the sphere of sheer contingency, as that which comes and goes, as that which occasionally and unforeseeably erupts into our lives and affairs, but which is nonetheless epiphenomenal to the central concerns of philosophy. Because the domain in which the new typically appears is the domain of culture, philosophy is disinclined to treat it as possessing any philosophical import. The energies and phenomena of culture (especially popular culture) contrast sharply with the "serious" concerns of philosophy, and are regarded as a distraction from the daily business of philosophy, the agenda of which is set not by culture, but by the "autonomy" of the philosophical enterprise.

Philosophy's generally suspicious, and occasionally disdainful attitude towards cultural phenomena only partially explains its disinclination to think about the new as a *philosophical* problem. A fuller explanation would also take account of philosophy's relation to time, and, in particular, its attitude towards the present, the historical moment in which we now live. Given that our form of life is the life form of modernity, *Neuzeit*, the time of the new, the present is typically confounding and unsettling. To regard it all as merely a "cultural" matter, as optional, and not principally a philosophical matter, displaces the normative question of just what philosophy's relation to time and to culture should be.

Philosophy's traditional self-image is of serene, poised reflection, in time, but not of it. After all, a philosopher is not supposed to run around breathlessly in search of the new, like Baudelaire's *peintre de la vie moderne*. There is something embarrassing in the thought of philosophy having to exert itself to catch up to its own time, leaving it panting for breath, and possibly exposing just how out-of-shape it is. Besides, what possible obligation could the philosopher have to seek out and capture the transitory and fugitive elements of the present? Such an enterprise not only requires making the present intelligible in light of what is transitory and fugitive; it also supposes an attitude towards time that embraces rather than looks down upon, or keeps self-disciplined distance from, what is merely temporal. For philosophy to change its relation to its own time, it would need to bring about a change in self-understanding and a change in sensibility.

In his justly celebrated essay, "The Painter of Modern Life," Baudelaire distinguishes invidiously and polemically between two types of artists: the "artist" in the narrow, specialized sense, and someone he calls the "cosmopolitan."[48] The "artist" is "wedded to his palette as like the serf to the soil."[49] For the "artist," art is an autonomous enterprise, and its internal problems are understood as technical questions, a matter of finding and applying the correct techniques or procedures. For the "cosmopolitan," art transcends its own concept, and any current understanding of it embraced by the professional art world. For the "cosmopolitan," whose interests are worldly, not parochial, art is positively defined by its relation to what is not art. Art does not constitute its identity by distinguishing itself strictly from what it is not; rather, it constitutes its identity by "wedding" itself to its other.[50] For Baudelaire, the other of art is all that concerns the present in its presentness. In seeking to become as intimate as possible with one's own time, the Baudelairean artist, the "cosmopolitan," is seeking to see the possibilities of his time in a new way, in a freedom-enhancing way. As Foucault eloquently put it, the high value that Baudelaire attaches to the present "is indissociable from a

desperate eagerness to imagine it, to imagine it otherwise than it is, and to transform it not by destroying it but by grasping it in what it is."[51] Those new
possibilities will not emerge from the "depths of the unknown," but, improbably,
from the all-too familiar conditions of our own form of life, and because familiar,
not well known (as Nietzsche, Hegel, Freud and Wittgenstein pointed out).

Now what would happen if philosophy transformed itself into a
"cosmopolitan" enterprise in Baudelaire's sense? What if it wed itself to its time
rather than to the timeless? How might that change how it conducts its business? How would its sensibility and not just its self-understanding be
transformed? Would philosophy turn into an aesthetic enterprise, practically
indistinguishable from literature and art, from cultural practices which cannot
deny or evade, indeed, must embrace, the time-bound and time-imprinted
nature of their undertaking under conditions of modernity? And would philosophy not then lose the cognitive power critically and reflectively to transcend
its own time? That question presumes that such time-transcending cognitive
power resides *only* in the capacity to identify with and appeal to what is timeless. Can we really say of art and literature that by immersing themselves in
their own time they have forfeited the power insightfully to transcend their
time? Or do we have to admit that their immersion in their own time is
precisely, as Baudelaire claimed, what makes possible their ability to see it
otherwise, in a different light, not from a standpoint outside it, but from a new
normative standpoint generated from within it? Well, maybe that's good enough
for art, one might reply, but philosophy is strictly a cognitive medium; it does
not operate in the realm of appearance, fiction, etc., but in the medium of argument. True enough, but what counts as argument in philosophy is as unsettled
as the question of what philosophy's business should be.[52]

I would like here to distinguish the largely empirical question of how tight
the bonds of history and culture are, and the normative question of *how* philosophical inquiry should bind itself to time, consciously, reflectively, openly.
What is at issue is not just the recognition that we are, as a matter of fact,
affected and shaped by time, but an invitation to think about how we should *let*
ourselves be affected and shaped by time. It means regarding the imprinting of
one's thought by one's own time not just as an unavoidable (or even constitutive) fact, and as a process which we must also critically and reflectively resist; it
means regarding it as a process that we should *also* embrace, something we
should want to embrace for the sake of thinking and acting differently, for the
sake of making the new possible.

The question of how to bring about something new is as much a matter of
receptivity as it is of activity (if not more so). Since the new is not something we
can will or make happen; it is our *active* receptivity that facilitates the emergence
of the new.[53] And as we have already noted, given the form of life that is modernity, we are under some normative obligation to facilitate the emergence of the
new. If modernity defines a relation to time that renders it open to the novelty of
the future, then that openness can be understood as one of the conditions of our

modernity. By "one of the conditions of our modernity," I mean not only the social and historical conditions in which we find ourselves, but also one of the conditions that we as moderns must meet, that we are enjoined to meet. Romanticism can then be understood as an attempt to meet that very distinctive condition: the normative obligation to help make the new possible. In making the new possible, opening up the range of our currently restricted possibilities, and enlarging the horizon of the future, giving possibility a future, romanticism responds to and seeks to meet an inescapable condition of our modernity.

Making the new possible is continuous with a transformative encounter with one's own time, an encounter whose success presupposes a "cosmopolitan" or worldly relation to that which is different from, other to, oneself. Can philosophy afford to be "romantic" in this sense? Would it remain "philosophy" if it were to become "romantic?" Of course, we could also ask whether philosophy can afford *not* to be "romantic." Would it remain "philosophy" if it *fails* to be "romantic?" Each of these questions comes with its own particular worry. If it were to philosophize beyond itself, philosophy risks making a fool of itself, looking comical, undermining its credibility as a rational enterprise, putting in question its claim to be the "guardian of rationality." In responding to demands that arise outside it, philosophy may find itself on unfamiliar terrain where it moves awkwardly, and speaks without its customary authority. On the other hand, if it fails to philosophize beyond itself, philosophy fails to risk itself. Without being ready to risk itself, to unsettle itself, philosophy may find that its evasion of its own time, its evasion of the new, renders it both alienated and parochial, unable to translate itself into worldly, "cosmopolitan" speech.

To rethink philosophy's relation to the new would not only require of philosophy an acknowledgment of the time-bound, time-imprinted character of thought itself; it would also require some sustained and ongoing reflection on the nature of philosophy's modernity, and on its position within the culture of modernity. As has been pointed out by a number of contemporary philosophers, the bulk of professional philosophy, so-called "analytic philosophy," takes its modernity for granted, as unproblematic and settled.[54] It was in response to the question of the normative relation of philosophy to its time that prompted the young Hegel to speak of the "need of philosophy." According to Hegel, this need arises from the experience of *Entzweiung* – the experience of breakdown, crisis, of things having gone very wrong: "The need of philosophy arises when the power of unification disappears from human life, when oppositions become independent, and lose their living connection and reciprocal relation."[55] Thus, for Hegel philosophy's responsiveness to its own time is a condition of its capacity to be responsible to its own time.

To prevent misunderstanding, it is essential to point out that the "need" that gives rise to philosophy is not one philosophy already comprehends and to which it is already in a position to respond. The "need" that gives rise to philosophy also instructs philosophy about its own need – about what philosophy is itself in need of, if it is properly to respond to the need which gives rise to its own activity. Philosophy is called upon to speak without knowing in advance what can answer the need that calls upon it to address, to intervene in, its own time. In this respect, philosophy *receives* its concept of itself from its time; and it is from this stance of receptivity that it is then able to recognize its obligations to its time, able to recognize its own concerns in the concerns that bedevil its own time.

> Philosophy's virtue is responsiveness. What makes it philosophy is not that its response will be total, but that it will be tireless, awake when the others have all fallen asleep. Its commitment is to hear itself called on, and when called on – but only then, and only so far as it has an interest – to speak.[56]

Cavell's variation on the young Hegel's idea that philosophy's responsibility to its own time is a function of its time-responsiveness, adds a further layer of complexity to the relation between philosophy and its own time, a layer that is concerned with the long-standing problem of philosophy's presumptuousness – which is, of course, the question of its cultural authority, the authority of its voice. Philosophy's self-education not only requires hearing itself called; it requires hearing *when* it is called to speak. The point Cavell is making is that philosophy ought not to speak first, since it does not *yet* know what to say, or, for that matter, *how* to say it. In this construal of philosophy, its role is determined by its position as the respondent, as the second speaker.[57] As the respondent, it occupies a position analogous to the position of the child first learning to speak, and so, finds itself in a situation analogous to a scene of instruction, education. When learning to speak our mother tongue, or any other tongue, we speak second. From the position of the respondent, philosophy discovers that the nature of its business is not determined by it alone, but rather, by something that it (willingly, receptively) inherits, as a child inherits a language and culture.

That discovery seems to involve a continual rediscovery of not only what to say when called upon to speak, but also of how to speak, and in what voice. And so it constitutes the task of philosophy as a task of re-inheritance – i.e. as a task that is concerned with the proportion of continuity and discontinuity in the forms of modernity philosophy inherits and passes on. It is the recognition, then, that philosophy's responsiveness, its capacity to respond to the demands that arise outside it, burdens it with the responsibility of keeping the future open, preventing the foreclosure of the future by facilitating the emergence of new possibilities for thinking and acting. This is indeed an improbable task, and in taking it on, philosophy may have to accept that in attempting to help make the improbable happen, it may end up looking pretty comical. But if it persists in its various efforts, surely to be bumbling and humbling, to rewed itself to its own time, philosophy may yet have reason to smile, taking its task seriously, but not itself.[58]

THE IDEA OF A NEW BEGINNING

Notes

1 We can safely assume of course that Buffy's teacher was voicing the common complaint of all teachers of the humanities and social sciences, who year after year must face succeeding generations of young people who know (or think they know) the present, but know nothing of the (pre-television) past. Scriptwriter Joss Whedon, who has an excellent ear for mallrat conversation, appears to be siding, correctly I think, both with Buffy and with Buffy's teacher, siding with a richer and more complex relation to the present and to the past.

2 Immanuel Kant, *Critique of Pure Reason*, trans. and eds Paul Guyer and Allen Wood (Cambridge: Cambridge University Press, 1997) p. 541.

3 Robert Pippin, *Modernism as a Philosophical Problem*, p. 67. I'm indebted to Pippin's formulation of the spontaneity issue in Kant and German Idealism, which he states in a particularly perspicuous way. On this issue, see also Pippin's "Kant on the Spontaneity of Mind," in *Idealism as Modernism* (Cambridge: Cambridge University Press, 1997) pp. 29–55.

4 Robert Pippin, *Modernism as a Philosophical Problem*, p. 47.

5 Jürgen Habermas, *The Philosophical Discourse of Modernity*, trans. Frederick Lawrence (Cambridge MA: MIT Press, 1987) p. 7.

6 Kant, *Critique of Pure Reason*, p. 610.

7 *Ibid.*, p. 5.

8 G. W. F. Hegel, "The Preface to the *Phenomenology*," in W. Kaufmann (ed.) *Hegel: Texts and Commentary* (Notre Dame IN: University of Notre Dame Press, 1977) p. 20.

9 Karl Marx, *Early Writings* (New York: Vintage Books, 1975) p. 206.

10 Kant, *Critique of Pure Reason*, p. 545.

11 Reinhard Koselleck, *Futures Past. On the Semantics of Historical Time*, trans. Keith Tribe (Cambridge MA: MIT Press, 1985) p. 257.

12 I think this "openness" to the novelty of the future is a crucial part of the explanation as to why so much "end" and "death" talk gets generated and reproduced in the high culture of modernity – the end of history, the end of philosophy, the death of the subject, etc., as well as the various "post-this's" and "post-that's" which seek to fill the evacuated spaces.

13 Reinhard Koselleck, *Futures Past*, p. 276.

14 *Ibid.*, p. 275.

15 Jürgen Habermas, "Historical Consciousness and Post-Traditional Identity: The Federal Republic's Orientation to the West," in *The New Conservatism*, trans. Shierry Weber Nicholsen (Cambridge MA: MIT Press, 1989) p. 263.

16 John Dewey, *The Public and its Problems*, in *The Later Works of John Dewey, 1925–1953*, vol. 2 (Carbondale IL: Southern Illinois University Press, 1984) p. 255.

17 See Nikolas Kompridis, "So We Need Something Else for Reason to Mean," *International Journal of Philosophical Studies*, vol. 8, no. 3, 2000, pp. 271–95, and Robert Pippin, "Brandon's Hegel," *European Journal of Philosophy*, 13:3, pp. 381–408.

18 On this, see Habermas, "The New Obscurity: The Crisis of the Welfare State and the Exhaustion of Utopian Energies," in *The New Conservatism*, pp. 48–70; Stanley Cavell, "The Future of Possibility," in this volume; and part VI ("In Times of Need") of Nikolas Kompridis, *Critique and Disclosure. Critical Theory Between Past and Future* (Cambridge MA: MIT Press, 2006).

19 Emerson, "Circles," in *Essays. First and Second Series* (New York: Vintage, 1990), p. 175.

20 Nietzsche, *The Gay Science*, p. 79, trans. Walter Kaufmann (New York: Vintage, 1974), p. 79.

21 Walter Benjamin, *Charles Baudelaire. A Lyric Poet in the Era of High Capitalilsm*, trans. Harry Zohn (London: Verso, 1983) p. 166.

22 Adorno, *Minima Moralia*, trans. E. F. N. Jephcott (London: Verso, 1974) p. 235.

23 *Ibid.*, p. 235, translation altered.

24 *Ibid.*, p. 236.

25 *Ibid.*

26 Edgar Allan Poe, "The Maelstrom."

27 Adorno, *Minima Moralia*, p. 235.

28 "The *flâneur's* last journey: death. His goal: novelty." Walter Benjamin, *Charles Baudelaire. A Lyric Poet in the Era of High Capitalism*, p. 172.

29 William Gibson, *Pattern Recognition* (New York: Berkeley Books, 2003) p. 8.

30 *Ibid.*, p. 12.

31 *Ibid.*, p. 23.

32 *Ibid.*, p. 24.

33 *Ibid.*, p. 23.

34 *Ibid.*, p. 65.

35 Of course, that is just what makes her "valuable" to the Bigends of the world, and why they can instrumentalize that yearning for their own purposes, as Gibson's novel shows.

36 Hannah Arendt, *The Human Condition* (Chicago: University of Chicago Press, 1958) p. 246.

37 Susan Bordo, *Unbearable Weight: Feminism, Western Culture, and the Body* (Berkeley CA: University of California Press, 1992) p. 246.

38 Stanley Cavell, "The Future of Possibility," in Nikolas Kompridis (ed.) *Philosophical Romanticism* (London: Routledge, 2006), my emphasis.

39 Kant, *Foundations of the Metaphysics of Morals*, trans. L. W. Beck, in *Kant Selections* (New York: Bobbs-Merrill, 1969) p. 80. On this issue see Robert Pippin's richly informative essay, "Kant on the Spontaneity of Mind," in his *Idealism and Modernism. Hegelian Variations* (Cambridge: Cambridge University Press, 1997) p. 36.

40 Here I'm just beginning to draw these connections together, but I hope to make them as tight and compelling as I can in a new book tentatively titled *The Idea of Freedom as a New Beginning*. See also *Critique and Disclosure*, parts V ("Alternative sources of normativity") and VI ("In times of need").

41 See Charles Taylor's "Heidegger, Language, and Ecology," in his *Philosophical Arguments* (Cambridge MA: Harvard University Press, 1995) pp. 100–26, and part III ("Another voice of reason") of my *Critique and Disclosure*.

42 Dewey, *Experience and Nature* (La Salle IL: Open Court, 1929) p. 156, my emphasis.

43 Hannah Arendt, "What is Freedom," in *Between Past and Future* (New York and London: Penguin, 1993) p. 151.

44 Hannah Arendt, *On Revolution* (London and New York: Penguin, 1990) p. 211.

45 Hannah Arendt, "Freedom and Politics," in A. Hunold (ed.) *Freedom and Serfdom* (Dordrecht: Riedel, 1961) p. 215.

46 For Cavell's interpretation of this scene, see *The Pursuits of Happiness*, (Cambridge MA: Harvard University Press, 1981) pp. 256–9, and his recent reprise of this interpretation in *Cities of Words* (Cambridge MA: Harvard University Press, 2004) pp. 377–8.

47 In liberated moments, we know that a new picture of life and duty is already possible; the elements already exist in many minds around you, of a doctrine of life which transcends any written record we have. The new statement will comprise the skepticisms as well as the faiths of society, and out of unbeliefs a creed shall be formed. For, skepticisms are not gratuitous or lawless, but are limitations of the affirmative statement, and the new philosophy must take them in and make affirmations outside of them, just as much as it must include the oldest beliefs.

(Emerson, "Experience," *Essays*, p. 257)

48 For the sake of gender-neutrality, I have substituted "cosmopolitan" for "man of the world." Since the "worldliness" of the "man of the world" is meant to contrast with the parochial attitude of the "artist," the substitution is not inappropriate.

49 Charles Baudelaire, *The Painter of Modern Life and Other Essays*, trans. Jonathan Mayne (London: Phaidon Press, 1964) p. 7.

50 As Marshall Berman already remarked in his very fine study of Baudelaire, the French verb *épouser*, which Baudelaire uses to describe the relation between the "cosmopolitan" artist and the world (the everyday world of the "crowd,") carries the literal meaning of wedding oneself to an other, and the more carnal figurative meaning of sexually embracing an other (Marshall Berman, *All That is Solid Melts into Air* [New York: Simon and Schuster, 1982] p. 145). But it also carries the meaning of mimetically giving oneself to an other, aligning oneself with, entering into, the meanings and struggles of the present in which one lives.

51 Michel Foucault, *The Foucault Reader*, ed. Paul Rabinow (New York: Pantheon, 1984) p. 41.

52 For a systematic discussion of this question, see part IV ("The business of philosophy") of my *Critique and Disclosure: Critical Theory Between Past and Future* (Cambridge MA: MIT Press, 2006).

53 For a systematic discussion of receptivity and its role in making a new disclosure of the world possible, see my *Critique and Disclosure*, part V (section 2 – "Receptivity, not passivity").

54 For a useful discussion of this issue in connection with the work of Taylor, Rorty, and MacIntyre, see Gary Gutting's *Pragmatic Liberalism and the Critique of Modernity* (Cambridge: Cambridge University Press, 1999).

55 *Differenz des Fichteschen und Schellingschen Systems der Philosophie*, in *Werkausgabe Band 2* (Frankfurt: Suhrkamp, 1970) p. 22. English translation in *The Difference Between Fichte's and Schelling's System of Philosophy* (Albany NY: SUNY Press, 1977) p. 91.

56 Stanley Cavell, *This New Yet Unapproachable America*, p. 74.

57 I owe thanks to Stanley Cavell for taking the time to discuss this passage with me.

58 I want to thank Richard Eldridge and Allison Weir for their valuable comments on an earlier draft of this essay.

3

AUTHENTICITY WITH TEETH

Positing process

David Kolb

Shakespeare's Polonius announces the kinds of drama offered by the players Hamlet has invited.

> The best actors in the world, either for tragedy, comedy, history, pastoral, pastoral-comical, historical-pastoral, tragical-historical, tragical-comical-historical-pastoral, scene indivisible, or poem unlimited.
>
> (*Hamlet*, act II, scene 2)

This multiplication is based on accepted types of drama. Any set of social or artistic or behavioral norms can generate new types by combining the old. We have rock, rap, country music, country-rock, and could have country-rap. But changes can go far beyond this, providing new types to be combined and new modes of combination. Goethe's *Faust* is none of the player king's types, and then Beckett invents more. Impressionists and post-impressionists did not just add to the genres of painting; they changed the goals and practices of painting so that older genres were redefined in the new context. Modern capitalism and representative democracy brought new modes of social individuation, new kinds of associations, new dimensions of combination and mutation. The whole space of possible actions was reconfigured.

As moderns or postmoderns we cherish such novelty. We live within ranges of normatively sorted possibilities, from explicit social rules to artistic genres and scientific methods, from language rules to codes of law to appropriate behaviors for courthouses and ballparks. Norms define acceptable individuals and actions: more tightly in the law and older norms of politeness, less so with recent politeness norms and artistic genres.

With the shattering of the ideal of a static traditional society, we expect changes in such norms. The changes come sometimes with fanfare, sometimes in ways unnoticed until later retrospection reveals them. They accelerate as older norms are experienced as restrictive. Yet novelty by itself is not always good. Merely replacing old by new systems of government or artistic genres is not enough. If galactic aliens arrived and enforced on us a new religion or social system, the novelty alone would not make that change something to be approved. If art moved towards more restrictive artistic genres, or society toward less social mobility, such novelty might not be welcomed. We hope for changes that enlarge the space of possible actions.

In what sense can the space of possibility be enlarged? When the rule of castling was introduced into the game of chess, the game changed. It was possible physically to have moved chess pieces in a castling way before, but it would not have been possible within the rules of the game. Austin's observations about when performatives succeed are apropos here. Speaking strictly, what is achievable after a change of norms was possible beforehand, though not approved or perhaps even recognized as possible. A castling move was not included in the state space of the allowable moves, though it was included in the larger space of possible arrangements of pieces of wood on the board. Impressionism was possible in 1500, in the sense that paint could have been laid on canvas in those patterns. But its real possibility had to wait for social and artistic developments to make room for its act of making new room.

We would like to understand new possibilities and norms as resolving tensions or meeting unmet needs. What the new completes or improves may not be an explicit aspect of the previous set of normative practices. It could be an implicit problem or unnoticed contradiction. Yet the new should not just be extruded from the old by an algorithmic process or inertial continuation. It should be more than a recombination of elements already present. We hope for genuinely novel expansions of possibility that yet remain authentic to what we have been.

The most familiar notion of "authenticity" demands that an individual or society stay faithful to some normative content. This might be an individual's ideals or family tradition. It might be a social patrimony of values, roles, practices, institutions, or teachings. But through time in the history of the individual or the society, the patrimony must be handed on to future selves or generations. There is no avoiding the hermeneutic task of interpreting, and perhaps reforming or attempting a return to some original meaning of the patrimony. But then the problem of defining the criteria of authenticity challenges the direction of any reinterpretation.

If authenticity is seen as involving a fixed patrimony, then change will be an external event that happens to that content. An authentic core is to be sheltered from the change, but skepticism attends any attempt to define that core or its legitimate successors.

However, there is another way to envision authenticity. Social formations could be seen as concretions within some larger process that itself provides guidance. It can do so, not because the process has a fixed goal that provides a criterion, but because the process has internal conditions, structures, or moments that demand their own expression.

In the following sections I take Hegel as an example of this way of conceiving authenticity. I make some references as well to Deleuze, a most resolute anti-Hegelian. Though Deleuze would violently repudiate the historical directionality of Hegel's analyses, they share an approach to authenticity where the "being" of the current social formation comes in a process with moments or aspects that should be made explicit elements in our social formations. The goal of authenticity might acquire some bite from these ideas, so that it could help judge changes that go beyond recombinations of the past.

Hegel and change

Hegel attempts to think social and artistic changes that provide both novelty and continuity. His dialectical investigations present a self-developing structure of concepts and follow temporal developments in thought, art, and institutions. He tries to show unpredictable novelty that nonetheless deals with tensions in earlier formations.

In his treatments, changes are not just added on to what went before. Each new logical concept reconfigures the whole, each new shape of spirit redefines everything in the practice of thought or art or society. Basic notions of individuality change, as do the kinds of relations and combinations that are possible. Such novelty is deeper than combinatorial play with previously defined individuals and relations.

Hegel is applauded for providing novelty that goes beyond recombinations of the past. But he is accused of reabsorbing the changes into a unitary developmental process. Hegel's situation is more complex, though, and even if we doubt his overall program we can learn from his treatment of normative change. There are three features in his approach that are relevant: how goals are conceived, how forms are related, and how the process posits its own form.

First, Hegel argues that while there are ongoing goals for the overall series of changes, those goals are not adequately describable by the earlier formations in the series. The dialectic introduces structures and norms that are unthinkable in terms of earlier structures that they encompass and replace.[1] For instance, Hegel thinks that fully actualized and institutionalized human freedom is the goal of history, but that this goal cannot be adequately conceived until it is well nigh achieved. Particular changes are also new: Roman citizenship could not be understood nor predicted in terms of Greek city membership. Medieval cathedral sculpture will not fit the concepts or practices appropriate for Greek temple sculpture, and neither of them can show art's ultimate self-transcendence. We come to self-presence within systems of thought and practices of politics and culture that are already underway trying to accomplish their own explicit goals, but which are stages of processes that turn out to have fuller goals, though those goals are not graspable within the current formation.

Second, Hegel sees the structures of a given intellectual or artistic or social formation as themselves inclining toward change. It is not necessary to shock them from outside. A social formation can be described abstractly as embodying this or that complex pattern or structure. But for Hegel this is not an adequate description. The connections of the abstract pattern must also be seen, and those connections go beyond similarities and differences. Abstract patterns and structures have their own internal tensions and mutually constitutive relations with those they arise from and those they transition into within a larger process that supports the being of any formation. These continuities and connections go beyond resemblance and formal overlaps, since they are in an order of connection and generation. The process, as the condition for the possibility and existence of the current formation, also brings the novelty that will transform that formation. Hegel's logic follows a series of conceptual structures as they reveal their constitutive relations with their opposites and their mutual dependencies within larger structures.[2] Dynamism does not need to be added from the outside, since the conditions for the stability of a current formation also require or offer novelty.

Third, and most important for this essay, the process of form and change develops toward its own self-presentation. Hegel argues that the final content of the process of development will be the explicit manifestation of all the moments that comprise the form of that process. What exists as philosophies, arts, or institutions is not a collection of finished or static results of the process of thought and social development, but rather is that process showing itself to itself. The process is defined neither by its present shape nor by any static structure. The process of manifestation manifests itself.

> The manifestation of itself to itself is therefore itself the content of spirit and not, as it were, only a form externally added to the content; consequently spirit, by its manifestation, does not manifest a content different from its form, but manifests its form which expresses the entire content of spirit, namely, its self-manifestation. In spirit, therefore, form and content are identical with each other.
> (Encyclopedia, 383z)

> All that remains here as form for the idea is the method of this content – the determinate knowing of the currency of its moments.
> (Encyclopedia, 236)

> The absolute idea has for its content only this, that the form determining is its own fulfilled totality, the pure concept.
> (The Science of Logic, 825)

The process of thought and socially mediated self-consciousness manifests itself by positing its own motions and moments. To posit a moment is more than to become aware of it. It is to let that moment be the dominant feature of a forma-tion, after which it will be taken up explicitly into a more complex whole.[3]

> In this way, the method is not an external form, but the soul and the concept of the content. It is distinct from the content *only inasmuch as the moments of the concept, each in itself, in its determinacy, reach the point where they appear as the totality of the concept.* Since this determinacy, or the content, leads itself back, along with the form, to the idea, the latter presents itself as a systematic totality, which is only one idea. Its particular moments are in-themselves this same [idea]; and equally, through the dialectic of the concept, they produce the simple being-for-self of the idea. – as a result the science [of logic] concludes by grasping the concept of itself as the concept of the pure idea for which the idea is.
>
> (*Encyclopedia*, 243, my emphasis)

In philosophy, some particular concept of reality or subjectivity central in a philosophical system can then be redefined as a subordinate aspect of a new system. Hegel sees these developments in actual fact as well as in the pure thought of logic. In politics, for instance, authoritative unified subjectivity appears as royal power, which has its day and is then reduced to a functioning aspect of the more supple whole of constitutional monarchy. Genres of art, ethical systems, and sets of social institutions all emphasize different moments as they refigure their overall process.

Hegel's logic aims to provide the basic moments of spirit's process. It defines a self-coincidence that is not from any one subject position, but is the self-presentation of the process that generates subject positions. The overall logical form of the process tells Hegel what moments need to be explicitly posited. But this overall logical form must then be itself treated in terms of itself, that is, the abstract form of the process must be explicitly posited as a "real" process in appropriate spheres of objectivity, and so fully developed and brought to itself.[4]

This is not some mysterious ontological dynamism but the process of thought and socially mediated self-consciousness coming to be and know itself. Less adequate normative formations cannot handle the self-reflections and inter-twined moments involved. In social structures, inadequacies show up as a growing inability to provide full freedom to individuals who are nonetheless becoming more defined by that freedom. In art, inadequacies show up when artistic content and form refuse to fit well together, and the role of the artist becomes unstable. In philosophy, inadequacies show up as an increasing inability to take fixed categories and binary oppositions as final even while they are being asserted. No pattern is stable unless it has explicitly posited all the mediations and moments necessary for its own existence, and those usually lead beyond it.

As Hegel turns to nature and history, the patterns from the logic show up in governmental institutions, the history of religions, the basic functions of organisms, and so on. Critics charge that Hegel is applying what amounts to an algorithm for the generation of normative formations. There are some defenses that Hegel can offer. One is that the overall logical form of the process is not available until the final moments in the process. Thus there is no distant meta-view; no algorithm is applied from the outside. Another is that the moments of the process are embodied within contingent detail. Once he is faced with a particular historical formation, such as the politics of his native Württemburg, or a proposal such as the English Reform Bill, Hegel can compare the situation or the proposal to the requirements for the full positing of the form of the social process, and so make criticisms and suggestions. But he cannot move from the a priori structures to concrete details, for these latter are truly contingent.

Whatever the success of these defenses, there are also more sweeping objections that can be raised about the success of Hegel's logical closure and transparency, and against the necessity of his list of moments. In this essay I am not trying to judge Hegel against these and other charges, though I doubt that his project can fully succeed. I want rather to point out that whatever the success of his particular project, his ideas provide lessons worth considering when we are trying to elaborate a concept of social authenticity.

This essay explores the idea that by positing the moments[5] of their own process, intellectual, artistic, and social formations could expand their possibilities, and so could arrive at normative formations that are truer to the way that norms come about. The results would be more authentic. In what follows, I first investigate how a normative formation can be expanded through the positing of the form of its process.[6] Then I ask whether such expansion always produces a better formation. Then I consider whether deviations from Hegel undermine the effort to learn from him, and close with a few remarks about the situation today.

Positing moments

Positing is not a self-interpretation performed in the privacy of one's mind or in the implicit self-consciousness of a group. It puts a moment "out there" in public as recognized in the explicit working of an institution or a cultural practice. This is more than a linguistic act, though it could happen through the development of institutionalized linguistic practices. Aspects of a normative formation which were subordinate and somewhat indefinite become more prominent and explicitly defined, and the whole formation reconfigures. This expands the set of norms, since new explicit dimensions of action become recognized and governed.

One way of describing this expansion, taken from physics, might be to say that it complicates the state space set up by a system of norms. A set of elements (which could be types or individuals) plus their qualities and relations create an abstract space containing all the possible states the system could be in. For instance, two individuals, each of which could have either of two qualities, generate four possible descriptions of the whole. Individuals A and B, each of whom can be either blue or red, give four possible system states (AbBb, AbBr, ArBb, ArBr). Add relations (A could be above or below B) and the number of combinations multiplies. This could be imagined as a space with a dimension and axis for each quality. The system as a whole would then occupy one location in this abstract space, and its changes could be mapped as a trajectory through this space of states. The state space, no matter how complex, depends on the specification of the initial individuals or types and measurable qualities. "Measurable" here need not refer to scientific measurement – instead of a physical system, think of a system of etiquette rules. This system sets up a space of possible actions. Each addition of a new individual (say, single parents) or a new type or a new quality (say, Friday informal dress) adds a dimension to the whole space and enlarges the number of possible states for the system. Norms identify preferred regions of this state space. More radical changes may reconfigure all the dimensions of the state space. This will likely enlarge the total repertory of possible actions available to a society but it might also, for instance in a modern bureaucracy, reduce the number of possibilities open to a single individual, because the new roles had more tightly defined spheres of operation.

Such changes are not primarily those personal self-redefinitions that revolutionize an individual's life history. Hegel would say that the content of such new selves is not an individual product; the alterations move within an intersubjective space of alternatives that has been enlarged through other than individual creativity. Similarly, authenticity to process will not be primarily a quality of a particular individual. It is on the social level that the process can make its own structure and movement actual for itself, in the development of forms for life that are truer to the way that action possibilities and norms come to happen.

In Hegel's aesthetics artworks always unite form and content, but in the first phase of art, symbolic art, the issue of the adequacy of form to content is not a matter of concern. With the development of classical art, a proper balance of content and form becomes an explicit norm. In romantic art, the action of social and individual subjectivity in going beyond the union of form and content becomes explicitly recognized, although it was implicitly functioning all along. With each phase the self-interpretation of what artists do changes, and the institutional norms change as well, so the space of possible art works is reconfigured. In politics, the moments Hegel describes as the universal, particular, and individual are present in any formation, but as they are explicitly recognized and given interacting institutional roles, government moves from tribal leadership toward a representative democracy with intricately intertwined governmental agents.

But we need not stay with Hegel for examples. Gilles Deleuze would never be labeled Hegelian, and his concepts of identity, sense and possibility are very far from Hegel, yet there are parallels in his thought to the motions just described. Deleuze offers an ontology of events which, though it has no dialectical moments in Hegel's sense, has interacting elements (pre-individual singularities and forces, ideas, concepts, problems, etc.) These are active in the being of any normative formation. There is no goal-oriented historical development, but some normative formations will more fully express the interplay of these elements than others.[7] Deleuze urges us to create individual and social structures which embody this interplay more explicitly. Avant-garde art is an example, where the explicit creation-discovery of new possibilities becomes an institutional norm.[8]

Oppression for Deleuze is not just a matter of particular factual structures getting in the way of particular wills and desires. A society organized as much as possible in terms of striated space and its social analogues is oppressive, for Deleuze, not just because of factual repressions of this or that particular desire, but because that sort of society ignores or represses constitutive elements of the process that allows societies to exist at all. The mode of being of any structure is within a process that is "for" novelty and new intensities. We are called to be that newness and so to create normative formations that allow us to enact the whole process more explicitly.

Deleuze's notions, applied to institutions, challenge the modernization that Hegel applauds. Rational transparency is seen as limiting human possibilities by imposing centralized and striated systems that classify and assign to each a fixed place, caging the dynamism of individual and pre-individual desires. Still, while Deleuze's writings are full of images of flight, nomadism, schizoid break-outs and anti-systems, total discontinuity is not a goal.[9]

Hegel distrusts the notion of genius and other eruptions, preferring to see individual insights as part of rational social processes. Deleuze on the other hand sees rationality as a normalizing pressure on individual and social eruptive events of new forces and wills. What I want to point out is that despite their opposed orientations, both Hegel and Deleuze affirm a self-becoming process whose interacting elements or moments need to be explicitly and publicly posited within normative formations to allow for full freedom. In both cases an enlargement of normative formations occurs through explicitly positing the underlying process's moments and elements.

Authenticity and value

But is there any reason to conclude that such changes lead to normative formations that are better than the earlier ones? Do such expansions automatically produce normative formations that should be valued more highly?

An enlargement of possibilities may remove an earlier restriction, perhaps one unfelt until the new space opened up. But is it enough to show that some restriction has been lifted? Why should this be better? It fits with modern sensibilities, but that does not establish that it was an improvement. The enlargement of possibilities might dilute and dehumanize, as with the increasing specialization of factory labor. Or it might open up a nihilistic expansion leading away from any concentrated goals and toward a consumerist thirst for novelty without significance.

One possible response to such worries might be to seek an independent criterion that distinguished those cases when expansion and complexification were positive values. Hegel argues that they are positive when at the service of authentic freedom defined in terms of the rational self-presence of the whole process. He avoids endless dilution by finding structures that close upon themselves, though they leave open their lower-level determinations. Deleuze sees the value of expansion and complexity depending in Nietzschean fashion on the type and direction of the willed intensity. He favors openness over closure, but with the proviso that affirmative forces repeat and maintain generous intensity.

Another response might be to dodge the question by claiming that what should be judged better or not, virtuous or not, is not the normative formation itself but particular paths through the space of possible actions it opens. This leads to familiar debates about relativism and about what criteria should be used to judge the paths.

A more exigent response would be to show that a previous normative formation was unable in practice to provide paths of action that would be judged virtuous and good even on its own terms. This resembles Hegel's procedure in the *Phenomenology of Spirit*, which narrates the failure of shapes of consciousness to provide paths of action that fulfill their own internal norms. Their failure stems from their inability to posit crucial moments in the process of their own becoming.

The *Phenomenology* is Hegel's richest and his most questionable self-developing sequence. Many commentators find segments of it convincing, but few are persuaded that the whole has the kind of necessity Hegel claims. Even if the book's progression does not work out in its own terms, nevertheless it suggests a method: to examine a normative formation as to whether it can meet its own criteria, with an eye to the self-affirmation of larger processes. If such evaluations are possible, and lead to changes, they will bring new dimensions that enlarge the space of action when the earlier formation is enfolded into the new.

Some normative formations demonstrate their failure to posit crucial moments by changing into new formations that are more authentic to the structure of the process. In such cases, even when the change leads to a breakdown of previous social patterns, the new formation can be judged an improvement.

One historical example Hegel offers is drawn from pre-revolutionary France. It is a social formation that officially defines itself by an interplay between a central royal power representing universal goals and duties, and talented and noble people finding their self-identity in serving those universal ends. This seems on the surface a stable and clear set of norms and social roles, but the paths of action defined by the norms do not lead where they are supposed to lead, because a crucial moment demands to be posited explicitly: individual free subjectivity.[10]

The self-definition of the nobility depends on honor given from a central source. This nobility must fashion itself according to norms that gradually change from military glory to witty court service. Others become dependent on wealthy bourgeois, who are also fashioning themselves according to changing norms. Hegel focuses on a growing awareness in all groups that their selves are both identified with and alienated from the social role definition they receive from others. As the act of receiving a normatively valid identity from another becomes increasingly self-aware, the person's inner self is perceived as a pure process of choice and reception without any given natural normative content.

> It finds confronting it its own, but alienated, self as such, in the shape of an objective fixed reality which it has to receive from another fixed being-for-self.
>
> (*Phenomenology of Spirit*, 516)

> As regards the aspect of that pure actuality which is its very own, its own "I," it finds that it is outside of itself and belongs to another, finds its personality as such dependent on the contingent personality of another, on the accident of a moment, on a caprice, or some other utterly unimportant circumstance.
>
> (*Phenomenology of Spirit*, 517)

> It is absolutely elastic and ... rejects this disowning of itself which would make its being-for-itself into something alien, and rebels against this reception of itself, and in this very reception is conscious of itself.
>
> (*Phenomenology of Spirit*, 518)

> The self-consciousness which rebels against this rejection of itself is immediately absolutely self-identical in its absolute disruption, the pure mediation of pure self-consciousness with itself.
>
> (*Phenomenology of Spirit*, 520)

The honest culture of service evolves into a culture of flattery and deceit, together with a group of purer people announcing that they are above such decadence. But that belief is punctured by a cynical talk that sees through and ridicules these pretensions, as well as the honor and goodness of the noble ideals.

> When the pure "I" beholds itself outside of itself and rent asunder, then everything that has continuity and universality, everything that is

called law, good, and right, is at the same time rent asunder and is destroyed. All identity dissolves away.

(*Phenomenology of Spirit*, 517)

The self no longer defines itself in terms of universal principles of right and duty. "It exists in the universal talk and destructive judgment which strips of their significance all those moments which are supposed to count as the true being and as actual members of the whole" (*Phenomenology of Spirit*, 521). This historical process, for which Hegel cites Diderot's *Rameau's Nephew*, begins to posit a new moment of negation and pure subjectivity that was not explicit in earlier normative formations.[11] Hegel sees the Enlightenment as an attempt to find public content for this empty self. Later Hegel argues that the Terror in the French Revolution attempts to institutionalize a version of this free selfhood, but fails spectacularly.[12]

The reason for that failure is revealed in the sections of the *Phenomenology* where this free selfhood turns out to have its own internal moments of universality and particularity that need to be posited if it is to be lived without destructive results. The interaction and increasing recognition of these moments develop in the Morality section, and they are posited affirmatively in the "reconciling yes" at the end of that section. Though public, this mutual recognition still lacks institutional authority. Hegel's *Philosophy of Right* tries to develop a theory of institutions adequate to such a complex notion of self and freedom.

The move from a medieval normative formation focused on honor and service to the cynical norms of pre-revolutionary France appears to be a degeneration from honesty and noble intention. But Hegel sees it as progress because it posits structural moments of human freedom that were not given their full due before. The bad effects of the change will be repaired not by a return to an earlier simplicity but by positing further moments and mediations still obscured in the Rameau formation. So this change can be judged progressive because it moves along the process of making human selfhood in society fully self-present and publicly recognized in all its dimensions.

The goal is to develop institutions that show in their operation the process that creates and sustains them. In this example the seeming degeneration makes explicitly operative a moment of that process. The resulting normative formation is then truer to its own mode of being as embedded in a historical process involving the moments that are gradually being posited. In this sense it is more authentic.

Authenticity provides value not so much on its own but as a condition for other important values. For instance, in Kierkegaard and Sartre the authenticity of the mode of choosing is supposed to guarantee that the values of freedom and subjectivity are affirmed. In Heidegger, who rejects talk of values, authenticity demands that a choice or a normative formation be more open to its structural temporality and so to the possibility of creative responses and responsibilities, which Heidegger judges positively.

But authenticity to process demands that there be some internal structure to the process that creates and sustains normative formations. In his novels and plays, Sartre writes powerfully about people caught in situations that demand revision of their values, and he describes the agonies of people torn by past loyalties, their own desires, and envisioned futures.[13] Yet in his early theoretical writings the moment of decision is insulated from all determination by the past or by any personal or social content or inclination. In *Being and Nothingness*, the man on the cliff path is not in anguish at the difficulty of the choice facing him, but at the possibility that a choice will occur. He is not in anguish while deciding whether or not throw himself off the cliff; his anguish occurs because he cannot know whether or not in the next moment a redefining irruption unconnected with his current self might decide to jump off the cliff. The self, in the ordinary sense of an ongoing actor with a definite set of values and tendencies, emerges from a choice that has no internal structure and can give no reasons, since that choice creates the framework within which reasons will be evaluated. Sartre tries to buttress this theory with a doctrine of the fundamental project. A basic choice of style of being provides a framework to which other choices can be faithful. But the fundamental project itself exists as a willed continuity that can be broken and changed at any moment.[14] There is no fixed patrimony and authenticity is reduced to formal compliance with the process of choice, but that blank process can offer no internal guidance.

Heidegger shows another variant of the problem. In *Being and Time* he does not propose a disconnected blank choice. He speaks of us as "thrown projects" that find ourselves cast into activities and goal orientations already ongoing. We are never in a state of sovereign independence with respect to values and possibilities. There are projects and goals that we did not establish but that themselves establish our activity. The task of authenticity is not self-creation but decisive self-reinterpretation. The general lines of our selfhood are predefined by the overall "meaning of being" of our time, and by the more particular tasks of our generation. Those determinations are not thing-like presences but openings and calls that require further definition and interpretation. We can return to the call or project that has opened our situation, and find new possibilities not developed in the current configuration of meanings and norms. We retrieve the new by moving decisively and creatively as we break through everyday average sets of norms and possibilities. This authentic return, however, requires a privileged insight about what counts as an appropriate retrieve from the origin. Heidegger had trouble giving content to this advice, and his notorious embrace of the Nazi movement shows that the reinterpretation and discernment called for lack usable criteria and slip toward social determinism despite his rhetoric of heroic isolation. Though Heidegger would not use Hegel's term, the "moments" he finds within the process of meaning and norm creation cannot offer the guidance Hegel finds. Heidegger's analysis remains formal in a way that Hegel avoids with his self-referential form-as-content, though this last is purchased at a price too high for Heidegger.[15]

In Sartre and Heidegger the process that is to become authentic does not have the kind of internal structure that might provide guidance about what kinds of choices and changes would be authentic and better than their alternatives. Deleuze, by contrast, can recommend particular cultural trends and modes of life as more authentic and as providing human freedom and flourishing in the terms defined by his ontology of events. In addition, he would say that the acceptance of the new formation enacts a criticism of the old, showing where it failed in comparison with the new. If this were translated into his own concepts, Hegel would agree.[16]

Juxtapositions

I have been suggesting that something akin to a Hegelian strategy might be implemented without the full Hegelian system. But there is a problem: Hegel's logic is meant to provide a definite and finite list of the correct moments of the self-positing process. The ways in which those moments might be found posited in the spheres of actuality are many and contingent, but the logical moments themselves come in a self-generated and closed series. If we have doubts about the success of Hegel's self-generating series, should we continue to talk about a process of self-positing?

Positing means putting the moments out there institutionally, where they open spaces for action. If there are correct moments to the process, and if we have misconceived them, our misguided attempts to enlarge our sphere of action should create friction between what we posited and what ought to be posited, as in the Rameau example. This is another point on which, for very different reasons, Hegel and Deleuze (as well as other more naturalistic thinkers) might agree.

But what if there is no finished list of moments to be posited? Why not endless additions and complexities? Another and yet another new political scheme or cultural norm? For instance, new artistic movements can be multiplied indefinitely, each further complexifying the institution of art. However, even if the process has no end, at some point – art has already reached it – the institution can explicitly posit the repetitive process itself. Creating new art genres becomes a criterion of artistic stature. Novelty is expected; the endless series becomes a return of the same. A kind of self-conscious closure envelops the ongoing lower-level novelties.[17] This "modern" turn is the self-grasp of the structure of processes of change. Such moves to a higher-level sameness are typical of modern institutions in politics, art and science. Fundamentalisms in all these areas resist such moves.

The same objection can of course be repeated against the second-level process. But the same answer applies: The process that needs institutional positing is the reflective-regressive move itself. Positing the process of reflection in institutional terms that can be shared by multiple coexisting normative formations – that is our social, political and artistic task.

But who are we? The world is filled with migrants and media. The galactics mentioned at the beginning have shown up and, rather than forcing their ways upon us, have settled down next door, showing off their ways and wares. Today's world points up limitations in Hegel's version of authenticity to process. He thinks about linear, one-stage-at-a-time changes. But we are surrounded by juxtaposed normative formations that have no inner relation to our own yet are offering themselves along many different directions. We do not have to wait for our possibilities of action to be expanded by dialectical development. Possibilities get enlarged by juxtaposition. A song here, a food there, a different mode of address, a few foreign words learned, and new norms establish themselves.[18] Or norms are forced by education, or by economic or political pressures. And besides the social osmosis and the social engineering there is the omnipresent marketing.

In this situation, is a notion of authenticity still useful? It can still be useful, because the authenticity discussed in this essay is not a matter of faithfulness to some particular pattern or value expressed in an earlier normative formation. It is authenticity to a process rather than to a patrimony. What makes a change authentic in this sense is that it posits or makes institutionally explicit more of the moments or elements of the process that sustains normative formations. In the contemporary situation, this could help choose among proffered new customs and values, and to distinguish authentic enlargements of action from those resulting from manipulated desires.

Cultural and social juxtapositions need further investigation that might look at such encounters in terms of a second-level process analogous to the institutionalization of novelty in art. Many social critics have emphasized overarching processes which treat juxtaposed cultural differences as material for fads and consumerism. This returns the discussion to the issue mentioned briefly above about personal life choices and social possibilities. The issue would be whether juxtaposition requires an antecedent open field so that the fragments can touch one another. This then connects to a basic issue present in most philosophical traditions today: what kinds of unity and self-reference are required for the space of meaning and norms to function? And that lands us in the middle of discussions pioneered by Kant, Fichte and Hegel, which lead toward a richer notion of social authenticity as authenticity to process.[19]

Notes

1 For example, in Hegel's logic, the paired categories in the second section (ground and grounded, essence and appearance, cause and effect, and the like) are not extensions of the single categories of the first section (quality, quantity, and the like), and neither section can properly enunciate the full goal of the logic.
2 Strictly speaking, for Hegel "process" is a term more applicable in the philosophy of nature and spirit than in the logic itself.

3 "True spirit, however, is just this unity of the absolutely separate moments, and, indeed, it is just through the free actuality of these self-less extremes that, as their middle term, it achieves a concrete existence" (*Phenomenology of Spirit*, 521).

4 The logic is not useful for guiding future developments, because the explicit knowledge of the logical moments comes late in the game, and also because Hegel does not think that historical change is consciously guided. The rational present was to transform itself, and Hegel did not think in terms of avant-garde groups leading the way. He was at best very cautious about the self-appointed artistic and political radicals of his day. The major motors of change in society and thought do not operate under conscious control; self-awareness is more a result than a cooperating cause. In the preface to his *Philosophy of Right* Hegel famously urged us to seek the rose in the cross of the present, and he claimed that whatever is effective and actual is by that very fact also deeply rational. He seems to urge quiet acquiescence since "whatever is, is right." Yet we know that Hegel also wrote extensively about the inadequacies of German political and social systems, and that he worked with government bureaucrats and students who sought significant changes. Comprehension is retrospective, yet it can enable criticism. Once a new formation is coming into being, for instance democratic constitutional government, it can be invoked to criticize lagging institutions, as Hegel did for German governmental arrangements.

5 Although the non-Hegelian examples cited later involve elements or aspects rather than moments in the Hegelian sense, I will continue to use the word as a placeholder for whatever a particular analysis reveals to be the internal structure of the process.

6 I am ignoring Hegel's discussion of how moments are posited in nature, and concentrating on social and artistic formations, although the non-Hegelian examples I suggest, Deleuze and Whitehead, do apply their ideas to nature as well as to social and artistic examples.

7 An earlier thinker whom Deleuze quotes with approval, Alfred North Whitehead, again no Hegelian, also develops an ontology of events in which various factors (eternal objects, creativity, past formations, subjective aim, etc.) cooperate in any concrete actual entity. He too urges us to develop social structures and artistic practices that make more room for the explicit interplay of these elements, and in so doing increase the sphere of possible actions and creative expressions. (See, for instance, Whitehead's discussions in the later chapters of *Adventures of Ideas*.)

8 See Deleuze's analyses in *Difference and Repetition* and the comparative evaluations of cinematic forms and social realities in *Cinema* 1 and 2. His institutional judgments are most fully expressed in *A Thousand Plateaus*. There is no doubt that talking about Deleuze in the context of Hegel tends to present Deleuze as more rationalistic and more interested in continuity than he really is. But making corrections by talking more about bodies, forces, breaks and becomings will only emphasize further that Deleuze has a theory of the becoming of normative formations that wants to have all its elements recognized and functioning explicitly. I am not suggesting that Deleuze derives this from Hegel; both of them are dependent on Spinoza and Leibniz for the basic strategy.

9 According to Deleuze:

> Staying stratified, organized, signified, subjected – is not the worst that can happen; the worst that can happen is if you throw the strata into demented or suicidal collapse, which brings them back down on us heavier than ever. This is how it should be done: lodge yourself on a stratum, experiment with the opportunities it offers, find an advantageous place on it, find potential movements of deterritorialization, possible lines of flight, experience them, produce flow

conjunctions here and there, try out continuums of intensities segment by segment, have a small plot of new land at all times.

(A Thousand Plateaus, 161)

10 The section is "The world of self-alienated spirit: culture and its realm of actuality," in the Phenomenology of Spirit, paragraphs 488–526, especially paragraphs 512–22. For a fuller discussion, see Pinkard's The Sociality of Reason, 157–65.

11 The moment of self-consciousness for itself is pure self-presence but without the ability to generate content out of itself because it is too negatively defined. "The self sees its self-certainty as such to be completely devoid of essence, sees that its pure personality is absolutely not a personality" (Phenomenology of Spirit, 517). This empty self-affirmation will be taken up and reworked in the Morality section, with its Kantian echoes. In the complex structure of the Phenomenology there are prefigurings of this movement in earlier sections such as those on skepticism and the "unhappy consciousness."

12 The failure of the Terror is foreshadowed in this comment about the cynical discourse:

> In such talk, this particular self, qua this pure self, determined neither by reality nor by thought, develops into a spiritual self that is of truly universal worth. It is the self-disruptive nature of all relationships and the conscious disruption of them; but only as self-consciousness in revolt is it aware of its own disrupted state, and in thus knowing it has immediately risen above it. In that vanity, all content is turned into something negative which can no longer be grasped as having a positive significance. The positive object is merely the pure "I" itself, and the disrupted consciousness in itself this pure self-identity of self-consciousness that has returned to itself.
>
> (Phenomenology of Spirit, 526)

It would be interesting to compare this with contemporary postmodern attempts to disrupt false consciousness and false unities; there are significant similarities and equally significant differences.

13 See for instance the plays in Sartre 1949, especially Dirty Hands.

14 Sartre tries to argue that authenticity provides a criterion that can guide choice, or at least exclude some choices as inappropriate, but his Kantian maneuvers in Existentialism Is a Humanism are not successful. Sartre's ideas resemble the thesis of Descartes (and earlier of Al Ghazzali and the Muslim Asharites) that God remakes the world anew at each successive moment, and can alter its laws and patterns at any time. Al Ghazzali uses the conception of continuous re-creation to deny any notion of necessary connection among events, and draws Hume-like conclusions about causality being a fiction resulting from habituation. For Al Ghazzali this allows for divine interventions and miracles, because God can choose to have any event followed by any other, so the corpse could speak, the cotton refuse to burn. The early Sartre allows similar discontinuities within the self. Later, in his rapprochement with Marxism he develops a doctrine of dialectical constitution of the self in mutuality, as opposed to any simple causality either by social reality or by individual freedom. Whether this succeeds is debated, but at least it softens the dualisms of the early Sartre.

15 See the discussions of Heidegger's notion of authenticity in Zimmerman's Heidegger's Confrontation with Modernity and his Eclipse of the Self, and the comparisons with Hegel in my Critique of Pure Modernity.

16 Even someone as pluralistic as Derrida, who sees an indefinite multiplication of modes of self-reference and self-reflection, still has them stand under some quasi-transcendental conditions that can judge some normative formations more explicit

than others about the unconditional demands and the porous unities of the process that lets them be. Thus he can write in criticism of some modes of conceiving European unity in *The Other Heading*, or discuss Marxist visions in *Spectres of Marx*.

17 In Hegel's terms, this is a move from bad to good infinity. Hegel sees this as inevitable, but Deleuze fights against this modernist move by urging the creation of new modes of life that are incommensurable with older artistic or cultural institutions. Nonetheless he still talks about the overall moments of the process of innovation.

18 Hegel himself lived in a world where such juxtapositions were beginning to happen, but he conceptualized them in terms of one dynamically changing cultural formation, northern Europe, faced with frozen remnants of older cultural formations such as China and India. He relied on the insulation given by spatial distance, and did not think through the relations of non-dialectical difference among those formations in their growing presence to one another. Hegel did think about how the pressures of bourgeois social economics would lead to colonial trade and exploitation, but he conceptualized that as the European model transforming backward formations, not as a relation of difference and mutual juxtaposition.

19 In this regard one could ask, in Wittgensteinian fashion, whether there is any such thing as "*the* process of reflection" (or of norm creation and sustaining) rather than a motley assemblage of varied mechanisms. As in other debates about transcendental conditions, the issue turns on what justifies and makes possible gathering the assemblage together, on the temporal continuity of the process, and on whether the gathered elements are what they are only in the implicit context of the other elements in some kind of whole that includes the self-reference of thought and action.

Bibliography

Deleuze, Gilles, *Cinema 1: The Movement-Image*, trans. Hugh Tomlinson and Barbara Habberjam (Minneapolis MN: University of Minnesota Press, 1986).

——*A Thousand Plateaus: Capitalism and Schizophrenia*. Written with Felix Guattari, trans. Brian Massumi (Minneapolis MN: University of Minnesota Press, 1987).

——*Cinema 2: The Time-Image*, trans. Hugh Tomlinson and Robert Galeta (Minneapolis MN: University of Minnesota Press, 1989).

——*Difference and Repetition*, trans. Paul Patton (New York: Columbia University Press, 1994).

Derrida, Jacques, *The Other Heading*, trans. Pascale-Anne Brault and Michael Nass (Bloomington IN: Indiana University Press, 1992).

——*Spectres of Marx*, trans. Peggy Kamuf (New York: Routledge, 1994).

Hegel, G. W. F., *Philosophy of Right*, trans. T. M. Knox (Oxford: Oxford University Press, 1952).

——*The Science of Logic*, trans. Arnold Miller (London: Allen and Unwin, 1969). Reference by page number.

——*Phenomenology of Spirit*, trans. Arnold Miller (Oxford: Oxford University Press, 1977). References by paragraph number. I have slightly altered some of the translations.

——*The Encyclopedia Logic*, trans. T. F. Geraets, W. A. Suchting and H. S. Harris (Indianapolis IN: Hackett, 1991). References by paragraph number.

Heidegger, Martin, *Being and Time*, trans. Joan Stambaugh (Albany NY: SUNY Press, 1966).

Kolb, David, *The Critique of Pure Modernity: Hegel, Heidegger, and After* (Chicago: University of Chicago Press, 1986).

Pinkard, Terry, *Hegel's Phenomenology: The Sociality of Reason* (Cambridge, Cambridge University Press, 1996).

Sartre, Jean-Paul, *Being and Nothingness*, trans. Hazel Barnes (New York: Philosophical Library, 1956).

——*Three Plays*, trans. Lionel Abel (New York: Knopf, 1949).

Whitehead, Alfred North, *Adventures of Ideas* (New York: Free Press, 1933).

Zimmerman, Michael, *Eclipse of the Self: The Development of Heidegger's Concept of Authenticity* (Athens OH: Ohio University Press, 1981).

——*Heidegger's Confrontation with Modernity: Technology, Politics, and Art* (Bloomington: Indiana University Press, 1990).

Part II

SELF-DETERMINATION AND SELF-EXPRESSION

4

LETTING ONESELF BE DETERMINED[1]

A revised concept of self-determination

Martin Seel

1

Philosophy has said a lot about doing, but little about letting-be-done. Granted, the polarity of doing and undergoing, and the virtue of tranquillity, has played a major role in its history. And yet, what has been understood as unique to human life is primarily the capacity actively to explore and give shape to the conditions of its own life – a life that is reflectively directed rather than instinctively or affectively regulated. This has obscured the element of passivity which inheres in all our activity. Little thought is devoted to the state of being determined [*Bestimmtsein*] that lies at the heart of human determining [*Bestimmendsein*]. The unity of doing and letting-be-done is most often ignored where it – in theory as much as in praxis – is most important: namely, in dealing with the human capacity for self-determination.

The liberation of human being from alien determination is one of the oldest motifs of philosophy. To actively direct and orient one's life under essentially indeterminable circumstances has always been regarded as the constitutive core of a successful life. Where opinions continue to diverge is the question of how this autonomous conduct of life is to be achieved under conditions of far-reaching heteronomy. How is it possible to orient oneself along life's path by one's own agency even when there are internal and external forces at work, uncontrolled and maybe uncontrollable, undetermined and perhaps indeterminable? How can self-determination under conditions such as these be anything more than an unreachable ideal? But philosophy, if it is to have any practical consequences, must not be satisfied with such a conclusion. After all, we can invoke or defend self-determination – be this in personal, moral, or political contexts – only when we can give it reality as something fundamentally attainable. Much depends then on rethinking the possibility of self-determination in a way that makes it a real possibility for us.

Trusting in such a possibility is not the same as believing in the attainability of complete and full self-determination, for it is one of those aspects of living in which we must succeed each time anew, and thus are liable to fail. Even when we succeed for a time, we always find ourselves in danger of failure. One is tempted to say that the potential for successful self-determination is drawn from the training one receives from the experience of failing. This tenuous possibility, however, is what philosophy has to bet on if it is to meet seriously the demands of a practical philosophy.

2

Socrates's interlocutors already registered vigorous doubts as to whether the road to the proposed good life was actually open to real human beings – even if the imposing presence of Socrates himself seemed to be overwhelming evidence that travel down that road was indeed possible. Nonetheless philosophers have never ceased doubting the power and the glory of a life guided by reason. David Hume, for example, toppled the platonic-Christian conception of self-determination when he remarked that reason is not the lord but the slave of the passions. But Hume thought that crowning the passions as the first and last causes of action was an act of liberation – the liberation from traditional notions of human nature. We have to reflect on that which actually guides our actions, Hume says. And that which guides them consists of impulses which, in accordance with our nature, we passively accommodate. Thus, we need to recognize that in all our practical determinations we are always already determined – by ourselves. We can respond to this determination in wise and unwise ways, but that's all. In determining ourselves, Hume might have said, we actually let ourselves be determined by the functions of our affective and appetitive reactions.

Deflating reason to an essentially executive organ (whose responsibilities are limited to the discovery of objective mistakes and the choice of appropriate means), Hume explicitly abandons any robust conception of self-determination – such a conception would be illusory. Self-determination in the strong sense would require the ability to set up the directions of one's own actions – and thus the course of one's own life – on the basis of one's own reflection alone. Since these basic directions are always already given affectively, reflection cannot claim to provide them. Our basic practical stances, however well reflected upon, turn out to be consequences of our stance within the force field of our passions. In Hume, then, being determined and active determining are out of balance.

3

One could claim that Kant set this balance right again, but things are not in fact that simple. For as far as the human drive for happiness is concerned, Kant follows Hume in regarding practical reason as pathologically conditioned. Kant too sees our factual inclinations as determining the direction we ultimately choose. "The will would not give itself the law but a foreign impulse would give the law to it."[2] This reinterpretation of one's own drive as an external impulse makes of course very clear that Kant, as opposed to Hume, sees here a heteronomous relation to one's own drives. "I ought to do something because I will something else."[3] In this cycle of arbitrary willing [Kreislauf der Willkühr], every reasonable wanting is tied to a factual drive. According to Kant, human autonomy occurs only when one gives oneself a law capable of guiding one's conduct based on reason alone. Self-determination in the actual sense of the word is possible only when strictly universal reasons and not one's own sensuous drives set the framework for individual orientation. Only reason born of morality lends the will its autonomy. Only when one determines not one's goals, which are at base contingent, but rather the form of one's actions, says Kant, does one really act according to one's own determination. In this way, we can achieve autonomy under inescapable conditions of heteronomous determination.

This combination of heteronomy and autonomy marks the entirety of Kant's practical philosophy (excepting perhaps the ambivalent attempts at mediation in the Critique of Judgment). While Kant's theoretical philosophy posits – by the connection between receptivity and spontaneity – a unity of being determined and being able to determine, the practical philosophy emphatically excludes the possibility of such integration. Just like Hume, albeit for different reasons, Kant gives up the notion of self-determination as an activity (and ability) that can lead our lives all the way through.

<h1 style="text-align:center">4</h1>

This splitting of practical reason into an heteronomous and an autonomous component – or, perhaps more appropriately, into a relative and an absolute concept of self-determination – has been subject to much critique, among others by Fichte, Schiller and, of course, Hegel. It is one of the central aims of Hegel's practical philosophy to correct the distortions resulting from Kant's "creative" division of labor within practical reason. His starting point is the balance between being determined and active determining as it appears in the relation between subjects, particularly under conditions of mutual recognition. As in Fichte, there is a mutual determination not only between subject and world, but between subjects, who, through their mutual interaction, manage to find an unforced place in the world. In explicating this interactive autonomy in the Philosophy of Right, Hegel took recourse to the intersubjective model of love.[4] In the case of love, "we are not one-sidedly within ourselves, but willingly limit ourselves with reference to an other, even while knowing ourselves in this limitation as ourselves."[5] Hegel extracts from this observation a far-reaching maxim that is intended to show how the dualism of active determining and being determined can be overcome in the context of successful living. "*In this determinacy, the human being should not feel determined.*"[6] Or to put it differently: One should not experience this act of self-limitation as an alien imposition.

Hegel, however, yokes this interpretation of individual freedom as a freely willed and freely permitted openness to letting oneself be determined, to a much stronger thesis: the sublation of all one-sidedness, otherness, and limitation that is supposed to belong to the interactive character of the self. This entails a disavowal of the elements of passivity and dependence characteristic not only of friendship or love, but perhaps all human relations to the world. Accordingly, Hegel says of the free will which makes itself the object of the exercise of its freedom: "Only in this freedom is the will completely with itself [*bei sich*], because it has reference to nothing but itself, so that every relationship of dependence on something other than itself is thereby eliminated."[7] At precisely the point at which Hegel characterizes human autonomy as one internal, equilibriated complex, at precisely the point at which he recognizes being determined by oneself or by others as a constitutive element of self-determination, he backpedals. He places this freedom in – one wants to say, abstract – opposition to *dependence* on something else. But "being with oneself" [*bei sich sein*], that is, living as one wants to live, is not actually possible without a relation to someone or something other than oneself – and that means, to live in a way that does not originate in or coincide with one's own self-concept.

5

Kant's bifurcation of practical reason is one of Nietzsche's main points of attack as well. Nietzsche wants to reclaim an intact concept of the self as a practical undertaking. In doing so he harkens back to motifs of antiquity, all the while giving the notion of self-determination an extraordinarily constructivist sense. Artistic humanity, capable of powerful cultural achievements, creates the values by which it will let its life be determined. Much more radically than in Kant, being able to determine is given precedence over being determined, even if self-determination in the final analysis takes the shape of arbitrary willing and is thus once again a limited determination. Essentially, the self is determined by corporeal impulses, namely, by the appetite and taste for life-possibilities, impulses it freely follows and inventively shapes.

When Nietzsche says in the prescript to aphorism 304 of *The Gay Science*, "by doing we forego,"[8] he's talking primarily about the decisiveness with which one follows one's own preferences without letting oneself be swayed by a supra-individual standpoint. "What we do should determine what we forego; in doing we forego – that's how I like it; that is my *placitum*."[9] Here, too, what is proposed is not a balance or integration of doing and letting-be-done; rather, doing is supposed to set the framework for letting-be-done. And so we should refrain from whatever is not on our personal agenda for self-creation. Letting-be-done does not govern doing (as Nietzsche presents Kant's picture of human autonomy); doing governs letting-be-done. Under inverted premises, Nietzsche maintains a questionable hierarchy of passive and active components of action.

6

This is where Heidegger enters the picture. It is Heidegger who explicitly seeks to correct the one-sidedness of Nietzsche's hyper-activism in his analyses of the theory of action in *Being and Time*. On first glance it may seem as though the Kierkegaard-inspired polarity of "thrownness" [*Geworfenheit*] and "project" [*Entwurf*] finally yields a real balance between the vectors of self-determination. In my view, however, this does not turn out to be the case.

In "thrownness," Heidegger says, "Dasein, as my Dasein" reveals itself as "always already in a determined world and alongside a determined range of determined innerworldly entities."[10] We find ourselves thrown into concrete conditions of life, which have determined us, and which continue to determine us. As something thus thrown, Heidegger expounds, Dasein "is thrown into the kind of being we call projection."[11] This "projection" [*Entwerfen*] refers to an individual self-understanding that arises from culturally and socially preformed possibilities for action, which are themselves surrounded by a wide horizon of as yet undetermined possibilities. In this historically disclosed world, human beings are attuned to the general framework of their praxis, long before they determine courses of action, or design particular projects through imagination and reflection. Thus, what Heidegger means by "project" is not to be understood as designating the accomplishment of free self-determination; rather, it is meant as a letting-be [*Seinlassen*] – a letting-oneself-be-conveyed [*Sicheinlassen*] into the possibilities of existence. Human beings are *seized* by these received possibilities long before they are able to grasp their *own* possibilities.

Even in the mode of "authentic" existence, not much changes in the priority of being determined to determining. Here too, the human being is conceived of as primarily receptive: it holds itself "free and open . . . for its own actual [*faktische*] possibility."[12] For Heidegger, this "holding oneself open" for the indeterminate possibilities of one's own existence comes before any grounding or decisive resolution of a determining mode of will. Holding oneself open precedes any determination of the self. The authentic capacity for being-oneself, which in Heidegger replaces self-determination, is an *involuntary* submission to letting oneself be determined.

7

Of course, my title and my message is precisely this: self-determination, correctly understood, is the ability to let oneself be determined. However, a lot depends on which part of that formula is stressed. Heidegger stresses – increasingly so in his later years – the "letting." Kant and his followers[13] put the stress – with varying degrees of radicality – on the "self." I am trying to read the formula with an equal distribution of stress on the "(one)self" and the "letting" thus meaning "being determined" in the double sense of the phrase. This achieves the balance, which I believe the tradition has aimed for, and has so often missed. For now this is of course merely a syntactic balance; but I want to show that it actually corresponds to an objective balance that directs us to a robust yet plausible understanding of self-determination.

Throughout, I will be using the concept of self-determination in a very elementary sense. I am not speaking of moral self-determination in contradistinction to individual self-realization; and I am not speaking of subjective self-limitation in contradistinction to intersubjective self-binding, nor of aesthetic self-creation in contradistinction to ethical self-obligation. In a methodological analogy to Heidegger, I am trying instead to characterize a relationship of the self on which all of these are grounded. Long before "self-determination" becomes a specialized topic in ethics or in political philosophy, it is one of philosophical anthropology. (Only in closing will I shift from there to a few points on moral theory.)

8

Our point of departure will be a consideration of what it means to have oneself as subject and object of one's own determination. A person who exercises her ability to determine herself, applies it practically on a spectrum of life-possibilities – propitious to unpropitious, promising to futile – that are open to her. She determines for herself which one of these possibilities will indeed be grasped, and thereby determines simultaneously how she wants to understand herself within the continuity of her actions, and thus, to understand who she essentially wants to be.

This is of course not the only form of determining something or oneself, but rather, a particular and particularly complex form. More often we determine merely on the basis of an opinion or intention. But even in such cases we do not take each particular position separately. Each opinion or intention is always already connected to others. Each of them contains a determination *vis-à-vis* other persons, who may, in turn, arrive at these same or quite different decisions and resolutions. In general I use "determining" to refer to the *reflective commitment* to a certain claim or a certain course of action. "Commitment" means in this case an action in which a position is taken, which assumes a particular contour *vis-à-vis* other possible positions: *vis-à-vis* commitments to *other claims* or courses of action as much as to commitments that are undertaken by *others*. It is only within this two-dimensional space that we can commit ourselves to claims with a determinate content. I call commitments "reflective" if they rest on an exploration of different possibilities. That means that reflection is to be understood as a striving for understanding, regardless of whether it is attained or not. Whoever commits herself reflectively – be it to a proposition or a resolution, a theory or a way of life – has reasons, or believes she has reasons, to bind herself to it. She grants herself – and we grant her – the capacity for rational orientation in the different concerns of her life. Supreme amongst these concerns, however, is the individual's life itself – and it is for now quite uncertain, if and in what sense, rational orientation is possible in this area at all.

It is uncertain because nothing like final grounds is available. As both Heidegger and Wittgenstein have correctly stressed, whatever has previously played a practically determining role cannot go on doing so indefinitely. But this does not herald the end for the possibility of a life lived rationally. Rather, one sees that practical reflections and delimitations necessarily unfold within a historically structured and socially shared world. They unfold in the face of givens and opportunities, which are not at anyone's disposition; they unfold under conditions of receptive and responsive behavior, which give the spontaneity of action a basis and a perspective at once. Every determination of ourselves that we undertake involves entrusting ourselves to a particular horizon of possibilities, a horizon within which the possibility of undertaking commitments by and with regard to oneself arises.

Determination of any sort – be it with theoretical or practical intentions – involves multiple ways of letting-oneself-be-determined: by the content, by the medium, and by the motive of determination. Each reflective commitment has to take into account its *object* of concern. In this way, commitment also involves access to intersubjective *media*, through which one is able to articulate aspects of oneself and the world – even if one is in the process of developing one's own view of things. And finally, every theoretical or practical striving for understanding is guided by *motives*, by which we can clarify or at least register in advance, what counts as relevant knowledge and relevant willing in the context in question. In these dimensions we must definitely let ourselves be guided, when we will for ourselves. To be able to determine (actively), we must be capable of letting ourselves be determined.

9

The passive components of determination are legion; it is thus important to mark those components that are decisive for a theory of self-determination. Three dimensions can be differentiated, ones in which any determination of the self involves at once an element of being determined. The first of these is being determined *ex ante*: We are always already determined by past events, and by, among other things, ourselves. That is largely the trivial meaning of the conditionedness of our active being. The combination of genetic disposition, historical and cultural context, familial and social origin, economic and political circumstances, and an individual's own experiences and past actions, place her in a diversely and, in many cases, irreversibly pre-determined situation. Only in such a situation can self-determining freedom exist.[14] The individual who is not in some respect determined would be incapable of determining anything whatsoever, for there would

87

be no counterweight against which self-determination could have any leverage. Being determined is a constitutive *basis* of self-determination.

The second element is being determined *ex post*: Setting practical limits also means deciding by what we would like to *be* determined – and thus, by what we would like to *let us* be determined, currently or in the future. This element is anything but trivial, since here we are dealing with the content as much as with the consequences of our own decisions. Often, we determine the goal of our actions by ourselves so that we are able to be determined by that very goal in major respects. This determinability pertains not only to existential commitments, but also, at one and the same time, to *that* to which we commit when we determine what we will in our life. Whenever we do this, we exert an influence over how we are going to let ourselves be determined in the future. I am thinking here of the decision to watch a particular movie or to subscribe to a particular newspaper; in performing each of these actions we accept being subject to factors the exact extent of which we cannot judge. Much more far-reaching is of course one's choice of profession, place of residence, of partners, sexual or otherwise, or, an extreme example, the decision to bring a child into the world or to write a book. In whichever way we allow ourselves be determined by these choices, in each case we attune or orient ourselves towards situations in which we will be determined in an unforeseeable way – and by which we would like to be determined, so far as we can tell. Self-determination in life includes the good fortune of finding oneself in situations in and by which one would like to be determined. Letting oneself be determined is a constitutive *telos* of self-determination.

This second element has been given short shrift in the theory of action, to say nothing of the third one: being determined *in actu*. After all, being determined and letting oneself be determined are not only an ineluctable precondition or simply an intention of self-determination; they are, moreover, integral markers of the exercise of self-determination. No act of self-determination and certainly no self-determined praxis can be felicitous without developed receptivity. Letting oneself be determined is not merely a basis and an aim, it is a constitutive *component* of the process of self-determination.

In the following, I will focus in particular on this *processual* aspect of being determined. I would like to characterize the process of a self-determined life under appropriate consideration of its passive capabilities.

10

Whether it is ourselves or something else that we determine, understanding can be achieved, if it is achieved, only when we let ourselves be engaged by that about which we seek orientation. Even the most elementary cognitive determination can clarify this. One has to look to find out how many seats are in a particular room. This material determining of our cognition is not thinkable without its complement, a determining by a medium.[15] After all, determining something proceeds only insofar as the medium of concepts allows us to see that something as something. That we can determine anything at all is owed to the fact that we are already diversely pre-determined by the material and media of our determining activity. The vocabulary of a language, to use an example that suggests itself, provides a range of possibilities of mental or objective interconnections, in which we always already find ourselves (into which we are always already "thrown") whenever we make a determination. We are committed to use a particular chain of distinctions, even when we only make one distinction. We are committed to a particular range of opinions, even when we are forming only one opinion. But such (pre-reflective) commitment can be understood normatively – and thus as fundamentally open to revision – only in combination with the possibility of an active (i.e. reflective) undertaking of commitments. In our theoretical determining we are always already determined by the media and materials of determination; but we are thus determined only because we can be determining by way of our capacity actively to explore and reflect upon what to think or to do. For this is the only way to conceive of the maneuvering room [Spielraum] of our determinations – a field of uncharted and by-and-large unavailable possibilities, which are possibilities precisely because we can take hold of them or reject them.

But if theoretical cognition is a doing – an "action," as Kant calls it – then the point of this action needs to be taken into account. Theoretical behavior does not intend simply toward a collection of statements, but intends instead toward an orienting kind of knowledge. It aims at the formation of relevant and true opinions. Its purpose is to provide an account of the world. Thus, the formation of knowledge stands always in relation to what we draw from experience, what we want to know. That's why our theoretical behavior is determined not only by the medium and material of cognition, but also by its motives. These motives remain often unthematized, taking the shape of interests, which determine our turning toward the objects of cognition. (What counts as a "seat", for example, depends on the occasion for which we are seeking a seat.) If we were not in one way or the other motivated and thus moved by the world's events, no movement of cognition would be possible. Without such a drive, no will to knowledge demanding the determination of the undetermined would ever arise. In being determined by the material and by the medium, we allow ourselves to be determined by our positive or negative affinity to the circumstances of the world.

11

In practical deliberations, this affinity becomes the object of reflection. In such deliberations, we try to set parameters for how to direct our actions. We attempt to identify what our interests are, and what we wish to have a stake in. In doing so we are not only adducing reasons for this or that; we are adducing motivating reasons, which can give direction to our doing and undergoing. This is based on a clarification of our identified interests, on what we wish to stake our lives, and, thus, on an historical and imaginative review of our life-situation. Only so is it possible to recognize which possibilities we have and, of these, which we want to have. These possibilities cannot be invented wholesale; they have to be discovered in an observant encounter with the world. To let oneself respond to the possibilities of a particularly historical world is not merely a precondition and a consequence of practical determination; it is more than a mere procedure; it is almost its purpose. In practical reflection, when we are dealing with questions of existential import, we try to determine by what we *wish* to be moved.

But how does this basic determination look from a practical perspective? Well, it does not conform to Hume's view, according to which certain motives in the end gain the upper hand; or to the view of Kant's moral theory, according to which external reasons become defining. It does not conform to Hegel's view, according to which all dependence of will falls away as soon as the will establishes a free relation to itself; or to Nietzsche's, according to which we freely invent ourselves in an act of willing. And it does not, finally, conform to Heidegger's view, according to which we are to sustain an open relation to what happens, to events that take on the character of fate. In any case, it is not exactly like what these authors describe. A helpful corrective to their emphatic one-sidedness, are Harry Frankfurt's valuable studies on the practical relation to self. In our basic practical attitudes, Frankfurt claims, we voluntarily delimit ourselves to a project by experiencing ourselves *as* limited. We affirm something that we notice we are passionate about, something to which we are bound, both in terms of affect and volition.

By linking of the involuntary with the voluntary Frankfurt helps us see that we make our most weighty existential determinations not by first making a conscious and reasoned choice of this or that goal which seems to us worth achieving, which we then take steps to realize. Rather, it is the passion for something that first constitutes the value which that something has or gains for us (as Frankfurt makes evident in the case of love).[16] Often, to our own surprise, we experience ourselves as people who, of all the things we care about, care most about those particular things. However, such an experience alone does not constitute a binding orientation. It results, rather, from the affirmation of the affinity which we feel for a person, situation, activity or project. This is true for the central directives of a self-determined life. We do not have command over them when we follow them by our own accord. If we want to be self-determining, we must as well let ourselves be self-determined.

12

Here, "to let" means allowing something to be undergone. No self-determination can rise above the factual drives and affinities of one's particular way of responding to the world [*Gestimmtseins*]. Only when a person lets herself be carried by motives, which she in fact has, can she determine what kind of life she might want and – much more narrowly – which kind of life she actually does want. This is possible only for someone who knows how to pay attention to his or her own drives or affinities, and who is capable of moderating and modifying them. After all, not every possibility to which one is attracted is a possibility that one should then affirm. Otherwise, the freedom of voluntary affirmation or negation of one's own drives simply would not exist. But this freedom is primarily a freedom to affirm or endorse the direction of one's own drives. After all, only based on such affirmation can one successfully negate or modify them. Only by determining ourselves to *let* ourselves be determined by a determinate number of motives, are we free to determine the basic dimensions of our existence. The governing outcomes of our life happen – in the double sense of the phrase – *with our consent*.

Of course, none of this takes place in a void. It takes place – as mentioned before – within a historically and culturally disclosed world, a world in which all individual experience is always contextualized by social experience. It takes place in contexts of shared or shareable convictions as to what is valuable or important in one's own life situation. Even if the existentially founded will [*Wollen*] is not fully subject to rational grounding, it does not lie outside the intersubjective "space of reasons," in which alone binding orientations can exist.[17] An autonomous conduct of life is thus supported by a will that has not arisen from deliberation, but can nonetheless stand up to reflective scrutiny. The decision for this or that course of action remains contestable by reasons throughout. This critique can question the unintended consequences of a particular course of action just as much as its incompatibility with other vital goals. Moreover, it can call into doubt the desirability or advisability of the situation to be brought about. Critique can thus be the occasion for a revision of basic subjective willing. And with this alteration, the basic standpoints from which we evaluate our life circumstances change as well.

An analogy to perception may prove helpful. The convictions at which we arrive by way of perception are just as little the result of conclusions. But there are conclusions to be drawn from them, and these in turn can be tested by reasons. Correspondingly, one's attitudes or dispositions, attitudes and dispositions that shape what most matters, occupy a non-neutral position in relation to one's judgments concerning what counts as good for oneself or in general. When strongly held subjective values are involved in the position we take on some matter, we are taking a position not only toward various possibilities for living and acting, but also toward the evaluative convictions to which until now we have been bound. Thus, we not only modify the economy of our endeavors and strivings, we also modify the contents of our view of the world.

13

It is on account of this embeddedness that I labeled not only theoretical but also practical determination as a reflective commitment. The direction of our practical commitments display a cognitive character, even when, in contrast to theoretical commitment, they pertain first and foremost not to an opinion or proposition, but to a wanting or intending. First, I cognize and recognize that I want this or that. I discover something about myself; I learn that I am someone for whom this or that is really important. Moreover, I accept that this is so. Second, an affirmation, this act of the will which is decisive for any free wanting of something, is only possible when that to which I am committing myself makes sense to me – when I see (or believe that I see) that I can sensibly will it. This I can only do if there exists a possibility, however small, that my project can be realized (even if it consists merely in "attempting the impossible." i.e. in seeing the attempt as the realization). In any case, that which I care about in this way cannot be diametrically opposed to other basic options (however tense their relation, since this tension may in fact be desirable). Tied up with this is, third, that I encounter the situations of my life in a new fashion – in light of this now revised or perhaps merely reinforced notion of what it means to want something, such that in my own experience and thought, I regard myself and my world in a new way.

Even if they do not owe their existence to any explicit justification, these basic practical commitments unfold within a holistic context of reasons. This consists of a totality that cannot be surveyed as a whole, but rather is comprised of an extensive range of relations, an indeterminate number of which pertain to the understanding of the situation from which we form our convictions.[18] The affirmation of value-forming passions, which first makes evaluation possible, is thus not the final decision. Rather, such affirmation unfolds from within a force field of reasons, the lines of which are merely put into new order by a revised demarcation. The fundamental practical attitudes constituting the framework of a self-determined life cannot be considered in isolation from the remaining praxis of life. After all, a self-determined life is a genuine possibility only when we are capable of experiencing our own decisions as binding. And that means, having intelligence and imagination enough to shift the perspective they open up throughout all the likely and unlikely situations of our lives. At the same time a self-determined life is not worthy of the name if it is a life that is determined *only* by one's practical attitudes – if it is unwilling and incapable of responding to the transformations to which our affinity to the things in our lives is subject.

14

We have to commit to this open-ended process of self-direction, if we want to play a guiding role in the actions of our own lives.[19] A certain degree of play within, as well as an enlargement of, the space of one's reflections, is probably the best way to take part and to have a stake in one's own life. To have this degree of play and to maintain such an open space of reflection, requires that one be and that one remain responsive – and, thus, vulnerable – to the world, to others, and to oneself. The freedom of a self-determined life consists in precisely this: to allow a provisional determination in indeterminacy, and to allow within one's own sense of determination a sense of the indeterminate.

The co-extensiveness of determinacy and indeterminacy, of being determined and being determining, is central to a non-illusory *concept* of, and to a non-illusory *relation* to, self-determination. We are able to bind ourselves to something or someone only because we are already bound to the world, connected to it through others and through ourselves. This is the moral that the Sirens episode in the *Odyssey* has provided to philosophy. We can only live successful self-determination when we are open to the perception of external and internal possibilities, possibilities that have not been determined by us, and that in many respects appear indeterminate to us. At the same time, only those for whom the indeterminacy of their own life-context remains open have the ability to find their own answer to the conditions that they happen to encounter. They will find the answer to those conditions only when they find their own response to those forces at work within their thoughts, emotions and actions. To *let* oneself be determined as one lets oneself be *determined* – this is the most propitious position. We can thus speak of successful self-determination only insofar as we grant the subjects of these determinations the capacity to enter into the relations in which they are already embedded in their own way.

But this capacity also includes, as becomes clear again, a comprehensive ability that is also called upon in theoretical determination as well. For herein lies an integral characteristic of rationality, be it theoretical or practical or of any other mode. We can only behave rationally so long as we are determined by reasons. But we can only be determined by reasons so long as we are capable of letting ourselves be determined: either by that upon which these reasons are based or by that to which they refer. But we would not be able to let ourselves be so determined, unless we were capable of making a determination, whether in our use of media, in our interaction with others, in the handling of objects, or in recourse to motives, all of which determine us there where we determine ourselves.

15

But who loses oneself in this way and who finds oneself in this way? It is someone amongst others – a definite someone who experiences herself in relation to others as someone who is different from those others. All who are "others" to others can find their temporary determination only in response to others. They cannot stand on their own without standing in some relation to an other. This relation has many aspects. It shows up where reasons are formulated and also where there is (inter)action with and against others. No one can let oneself be determined without letting others be determining. This possibility belongs to the capacity of self-determination right from the beginning.

That does not mean, however, that self-determination is always also a moral undertaking. Rather, the capacity for self-determination is the basis of the possibility of acting morally or immorally. The constitutive intersubjectivity of self-determination creates the space for morality and immorality. It opens the possibility, to let oneself be determined by others in this way or that, and thus, to respond to others in this way or that. If, as Kant put it, everything is practical "that is possible through freedom,"[20] then it is especially morally questionable behavior that belongs to the possibilities released by self-determination. But since this is basically a mode of self-conduct amongst and in connection with others, there is no self-determination outside of the purview of morality. Only when we have the capacity for self-direction, do we also have the capacity to make moral use of this freedom. If and when it actually comes to this use and what exact shape that use might take – that is something that must show itself in each instance. The moral standpoint is an important modification of self-determination, but not its essence.

16

We are used to understanding this modification as a restriction on action. We are supposed to desist from a particular behavior, however expedient or profitable, because it humiliates or disrespects others. In this respect, morality is a delimitation of the circle of permissible actions. But the basis of this restriction is not itself a limitation, but actually a derestriction of our behavior toward others. As especially Emmanuel Levinas has seen, it is not restriction that stands at the inception of morality, but rather the lifting of this restriction: namely, the readiness to let the well-being and suffering of the other determine one's own actions. One can thus only have a sense of morality as long as one remains receptive to others and thus remains determinable by them.

This openness to others is not a consequence of duty. It is much more the case that moral rules and duties are consequences of our openness to others. The source of morality is a freely willed and reciprocal engagement with the situation of the respective other. This turning toward the other is the source of the particular attachments that arise in relation to the other. They result from the situation in which I and the other find ourselves – a situation in which I and the other share a space in which we can be an interlocutor for one another or in which we can let each other be. We recognize one another as beings belonging passionately or indifferently – or passionately and indifferently – to one another. It is this intimate recognition of *certain* others from which spring the reasons for the recognition of *any* others. Those reasons follow upon the understanding that the space for a free encounter with the world is just as important to distant others as it is to me.

The road to this enlarged understanding is anticipated in intimate relations of recognition. For the recognition of a particular other is always already more than recognizing a determinate someone, just as from the point of view of the other it is always already more than being recognized by a determinate someone. In relations of recognition the role of the participants is essentially indeterminate. After all, nobody is certain of his or her position, of his or her capacities – of his or her face. Everyone is someone "other," or can be so for others. That means that the third person is already contained in the "other." The recognition of a particular other contains already the moment of recognition of any other. Morality is thus in the final analysis a consequence of recognition, as experienced and accorded, at least partially, in contexts of successful self-determination. When and how this consequence comes about depends on to what extent we allow our behavior to be determined by the claims of others.

However, the idea of moral determinability is given short shrift, if all over again we erect barriers – as happens in Levinas as well as in his contractualist opponents – between active and passive, symmetrical and asymmetrical bonds. Moral recognition is always at once active and passive, symmetrical and asymmetrical.[21] It is a letting-oneself-be determined, which leads to a respectful determinedness in intercourse with others. It is a perception of elementary equality possessed by its addressees in full cognizance of their comprehensive differences. What it involves is not the wish to determine others, but – as far as possible – to determine *in concert* with them. But this intersubjective coordination fulfills its purpose only when all are also allowed to resist being determined by others.

Notes

1 Translated by Adrian Daub and Nikolas Kompridis.
2 Immanuel Kant, *Groundwork for the Metaphysics of Morals*, in Immanuel Kant, *Practical Philosophy*, Allen Wood (ed.), trans. Mary J. Gregor, Cambridge, Cambridge University Press, 1996, p. 92.
3 *Ibid.*, p. 89.
4 Axel Honneth, *Suffering from Indeterminacy. An Attempt at a Reactualization of Hegel's Philosophy of Right*, trans. Jack Ben-Levi, Assen, Van Gorcum, 2000.
5 G. W. F. Hegel, *Philosophy of Right*, Allen Wood (ed.), trans. H. B. Nisbet, Cambridge, Cambridge University Press, 1991, p. 42.
6 *Ibid.*, p. 42.
7 *Ibid.*, p. 54.
8 Friedrich Nietzsche, *The Gay Science*, Bernard Williams (ed.), trans. Josefine Nauckhoff, Cambridge, Cambridge University Press, 2001, p. 173.
9 *Ibid.*, p. 173.
10 Martin Heidegger, *Being and Time*, trans. John Macquarrie and Edward Robinson, New York, Harper and Row, 1962, p. 264, translation amended.
11 *Ibid.*, p. 185.
12 *Ibid.*, p. 355, translation amended. In his later reflections on "letting-be," Heidegger adds, "In waiting we keep open that upon which we wait" ["Im Warten lassen wir das, worauf wir warten, offen."]. Heidegger, *Gelassenheit*, Stuttgart, Neske,1999, p. 42.
13 For example, Ernst Tugendhat, *Self-Consciousness and Self-Determination*, trans. Paul Stern, Cambridge MA, MIT Press, 1986; and Jürgen Habermas, *Justification and Application. Remarks on Discourse Ethics*, trans. Ciaran Cronin, Cambridge MA, MIT

Press, 1993. An extreme version of autonomy can be found in Volker Gerhard, *Selbstbestimmung*, Stuttgart, Reclam, 1999. For a critique of Gerhard, see Martin Seel, "Aktive und Passive Selbstbestimmung," in *Merkur*, 54/2000, pp. 626–31.

14 This has been made quite clear recently by Peter Bieri, *Vom Handwerk der Freiheit*, Munich, Hanser, 2001.

15 Martin Seel, "Bestimmen und Bestimmenlassen. Anfänge einer Medialen Erkenntnistheorie," in *Sich Bestimmen lassen. Studien zur theoretischen und praktischen Philosophie*, Frankfurt, Suhrkamp, 2002, pp. 146–66.

16 It is, according to Frankfurt, precisely this comprehensive and involuntary determination, which opens within the life of an individual the contrasting meaningful commitments. Harry Frankfurt, *The Importance of What We Care About*, Cambridge, Cambridge University Press, 1988.

17 Following Wilfrid Sellars, John McDowell and Robert B. Brandom have emphasized this. At this point, the one-sidedness of Heidegger's analysis becomes especially clear: he places the disclosure of authentic Dasein outside the space of reasons.

18 For more on this see, "Für einen Holismus ohne Ganzes," in Martin Seel, *Sich Bestimmen lassen. Studien zur theoretischen und praktischen Philosophie*, pp. 89–100.

19 In order to understand this correctly, we need to reject once again one-sidedly activist or passivist interpretations – in this case, interpretations of the game metaphor – as they are presented by Schiller and Nietzsche, on the one side, and Heidegger and Gadamer, on the other. For more on this see, "Heidegger und die Ethik des Spiels," in Martin Seel, *Sich Bestimmen lassen. Studien zur theoretischen und praktischen Philosophie*, pp. 169–96.

20 Immanuel Kant, *Critique of Pure Reason*, trans. Paul Guyer and Allen Wood, Cambridge, Cambridge University Press, 1998, p. 675, translation amended.

21 I explore this further in, "Moralischer Adressat und moralisches Gegenüber," in Martin Seel, *Versuch über die Form des Glücks*, Frankfurt, Suhrkamp, 1995.

5

ROMANTIC SUBJECTIVITY IN GOETHE AND WITTGENSTEIN

Richard Eldridge

As a result of the fine work of Mark Rowe, Joachim Schulte, Gordon Baker and Peter Hacker,[1] it has now been evident for some time that there are deep affinities – affinities in style and textual organization, in conceptions of elucidatory explanation via comparisons, and in a sense of subjectivity housed within nature – between the Goethe of the *Farbenlehre* and the Wittgenstein of *Philosophical Investigations*. Among the very deepest of these affinities is their shared sense of the limits of metaphysical explanation. The identification of simple elements is always relative to purposes and circumstances, never ultimate. Hence there is no single kind of ultimate explanation running from the nature and behavior of ultimate simples to the nature and behavior of complexes composed out of them. There are often useful explanations to be found of how the behaviors of complexes are determined by the behaviors of their parts, but this kind of explanation is one among many. Comparative descriptions of complexes – whether of organisms, human practices, works of art, or chemical and physical structures – are not to be supplanted in favor of ultimate metaphysical explanation.

Valuable and sound though these ideas are, they are, however, not my theme in this chapter. Instead, I am concerned with a different form of affinity between Goethe and Wittgenstein, an affinity in their senses of what it is to be a human subject. To be sure, I will practice some comparative description of their respective senses of subjectivity in the hope that some illumination may result, but I will dwell more on the substance of the comparisons than on the logic or methodology of the illumination pursued.

Thomas Mann's remarks on *Die Leiden des jungen Werthers* provide a useful starting point. "It would," Mann observes,

> not be a simple task to analyze the psychic state that determined the underpinning of European civilization at that time [1774, the date of publication of *Werther*]. . . . A discontent with civilization, an emancipation of emotions, a gnawing yearning for a return to the natural and

elemental, a shaking at the shackles of ossified culture, a revolt against convention and bourgeois confinement: everything converged to create a spirit that came up against the limitations of individuation itself, that allowed an effusive, boundless affirmation of life to take on the form of a death wish. Melancholy and discontent with the rhythmical monotony of life was the norm.[2]

It is likewise not a simple task to say what may have made such melancholy and discontent the norm, at least in certain circles. Secularization, bringing with it a sense of lost meaningfulness as religious ritual became a smaller part of daily life, and modernization, bringing with it a market economy and new but very uncertain life chances, are surely part of the story. But secularization and modernization are themselves interwoven with deep, largely tacit self-understandings about what is worth doing, in ways that are difficult to disentangle. Charles Taylor, in his monumental survey of the making of the modern identity, describes what he calls

> three major facets of this identity: first, modern inwardness, the sense of ourselves as beings with inner depths; second, the affirmation of ordinary life which develops from the early modern period; third, the expressivist notion of nature as an inner moral source.[3]

These facets of identity that come to the fore in modernity are as much a part of a generally possible human repertoire of identity as they are byproducts of something else. They are, according to Taylor, an inescapable part of our moral framework, a set of commitments that we cannot help but have.

One important result of these commitments is an undecomposable intermingling of moral discovery with moral invention. We no longer think of ourselves as simply living out in one way or another basic human tendencies that are simply given. Rather, drawing on our inwardness, on ordinary life, and on nature, we partly make ourselves what we are. As Taylor puts it, "We find the sense of life through articulating it. And moderns have become acutely aware of how much sense being there for us depends on our own powers of expression. Discovering here depends on, is interwoven with, inventing."[4] Finding is inseparable from founding.

But why should this occasion what Mann noted: discontent, yearning, shaking, revolt, melancholy, and a death wish? It is easy enough to see why a certain improvisatoriness and independence of mind might be valued. But how and why did our moral improvisations come to be freighted with all that? – Here the answer has to do, I think, with a certain lack of both ground and closure to our moral efforts. Without fixed tendencies and *tele* as starting points and endpoints, it becomes uncertain what moral progress and human achievement might look like, even uncertain whether they are possible at all. Philippe Lacoue-Labarthe and Jean-Luc Nancy note the uncertainties that attach to our moral efforts in the wake of the felt absence of any fixed presentation of the self and its powers, as they describe the conception of the subject in Kant's moral theory.

> Without oversimplifying or hardening the contours of a question that merits extended analysis, we cannot fail to note that this "subject" of morality can be defined only negatively, as a subject that is not the subject of knowledge (this knowledge suppressed "to make room for belief"), as a subject without *mathesis*, even of itself. It is indeed posited as freedom, and freedom is the locus of "self-consciousness." But this does not imply that there is any cognition – or even consciousness – of freedom. . . . [T]he question of [the moral subject's] unity, and thus of its very "being subject," is brought to a pitch of high tension.[5]

Lacking a fixed ground and definite *telos*, efforts at articulating and enacting "a sense of life" come to be marked by a desperate intensity. Different subjects become variously lost within different ongoing projects of articulation, each maintaining its sense of its place and progress not through ratification by an audience, which is all too caught up in its own projects, but rather through an hysterical lingering in process. Articulation "sets out to penetrate the essence of poiesy [poetic making], in which the [articulation] produces the truth of production itself, . . . the truth of production *of itself*, of autopoiesy."[6] The manifold modern *Bildungsromanen* and personal epics of coming to self-consciousness and assured social vocation, but *Bildungsromanen* and epics that have difficulty in reaching their own conclusions (other, perhaps, than by taking the artistic making of the very work in hand as the achieved *telos*), are evidence of the dominance of the project of autopoiesis in the modern moral imagination. Human moral self-imagination and achievement become a "question of the *becoming* present of the highest,"[7] not of its *being* present.

The three inescapable parts of our moral framework that Taylor identifies – inwardness, ordinary life, and nature as an expressive resource – conspire in our experience with and against one another to inhibit the achievement of a stable sense of life. Either nature in the aspect of the sublime conspires with inwardness to resist the sways of ordinary life and conventionality, thus setting up the image of the chthonic genius as the exemplar of moral achievement, as in Nietzsche, or nature in the aspect of the beautiful conspires with ordinary life and conventionality, thus setting up an image of pastoralized domesticity as the exemplar of moral achievement, as in certain moments in Rousseau. Each image then stands in immediate criticism of the other, and no stable image of moral achievement persists.

Under such uncertainties and instabilities, it is all too plausible that one might not only become melancholic, but come to wish for nothing more than surcease, even to regard the taking of one's own life as the only possible creative act with a fixed endpoint, as the only meaningful act. Or of course, more modestly, one might forego efforts to live according to a sense of life or to what is highest and assume instead an instrumentalist stance toward the things of life, seeking only modest satisfactions. This strategy is common in modernity, and it is surely honorable. But does it quite escape the silent melancholies, quiet desperations and covert nihilisms about which Emerson and Thoreau and Nietzsche variously warned us?

To come now specifically to *Werther*: Werther's own character is torn between the idealized images of chthonic originality, represented for him by the wild excesses of his own inner emotional life, and pastoralized domesticity, represented for him by the figure of Lotte, maternally feeding bread to her younger brothers and sisters. There are interesting historical specificities that surround the split in Werther's character – and in Goethe's – between these two ideals. In his monumental study of Goethe's development, Nicholas Boyle suggests that these ideals are posed, and posed as irresolvable, for Werther and for Goethe, by certain strains in eighteenth-century German culture. "Werther's innermost life," he writes,

> is determined by a public mood; he lives out to the last, and inflicts on those around him, the loyalties which – because they are literary, intel-lectual, in a sense imaginary loyalties, generated within the current media of communication – most of his contemporaries take only half-seriously. His obsessions are not gratuitously idiosyncratic – they belong to his real and socially determined character, not just to a pathologically self-absorbed consciousness.[8]

Specifically, Boyle suggests that Leibnizianism, Pietism, and Sentimentalism offered images to Goethe of "the self thirsting for its perfectly adequate object."[9] This thirsting of the self for a confirming object took an especially inwardized turn in Germany, since it could not plausibly be welded to a project of political nation building. Autonomy or achieved selfhood had to be found within, and its prin-cipal marks were inner intensities of imagination, feeling and devotion. Goethe's subjectivity, like Werther's, is dominated by "his belief in binding moments of insight"[10] to be achieved fitfully against the sway of official and conventional culture. At the same time, however, Goethe also absorbed a certain political realism and social consciousness from the Storm and Stress (*Sturm und Drang*) movement. He had an awareness of individual character types, including his own, as specific social roles – a novelist's sense (unlike anything in Werther himself) of social reality as narratable from multiple points of view. In *Werther*, as Boyle char-acterizes it, "the Sentimentalist content of the novel is in perfect but momentary balance with a Storm and Stress aesthetic which determines the manner of its presentation."[11] Like Werther, Goethe in writing *Werther*

> endeavored to find roles for himself to act out which both had some general moral or historical significance and could be filled by him with

a sense of selfhood: roles which fused both a [social] character and [an intensely individual] consciousness.[12]

Inwardness and the pursuit of chthonic originality alone lead to empty solipsism; acceptance of oneself as a social type and conformity to convention alone lead to derivativeness and imaginative death. The task is to combine the pursuit of originality with acceptance of oneself as a social type. Unlike Werther, Goethe himself carried out this task through the act of writing about his innermost emotions and self-imaginations in a social setting. This act of writing gave him the opportunity both to cultivate his inner life and to achieve a certain realistic distance from it. For Werther himself, faced with the same task and torn between his hyperbolic idealizations of originality on the one hand and domesticity on the other, things do not go so well. The "very impetus to self-destruction is being imposed on him by the German public mind" – itself faced with the problem of cultivating both autonomous selfhood and continuing sociality – "commerce with which he cannot avoid, or wish to avoid, if he is to express himself at all."[13] The task of blending selfhood with social identity is neither unique to Werther, nor to Goethe, nor to the German public mind of the late eighteenth century. It is the fate of modern subjectivity as such either to face or to evade it.

Like Boyle, Mann too characterizes Werther as "the overrefined final product of the Christian-Pietist cult of the soul and of the emotions."[14] What this means, above all, is a desire for singularity, specifically a desire to desire, intensely and infinitely. As Mann puts it, "the desire to exchange that which is confining and conditional for that which is infinite and limitless is the fundamental character of Werther's nature, as it is of Faust's. . . . He is in love even before his love has an object."[15] Even Lotte asks Werther, "Why must you love me, me only, who belongs to another? I fear, I fear, that it is only the impossibility of possessing me that makes your desire for me so strong."[16] Only a desire for the impossible can certify itself as genuinely singular and original, capable of confirming selfhood against the grain of conventionality.

In the grip of such a desire, impossibly seeking original selfhood both against the grain of all conventionality and yet blended with social identity, no one knows what to do. Our desires are original if and only if impossible, unrecognizable; and they are recognizable and satisfiable if and only if they are mimes of the conventionalized desires of others. No wonder that Werther observes that

> All learned teachers and tutors agree that children do not understand the cause of their desires; but no one likes to think that adults too wander about this earth like children, not knowing where they come from or where they are going, not acting in accord with genuine motives, but ruled like children by biscuits, sugarplums, and the rod – and yet it seems to me so obvious.

(9)

Werther cannot anywhere recognize, act on, and satisfy his own desire as his own. As he then himself wanders the earth, impossibly seeking fully original selfhood blended with social identity, Werther alternates in his moments of attachment and identification between surrender to beautiful scenes of sociality, composure, convention, and pastoralized domesticity, on the one hand, and ecstatic abandonment to sublime scenes of wild creative energy, on the other. In neither moment is the attachment or abandonment either ordinary or in fact achieved; in both cases it is hyperbolized in Werther's imagination into something exceptional, and his hyperbolizing imagination blocks his actually doing anything.

The emblem in nature of the beautiful, of pastoralized domesticity, and of attachment, in Werther's imaginative perception, is the cozy valley of Wahlheim – "Home's Choice." "It is," Werther writes early on,

> interestingly situated on a hill, and by following one of the footpaths out of the village, you can have a view of the whole valley below you. A kindly woman keeps a small inn there, selling wine, beer, and coffee; and she is extremely cheerful and pleasant in spite of her age. The chief charm of this spot consists in two linden trees, spreading their enormous branches over the little green before the church, which is entirely surrounded by peasants' cottages, barns, and homesteads. Seldom have I seen a place so intimate and comfortable.
>
> (10)

The force and direction of Werther's idealization is evident in his litany of adjectives: "kindly," "small," "cheerful," "pleasant," "little," "intimate" and "comfortable." Here he would – originally and creatively – surrender himself to a domesticated, given, human life in nature. But to desire to do this originally and creatively is to make one unable to do it, and Werther simply gazes on the scene, until, as he thinks of himself, he reverts in thought to the idea of nature as also a source of iconoclastic creative energy.

The counterpart scene in which Werther imagines ecstatically abandoning himself to the sublime comes late in his correspondence, as things are not going well. On 12 December, he writes,

> Sometimes I am oppressed, not by apprehension or fear, but by an inexpressible inner fury which seems to tear up my heart and choke me. It's awful, awful. And then I wander about amid the horrors of the night, at this dreadful time of the year.
>
> Yesterday evening it drove me outside. A rapid thaw had suddenly set in: I had been told that the river had risen, that the brooks had all overflowed their banks, and that the whole valley of Wahlheim was under water! I rushed out after eleven o'clock. A terrible sight. The furious torrents rolled from the mountains in the moonlight – fields,

trees, and hedges torn up, and the entire valley one deep lake agitated by the roaring wind! And when the moon shone forth, and tinged the black clouds, and the wild torrent at my feet foamed and resounded in this grand and frightening light, I was overcome by feelings of terror, and at the same time yearning. With arms extended, I looked down into the yawning abyss, and cried, "Down! Down!" For a moment I was lost in the intense delight of ending my sorrows and my sufferings by a plunge into that gulf! But then I felt rooted to the earth and incapable of ending my woes!

(69–70)

If only he could give himself over to this energy in sublime nature, to this wild torrent, the problem of the satisfaction of impossible desire would at least be ended, if not solved. Werther's itinerary lets itself be read as a move from some-time attachment to the beautiful to complete domination by the sublime, ending in the realization that only this end is possible. In some earlier scenes of the perception of nature, Werther's awareness shifts abruptly and jarringly back and forth between a sense of the "overflowing fullness" of nature, before which he feels "as if a god myself" and a sense of nature as "an all-consuming, devouring monster" (36–7). At this late moment in December, he remains in the condition that he had earlier ascribed to humanity in general: "we are as poor and limited as ever, and our soul still languishes for unattainable happiness" (20). His death looms, but he does yet quite grasp it: "My hour is not yet come: I feel it" (70).

Werther's relations to Lotte directly mirror his relations to nature. Both are dominated by his hyperbolizing imagination, as he sees her now as beautiful, now as sublime. When he first sees her, he finds

Six children, from eleven to two years old . . . running about the room, surrounding a lovely girl of medium height, dressed in a simple white frock with pink ribbons. She was holding a loaf of dark bread in her hands, and was cutting slices for the little ones all round, in proportion to their age and appetite. She performed her task with such affection, and each child awaited his turn with outstretched hands and artlessly shouted his thanks.

(15)

Everything here is simple, cozy, natural, and artless, in forming a scene of mildness with which Werther would like to identify. But then he also dreams that "I pressed her to me and covered with countless kisses those dear lips of hers which murmured words of love in response. Our eyes were one in the bliss of ecstasy" (70).

In each case, Lotte is more a posited object of Werther's fevered imagination of himself in relation to her than she is a being seen by him in her own right.

103

She is an occasion for him to fantasize himself complete, both original and at home. Lotte here plays the same role as was played by the earlier object of his affections, whom Werther describes wholly in terms of her effect on him:

> I have felt that heart, that noble soul, in whose presence I seemed to be more than I really was, because I was all that I could be. God! Was there a single power in my soul that remained unused? And in her presence could I not develop fully that intense feeling with which my heart embraces Nature?
>
> (8)

Here, as ever, the real object of Werther's consciousness is *my soul, my heart, my seeming to be more than I really was.* No wonder, then, that when he imagines that she loves him, Werther rhapsodizes in the same egocentric terms: "That she loves me! How the idea exalts me in my own eyes! And . . . how I worship myself since she loves me!" (27).

Werther's self-claimed exceptionalism, his sense that unlike ordinary people "there lie dormant within me so many other qualities which wither unused, and which I must carefully conceal" (8), leads him consistently to scorn ordinary life and the achievements of reciprocity, decency, and human relationship that are possible in it. In particular, he scorns, while also envying, Albert's staid conventionalism and decency. But he here finds Albert only to be typical of what most people are like. "Most people," he writes, "work the greater part of their time just for a living; and the little freedom which remains to them frightens them, so that they use every means of getting rid of it. Such is man's high calling!" (8). In contrast, Werther seeks for himself a genuine high calling and exemplary, commanding achievement, outside the framework of the ordinary. Not for him "the gilded wretchedness, the boredom among the silly people who parade about in society here" (44) at court, a world in which he stands "before a puppet show and see[s] the little puppets move" (45) as they are "completely occupied with etiquette and ceremony" (45). Unable to mix with them, he argues that real love, constancy, and passion "exists in its greatest purity among that class of people whom we call rude, uneducated" (55), as he again hyperbolically idealizes a pastoralized ordinary life. Yet he is unable, with his dormant qualities which he must carefully conceal, to mix with ordinary people either.

Work, too, is treated by Werther as something either stalely conventional and meaningless or idealized as salvific. On the one hand, "the man who, purely for the sake of others, and without any passion or inner compulsion of his own, toils after wealth or dignity, or any other phantom, is simply a fool" (28). On the other hand, "Many a time I wish I were a common laborer, so that when I awake in the morning I might at least have one clear prospect, one pursuit, one hope, for the day which has dawned" (37). In both cases, his attention is on the work as the vehicle of the exalted expression of his personality, not on the work itself and those who do it. Even when he imagines doing a small bit of work in first arriving at the court of Count C., his thoughts remain on himself and his superiority to others.

> But when, in spite of weakness and disappointments, we do our daily work in earnest, we shall find that with all false starts and compromises we make better headway than others who have wind and tide with them; and it gives one a real feeling of self to keep pace with others or outstrip them in the race.
>
> (42)

Werther's God is similarly exceptional – a being whom he assumes either specifically listens to his pleas or specifically avoids them, without any mediating institutions or any involvements in the lives of others. On 30 November, as he approaches his end, he addresses God directly and intimately, presuming to be his particular and special son.

> Father, Whom I know not – Who were once wont to fill my soul, but Who now hidest Thy face from me – call me back to Thee; be silent no longer! Thy silence cannot sustain a soul which thirsts after Thee. What man, what father, could be angry with a son for returning to him unexpectedly, for embracing him and exclaiming, "Here I am again, my father! Forgive me if I have shortened my journey to return before the appointed time. The world is everywhere the same – for labor and pain, pleasure and reward, but what does it all avail? I am happy only where thou art, and in thy presence I am content to suffer or enjoy." And Thou, Heavenly Father, wouldst Thou turn such a child from Thee?
>
> (64)

His address here is strikingly reminiscent of his earlier thoughts about Lotte, whom he similarly regards as his unique savior. "I cannot pray except to her. My imagination sees nothing but her; nothing matters except what has to do with her" (38).

What does it all avail? Seeking absolute and perfect ratification of his exceptional personality and talents, and perfect, autonomous selfhood joined to continuing sociality in a life of daily self-affirming divinity, but finding only ordinary people and his own tortured thoughts and fantasies, Werther can in the end hit only on the strategy of giving it all up. The only freedom from continuing failure is death. "We desire to surrender our whole being" (20) and if partial, egocentric surrender to Lotte, to art, to nature, or to work is received and ratified by no one, ordinary as they all are, then genuine surrender must be complete, an escape from life itself.

> I have heard of a noble race of horses that instinctively bite open a vein when they are hot and exhausted by a long run, in order to

breathe more freely. I am often tempted to open a vein, to gain ever-lasting liberty for myself.

(50)

As he recalls almost kissing Lotte, "And yet I want – but it stands like a barrier before my soul – this bliss – and then die to expiate the sin! Is it sin?" (62). In the end, "The body was carried by workmen. No clergymen attended" (87).

Goethe himself, of course, did not commit suicide, despite the autobiographical character of the novel. Mann suggests that Goethe's willingness to go on living had to do with his sense of his identity as a writer. "Goethe did not kill himself," Mann writes,

> because he had *Werther* – and quite a few other things – to write. *Werther* has no other calling on this earth except his existential suffering, the tragic perspicacity for his imperfections, the Hamletlike loathing of knowledge that suffocates him: thus he must perish.[17]

How did Goethe himself, then, come to have and to be aware of having another calling, one that made life for him worth living? As Mann suggests, the answer has to do, I think, with the very act of writing *Werther*, as well as with the ongoing activity of writing for a public already begun with *Goetz von Berlichingen*. For Goethe, the act of writing in general, and of writing *Werther* in particular, combined a kind of catharsis – both a clarification and an unburdening – of his emotional life with the achievement of a kind of distance or perspective on himself. He came through writing to achieve a sense of himself as having a social identity as a writer, so that the problem of wedding autonomous selfhood to continuing sociality did not for him go fully unsolved. It would be addressed again and again in the act of writing, from *Faust* to the lyric poetry to *Elective Affinities*, though with more maturity and never quite perhaps with the immediate cathartic intensity of address of *Werther*. Yet even in his maturity Goethe retained an intense subjectivity, capable of responding to others as though they were vehicles of salvation for him. Mann notes that at the age of seventy-two he fell in love with the seventeen-year-old Ulrike Sophie von Levetzow. Though address and partial solution to the problem of subjectivity are possible, perhaps full solution is not.

Ludwig Wittgenstein's character strongly resembles those of Goethe and Werther. Both his personal and philosophical writings combine an intense wish for attachment to others or to activities as vehicles for the expression of the higher self he felt himself to have with an equally intense critical scrutiny of that wish. The subtitle of Ray Monk's biography, *The Duty of Genius*, captures this feature of his character well. For the young Wittgenstein in particular, the realization and confirmation of genius was, in Monk's words, "a Categorical Imperative," and the only alternative to failing to follow it was death: genius or suicide. "Wittgenstein's recurring thoughts of suicide between 1903 and 1912, and the fact that these thoughts abated only after Russell's recognition of his genius, suggest that he accepted this imperative in all its terrifying severity."[18]

Monk traces Wittgenstein's submission to this imperative to his reading of Otto Weininger's *Sex and Character*, published in 1903, the year of Weininger's own suicide. Brian McGuinness accepts this connection but goes further to read this imperative into the composition of the *Tractatus* and to situate it in the context of Wittgenstein's family life and surrounding culture. McGuinness characterizes what he calls "the final message of the *Tractatus*" as

> Perhaps a clearer, a more concentrated view . . . would enable him to see the world aright. At any rate, if there was no real prospect of this: if he could not reach this insight, and if he could not get rid of his troubles by reconciling himself to the world, then his life was pointless.[19]

What made this question – genius or suicide – arise with special force in Wittgenstein's case, McGuinness argues, was not only the example and influence of Weininger or the general sickness of pre-war Austrian culture, but also and more deeply the influence on him of his father. The Wittgenstein family

> formed a sort of enclave, fortified against the corruption and inadequacy that surrounded it by severe and private moral standards, which, it seemed, some of them had not the temperament to match or meet. Ludwig's case . . . seems to have been that of a phenomenally strong assent and attachment to these standards, often at war not only with the normal human failings that became glaring in their light, but also with a particularly soft and affectionate nature.[20]

Yet McGuinness immediately goes on to add that Wittgenstein himself "was not one to see his problem as that of being unable to do what his father required,"[21] and he further comments that "what we are describing here is no disease. As Tolstoy says: 'These questions are the simplest in the world. From the stupid child to the wisest old man, they are in the soul of every human being.'"[22] With the example of *Werther* before us, we can see the problem of genius or suicide as forming a strong theme in German culture in its response to the yet more general problem of wedding autonomous selfhood to continuing sociality.

Wittgenstein's preoccupation with autonomy and with the realization and confirmation of genius against the grain of culture is pronounced in the remarks in his own voice published as *Vermischte Bemerkungen* (*Culture and Value*). "It's a good thing," he writes, "I don't allow myself to be influenced."[23] As is typical in the post-Kantian, post-Goethean German tradition, the realization of genius is conceived of as a matter of letting something natural and divine come to the fore in one's thought and life, often under the prompting of nature itself. "Just let nature speak and acknowledge only *one* thing as higher than nature, but not what others may think" (1e). "Don't take the example of others as your guide, but nature!" (41e).

107

When one is thus guided, one's thinking and acting happen with significance, in and through one, rather than under one's personal control. "One might say: art *shows* us the miracles of nature. It is based on the *concept of the miracles of nature*. (The blossom, just opening out. What is *marvellous* about it?) We say: 'Just look at it opening out!'" (56e). It is just this kind of natural yet significant opening out of his own features of character that Wittgenstein anxiously hoped might inform his own thinking and writing.

> Schiller writes of a "poetic mood." I think I know what he means, I believe I am familiar with it myself. It is a mood of receptivity to nature in which one's thought seem as vivid as nature itself. . . . I am not entirely convinced that what *I* produce in such a mood is really worth anything. It may be that what gives my thoughts their lustre on these occasions is a light shining on them from behind. That they do not *themselves* glow.
>
> (65e–66e)

Something hidden, powerful, and natural within oneself is to come to the fore, in a way that is not under one's egocentric control. One is to be swept along by one's genius into a natural-supernatural movement of thinking.

Yet talent can also be betrayed or misused, and so fail to confirm itself in its products. "Talent is a spring from which fresh water is constantly flowing. But this spring loses its value if it is not used in the right way" (10e). As a result, the most important thing is to come to think and write naturally, in faithfulness to one's talent and against the grain of culture. But the effort to do so takes place within the conventionalized space of personally controlled and discursive reflection, so that it is crossed by an anxious self-scrutiny. "Am I thinking and writing as it were beyond myself, out of the depths of the natural?", one egocentrically and discursively wonders, or Wittgenstein wonders, in just the sort of tragic perspicacity about his own imperfections that Mann saw in Werther.

> Working in philosophy . . . is really more a working on oneself. On one's own interpretation. On one's way of seeing things. (And what one expects of them.)
>
> (16e)

> No one *can* speak the truth; if he has still not mastered himself. He *cannot* speak it; – but not because he is not clever enough yet. The truth can be spoken only by someone who is already *at home* in it; not by someone who still lives in falsehood and reaches out from falsehood towards truth on just one occasion.
>
> (35e)

All or nothing; natural-supernatural, non-conventionalized, poetic truth and expressiveness or imitative, derivative, non-existence; genius or suicide.

Domination by this imperative produces the same complex of attitudes toward work and toward religion that we find in Werther. On the one hand, Wittgenstein idealizes ordinary manual work as something beautiful and honest, more honest than intellectual chatter: "what is ordinary is here filled with significance" (52e)[24] if the manual work is done with respect and integrity. It is no accident, but rather deeply part of his anxious self-scrutiny and his attitudes toward culture and value, that Wittgenstein so often urged others to take up this kind of work. On the other hand, "Genius is what makes us forget skill" (43e). It is beyond the ordinary. So how can one express genius within the framework of the ordinary? How can one write poetically – originally and yet in a way that draws on the common and is accessible to others? How can one wed autonomous selfhood to continuing sociality?

> I think I summed up my attitude toward philosophy when I said: philosophy ought really to be written only as a *poetic composition*. . . . I was thereby revealing myself as someone who cannot quite do what he would like to be able to do.
>
> (24e)

Religious faithfulness offers a paradigm of significant expressiveness, but a paradigm that in its traditional, institutionalized form is dead for us, shot through with the conventionality that expressiveness is to overcome. "What is good is also divine. Queer as it sounds, that sums up my ethics. Only something supernatural can express the Supernatural" (3e). What is needed is "a light from above" that comes to the individual soul, not religious institutions and ordinary religious training. "Is what I am doing really worth the effort? Yes, but only if a light shines on it from above. . . . And if the light from above is lacking, I can't in any case be more than clever" (57e–58e). Religious belief cannot be something that is simply given and shared. It must rather be achieved through the dormant qualities of one's soul coming actively to take religious life as the vehicle of their expression, as the terms of deep significance.

> It strikes me that a religious belief could only be something like a passionate commitment to a system of reference. Hence, although it's a *belief*, it's really a way of living, or a way of assessing life. It's passionately seizing hold of *this* interpretation.
>
> (64e)

Above all, what Wittgenstein wants from religion, from work, from the guidance of nature, from his genius, but can never quite find, is full-blooded and continuing significance in the face of mere conventionality and cleverness: a new life. "A confession has to be part of your new life" (183). And if not a new life, then death: genius or suicide, or suicide as the creative act of voluntarily removing oneself from a cycle of unending self-defeat. In 1946, in the middle of remarks about music, thought, Shakespeare, God, heroism, and the difficulty of philosophy, there occurs in *Culture and Value*, in quotation marks, the very last words of Werther to his correspondent Wilhelm: "Lebt wohl!"[25]

The intensities of Wittgenstein's character have been well documented in the biographical literature. Yet one might argue that these intensities have little to do with his actual philosophical thinking and writing, or at least with what he chose to have published. After all, he also wrote in *Culture and Value*, "My ideal is a certain coolness. A temple providing a setting for the passions without meddling with them" (2e). Yet it would be striking were his official philosophical writing to be wholly uninformed by the otherwise deepest preoccupations of his character. Even in this remark, he presents *a certain coolness* as an ideal, not as something that he has actually achieved, and he did note that he was "someone who cannot quite do what he would like to be able to do" (24e). Is *Philosophical Investigations* in any sense *about* the problem of the realization of talent against the grain of but always in relation to the affordances of culture and the ordinary, *about* the problem of wedding autonomous selfhood to continuing sociality? That *Philosophical Investigations* is about this, in detail, line by line, as well as being about the nature of meaning, understanding, the will, and so on, and about this *by* being about these latter topics, is a main line of argument of my *Leading a Human Life: Wittgenstein, Intentionality, and Romanticism*. I cannot recapitulate the whole of that argument here. But I will offer a few brief pointers to it.

In section 125 of *Philosophical Investigations*, we find that "das philosophische Problem ... ist ... die bürgerliche Stellung des Widerspruchs, oder seine Stellung in der bürgerlichen Welt"; in English, and appropriately, that "the philosophical problem ... is ... the civil status of a contradiction, or its status in civil life."[26] "Our entanglement in our rules is what we want to understand" (§125). This entanglement "throws light on our concept of *meaning* something" (§125). – What is it to be entangled in rules in civil life, in ordinary life, in the ordinary, civil "bürgerlichen" world? Not to "know one's way about" (§123) is not to know how to engage with this world, how to bring one's talents and self-hood to authentic, non-derivative, and yet ratifiable expression within it. To ask "what does this knowledge [of how to go on in applying a rule] consist in?" (§148) is to ask what there is in me – what talent, what locus of understanding, what source of mastery – that enables me to go on and *how* to bring this talent, locus, or source to apt expression. Something must be there in me. I can do something, and we are not in using language aptly either machines or other animals. But what is it? And do I bring whatever it is to expression aptly? How? I seem caught between an anxiety that the only routes of expression are those already laid down in surrounding practice, that I contribute nothing, that I am ordinary, and hence non-existent: call this the anxiety of expressibility; and an anxiety that I cannot express that whatever-it-is in the ordinary, that I am alone, and mad: call this the anxiety of inexpressibility. To be able to mean something, to understand something: these are the results of the mysterious engagement of spontaneity in me, the source of originality, with the routes of expression that are given in practice, as though a seed in me – but one I can never identify or cultivate deliberately – grew in relation to its environment. "Each morning you have to break through the dead rubble afresh so as to reach the living warm seed. A new word is like a fresh seed sown on the ground of the discussion" (2e). It may well be that there is for the language user "a special experience" of understanding, but this special experience cannot be grasped and deliberately deployed independently of engagement with the affordances of culture. "For us it is the *circumstances* under which he had such an experience that justify him in saying in such a case that he understands, that he knows how to go on" (§155). The always mysterious interaction of circumstances, that is, of the affordances of culture in providing routes of expression, with the powers of self-hood is something to be accepted, not explained in either a scientific or intellectualistic theory.

Wittgenstein too, like Goethe but unlike Werther, did not commit suicide. His last words, famously, were "Tell them I've had a wonderful life."[27] Like Goethe, he achieved through the act of writing, repeatedly and day to day, a kind of catharsis, *some* distance or perspective on his anxieties as a subject, and a sense of himself as having a social identity as a writer. Hence there is some point to thinking that the second voice of the *Investigations* (if there are only two) – the voice that rebukes the tendency to seek scientific or intellectualist explanations of our cognitive abilities and that recalls us instead to the ways of the ordinary – *is* Wittgenstein's more mature voice. At the same time, however, the first voice – the voice of temptation and of intensities of perfect explanation and attunement – is his too, a voice he cannot quite give up, much as Goethe in his maturity would not give up intensities of infatuation and would still also identify himself with such intensities in Edward in *Elective Affinities*. The mature voice of the ordinary, the voice of survival, comes to the fore and is allowed the last word within a section, but always in continuing critical engagement with the voice of perfectly grounded and explained attunement, the voice of temptation.

Wittgenstein knew all this about himself. In 1931, in one of the remarks of *Culture and Value*, he wrote: "The delight I take in my thoughts is delight in my own strange life. Is this joy of living?" (22e). It is perhaps the kind of joy in living, arising out of the acknowledgment of the weddedness of one's selfhood to others and to the given and out of gratitude for that weddedness and the always partial expressiveness it enables, that is open to us as subjects who seek to achieve both autonomous selfhood and continuing sociality.

Notes

1 See M. W. Rowe, "Goethe and Wittgenstein," *Philosophy* 66, 1991); Joachim Schulte, "Chor und Gesetz: Zur 'Morphologischen Methode' bei Goethe und Wittgenstein," *Grazer Philosophische Studien* 21, 1984; and G. P. Baker and P. M. S. Hacker, *Wittgenstein: Understanding and Meaning*, Oxford, Basil Blackwell, 1980, pp. 537–40. I summarize and comment on this work in my *Leading a Human Life: Wittgenstein, Intentionality, and Romanticism*, Chicago, University of Chicago Press, 1997, pp. 177–81.

2 Thomas Mann, "On Goethe's *Werther*," trans. Elizabeth Corra, in *The Sufferings of Young Werther and Elective Affinities*, Victor Lange (ed.), New York, Continuum, 1990, p. 2.

3 Charles Taylor, *Sources of the Self: The Making of the Modern Identity*, Cambridge MA, Harvard University Press, 1989, p. x.

4 *Ibid.*, p. 18.

5 Philippe Lacoue-Labarthe and Jean-Luc Nancy, *The Literary Absolute: The Theory of Literature in German Romanticism*, trans. Philip Barnard and Cheryl Lester, Albany NY, State University of New York Press, 1988, p. 31.

6 *Ibid.*, p. 12. The subject term of Lacoue-Labarthe and Nancy's clauses is "literary production," not "articulation," but with the migration of human self-production toward the literary, in a mix of discovery and invention, the latter, more general term makes their characterizations appropriate to human moral efforts in general.

7 Rodolphe Gasché, "Foreword" to Friedrich Schlegel, *Philosophical Fragments*, trans. Peter Firchow, Minneapolis MN, University of Minnesota Press, 1991, p. xix.

8 Nicholas Boyle, *Goethe: The Poet and the Age – Volume 1: The Poetry of Desire*, Oxford, Clarendon Press, 1991, p. 176.

9 *Ibid.*, p. 124.

10 *Ibid.*, p. 110.

11 *Ibid.*, p. 177.

12 *Ibid.*, p. 162.

13 *Ibid.*, p. 176.

14 Mann, "On Goethe's *Werther*," p. 9.

15 *Ibid.*, pp. 9, 10.

16 Johann Wolfgang von Goethe, *The Sorrows of Young Werther in Goethe: The Collected Works*, vol. 11, ed. David E. Wellbery, trans. Victor Lange, Princeton NJ, Princeton University Press, 1994, p. 72. Subsequent references to *Werther* will all be to this edition and will be indicated in the text by page number.

17 Mann, "On Goethe's *Werther*," p. 8.

18 Ray Monk, *Ludwig Wittgenstein: The Duty of Genius*, New York, The Free Press, 1990, p. 25.

19 Brian McGuinness, *Wittgenstein, A Life: Young Ludwig 1889–1921*, Berkeley CA, University of California Press, 1988, p. 156.

20 *Ibid.*, p. 50.

21 *Ibid.*

22 *Ibid.*, p. 156, citing Tolstoy, "A Confession."

23 Ludwig Wittgenstein, *Culture and Value*, trans. Peter Winch, Oxford, Basil Blackwell, 1980, p. 1e. Subsequent references to this work will be given by page numbers in parentheses.

24 This remark is about "an ordinary conventional figure" at the end of Schubert's *Death and the Maiden*, but it captures well Wittgenstein's attitude toward the manual work he repeatedly urged on others.

25 Goethe, *Die Leiden des jungen Werther*, Stuttgart, Reclam, 1948, p. 147. Werther actually adds one more line to Wilhelm: "wir sehen uns wieder und freudiger" (p. 147). But "Lebt wohl!" alone is what lives in the memory of his readers as his valedictory to life, particularly since his last diary entry, addressed to Lotte, concludes "Es schlägt zwölfe. So sei es denn! – Lotte! Lotte, lebe wohl! Lebe wohl!" (p. 150).

26 Wittgenstein, *Philosophical Investigations*, 3rd edn, trans. G. E. M. Anscombe, New York, Macmillan, 1958, §125, pp. 50, 50e. Subsequent references to this work will be given in the text by section number.

27 Wittgenstein, cited in Norman Malcolm, *Ludwig Wittgenstein: A Memoir*, Oxford, Oxford University Press, 1958, p. 100.

6

ON "BECOMING WHO ONE IS"
(AND FAILING)[1]

Proust's problematic selves

Robert Pippin

I

Oscar Wilde once noted that for antiquity and for long afterwards, the great imperative in human life was "Know thyself." This was the path to wisdom given by the oracle at Delphi, and was often cited by Socrates as his greatest task in life. It did not imply in antiquity what it might to us; it had much less the sense of "avoid self-deceit," or "be true to yourself" or "know your limits." It had much more the sense of "avoid ignorance about what it is to be a human being and what happiness for such a creature consists in." However, said Wilde, for us moderns, the major life task had become something different. It is now: "*Become* who you are." This imperative has also been of central concern in a strand of modern European and American philosophy (sometimes called a "romantic" strand) that stretches from Rousseau through Hegel, Emerson, Thoreau, Nietzsche (with whom the phrase itself is now probably most associated) to Heidegger and Sartre.[2] A kind of anxiety that we are not in our official or public roles really or authentically "who we are," that we are not what we are taken to be by others, now seems familiar to us as a characteristic problem in modern Western life.[3]

However familiar, the imperative and the issue also seem quite paradoxical. Why would you need "to become who you are?" Who else could you be? And even if that could be worked out, the idea of a contrast between the two maxims is paradoxical for other reasons. How can the imperatives be separated and contrasted? Doesn't one have to know who one is, before one can struggle to become who one is, struggle to resist the temptation to be false to oneself?

To answer the first concern we have to appreciate that the subject in question – the "you" that you are to become – at least in the explorations undertaken in the modern novel or confessional poetry – has little directly to do with the familiar philosophical questions about the minimum conditions of self-identification, personal identity, and so forth. The Humean worry about the possibility of an awareness of an enduring, stable self is not at issue, but some-thing like acknowledgment of (and faithfulness to) one's "practical identity," what is sometimes referred to as one's character, is clearly the issue being raised. (*What* one is "being true to" when one is "being true to oneself.") Or, as it is sometimes put, the problem is not the problem of individuation, but of individ-ualization; the problem of the self's unity is not so much the formal problem of possible continuity over time, but the substantive problem of self-knowledge, ego-ideals, grounding commitments, all understood as an ethical as much as an epistemological problem.[4] What most seems at stake is what is meant when, *in extremis*, someone might say: "I couldn't live with myself if I did that"; or, more commonly, "I don't know why I did that; I don't recognize myself in that deed." And, said the other way around, many people, after all, have self-images that they count as solid self-knowledge, but which are better described as self-indul-gent fantasies or delusions. They especially might be said to need to become in reality the person they take themselves to be (because they are not, or not yet). Put in a much more general way and anticipating my conclusion: being the subject of one's life, a subject who can lead a life rather than merely suffer what happens, who can recognize her own agency, the exercise of her subjectivity, in the deeds she produces, also means *being able to fail to be one*. That already indi-cates that being such a subject cannot be something one just substantially "is" over time and so can report. As we shall see several times, a "practically rele-vant self-knowledge" is the question at issue and such first-personal knowledge cannot be understood on models of introspecting an inner essence, on the model of *being S* or *not being S*, but is more like the expression of a commitment, usually a provisional commitment, which one can sustain or fail to sustain, and so is something one can always *only* "be becoming" (or failing to become).[5]

Accordingly, the answer given by philosophers like Nietzsche and novelists like Proust to the second concern (the apparent priority of self-knowledge over self-becoming) is to deny such priority, and so to suggest a deeper paradox. They want to say something like: any settled piece of self-knowledge or presumed fixed commitment or ego ideal is, because of considerations like those just advanced, *always*, necessarily, provisional, in constant suspense, always subject to pervasive doubt.[6] The reality of such a self-image, what turns out to confirm it, is not fidelity to an inner essence, but is ultimately a matter of action, what we actually do, a matter of engagement in the world, as well as, in a way, a kind of negotiation with others about what, exactly, it *was* that one did. (So, to determine that something is true about myself is much more like resolve than discovery.)[7] As such, our actual practical identity is always also the subject of contested interpretations and appropriations by others (another mark of its provisionality). And there is very often a kind of struggle to hold fast to such an image, or to alter it properly in the face of finding out that one "was not whom one took oneself to be." The idea is that it is only *in* trying to become who one (provisionally) thinks one is that one can begin to find out who one really is (what one would really do), even though that putatively discovered result is only

114

a provisional pledge of sorts to act in certain ways in the future. That is, this finding out does not discover a stable essential self thereby simply "revealed" in action. We get at best another temporary resting place which further demands on us could, and very likely will, dislodge. In this context, the question of whether there can ever be any end to this provisionality, re-formulation and re-engagement is obviously a pressing one.

So is another necessary struggle – for some perspective from which the unity of such deeds and manifestations can be made out. We need to achieve some such coherent connections among deeds – to be able to understand why someone who did *that* would do *this* – or we won't be able to recover the deeds as *ours*, to recognize ourselves in them. Some will seem strange, alien episodes, absent such connectability; more like things that happen to us rather than things we do. (And again, all such claims to unity by any individual, even to himself, are *claims*, are also subject to dispute and denial by others, especially when we act on such a self-understanding.)

This is the problem of recovering "lost time," attempting to retrieve what really happened as one's own, or to recover who one "really" was. It is the attempt to avoid being trapped in some wish-fulfilling fantasy or in yet another, merely successive provisional point of view. And it is the attempt to avoid being subject to the interpretive will of another. And this issue is the chief subject of Proust's great novel, at issue in questions like Marcel (or Swann) becoming "a writer," what it is to be truly "in love," why social prestige and snobbery (or radical social dependence) are so important, and why there is such an insistent repetition of the theme of "theatrical" selves, selves which seem to exist only as "displayed" and only in the perceptions of others – actresses, prostitutes, homo-sexuals and socially successful (Swann) or socially ambitious (Bloch) Jews.

Moreover, the suggestion of such maxims as "Become Who You Are" is that this possibility of a gap between self-image and reality must be *overcome*, that exercising your agency is always an active becoming, a struggle against some barrier, some temptation to conformism or forgetfulness or bad faith or inau-thenticity (or some unavoidable contestation with others about what it is that one did, over whom one is revealed to be or about whom one gets to be). This gap can either be some sort of real barrier to becoming who you are (like a polit-ical barrier or some social convention), where that struggle is based on already achieved (if still provisional) self-knowledge, or it could be required because of a gap between self-image and self-knowledge. Self-knowledge, on this view, should be understood as a product of long experience, profound struggle, and negotiations with others, never a moment of epiphanic insight. It is a retrospec-tive of what we learn in some struggle (with and often against others) to become who we believe we are.

I want to focus some attention on this theme ("become who you are") in Proust's novel, *Remembrance of Things Past*, by isolating four different facets of the novel where this problem is engaged and extensively treated, where the logic of such a provisional and developmental sense of self is thematized and explored. The four facets concern: (i) The extremely complicated narrative strategy of the novel. (Complicated formally, anyway. As has been pointed out, the plot of this massive work is very simple: Marcel becomes a writer.)[8] Here the surface of the novel, with the young Marcel apparently finally "becoming" the actual author, Proust, is particularly deceptive and elusive. (ii) Becoming a self-in-society. The suggestion above was that the basic struggle "to become who one is" is a *social* struggle, and involves a complicated negotiation of dependence and social independence that Proust explores with great subtlety. (iii) Selfhood and love. Here the possibility of failing to become who one is, at times it seems, *necessarily* failing, is most evident. One never seems to know who the (provisional, possible) beloved is, and one constantly finds that one is not who one assumed one was, or is frequently surprised at how different one is "in relation to A" when compared with "in relation to B." And (iv) Marcel's self-identity as an artist, and the role of artistic idealization, fantasy, self-fashioning and creation in, paradoxically, knowing the truth, especially the truth about oneself. More generally then, the novel invites us to entertain, as a premise for what it will work through, Marcel's unusual anxiety that he will fail to find, or will always have lost, his "self," whom he is to become, and this "in time" (that there might be no successful narrative point of view), in love (the beloved remains unknown, his desires never stabilize), in rejection from society, and in failing to become a writer. What is it to be worried about such a matter?

II

In the novel, a narrator, near the end of his life, now mostly isolated from society, alone, often ill, attempts to remember and reconstruct narratively the story of his boyhood and early adulthood. (At two and only two very isolated moments in the novel, this object of memory, the narrator's younger self, is called "Marcel.") For the most part, he is nameless and speaks in the first person, as the narrator seems to assume the persona of, seems to enact or re-enact the voice of this younger person, expressing things as this young Marcel would, as well as apparently sometimes stepping outside it to comment on what was really happening to the younger Marcel, as if this were not accessible to that character then, but which is to his older self. To complicate matters, the novel is also often interrupted by what appear to be long, independent philo-sophical reflections on love, jealousy, time, art, memory, and human psychology. It is often unclear whether these reflections capture the young Marcel's thinking at the time, reflect the narrator's considered view, or are philosophical inser-tions by the real Proust, the absent author of the narrator's reflections. Many readers have stumbled over this issue, taking it as simply unproblematic that the reflective passages are bits of "Proustean philosophy," meant to illuminate the narrative passages. But the presence and meaning of those passages are quite problematic indeed, something to be thought about, not a given, and it is more likely that Vincent Descombes has it right when he suggests in his recent book that the situation is rather the other way around: that the narrative helps us contextualize and understand the reflections and especially the limitations of the quite specific point of view which they express. A "philosophical reading" can only occur after this is appreciated.[9] Put much more simply, we have to be as constantly aware as Marcel that nothing is what it seems. Society matrons are ex-prostitutes, manly aristocrats are homosexual masochists, one's beloved is a lesbian, and the book we are reading does everything possible to convince us it is a memoir; a reportage of inner states, a psychological work. But it is not. There is no historically real Marcel, no real narrator. And characters report their inner states, even to themselves, in ways that turn out to be fundamentally untrustworthy, prompting a constant search for truth, and this more "in" social action than in deeper psychological insight.[10]

There is a passage from Proust's letters, quoted by Descombes, which sums up this problem:

> No, if I had no intellectual beliefs, if I were trying simply to remember and to create through memory a useless depiction of days gone by, I would not, ill as I am, take the trouble to write. But this evolution of a mind – I have chosen not to analyze it in an abstract way, but rather to recreate it, to bring it to life. And so I am forced to depict errors, but without feeling bound to say that I hold them to be errors. So much the worse for me if the reader believes I hold them to be the truth. The second volume will encourage this misunderstanding. I hope the last volume will clear it up.[11]

And the novel itself warns us, even if that warning appears hard to remember for most readers: "A book in which there are theories is like an article which still has its price tag on it" (III 916).

So, in testimony to the relevance of our problem (how one becomes who one is), the novel directs us to three main personae, and the relation among them is not clear. (And I should emphasize that I mean three *main* narrative "I's." Marcel Muller has argued for seven narrative voices sharing the first-person pronoun; Joshua Landy five.)[12] There is the younger Marcel, the object of the narration, as well as the imitated subject of thoughts and reflections in the novel, the older narrator, whom the younger is becoming – as if becoming who he is – and the absent authorial narrator, Proust himself. These characters are three, but as just noted we tend to collapse them into one, and want that one to be the real Proust.[13] This theme is expressed by the earliest object of Marcel's writing, the three church spires at Martinville, which look like three from one angle, but from another and farther away, meld visually into one spire (The more distant our perspective on the book, the less close our reading, the more likely we are to submit to an optical illusion, to mistake all three for one, for Proust himself?)[14]

And the specific problem in the novel is quite relevant to our theme: the young Marcel considers himself, from very early on, a writer; that is his self-understanding, and he is very much trying to become who he believes he is, trying to become a writer. And this is indeed portrayed as a struggle, and the struggle concerns the right relation to his audience, among many other things. (Again the deceptively simple "plot": Marcel wonders what it is to be a writer, is eager to imitate models, enters and succeeds in high society, where people become ever more (or less) socially prominent. Dinner parties are held. Beach resorts are visited. People grow old. Some die. Marcel becomes disillusioned about society, but finally does become a writer (while offstage, frustratingly enough, and during a long temporal gap in the narration), and, if we accept the conventional point of view, the book we are reading is the product of that decision.)[15] For a very long time, though, Marcel is a writer who does not write, or writes very little, as he struggles to understand how a writer lives, how one responds to and tries to understand the people around him "as a writer would," and struggles to find out whether he can ever become in reality, however much he actually writes, "a real writer."[16] The issue that he is most puzzled about – what does it mean *in this society* to become a writer? – is already prominent in the narrative or more formal structure of the novel, which is often built upon "surprising revelations."

That is, Marcel, in this quest to know who he is, to know whether he is a writer, finds that his beliefs about that issue and many others (especially about what he should do, given those beliefs), almost inevitably fail to correspond with how he actually does react to events, and are out of sync with the way in which what he does is understood by others. He is sure he is not in love with someone, and is then devastated by some slight or neglect or indifference; he is sure the attainment of some goal is crucial to his happiness, yet finds himself indifferent in acquiring it. (An important example: Marcel is frustrated by his father's opposition to his becoming a writer, but when, influenced by M. Legrandin, his father drops his opposition, Marcel immediately finds the prospect dubious.) We are thus shown that reports of self-knowledge are very likely not reports of mere inner facts, gained by some special access the subject alone has (as if one could discover whether one had a writerly essence or not). The relation between such beliefs and their expression in actions is much tighter than this; the latter turns out to be crucial to the truth of any such former claim, and such truths often turn out different from how a provisional, prior expectation would have it. Introspection is thus singularly unreliable, as in this extraordinary passage.

> Now, since the self is constantly thinking numerous things, since it is nothing more than the thoughts of these things, when by chance, instead of having them as the objects of its attention, it suddenly turns its thoughts upon itself, it finds only an empty apparatus, something unfamiliar, to which, in order to give it some reality – it adds the memory of a face seen in a mirror.[17]

118

As Sartre would later put it, these reports of self-knowledge reflect more provisional promises or pledges at a time (in effect promises to oneself and others) to act in certain ways, which one may fail to keep for all the sorts of reasons people fail to keep pledges.[18] To summarize several of these points at once: the fact that Proust's narrator is also a character in the novel we are reading is not merely the exploration of an unusual point-of-view technique; it manifests the paradox and tensions of any self-reflection, and so the necessary link between such reflection and action, manifests it more than perhaps any other book, or so I am trying to claim.[19]

And often these reflective failures are not matters of simple weakness or moral failure; they can be results of the simple pressures of time. One has to make such pledges at some moment, before one can even begin to know how to understand the implications of the commitment, something one only learns "as time unfolds," given some principle of narrative connectedness. For this reason, "the bluff" – pretending, when some situation calls for action, that one knows what one is about, knows what should happen, etc. – is an important, unavoidable and often hilarious social mechanism throughout *Remembrance*[20] and thereby also a valuable way to learn about oneself in a fairly standard (not absolutely unique, first-personal) way.[21] And for similar reasons the novel itself embodies, constantly exhibits, a narrative and point-of-view uncertainty and complexity consistent with the often confusing temporal and social instabilities exhibited in its details. While much in the novel conspires to have us believe that the vain, social climbing young Marcel grows into a wise, reflective narrator Marcel who writes the books we have just read, and that *that* narrator is "really" Proust himself, the novel does nothing to establish that there is or even can be any point of view "outside" the narrative flux and instability described, that Marcel's quasi-religious discovery of "real time past" in the last novel is anything other than *yet another* moment in a temporal story that has led Marcel in hope to, and then in disappointment away from, other idealizations: Swann, Berma, the Guermantes, his grandmother, art itself, Albertine, *time regained*, and so forth. There is no more reason to take Marcel's "death bed" conversion away from the radical temporal instability we have just seen as any more authoritative than these other putative moments of redemption. If Marcel is to become who he is, it will not be in any such moment of stalled or stopped time. We have just read the account that shows why it cannot be.

Put one final way, the problem I have called Marcel's "becoming who he is" amounts to his becoming a determinate agent, someone who leads his life, both carries the past into the future in a certain way, and does so, acts, in the light of some conception of the subject he is struggling to become. But this is mostly manifested by a kind of *via negativa*, the often palpable sense in the novel of the great and almost intolerable burden of the demands of such agency, or the sweet pleasures to be gained by avoiding such a burden. We are introduced to this theme in a famous archetypal theme, Marcel's intense pain at being separated from his mother, that great rip in the fabric of pre-subjective, harmonious being

119

which can never be avoided or ever healed. But the figure for this problem actually begins earlier in the first novel, in its first, most famous line: "For a long time, I used to go to bed early." We are thus subtly introduced to the odd desire for "earlier sleep," a desire for some release from the burdens of "waking" agency that introduces the recurring images of passivity and its many pleasures; being pursued, being a beloved, and even the later themes of masochism and betrayal, being made an object. It is enough to note here the importance and potential, perhaps very deep irony of this theme in Marcel's (that is, not "Proust's") enormous faith in "involuntary memories," supposedly the key to the novel's success.[22] This would be to make a point, by way of attention to irony, that Benjamin makes in a different way: that Marcel's near sanctification of involuntary memory figures a failure, a kind of breakdown, in modern temporal experience. For Benjamin that failure consists in a gap opening wide between individual and collective, inherited memory, or tradition, an inability to place oneself in such a collective memory that means it is wholly "a matter of chance whether an individual forms an image of himself, whether he can take hold of his experience."[23]

III

A great part of such a struggle to become who one is, an agent, obviously concerns our proper relation to people around us, concerns our social self. A self-image, for example, that is not at all reflected or accepted in practice by others, or especially that is contradicted by the way one is treated or regarded, would have to count as some sort of failure to become who one is. An obvious example: the reputedly large number of our contemporaries who think of themselves as poets, or novelists, or writers or artists but whose work (the objectification of such a self-understanding) is universally rejected. (At a certain level of rejection, that is, being such a bad writer has to count as not being a writer at all.) And the case is even more obvious in those who profess such self-knowledge, but who have not yet even begun to write, who know somehow that in their inner being, a great writer lurks, waiting only for the time and leisure to escape. A self-image never realized in social space, never expressed in public action, has to count as more a fantasy than a piece of self-knowledge, even though when expressed in such action, the public deed cannot be said to be exclusively owned by the subject, to have the meaning that the subject insists on. It is "up for grabs" in a certain sense. One's self-image becomes a social fact through action, and its meaning can then no longer be tied to the intention or will of the agent alone. This is of course, exactly why many people forever postpone such action; never write that book, send off that manuscript, finish that dissertation.[24]

And yet on the other hand, there are clearly people whose self-image, whose practical identity, has been formed so extensively by the expectations and demands and reactions of others, that, while their own self-image does circulate successfully in society, their view of themselves is indeed very well mirrored in how they are regarded and treated, it has to be said that they have become the person whom "*they*" want one to be, that one does not have one's own identity, has not become who one is. As noted above, this type of slavish conformism has to count as just as much a failure to become who one is as the fantasy-indulging narcissist we just discussed.

We are also often shown another implication of this theme: that the "you" who you can become is not entirely "up to you." For one thing, our self-identity is very much linked to some commitment to values, and we don't think of ourselves as committing to values arbitrarily, or of values themselves as just expressions of our preferences. *They* make some claim *on* us. When we say that we know ourselves very well, we often mean to imply that we know something like where we'd draw some line beyond which we would never cross, that our sense of self is essentially a sense of values we can't give up in the face of demands by others. (Having a practical identity – husband, father, professor, American – always involves something like commitment to a norm, something that I must initiate and actively sustain over time. I don't regard myself as having the option of just abandoning such a commitment.)

For another, the realization of such value must make some sense within the historical, social world in which we live. We can adopt the values of chivalry and try to become a knight in the modern world, but we won't be able to become a real knight; we'll end up a comic character, a Quixote.[25] (The growing absurdity of Charlus's aristocratic pretensions is connected with this theme. His decline into sadomasochistic farce is not at all simply a matter of psychological deterioration, but is both an effect of and a manifestation of "social deterioration," from the Guermantes to the middle-class Verdurins.[26] This is a new world in which his fantasy of feudal power is only sustainable if he can experience himself as creating his new submissive, dependent role, and so in sadomasochism. And Swann's inability to write his Vermeer book is not mere "writer's block." It has everything to do with Swann's sense of audience or lack of audience.)

Finally, such social treatments of the "real self" question (and the narrative factures and ambiguities they entail) are also presented within a specific socio-*historical* context by Proust. Geographically, the vast novel is divided for the most part into three regions. Combray, the country village where Marcel's parents have their vacation home, Paris, where Marcel's father is a doctor and where they have their principal residence (eventually sharing a building with the famous Duc de Guermantes' family) and Balbec, a seaside resort, both a kind of transition place for the young Marcel and a social scene where rigid class distinctions do not apply as much as in ancient Combray, but which is not yet as unstable as modern Paris. (He first visits Balbec with his beloved grandmother, and so it remains a piece of his boyhood, but it is also where he meets the fabulous Guermantes, especially the dashing whirlwind of a character, Robert de Saint-Loup, and the most complex, colorful and sad character in the book, the great Baron de Charlus.)

But these geographical regions also sound a historical resonance. Combray is an almost pre-historical social world; at least pre-modern and largely feudal. There is little historical time present. Life there is as repetitious as nature's own cycles, and it has a rigid and largely unchanging social hierarchy. It is important that the character most associated with this world, the maid Françoise, is the rock of ages in the book, outside of modern, historical time; supremely self-confident, unchanging, full of the opinions and superstitions her ancestors would have expressed. She has no need to "become who she is"; the question itself would no more arise for her than it would for Eumaios in the *Odyssey*.[27] But the world of Paris, and to a growing extent the intermediary world of Balbec, is a world where the experience of vast, rapid social change is omni-present, disorienting and, when properly appreciated, simply will not allow the intelligent and aware characters a "Françoise-like' solution. (Even characters like the Duchesse de Guermantes prefer not to observe rigid social hierarchies based strictly on family, and the Duchesse fancies herself a social adventuress, thus raising the question the Parisians must now face; what is it to "make" a society in these altered social conventions? How does one play the great and unbelievably complex "game" of invitations and refusals?)

The evidence for such change is often slipped in quietly in the narrative details, but begins to accumulate as the events in the novel head for two deci-sive historical and social crises, the Dreyfus affair and the First World War. These details include enormous technological change: the arrival of electric lighting in a home, the telegraph and railway, Marcel's first telephone call, and above all, the arrival of the automobile. (In a famous passage in *Cities of the Plain*, Marcel actually weeps when he first sees an airplane [II 1062].) These are all shown to contribute to a great "compressing" of social life, as if various communities grow more and more compacted together, making more and more impossible the isolation of little villages like Combray, and so exposing everyone more and more to more social pressures than before, resulting in greater conformism and anxiety about authenticity.[28] It is all presented as if these devices, by drawing people closer together, in ever more rapid physical and communicative contact with each other, rather than increase communica-tive closeness and daily intimacy, mostly increase the sense of being-regarded, of being monitored ever more constantly and effectively, by others, as if, in effect, there are fewer and fewer places to "hide," fewer reasons to avoid contact, fewer real opportunities for solitude and the development of a socially independent self.[29]

Finally, another consequence of the socio-historical Proustean world is even more important, but harder to summarize without a separate paper (or book). A simple term for it would be the untrustworthiness of direct or immediate experi-ence, something that seems linked to the inadequacy of the historically specific evaluative and descriptive terms available to Marcel. We all know that the offi-cial Proustean doctrine is supposed to be that immediate experience is experienced too quickly, caught in too great a jumble of associations and affec-

tive responses, to be fully intelligible. Experiences "according to Proust" supposedly reveal their true meaning in a *mémoire involuntaire*, when they supposedly
can jolt their way through the surveillance of quotidian consciousness and
appear as, it would seem, the thing in itself, an experienced moment in its original meaning and importance. But we sometimes neglect to note that such
"experiences of not clearly or reliably experiencing" in the historical present are
not treated as epistemological theses but as a record of such flux and uncertainty
in a certain historical world. Françoise's world, the largely pre-modern world of
Combray, we can easily infer, suffers no such confusions or uncertainties, since
within it the patterns of repetition and re-identification familiarize the familiar
and screen out what does not fit. Marcel however, in a world where the
unprecedented is common, a world always over-determined in meaning, cannot
even directly experience the greatest life-event in the novel, his grandmother's
death. He must later, at Balbec, re-experience what he paradoxically did not
originally experience. This is yet another image of the inevitably reflective and
thereby unstable characterization of experience in the novel, a feature that I
would argue is historically indexed, tied to the sort of world where sexual identities can seem to change instantaneously, information circulates rapidly and
often without context, and moral hierarchies crumble and are rebuilt unpre-
dictably. (It is also in, and probably *only in*, such a world that such extreme
claims about the power of involuntary memory can seem to make sense. That is,
we need again to be attentive as well to *Marcel's need* for such a touchstone –
something independent of any supposed Proustean theory – before we can properly evaluate what Marcel thinks he experiences in the novel's final volume.)[30]

IV

In the novel's many love affairs, the issue of being or becoming a lover or
beloved is raised in both a temporal and more directly psychological framework.
The temporal problem in human relations is pronounced and stressed very
frequently, almost ad nauseam. A typical passage:

> Every person is destroyed when we cease to see him; after which his
> next appearance is a new creation, different from that which immedi-
> ately preceded it, if not from them all. . . . Remembering a strong and
> searching glance, a bold manner, it is inevitably, next time, by an
> almost languid profile, a sort of dreamy gentleness, overlooked by us in
> our previous impression, that at the next encounter we shall be aston-
> ished, that is to say almost uniquely struck.

(I 979)

Because of this phenomenon of instability, the very attainment of desire is
treated as temporally complex and problematic. For when we achieve what we
thought we desired, we often find that we are "no longer the person who desired

that," that we formed the desire at a time and under conditions specific to that period, not, any longer to this new one.[31] (And I stress again the terrible complication: all we know is that this is what the *narrator* believes about such matters, perhaps for his own defensive, still obsessional motives. As always, we as readers have to try to figure out just who is speaking, as the speaker or rememberer is also trying to figure out who he is or was. These opinions are part of that process and so part of ours.)

Moreover, Proust treats imagination and fantasy as essential to desire, especially necessary to intense, powerful desires like romantic love, which are formed and sustained largely under the influence of fantastic idealizations of the beloved or lover. (In the language used here: one forms various aspects of one's self- and other-image under the inevitable sway of these erotic illusions.) Without such fantasies, love would become like that dreary contract between consenting partners for the reciprocal use for pleasure of each other's bodies that Kant so infamously defined as the basis of any ethical marital relation. Yet such fantasies – so essential to any person's self-identity – also cannot withstand the great pressure of having finally to acknowledge the humdrum reality behind such illusions, and so the identities of lover and beloved are in constant suspense.

For this and many other reasons (such as the unreliability of experience sketched above) the central plot event in the novel is disappointment after disappointment after disappointment. The great actress, Berma, whom Marcel yearned to see with every fiber of his body, turns out (at first, anyway) to be a prosaic disappointment. The imagined, ancient, church at Balbec is in reality prosaically stuck among some shops in a dull village. The great, mysterious Swann is a pathetic dilettante, captured in a love affair with a woman whom he does not even like, tortured by constant jealousy. The mysterious world of the Faubourg St Germain, the Guermantes, turns out to be a collection of petty, venal, essentially worthless people. In fact, society itself, the very necessary condition under which one forms a sense of who one is and should become, looks to be little more than a tissue of lies, evasions, delusions, vain pretensions, a hall of mirrors for social posturing, with each figure trying hard to imitate those regarded as the originals, the setters of fashion, who are themselves trying to imitate those who are trying to imitate them. (There is even a Groucho Marx element to this disappointment: Marcel's constant sense that the objects of his desire must be so valuable and rare and difficult to achieve that if he, poor Marcel, has attained them, they must be worthless in reality, thus confirming Groucho's law that he would not want to a member of any club who would have him as a member.)

In this doomed economy of love, the beloved wants the lover, but that means wanting the lover to want her, and so she wants to become what the lover wants to love. "Success" in such an enterprise is then obviously double-edged, since she is always left wondering whether the lover really loves *her*, the "real her," and about what will happen when he "finds out" who she really is, behind all the mystery, make-up, fine clothes, tailored persona, and so forth. And as she is assessing what the lover wants, she is also assessing the lover's self-presentation to the beloved, which is of course *his* attempt to be whom he thinks she wants a lover, or him, to be.

And we see over and over again that the enemy of love's intensity is the grinding, soul-deadening familiarization of habit and the everyday. (Cf. "stupefying habit, which during the whole course of our life conceals from us almost the whole universe, and in the dead of night, without changing the label, substitutes for the most dangerous or intoxicating poisons of life something anodyne that procures no delights," III 554.)[32] Proust suggests that it is almost as if we had a motive to *find* constant occasions for jealousy, to *want* to consider the beloved as eluding us, absent (thereby defeating habit, even if in a Pyrrhic victory). Marcel wants to convince himself that he does not really know Albertine and so must constantly experience a great anxious unsettled doubt about her life apart from his. This, though, however painful, means that their love has not been completely settled, has not become a matter of habit. The difficulty of becoming who one is, in other words, is something one easily and unavoidably and sometimes eagerly projects onto others too; one realizes the beloved may not really be the person that the lover, or even she herself, takes herself to be, or that she may suddenly, given some chance encounter with another, not just reveal herself to be in fact other than she appeared, but might become someone else. (Marcel's Law seems to be: anxiety and jealousy make the heart grow fonder.)

Now Marcel appears to react to this with an almost insane possessiveness, tries to keep Albertine a prisoner. But this too is treated with great irony by Proust. We see pretty quickly that Marcel is as much, if not much more, the captive of Albertine as vice-versa, and the situation itself is already paradoxical. (The jailer must be constantly on guard lest his prisoner escape; they are in effect chained to each other, the jailer as much a prisoner.)[33]

Finally, this whole set of considerations – escaping from habit, avoiding the dullness of familiarity and so forth – is another reason why, in a novel so much about remembering, forgetting is so important. Moments of past time must be lost, however painful that is, so that they can escape the control of habit and habitual associations and then be (apparently) re-captured in moments of sudden, unplanned, involuntary memory. Said another way, the picture Marcel presents suggests that our real life, wherein we can come to understand ourselves, understand what it is to become who one is, is so wholly false, routinized, saturated with habit, familiarity (and the contempt it breeds), as well as, paradoxically, so subject to radical temporal flux, that it can only really be *lived* "too late," afterwards, in (mostly involuntary) recollection and a kind of intense re-experiencing. (We can only become who we are when, in a way, we cease to be, at least cease to be so "in control.") In his famous, sad phrase, the "true paradises are the *paradises we have lost*" (III 90). (If they are lost, forgotten, they at least have a chance of escaping habit and can re-appear with some freshness and vivacity, as "true" paradises. This is a mirror of the earlier point – that the only successful (sustainable) love is unrequited love.) The suggestion is that while we like to think of ourselves as living our life forwards, as if a life were in the control of a subject, enacting a clear self-identity, in fact that direction would not make much sense unless we were able to live it constantly "back-ward" too, making sense later of what could not make sense at the time. This is already the beginning of a claim for what amounts to the priority of art to life itself in the novel, for a radical aestheticism as the solution of sorts to the "become who you are" imperative.[34] Since *lives* are such backwards-looking narrated *novels*, the best narrator is the wisest judge, the most successful at life; he is perhaps most of all "who he is." Or at least he is the most self-conscious. And this is also an answer of sorts to the obvious question raised by the book's title. *Why* must lost time be searched for? Because that is where your life lies hidden, Marcel seems to say. Contrary to the conventional wisdom – "Don't live in the past" – Marcel often suggests that one can only truly *live* in the past, at least live in a way that can make some sense, can be rescued from habit, the rush of time, the confusing swirl of immediate impressions, and from the diffi-culties arising from one being a character in the novel one is narrating – all if such lost time can be "found."

In the treatment of love in high society, what would otherwise seem a rather bizarre intense, frequent emphasis on male and female homosexuals (what Proust calls "inversion"), and prostitutes, is more intelligible as linked to the social dimensions of this identity theme. This is so because such characters allow Proust to raise frequently the question of the "theatrical self" (existing only in the beliefs and perceptions of others) or the importance of role-playing, acting, and so the nature of the difference between the public self (in conven-tional terms, often false, hypocritical, as with homosexuals who not only present a straight face to the world, but one full of hostility for gays, or prosti-tutes like Odette Swann, who have become society matrons and try hard to stay well to the right of any social issue of the day, as in the Dreyfus affair.) Indeed, this concatenation of themes – homosexuals, prostitutes, actors, Jews – all seem designed to raise the question of the relation between "inner" and "outer" self, and the link with the non-social/social dialectic noted earlier. For secularized Jews, it was the problem of what it was to "be" Jewish (or to deny being Jewish) in those heated times. For some women, it was a question at least as old as Mary Magdalene – how does one *become* a thoroughly "ex-" prostitute after one has been one? And the acting theme (and so the difference between pretense and reality) is everywhere, as one might expect in a work where Proust is in effect "acting the part of himself" all the way through.

This theatricality then also carries us back full circle to the romantic theme, and so to the question of how to distinguish regarding a persona as a finely crafted work of art, something which does express one's self or the artist's truth, but which takes account of what can be socially understood and circulated (and so which avoids the simplistic solution – just be who you are honestly and forget about what the world thinks), and, on the other hand, being inauthentic and deluded, a victim of a self-serving conformism. (A typical anxiety of Marcel's: "our social personality is the creation of the thoughts of other people," I 20.)

V

Now, if one tried to sum all this up too quickly, one would end up with a vast novel of horrible disillusionment. "Becoming who one is" would simply look impossible in such a society with no sense of what is worth wanting and why, trapped inside an endless cycle of snobbery, fashion, hypocrisy, without genuine worth, unsettled every second by the radically temporal, mutable nature of the human subject. Or such a goal seems possible only in a pure, rarefied aesthetic domain, bought at the price of a great distance from life-as-it-is-lived; at the price, to use such a frequent modern image, of an isolating illness, making real contact with others impossible, but just thereby allowing separation and insight, a living death or *nunc stans*, outside time but thereby outside life. (At one point in the last volume, the narrator remarks that people think he has looked at them under a microscope, but it was really a telescope, far away enough for distance, but with the power to magnify from that distance (III 1098).)[35] We seem left with a human world with no possibility of adult, romantic love; one where love is possible (if it is) only within the family.

And there is almost a religious dimension to such an attitude. It is in one sense true that Proust seems to show us only the vanity and corruption "of the world," in some Augustinian way (or the reduplication in the modern world of the diseases of court culture, an old, tried and true theme in French literature), and to propose salvation only in another realm, isolated, non-social (or proposed for a thoroughly idealized society), a religion of art.[36] But *real* society is also what makes possible Marcel's education, his *Bildung*, his meeting Bergotte, Elstir, Swann (all of which is made possible by his grandmother's social position and her social taste); there are genuine friendships (Bergotte's beautiful minis-trations to the grandmother when she is dying; the early friendship with St Loup); and there is the telling and rich spectacle of Charlus's disintegration, and what it teaches Marcel. So there are various things about the "human mystery" that appear to require not just a social existence but a complex form of social sensibility, refined over time, and which turns out to be indispensable for Marcel's vocation. How to state properly this relation of dependence (the novel is after all about the social world, and not in a moral, or condemnatory way) and social independence (there must be some break, the sanatoria stays, and his later isolation, for Marcel to gain the perspective he needs to write), remains the riddle that must be solved.

That is, the novel seems to suggest a kind of "capacity" view of one's prac-tical identity and unity, and the capacity in question is an ability to negotiate properly the relation of dependence and independence with one's fellow agents, what to accept of how others take up and interpret and react to one's deeds, what to reject. Swann seems at first to negotiate the aristocratic social world with some proper measure of independence and integrity, in what appears to the young Marcel anyway, an ideal way. Bloch's pretended integrity is as false as, ultimately, Charlus's. There seems an endless dance of domination and submission in all the love affairs. But the social world in which all this occurs, and its great temporal and psychological instability, seems to leave no place for such a settled balanced capacity, no space even for it to develop properly.

But such a pessimistic reading would be much too hasty. For one thing, neither our narrator nor the younger Marcel can be granted complete authority in what they pronounce about these issues. Marcel is shown to be vain, deceptive, weak-willed, neurotic, hysterical, untrustworthy; and he spouts a lot of half-baked philosophy about idealism, solipsism, egoism, the impossibility of love, the prevalence of vanity and so forth, views that have no independent weight in the book, and are opinions which themselves undergo considerable, manifest change over time. Accordingly, as in all great novels, we have to pay attention to what is shown much more than what is said, if we are to come to any conclusions about the possibility of becoming who one is.

And we are shown a great deal. We are shown how the possibility of "becoming who you are," and all that comes with that – sustaining a commitment to a value, living in a social world without living under the suffocating, conformist weight of that world, living a coherent, a relatively unified life (being able to narrate one's life, to live backwards as well as forwards and so forth) – should all also be understood as some sort of function of the kind of society one lives in as well as a result of a refined capacity one might develop. (All such that generalizing from such a society to the "in itself" or essential problem would be dangerous. Just consciously realizing *that* sort of socio-historical dependence is already a manifestation of some independence.) As the novel shows, a practical identity, our sense of our own individuality, is the coherent realization in deeds of such a self-consciousness and so such a capacity, a kind of (relatively fragile, easily lost) achievement, not a simple discovery, and in all such achievements one needs help from others, and the right kind of help. Social dependence need not itself mean a loss or qualification on independence and so a restriction of the achievement of individuality; it all depends on the sort of dependence.

And the most salient feature of the society of aristocrats that becomes Marcel's world is that they have nothing to do, are part of no social project larger than preserving privilege and the system that enhances them; they are desperately dependent on each other, and so some aspect of this theme in the novel must appear in a distorted way. They are, as Ortega y Gasset said, like plants; rooted in their natural spots, moving only to turn to catch the rays of the sun of flattery and esteem, without which they would surely wilt and die, and so they have no help to offer in any common project. They have no project. Or, they are more like strutting, well dressed animals in a zoo than human beings.[37] They have no historical time because they have no future, have no way of stretching the past on along into the future, the modern world. They only have one way of making sense of their past, "narrating backwards" as we said earlier: lineage and genealogy. (By contrast, the peasants of Combray are privileged with the burden of necessity; they must work and their lives are purposive and ordered by means of the structure of this work.) There is a description of Swann that is telling in this regard.

> The fact was that Swann had reached an age whose philosophy – encouraged, in his case, by the current philosophy of the day, as well as by that of the circle in which he had spent much of his life, the group that surrounded the Princess des Laumes, where it was agreed that intelligence was in direct relation to the degree of skepticism and nothing was considered real and incontestable except the individual tastes of each person – is no longer that of youth, but a positive, almost medical philosophy, the philosophy of men, who, instead of exteriorizing the objects of their aspirations, endeavor to extract from the accumulation of the years already spent a fixed residue of habits and passions which they can regard as characteristic and permanent, and with which they will deliberately arrange, before anything else, that the kind of existence they choose to adopt shall not prove inharmonious.
>
> (I 304–5)

For a good part of the novel, until a large temporal break at the end (Marcel's illness requires two very long stays at sanatoria) Marcel struggles (and fails) to become who he is in *this* sort of world, modeled on that world, struggles to become what would be an artist for this audience, at such a time. He clearly at first regards their leisure and education and worldliness as the key to their freedom from necessity and so their capacity for an undistorted view of the higher things. If there is any group, he seems to reason, where a free appreciation of the best aspects of human life can be had, especially an appreciation of beauty and nobility, this must be it. That is all, we are shown (especially in the case of Charlus, whose pretense of near god-like independence is finally revealed as in reality a craven masochism, as he enacts this cult of dependence in sexual-pathological terms), and it leads to a hopeless counter-fantasy about art. At first, it is only once free of such a community (one that regards art as an escape into some realm of purity and eternity, away from life) that can he write, can he be for-himself a writer.[38] Not being able to become who he is, is not the difficulty it is because of some intrinsic limitation, some inherent tragedy in human life, dooming us to perpetual alienation; and it is not due to some inherent falseness of the modern world. It has everything to do with Marcel's historical world.

What he comes to appreciate, I would suggest, is that artists have no secure place in this society because this society, both the remnants of the feudal, *l'Ancien Régime*, and the new "fast" society of consumption, rapid technological change, great social instability and a new power of fluid capital, is about nothing, stands for nothing, devours its artists as entertainment or fetishizes them as sacred priests, disguising in Mme Verdurin's paroxysms of aesthetic delight its own vapidity. Bergotte, Elstir, and Vinteuil are in the novel served by, their aims are realized by, their social reality largely determined by, acolytes like Mme Verdurin, Berma and Rachel, Swann, Charlus and Morel. The relations among patrons, artist, and audience have always been complex, but there is not much hope for the artist as such when he is bounded on either side by such unrelenting phoniness and self-servingness or, in cases like Swann, such cynicism and boredom.

Marcel's reaction to this realization is complex. He *does*, after all, become who he is in spite of all this, he becomes a writer, and the conditions for his success are presented in a complex or double-edged way; not just as an escape from a concern with society. (A flight that would suggest the naiveté of a claim for complete societal independence, a "beautiful soul.") In the simplest terms, he can become a writer when he gives up the search for something like the "writerly essence" inside him, ceases looking inward at all, and begins the act of writing and submits the product to the social world. And this is all of a piece with what we have seen before, Marcel's breaking free of understanding the first-person perspective as introspective and observational, that he comes to see that attitude as more projection than reportage, projections or pledges that must be sustained and backed up. His hesitancy in the writing case is a product of the somewhat ludicrous elevation of art's importance that he inherits through his grandmother and his grandmother's relation to art is, as Shattuck has pointed out so well, a kind of *idolatry*, an absurd project of investing in art virtually every dimension of human value and of thinking of that activity and its creators in essentialist, Platonic ("anti-temporal") terms. This is, after all, a woman who gives a small boy a George Sand novel, so risqué or adult that his mother must censor so much in reading to Marcel that nothing makes any sense. (The fact that the novel, *Francois le Champi*, is almost about a kind of incest, a foundling who marries a woman who is "like a mother to him," is a topic best left for another discussion.) Likewise, there is something hysterical and defensive about the "aristocratic" (and late-nineteenth-century) relation to art, as if in compensation for the sterility, the non-generative character of their lives (another link to the homosexuality theme), and both influences set up Marcel's hopelessly Platonic aspirations for art, as a way of rescuing truth from time, or communing with eternal essences and revealing them all to everyone.[39]

The central transformation that makes possible not only Marcel's success in becoming who he is, but which makes possible a Proustean way of thinking about such an issue in an age where such identities, practices and types are always in suspense and contestable, cannot be secured by anything, any value or reality that transcends the wholly temporal human world, is that his time so long away from society has broken the hold of such "Platonic" illusions.[40] He comes to understand that his world's not being redeemable in this sense *is* his subject, and an infinitely variable one it is too, making some sense now of the modern anxieties of love and jealousy, the prevalence of vanity, his constant disappointment with society. It was, in other words, by failing to become "what a writer is," to realize his inner "writerly essence" – as if that role must be some transcendentally important or even a definite, substantial role – that Marcel realizes that such a becoming is important by *not* being secured by the transcendent, *by* being wholly temporal and finite, always and everywhere in suspense, and yet nonetheless capable of some illumination. (Marcel thus accepts the idea that his own book "will never be completed.") This realization is expressed a number of ways.

> How much more worth living did it appear to me now, now that I seemed to see that this life that we live in half-darkness can be illumined, this life that at every moment we distort can be restored to its true, pristine shape, that a life, in short can be realized within the confines of a book.
>
> (III 1088)

And, when talking about the readers of his book, and pointing us away from the notion of the book's "content":

> For it seemed to me that they would not be "my" readers but the readers of their own selves, my book being a sort of magnifying glass like those which the optician at Combray used to offer his customers – it would be my book, but with its help I would furnish them with the means of reading what lay inside of themselves.
>
> (III 1089)

At another point, the emphasis on the instability and temporariness of any such putative inner "self" we might become is not invoked as a reason to despair.

> For I realized that dying was not something new, but on the contrary, since my childhood, I had died many times. ... These successive deaths, so feared by the self which they were destined to annihilate, so painless, so unimportant once they were accomplished and the self that feared them was no longer there to feel them, had taught me by now that it would be the merest folly to be frightened of death.
>
> (III 1094–5)[41]

And Marcel goes on here to contemplate with the same equanimity the death of his book itself. ("Eternal duration is promised no more to men's works than to men," III 1101.)

But how can the "illumination" of these successive deaths and even successive selves, this acknowledgment of contingent temporality as sweeping as that very soon thereafter embraced so famously by Heidegger, serve as some sort of answer to the question of "how one becomes who one is?" It seems to be saying, when all is said and done, you will be several (contested, provisional) "selves" in your life and most of these will not care very much about the past others and the ones to come, and the best thing to be said about all that is that at least you will be well prepared for your actual death.

Proust's treatment here is quite deliberately indirect, and his response to this question involves an even further shift away from thinking of one's self-identity as a kind of content revealed in a redemptive moment. This is of course to be expected. The emphasis we have seen on breath-taking temporal transformations (Marcel's friend St Loup being, for Marcel, one of the most painful, since it involves the death of a friend; the "death" of his love for Albertine another), the effects of habit on daily perception and understanding, the over-determination of possible meaning in the words and gestures of other people, are all just as relevant to self-understanding as the understanding of anything in society. If Marcel has become who he is, and this somehow continuous with and a product of the experience of his own past, it is unlikely that we will be able to understand that by appeal to a substantial or underlying self, now discovered, or even by appeal to successor substantial selves, each one linked to the future and past by some sort of self-regard.

If the details of the novel suggest that becoming an individual is a kind of achievement, one that involves an implicit, not formalizable or thematizable capacity to negotiate the social world in a way true to the inevitable dependencies and relative independence required, is there a right or better way to embody this, and a wrong or worse way? If one never becomes who one is, but is always, inevitably becoming and revising a practical identity in exercising this capacity, if one is always in a kind of suspense about who one will turn out, yet again provisionally, to be, what is the *proper* acknowledgment of this state of affairs?

Even the right formulation of the question suggests an important, required acknowledgment. It reveals that it is a matter of some significant Proustean irony that "Prousteanism" or "Proustean idealism" is supposed to consist in a solipsism beyond the merely methodological, or even epistemological; that it reaches metaphysical dimensions. Yet the questions that dominate the interior monologue of the narrator and Marcel – what do I really believe? What do I really want? – are revealed never to be asking, cannot be asking, "Do I *have* such a determinate belief?" "Do I *have* such a determinate desire?" Marcel constantly surprises himself by what he turns out to desire, and so in some sense learns (or at least we learn) that the content of the desires ascribable to him are manifest only in deeds, demurrals, social interactions, and actual struggles; "out there." And even "there," where it is manifest, it is not ever wholly or fully manifest. What is manifest is a subject of contestation, possible retraction; provisional yet again. That is why the book is a novel, not a lyric poem, and the "unfinished" character of this provisionality tells us something of why it is not a work of philosophy. (The logic of the claim Proust is implicitly making is important to stress. It is not that Marcel is simply self-deceived (although he often is), not that his true practical identity, the true commitments have already been made and lie somewhere hidden. Again: he only becomes who he is when he acts in some way, and even then what he intended to do and what he did are both subjects for much uncertain retrospective contestation.)

A different "answer" of sorts is suggested by a long passage about a musical concert in *The Captive*. What we are presented with is a different way of thinking about who one is, one that, oddly, undermines any way of thinking of such an achievement as a possible intentional goal that can finally be reached, and that shifts our attention from center to periphery in the "search for self." The concert occurs in one of the funniest and yet pathos-filled party scenes, this one organized by Charlus for his lover, the violinist Morel, at the home of Mme de Verdurin. The party is a social catastrophe, as Charlus's posh friends treat the Verdurins like the butler and maid, and titter openly about their social pretensions, thus ruining forever Charlus's relations with the Verdurins and so his relation with Morel. But at this party, Marcel hears a new piece of music, a "septet,"[42] by Vinteuil, a composer who, along with an earlier piano sonata, has figured intermittently and importantly in the novel since *Swann's Way*. The sonata serves as a figure for the Swann-Odette story and perhaps as well for what that story could have meant to us then, all to be contrasted with the now much more complex "septet," figuring as it does the culmination of our experience of love in the novel. (It is important too that the septet was written by Vinteuil in a kind of code or shorthand and required translation, especially since Marcel has already referred to the writer's task as translation. Whatever the meaning of Vintueil's notes, the record of temporal movement, they will require as much interpretive or de-coding work as is demanded of the reader of *Remembrance*.) Marcel's reflections on the differences between that earlier, "prettier" piece and this more complex, almost discordant, but much more "profound" work, provide a context for an indirect reflection on his own history, and his relation to art and identity. (It can even be read as an indirect manifesto for modernism in the arts, the aesthetic analogue to the social suspension of the self's stability.) The earlier works of Vinteuil are called "timid essays, exquisite but very slight, besides the triumphant and consummate masterpiece now being revealed to me" (III 253). This seems to be a reference to his own little pieces, his small essay for *Figaro*. He continues to use the language of youth and innocence to describe that sonata ("lily-white," III 256), and the language of a dawning maturity to describe the septet, but he also begins to realize that that the two pieces are profoundly linked, and his reflections on how they are linked seem like reflections on the question Marcel has always asked himself, "who am I?" While the earlier sonata is "so calm and shy, almost detached and somehow philosophical," and the later septet "so restless, urgent, imploring," they, Marcel realizes,

133

were nevertheless the same prayer, bursting forth like different inner sunrises, and merely refracted through the different mediums of other thoughts, or artistic researches carried on through the years in which he had sought to create something new.

(III 257)

Although the works are so different, Marcel realizes that they teach him that "in spite of the conclusions to which science seemed to point, *the individual did exist*" (*Ibid.*, my emphasis) and that that individual exists as a kind of "accent" throughout so much temporal change. (It is thus important that the image is musical, where such an accent is not exactly an inflection *on* content. Since there is no independent content in music, it, the accent, *is* the "content," the music, and by its existence serves as "a proof of the irreducibly individual existence of the soul," III 258.) All artists are thus like travelers from an unknown land that they have forgotten, but which stamps one's talk and manner none the less, to which fatherland we remain all our lives "unconsciously attuned," able thus to express "who we are" only as an "ineffable something" more than the substantial content of our roles and practices and ideals.[43]

We have thus come to the place and time that Marcel has come to; we understand who he is, but not by knowing anything substantial directly about him. We know what we know by having become "attuned" after 3,000 pages and months and months of reading, to this accent, the musical figure for his distinct capacity, his "attunement." And this result has a number of implications. It suggests that "one's true self" is not a thing one can pursue directly, that it is much more something like "the bloom of health in a youth." Trying to find "it" almost insures it will be artificial. (And many of the other grand themes have this quality: you cannot really seek love, or certainly cannot seek to be "in love"; you can't achieve social prestige by trying to achieve such prestige. Even Mme de Verdurin has to fake her aesthetic swoons of appreciation. In all such cases, including this practical identity, these are things that one can't achieve alone; they reflect quite a complicated social dependence.)

This would mean too that any expression of putative self-knowledge is always something provisional and hypothetical, a matter of dispositions with uncertain realizations, and commitments of uncertain strengths. (This position again bears comparison with Sartre's early position in *The Transcendence of the Ego*, with his claim that one's "self" is so linked to action and possible action that it can be said to be "out there," as much "in the world" as anything else.)[44] More importantly, less this sound like the familiar kind of aestheticism ascribed to Proust, accents also exist in being heard in contrastive contexts and interpreted for what they show about origin; they have their own social dimension as well, and in the same sense noted throughout, can never "settle" anything. Our own difficulty in settling on what we really believe, are committed to, is thus as much a problem as the reader's difficulty in identifying "which" Marcel is speaking, from what stage of development, in what relation to the absent

Proust. And that is paradigmatic for the problem itself in the novel. (To know anything about anyone is not to have prepositional knowledge about an object, but to be able to inhabit, to become the point of view of such a person. In a deeply paradoxical way, Proust is suggesting, this is just as true of self-knowledge. It is the task of "becoming who one is.") Indeed, finally, our narrator goes very far to make his point, so far as to say that it is only in art (or in the aesthetic dimensions of our own lives) that this "ineffable something . . . which we call individuals" can be known.

> A pair of wings, a different respiratory system, which enabled us to travel through space, would in no way help us, for if we visited Mars or Venus while keeping the same senses, they would clothe everything that we saw in the same aspect as the things of Earth. The only true voyage of discovery, the only really rejuvenating experience, would be not to visit strange lands, but to possess other eyes, to see the universe through the eyes of another, of a hundred others, to see the hundred universes that each of them sees, that each of them is; and this we can do with an Elstir, with a Vinteuil; with men like these we really do fly from star to star.
>
> (III 260)

Notes

1 I am much indebted to John Coetzee, Thomas Pavel, Glenn Most, and Nikolas Kompridis, for comments on an earlier draft of this paper, and to Jonathan Lear, James Chandler, Joshua Landy, Lanier Anderson, and Candace Vogler for conversations about its content.

2 There is a thoughtful comparison of Nietzsche and Proust by Alexander Nehamas in *Nietzsche: Life as Literature*, Cambridge, Harvard University Press, 1985, pp. 167–70. I shall be stressing here much more the ineliminable social dimension to any "self-fashioning." Cf. also my discussion in *Modernism as a Philosophical Problem: On the Dissatisfactions of European High Culture*, 2nd edn, Oxford, Blackwell, 1999, pp. 99–113.

3 Compare, though, Pindar's second *Pythian Ode* (2.72), where one is encouraged to "Become such as you are, having learned what that is." Pindar, *Olympian Odes; Pythian Odes*, ed. and trans. William H. Race, Cambridge MA, Harvard University Press, 1997, p. 239. Pindar, as the context reveals, *is* talking about a kind of integrity, being true to yourself no matter what the "cunning . . . slanderers" say. But there is no sense that *who* one is might just consist in a constant, experimental "becoming," one that never ends in a realization. Proust's vision is much more like this latter, ever suspended, unresolved becoming, I want to show. (I am grateful to Glenn Most for discussions about the topic.)

4 Contra, to some extent, the approach suggested by Joshua Landy in "The Proustean Self in Philosophical Perspective," *New Literary History* vol. 32 (2001), pp. 91–32.

5 Cf. Leo Bersani's apposite remark: "For Marcel, personality – his own and that of others – is by definition what has not yet happened or has not yet been revealed; it is in essence a secret." *Marcel Proust: The Fictions of Life and Art*, New York, Oxford University Press, 1965, p. 77. One might also put the point by stressing the non-propositional character of the content of self-knowledge. One must always "*make*

true" what one claims to know about oneself, rather than "*find* such true propositions." A contrast between "reports" and "avowals" in first-person knowledge is
discussed in Richard Moran's valuable book, *Authority and Estrangement: An Essay on
Self-Knowledge*, Princeton NJ, Princeton University Press, 2001, although he retains
a sense of first-person authority that, I think, emerges quite "scathed" in Proust's
treatment, even though it does not disappear.

6 Cf. the very typical "hesitation" style in this simple "report" on the Balbec elevator
boy and his reluctance to enter conversation.

> But he vouchsafed no answer, whether from astonishment at my words, preoc-
> cupation with his work, regard for etiquette, hardness of hearing, respect for
> holy ground, fear of danger, slowness of understanding, or the manager's orders.
>
> (I 715–6)

All references will be to the C. K. Scott Moncrieff and Terence Kilmartin translation, New York: Vintage, 1982. References will be cited in the text ands refer to the
volume and page number of this edition.

7 A typical passage indicating Proust's sense of this issue, from *The Fugitive* (Marcel is
hesitating after he has told his mother he will not leave Venice with her):

> I was well aware that in reality it was the resolution not to go that I was making
> by remaining here without stirring, but to say to myself: "I'm not going," which
> in that direct form was impossible, became possible in this indirect form: "I'm
> going to listen to one more phrase of 'O sole mio.'"
>
> (III 669)

8 Cf. Gérard Genette, *Narrative Discourse: An Essay in Method*, trans. Jane E. Lewin,
Ithaca NY, Cornell University Press, 1980.

9 Vincent Descombes, *Proust: Philosophy of the Novel*, Stanford CA, Stanford
University Press, 1992, p. 6. See also his very useful formula summarizing his
approach: "The thoughts reported *in the narrative* do not coincide with the thoughts
communicated *by the narrative*" (p. 30, my emphasis). Cf. also p. 272. Descombes'
book is invaluable, but I disagree with his interpretation of Proust's modernism in
chapter 8, and especially on pp. 138–9. ("For remembrance systematically eliminates
public events as a source of exaltation or despair. The Dreyfus affair is a mere topic of
conversation," p. 138.) My claim is that Proust (the "philosophical novelist" as that
notion is brilliantly deployed by Descombes, or the "implied author" as Wayne
Booth would deploy that term) has understood something essential about the relation between public and private, social and individual, not somehow dismissed the
former, and so has avoided the simplified dichotomies presupposed in such questions
as about the "sources" of inspiration. Also extremely helpful on this theme: Leo
Bersani's *Marcel Proust*.

10 There are signs throughout the novel that Proust is well aware of this problem. One
of the clearest occurs in *The Guermantes Way*, when Marcel realizes that "Elstir the
painter" is much "more daring" than "Elstir the theorist"; that in general, there need
be no tight connection between the two (II 436).

11 Quoted by Descombes, *Proust*, pp.4–5. See also Landy, "The Proustean Self," p. 109.

12 Marcel Muller, *Les voix narratives dans La recherche du temp perdu*, Geneva, Dorz,
1965; Joshua Landy, "The Texture of Proust's Novel," in *The Cambridge Companion
to Proust*, Richard Bales (ed.), Cambridge, Cambridge University Press, 2001, p. 124.
(Landy has a fine book, *Proust, Philosophy and Fiction*, forthcoming from Oxford
University Press, in which many of these narrative and chronological details are
clearly sorted out; some, as far as I know, for the first time.)

13 Indeed, the temptation to read the novel as a *roman à clé*, and such curiosity about
"who" the "real" author is, is what is thematized so explicitly in the novel, and is a

bit like the obsessive need to know if Albertine is a lesbian, if Odette was with Forcheville, and so forth.

14 This expands on a brief suggestion by Roger Shattuck. Cf. Roger Shattuck, *Proust's Way: A Field Guide to In Search of Lost Time*, New York, Norton, 2000, p. 32. I should stress that there most definitely *is* also a sense in which the three *are* one. So many readers automatically assume this, though (that what Marcel thinks, what the narrator says in his philosophizing, and what Proust believes, are the same thing), that while the three-in-one, one-in-three structure of the novel is the complete picture, the difficulty of simply identifying all the thoughts in the book with Proust's should be especially stressed. The view from far off can't be wholly deceptive, since the narrator himself uses the "distance" metaphor when he claims that he can only see from "far off," though with a telescope. I am indebted to conversations with Jim Chandler on this point.

15 Landy has established in his forthcoming book that this is not so, *even from the novel's* (narrator's) own point of view.

16 During this "apprentice" time Marcel pays very close attention to three ideal or model artists, the novelist Bergotte, the painter Elstir, and the composer Vinteuil, trying to understand what makes them artists, and how they are both formed by, and help to form, their milieu. (They appear to be arranged in some order of importance in the novel, and one of the most important passages is in the last volume; it presents a reflection on a septet by Vinteuil and its implications for the self. I discuss it in section V below.)

17 This is from a passage not included in the French edition used by Moncrieff; quoted by Bersani, *Marcel Proust*, pp. 106–7.

18 This despite the fact that Sartre almost willfully refuses to notice those passages in Proust so similar to the views of *Being and Nothingness*, and treats him as if wholly wedded to an introspective account of self-knowledge. Bersani is very good on this issue, *Marcel Proust*, p. 106.

19 I agree with Bersani that the absence of omniscient narrators in the work of novelists like Proust or Henry James is not merely a matter of technical experimentation, but evinces a historical and social crisis manifest in literary modernism and one ultimately most threatening to that bourgeois consolation that had been so often evoked as a refuge from the secular harshness and uncertainties of the bourgeois world – romantic love. See the discussion in my *Henry James and Modern Moral Life*, Cambridge, Cambridge University Press, 2000.

20 There is a fine description of the bluff and its dialectical twists in vol. III, pp. 360–1.

21 There are philosophical controversies aplenty here. As stated this "Proustean" theory is quite incomplete. It especially leaves unclarified our strong intuition that there nevertheless *is* something distinctive and unique about the first-person perspective on "who I am," distinctive that is from one's knowledge of other persons and objects. The novel is, in effect, "disputing" that. But for the purposes of this essay those refinements are not yet relevant.

22 In fact, reliance on such memories is what we might call ideological, something Marcel needs badly to believe rather than what is in itself believable. As Adorno pointed out, no past memory is ever safe, neatly stored away; it can be "revoked in its very substance by later experience. He who has loved and who betrays love does harm not only to the image of the past, but to the past itself" (MM, §106, p. 166). Cf. also Leo Bersani's remark: "And the act of memory seems to involve such a liberal re-creation of the past, rather than a mere fidelity to past impressions, that some of the theoretical positions that inspired the narrator's work are made obsolete by the work itself." *Marcel Proust*, p.18.

23 Benjamin, *Illuminations*, New York, Schocken, 1977, p. 158.

24 Cf. the formulation by Bersani, "Our knowledge of the outer world is, then, dramatic rather than conceptual; unable to describe it, we nevertheless spend our lives meeting it." *Marcel Proust*, p. 134.

25 As is often pointed out, a great deal of the nineteenth-century realist novel obviously involves such a "lack of fit" between idealistic expectation and the emerging social reality of bourgeois Europe.

26 Or it is a manifestation of the even more deflating revelation that there was essentially never any difference between these social cliques.

27 Descombes, *Proust*, p. 166, notes that because no real events happen in Combray (anomalies that might seem like novelties, like the social success of Swann or Legrandin, are successfully filtered out) this "world" is not a novelistic world, as is the world of Paris. Throughout his book, Descombes makes an interesting case, using Proust, for a historical theory of the novel, similar in ambition to Girard's.

28 Some aspects of technology also are shown to distort, narrow, or at least drastically affect aspects of social understanding, as when Marcel speaks to his grandmother on the telephone, hears her isolated voice, the voice of a frail old woman, not his grandmother. And when he rushes to see her, he now cannot avoid seeing her in this way, a "mad old woman, drowsing over her book, overburdened with years, flushed and coarse . . . a stranger whom he has never seen." Cf. Samuel Beckett, *Proust*, New York, Grove Press, 1931, p. 15.

29 Cf. Adorno's remarks in #20, *Minima Moralia*, "Die Entfremdung erweist sich an den Menschen gerade daran, dass die Distanzen fortfallen" (MM 45). ("Alienation is manifested precisely in the elimination of the distance between people.") Thomas Pavel has pointed out to me that people lived on top of each other, and complained about it, well before such technologies. But I mean to suggest here that the rapidity and efficiency of communication and travel introduces a qualitative change into this long-standing problem, a level and a kind of odd, paradoxical (because also anonymous) intimacy and regard that alters the nature of social experience. The line between "inside" and "outside" is harder to maintain and what one can regard as one's own point of view, developed by oneself, is harder to have some faith in. Marcel himself complains about how the automobile, by bringing villages "closer," is also homogenizing them.

30 See Walter Benjamin's discussion on involuntary memory, experience and Proust in "On Some Motifs in Baudelaire," especially pp. 162–3, in *Illuminations*.

31 To be able to be satisfied now with what we desired "then," is as "illogical," Beckett notes in his book about Proust, as "to expect one's hunger to be dissipated by the spectacle of Uncle eating his dinner." *Proust*, p. 3.

32 "Habit then is the generic term for the countless treaties concluded between the countless subjects that constitute the individual and their countless correlative objects." Beckett, *Proust*, p. 8.

33 There are many other examples of this issue in society. Cf. the story of Orianne, who in order to demonstrate or even create her independence, makes a show of not attending the party of Mme de Saint-Euverte and pretends a sudden desire to see the fjords of Norway. The suggestion is that she is no more free of social pressures than if she had accepted (II, p. 495; cf. also Descombes, *Proust*, p. 282).

34 At one point, Marcel can confuse relations of original and image to such an extent that he can describe the moonlight as "copying the art of Hubert Robert" (I 124).

35 As Walter Benjamin has pointed out, the significance of Proust's snobs extends far beyond French society. They are avatars of that deadly modern type, the consumer, who wants to be flattered for his discriminating taste, but whose taste amounts to nothing more than liking what will get him flattered, taking refuge in brand names and high-end merchandise much as the snob does in supposedly high-end people. A whole society looms where no one is or even wants any more to be "who one is,"

Another Nietzschean nightmare. See Walter Benjamin, "Zum Bilde Proust," in *Gesammelte Schriften*, vol. II, 3, ed. Rolf Tiedemann and Herman Schweppenhäuser, Frankfurt, Suhrkamp, 1974, pp. 310–24.

36 I am grateful to Thomas Pavel for noting the relevance of this Augustinian theme in French literature and its continuing relevance to Proust.

37 See Bersani on "Le royaume de néant," *Marcel Proust*, pp. 166–77.

38 It should perhaps be stressed that this is the opposite of many standard readings of Proustean "Platonism," the final aesthetic *defeat* of time. Beckett is often on a better course.

39 There are several hilarious send-ups of the members of the Verdurin salon on this score, and of the "High Art" religion of Charlus and his crowd. See *inter alia, The Captive*, vol. III, 250ff. Moreover, the narrator has set out these examples with some design in view. Elstir, the painter, is sometimes described as "stopping" time by painting moments of it; Vinteuil as composing a purely temporal art, leading to the suggestion that Bergotte and the novel form represents some possible synthesis.

40 In Beckett's apt phrase, "from the victory over Time he passes to the victory of Time, from the negation of Death to its affirmation." *Proust*, p. 51. See also p. 61ff. for Beckett's discussion of Proust's "romanticism."

41 This is the theme that begins very early. Cf. this passage from *Swann's Way*.

> And so it was from the Guermantes way that I learned to distinguish between these states which reign alternately within me, during certain periods, going so far as to divide each day between them, the one returning to dispossess the other with the regularity of a fever; contiguous, and yet so foreign to one another, so devoid of means of communication, that I can no longer understand, or even picture to myself, in one state what I have desired or dreaded or accomplished in another.
>
> (I 200)

42 This is the standard translation of "septuor," but it is a bit misleading. I quote Joshua Landy's note on the subject, from his forthcoming *Proust, Philosophy and Fiction*:

> In Proust, the term "septuor" does not appear to mean a piece for seven players – a septet – but rather a piece whose primary theme has seven notes. Thus Vinteuil's masterwork can be a "septuor," even though it is a "pièce pour dix instruments," because it is "a song on seven notes."
>
> (note 93, from the Introduction)

43 Cf. a similar image in Nietzsche's *The Gay Science*, §290, "One thing is needful – To 'give style' to one's character." Translated by Walter Kaufmann, New York, Vintage, 1974; and see the discussion in Nehamas's *Nietzsche: Life as Literature*, pp. 170–99.

44 J.-P. Sartre, *The Transcendence of the Ego: An Existential Theory of Consciousness*, trans. Forrest Williams and Robert Kirkpatrick, New York, Hill and Wang, 1989.

Part III

ART AND IRONY

7

POESY AND THE ARBITRARINESS OF THE SIGN

Notes for a critique of Jena romanticism

J. M. Bernstein

words without spirit, method without inner illumination, figures of speech without feeling.

(Moses Mendelssohn)

Introduction

Almost from the moment that modern aesthetics took on a distinctive shape in the middle of the eighteenth century, there arose claims that sought to make aesthetic reason or experience privileged. Aesthetic reason could come to have this privileged position because it could be seen as responding to a profound crisis of reason brought on by the disenchantment and dematerialization of circumambient nature that was the consequence of the mechanization and mathematization of nature by the new science, on the one hand, and the deworlding (and dematerialization or disembodiment) of freedom and subjectivity that arose as the necessary saving response to the loss of nature as habitat, on the other. The desubstantializing of the self into an empty form was but the flip-side of the emptying of the natural world of meaning.[1] Nature dematerialized and human subjectivity deprived of worldly substantiality in their interaction and re-enforcement of one another form the two struts supporting the various rationality crises of modernity to which art works and the reason they exemplify might somehow be a response. The privileging of aesthetic reason arose from the insight that unavoidably and uniquely art works bridge the abyss separating the new, transcendental separation of sensible nature from intelligible freedom and subjectivity – or so the conception of the aesthetic that arose from Kant's *Critique of Judgement* contended.[2]

The bald argument for this privileging runs like this: If art works are going to be a response to the crisis, to project or insinuate or promise or exemplify a resolution, then they must suspend the dematerialization of nature and the delegitimation of its voice, and, simultaneously, reveal the possibility of human meaningfulness becoming incarnated, materially saturated and embodied. Hence the core of art's rationality potentiality relates to the role and status of artistic mediums. By mediums I mean, minimally, the material conditions of a practice as they appear to an artistic community of producers at a given time; so, the medium of an artistic practice is the disposition of the material conditions of that practice at a given time, thus materials as conditions of possibility for making works. The medium(s) of sculpture at a given time would include not just the raw materials thought acceptable for sculpting (wood, marble, etc.), but what *kinds* of things are required to make stuff like that into works, what things minimally can or must be done to that stuff in order to transform it into a work, hence what potential for making works is perceived as lying in those materials, as projected on to those materials through the practices that might shape them. Working in a medium is working with a material that is conceived of as a potential for sense-making in a manner that is material-specific. Hence in art the medium is not a neutral vehicle for the expression of an otherwise immaterial meaning, but rather the very condition for sense-making. *The specificity of (modern) art-meanings is that their mediums are not regarded as contingent with respect to the meanings communicated;*[3] if that were so, if the medium were there simply as an instrument, a means, for conveying a meaning (the end) indifferent to it, then the work of art would disappear once the meaning it conveyed was grasped. But this is precisely what we think is not the case with the kind of sense-making that occurs in works of art. Art meanings, the kind of meanings art works have, are non-detachable from the medium through which they are embodied and communicated.

Artistic sense-making, then, is making sense in a medium. So mediums are the potential for sense-making. But since mediums are at least certain types of materials (as conditions of possibility for sense-making), then mediums are those materials, hence matter conceived of as a potential for sense-making. Since art is that kind of sense-making that is medium-dependent, and mediums are aspects of nature conceived of as potentials for sense-making, then art, its reason, is minimally the reason of nature as a potential for sense-making at a certain time. If art works make a claim at a particular time, then at that time nature is experienced as possessing a material-specific potentiality for sense-making. Hence, the experience of a work as making a claim at a time is to experience the dematerialization and delegitimation of nature as suspended. Or rather, that is how we come to understand and experience uniquely modern, autonomous works of art, and, in time, it is the claim that self-consciously modernist works make for themselves. The idea of an artistic medium is perhaps the last idea of material nature as possessing potentialities for meaning.

Working from the other side: in modern works of art freedom, the human capacity for autonomous sense-making, *appears*, that is, art works are *unique objects* that as unique sources of normatively compelling claims are experienced as products of freedom, as creations; their uniqueness and irreducibility are understood, experienced, as the material mark of an autonomous subjectivity. In autonomous works of art human autonomy appears; the autonomy of the former hence figures the autonomy of the latter. Beauty, Schiller tells us, is freedom in appearance. But the material bearer of appearing freedom cannot be neutral or indifferent, a mere occasion through which a meaning indifferent to its material substratum is transmitted. If meaning is indifferent to its material bearer, then freedom is not so much appearing as merely being transmitted. For freedom to appear, it must be embodied; but if truly embodied, then there must be an exchange between matter and meaning, a way in which that matter enables that meaning to be the meaning it is. Matter becomes a medium through artistic forming, but once formed it, retroactively, becomes matter-possessing-meaning-potential. So for freedom to appear nature must be truly amenable to human sense-making, implying, again, the idea of a medium as revealing nature as a potential for sense-making.

In modern, autonomous works of art nature in the form of an artistic medium appears as meaningful (e.g. the compellingness of modernist paintings derives solely from paint-on-canvas and not from conventional codes or representational illusions or culinary delight), and human sense-making is absorptively present in what is nonetheless simply a useless (purposive but without a purpose) material object. Artworks contest the duality of freedom and nature, and thereby suspend, displace, sublate, side-step, ignore, contest scientific and (immaterial) moral rationality. *Aesthetic reason is the rationality revealed in the production and comprehension of autonomous works of art in which there occurs an authentic binding of meaning and matter.* For the purposes of this chapter, this thesis is going to be assumed rather than defended.[4]

Because scientific and moral rationality really are constitutive of our empirical rationality, then what contests them is nothing empirical. So what makes art works *only* appearances, semblances, is that they abrogate the conditions that make empirical experience, cognitive and moral, possible. What makes such appearances substantive in their own right is that they reveal, however we construe the status of this revelation, through the compellingness or demandingness of the works, a rationality potentiality excised from the (normative and/or transcendental) repertoire of modern self-consciousness.

The cuckoo in the nest of aesthetic reason so understood is Jena romanticism, above all that of Friedrich Schlegel. What happened, in brief, is this: Beginning with Lessing, the argument arose that among the arts poetry should be accorded a privileged position because its medium, the arbitrary linguistic sign, enabled rather than constrained the freedom of the imagination.[5] This elective affinity between the arbitrariness of the sign and the freedom of the imagination provides poetry with a universality that the other arts, because they are bound by the materiality of their medium, cannot match. But the freedom of the imagination is equally not just any power of the subject: with Kant and Fichte, it became tempting to conceive of the freedom of the imagination as the essence of modern subjectivity. Hence poetry becomes the unique vehicle for expressing the essence of subjectivity. But once poetry is conceived of as having this task, then the constraints of material mediums become otiose, and this new, romantic privileging of aesthetic reason dissolves the specificity of the aesthetic, the linking of nature and medium, which had been the source of its original privileging.[6]

My explicit argument here will be that what is meant by romantic poetry as "progressive, universal poetry" (AF 116),[7] which is the idea of poetic works becoming explicitly and self-consciously the bearers of the idea of art as the fullest embodiment of human freedom, is very approximate to, because originally derived from, Lessing's understanding of poetry minus Lessing's qualification that what, in fact, makes poetry poetry, poetry art (and not the prose of the world) is the requirement that in it linguistic presentation be maximally sensuous or sensate, *sinnlich*. In order for a linguistic presentation to be sensate, Lessing argues, it must be, in essence, painterly:

> A poetic picture is not necessarily one that can be transformed into a material painting; but every feature, and every combination of features by means of which the poet makes his object so sensate that we are more clearly conscious of this object than of his words, is called painterly [*mahlerisch*], is called a painting [*ein Gemählde*], because it brings us closer to that degree of illusion of which the material painting is specially capable and which can most readily and most easily be conceptualized in terms of a material painting.[8]

In Lessing, the idea of painting as a constitutive constraint on poetic language is the final moment of resistance to the emptying of the natural world of any authority, since what it means for Lessing to make poetic language painterly is to make linguistic meaning appear as if natural. The claim for the universality of poesy, as premised on the arbitrariness of the linguistic sign, necessarily dissolves even this constraint. With it gone, the duality between deworlded subjectivity and disenchanted nature necessarily returns. Hence, the romantic defense of aesthetic reason terminates, despite itself and perhaps all unawares, in a radical anti-aesthetic that represses both the crisis of rationality and the uniqueness of the aesthetic that, arguably, was the magnificent achievement of idealist thought.

In Jena romanticism, a version of the idea that art must become self-conscious about itself, must become the philosophy of itself, is acknowledged and embodied in a practice that veers from the philosophical to the artistic, but artistic in a manner that is all the more theoretical and philosophical. Each of the characteristic gestures of Jena romanticism – its conception of irony, the fragment, incomprehension, genre indifference, and works as critically self-conscious – involves a further relinquishing of the idea of an artistic medium, and hence a further colluding with the forms of rationality that art was meant to be resisting.

The emergence of the universality of poesy

Probably as a consequence of Schelling's *Letters on Dogmatism and Skepticism*, along with the continuing influence of Spinozist pantheism as a counter to the dominance of the methodology and metaphysics of Cartesian subjectivity, the intense experience of nature as disenchanted that, for example, so stamps Schiller's and Hölderlin's thought (call it their orthodox Kantianism) simply does not appear in the writings of Novalis and Schlegel. On the contrary, in their writings there occurs a repeated taken-for-granted proposing of nature as itself forming the paradigm of poetic action which is participated in and imitated by human poetic activity. At the very beginning of the "Dialogue on Poesy" (1799) we find:

> And what are these [poems] compared to the formless and unconscious poesy that stirs in a plant, shines in light, that smiles in a child, shimmers in the bloom of youth, glows in the loving breast of women? But this is the first, originary poesy without which there would surely be no poesy of words. . . . We are capable of hearing the music of infinite chimes, capable of understanding the beauty of a poem, because a part of the poet, a spark of his creative spirit, lives in us as well and never ceases to glow with a mysterious force deep beneath the ashes of self-made unreason.[9]

Nearly from the outset, romanticism transformed the critical awareness of the disenchantment of nature and the requirement that the idea of nature as a source of meaning be kept alive artistically, which is to say, the critical awareness of the necessity and impossibility of thinking of nature as a source of meaning which Schiller salvages from the *Critique of Judgment*, into the philosophical/poetical presumption of nature as an originary source of meaning, as an everlasting poem. Any depth experience of disillusionment is no part of the romantic outlook; hence, one will not find in their writings the kind of tragic self-consciousness of loss that scores Hölderlin's early writings, for example. The absence of this tone and outlook derives from the absence of the disenchantment of nature from their thought.

Against the background of its enchanted conception of the natural world, how is it, then, that romantic poetics has been appropriated as a distinctly and radically modern philosophical poetics? If the romantics take for granted nature's enchantment, then the question to which their philosophical poetics is the answer must be systematically different from the question underlying

Lessing and addressed by Kant and Schiller. Till this juncture I have written as if, since the two sides of the crisis of modernity – the dematerialization of nature and the de-substantialization of the self – re-enforce and complement one another, then to the degree to which works of art are conceived as responses to the dilemma, what counts as a response to the one side will *a fortiori* count as a response to the other. To what extent distinctly modern works of art must or even can be conceived as resolving the simultaneous equation requiring the re-enchanting of nature (via the medium) and the objectification of freedom (the material binding of the arbitrary social sign) is perhaps the most difficult and significant question in the interpretation of modern art.[10] That there exists at least the possibility of divergence derives from each side of the dilemma possessing a metaphysical specificity that is not shared by the other. Metaphysically, nature as a potential for significance conflicts with nature as a closed causal order fully explainable through mathematical laws. Metaphysically, whilst the insubstantiality of subjectivity can be conceived of as an inwardizing of the subject demanded by the loss of nature as human habitat, one can also conceive of freedom (autonomy) as the power of transcending any given state of the self, and hence as what is intrinsically incommensurable with a fully mate-rial objectivity. Any material determination of freedom in an object would be, by that very fact, not free. Freedom cannot materially *appear* and still be freedom. Consider this the sublimity of modern freedom. Yet, still, one would suppose that for us works of art are paradigmatic products of free action. So somewhere close to the center of the concerns of the Jena romantics is the ques-tion: How is it possible to have a non-self-defeating, non-skeptical aesthetics that is premised upon sublime human freedom? This question spreads out to become all but all-encompassing once, following Fichte, freedom is identified as the essence of human subjectivity. What Friedrich Schlegel offers, and it is with his thought I will be concerned for the remainder of this chapter, is an aesthetics of production; poesy, the romantics' metaphysical conception of the linguistic arts, is a way of thinking subjectivity-as-freedom. This aesthetics of production can be shown to be an elaboration of Lessing's notion of poetry minus Lessing's concession to the idea of painting.

In pressing this negative thesis, I do not mean to deny that Schlegel's romantic poetics contains more *explicitly* modernist ideas about the work of art than any of his idealist predecessors. In scanning Schlegel's theory those modernist notions will be highlighted since they belong to his achievement and the seduction his theory poses: they form the compelling bridge to the collapse that occurs in its denouement. Indeed, it is because his modernist moments are so utterly lucid and prescient that the eventual collapse is so dispiriting. Nor is the collapse arbitrary: it represents the exemplary aesthetic denial of the aesthetic, the way art in seeking to be all, an apotheosis of modern reason, becomes a philosophical critique of art. What is worse, it is just the moment in which aesthetic reason undermines the aesthetic, in which there occurs what I shall frame as the philosophical disenfranchisement of art, that Schlegel's supporters celebrate and make their own. All this, I am contending, is what is hibernating in Lessing's notion of pure poetry, poetry stripped of the idea of painting, poetry as the repudiation of the notion of art as medium-bound.

The seeds of Schlegel's conception of poesy are planted in *On the Study of Greek Poetry* (1795),[11] an essay in which the characteristic Schlegelian comprehension of the relation between ancient and modern literature is first laid down. Equally here, Schlegel develops a conception of poetry in relation to the other arts that explicitly borrows from and elaborates Lessing's. For Schlegel the singular experience of modernity is the collapse of traditional authority, the loss of the self-evidence of the classical, the sense that even in our appreciation of the authority of Greek art we stand outside it. Hence, the study of Greek literature faces the problem of explicating how it is possible for us to represent the kind of authority and perfection it exemplifies whilst acknowledging its inaccessibility to us; we cannot create works nor perfect ourselves on the model of the Greeks, yet they remain somehow a model and a paradigm. Although no fully compelling solution emerges, Schlegel's thought is to configure the relation of ancient to modern poetry as natural to artificial *Bildung*. *Bildung* is the bridge between ancient and modern; in this context it possesses the full range and imbrication of its various senses: culture, formation, development, education, maturation. To consider the progress of Greek literature a *Bildung* is thereby to relate it explicitly to history and implicitly to human freedom. The conceptual energy of the essay requires us to hear *natürliche Bildung* as nearly oxymoronic, to hear the ambiguity and tension in the thought of culture unfolding, developing in accordance with nature. Taking the paradox out of the expression is the essay's achievement. To think the development of Greek literature as a natural *Bildung* is to consider that development as owing nothing to subjectivity or individual self-consciousness, an artist's awareness of himself as separate (as a source of meaningful claims) from the community of which he is a part. Without a sense of subjectivity, apartness from the community, the subjective/objective distinction becomes idle; hence, the progress of culture occurs under the presumption of fidelity to "nature," where nature, what is "natural," rather than being posed against culture, figures the experience of normative ideals as always socially actual; that is, a world in which there occurs *natürliche Bildung* is one without a systematic separation of ideal from actual – as does occur, for instance, in social worlds in which there are competing ideals. But without a separation of ideal and actual, there is equally no requirement for self-consciousness, a sentimental awareness of the self's relation to its ideals, on the one hand, and actuality on the other from which the self remains separate, which have to be put into relation by the self. Greek unity of ideal and actual explains the cohesion of Greek culture. So the development of Greek literary culture is one that emerges from the requirement of fidelity to nature in this expanded sense.

Conversely,

> with greater intellectual development [*Bildung*], the goal of modern poetry naturally becomes *individuality* that is *original and interesting*. The simple imitation of the particular is, however, a mere skill of the *copyist*, not a free art. Only by means of an *arrangement* that is *ideal* does the characteristic of an individual become a philosophical work of art.[12]

Individuality, what will become the ideals of autonomy and authenticity, emerges when self-realization can no longer occur through identification with established social roles. Individuality is expressed through originality and the interesting; they are what make an individual *individual*, this unique one distinct from all others. The interesting for Schlegel is a provisional aesthetic totalization manifesting as such the disappearance of taken-for-granted universality. Sophocles wrote objective tragedies, Shakespeare interesting ones; Sophocles summoned the fate of a culture as a whole, Shakespeare narrated the experience of individuals who are etched by the absence of a governing culture. Modern works stand in relation to an ideal that remains separate from the work; the gap between the ideal and the actual, the infinite and the finite, is what makes the modern an ever open and incomplete striving. The modern age is an artificial formation (*künstliche Bildung*) because objectivity is at best an achievement, something striven for, but striven for without fully determinate ends or criteria. This is why our perfectibility and corruptibility go together, why our world lacks cultural cohesion. Schlegel labels the modern work of literature "philosophical" because its arrangement occurs by means of a *concept* whose ideality, again, both informs and stands apart from the work. So modern works of art are riven with a reflective, critical self-consciousness of themselves as works of art in relation to (postulated, posited, proposed, invented) indeterminate ideals from which they remain forever separate. However crudely, most of the fundamentals of Schlegel's *Athenaeum* conception of literature are already on display in *On the Study of Greek Poetry*.

It is in this context that Schlegel's direct borrowings from Lessing occur. His first borrowing occurs in the context of a discussion of the universality of the arts. It may be the case, Schlegel concedes, that not all circumstances, cultural and/or geographical, are propitious for the production of the plastic arts; but this cannot be so with respect to poetry. It is a "universal art" because "its organ, *fantasy*, is already incomparably more closely related to freedom, and more independent from external influence. Poetry and poetic taste is thus far more corruptible than plastic taste, but also *infinitely more perfectible*."[13] Poetry's reliance on only the imagination, fantasy, makes it proximate to pure freedom and hence independent from the constraints of external circumstance. This independence is the ground of both poetry's anthropological universality, in comparison to the other arts, and its infinite perfectibility. When Schlegel picks up this problem again somewhat later poetry's relative universality has become absolute; poetry is the "single actual *pure art* without borrowed vitality and external assistance."[14] The other arts, Schlegel now contends, are "hybrids that fall between pure nature and pure art";[15] the vitality and particularity that are the advantages of the plastic arts and music are not intrinsic to those arts as arts, but are rather borrowed from nature. The appeal to the senses, the kind of sensuous particularity that might be thought, was thought by Lessing, to distinguish art-meanings from non-art-meanings, here become the remnant of nature intruding upon art, making any art so dependent on nature a hybrid thing, human and inhuman at once. Hence, nature, even as a principle of sensible vitality, is conceived of as essentially extrinsic to pure art; only poetry, "whose tool, an arbitrary sign-language, is the work of man, and is endlessly perfectible and corruptible."[16] So an argument that begins by asserting, in typical Lessing fashion, that it is only poetry's "unrestricted compass" that gives it an advantage over the other arts, concludes by making the other arts hybrids between nature and art, and poetry alone pure art. Pure art, the meaning of art, is thus to be aligned directly with imaginative freedom and universality, which are our capacity for infinite perfectibility, in opposition to the limiting character of what belongs to intuition and sensibility which now are regarded as falling squarely within inhuman nature.

The Lessing origin of this defense of poetry as the only pure art is underlined in the next paragraph in which Schlegel compares the kinds of unity achievable by the different arts. Because an action can only be completed in time, then sculpture cannot truly represent an action.[17] Equally, the most fully determined sculptural character must presuppose a world in which it belongs, a world that sculpture itself can never provide. Hence, "the most perfect statue is still only a sundered, incomplete fragment, not a whole perfect unto itself. The most that images can attain is an *analogon of unity*."[18] The second great advantage of poetry is that it can offer the perfection of artistic integration since it alone can present a complete action, which, Schlegel contends, "is the sole unconditioned whole in the realm of appearance."[19] This sounds unconvincing, since, first, it is not evident that empirical actions are ever fully complete, so unconditioned; and, second, it appears to make the perfected integration of artistic works parasitic on the unity or integration of the object represented. In fact, Schlegel compellingly argues the thesis from an opposed direction: "An entirely accomplished act, a completely realized objective yields the fullest satisfaction. A completed poetic action is a whole unto itself, a *technical world*." So it is the integration of the work as poetic action that enables the poetic work to be an actual unity, and it is the model of the poetic action itself, the model of the work as act, that offers the notion of completion and fulfillment to action. Works as actions, or actions realized as works, yield a "technical" world, that is, a whole that is unconditioned, wanting nothing from without. Or: spatial unity, no matter how complex, must finally correspond to a natural unity, the unity of a material object or a geometric unity. Only essentially temporal items, in being essentially non-spatial and therefore non-material (the material being what fills space), can have a human unity. The primary meaningful unity of a temporal duration is the unity of an action; indeed, only through conceiving of temporal moments as bound together through an action can there be non-natural unity: no meaningful unity without unification.[20] Since unifying itself takes time, then, again, only the purely temporal can be humanly unified. In narrative works of art, the unity of the work is the unity of its forming action; so the form of a narrative, its narration, what makes it a technical world, is the unity of the action forming it. Feelings of satisfaction in response to narrative works is feeling the satisfaction of an action (improbably but necessarily) completed; the satisfaction in the representation is in reality a satisfaction in the achieved representing.

So again the thought is that the unity of a work of plastic art is either borrowed from nature, the material unity of the representing medium, or, since bound to an atemporal medium, then, at the level of representation, a fragment of a whole it presupposes but cannot provide. Only escaping the constraints of materiality, the constraint of a resistant medium, allows the unity of action to appear – the infinite perfectibility which "arbitrary sign-language" provides to poetry derives from its indefinite plasticity. So the linguistic medium is ideally not a specifically artistic medium at all; that is its strength. The arbitrariness of the sign-language, there being no causal or material reasons for relating this sign to that object or meaning, is the profound source of its universal power.

The argumentation of On the Study of Greek Poetry is unsteady at best: Schlegel appears to be still thinking about Greek tragedy in his defense of the unity of the work as act,[21] and once he emphasizes the unity of the poetic act over the act represented, then he has no grounds for discriminating between poetry, widely understood, and the other temporal arts. Nonetheless, what is evident is that there is a more than elective affinity between modern, artificial Bildung and the Lessing-inspired notion of poetry, and that it is this constellation which is deepened by the characteristic gestures of Athenaeum philosophical poetics.

"On Goethe's *Meister*" or transcendental poesy

Athenaeum fragment 216 sets the terms in which modernity and romanticism are to be aligned: "The French revolution, Fichte's philosophy, Goethe's Meister are the greatest tendencies of the age." The mutual references of these three items forms the constellation composing Jena romanticism.[22] They share: the experience of the collapse and overturning of traditional authority; the premising of all forms – social, political, theoretical, literary – on freedom and autonomy; the necessity for including within forming action a reflective account of it ("the new version of the theory of knowledge is simultaneously philosophy and the philosophy of philosophy" (AF 281); so revolution must include, implicitly, beyond political events, an account, a philosophy of revolution – which is in part what Schlegel thinks Fichte's philosophy and Goethe's *Meister* provide: they are the self-consciousness of the Revolution); the removal of hierarchy (so the leveling out and mixing of classes and genders in society, and genres in literature); the affirmation of becoming and history (hence the infinite perfectibility of literature as paradigmatic for the infinite perfectibility of the self); and the accounting for that history through a process of self-creation (self-positing), self-destruction (positing of the other as not self), and self-restriction (LF 37).[23]

What is meant primarily by the idea of romantic poesy is the novel (*Roman*), beginning with Shakespeare's tragedies and *Don Quixote*, and becoming self-conscious in the paradigm *Bildungsroman*, *Wilhelm Meister's Lehrjahre*. Even at the representational level *Wilhelm Meister*, for Novalis "the Absolute Novel," embraces not just "spectacle, drama, representation, art, and poetry" (GM 274),[24] but equally "the art of all arts, the art of living. . . . The intention is not to educate this or that human being, but to represent Nature, Education itself in all the variety of these examples and concentrated into single principles" (GM 283–4; note the elision whereby nature is identified with *Bildung*; culture is our nature). If *Meister* represents the art of all arts, the art of living, the art of living becomes visible through the art of the novel; which is to say that the phrase "the art of all arts" is not metaphorical: life is the formation and cultivation of the self on the model of the progressive formation of a work. The notion of an autonomous subject, whose emblem is the (romantic) artist, and the notion of the romantic work of art, the novel, translate one another: "Then what philosophy is left for the poet? The creative philosophy that originates in freedom and belief in freedom, and shows how the human spirit impresses its law on all things and how the world is its work of art" (AF 168).

In "On Goethe's *Meister*" (1798), Schlegel's exegesis of the third element of his constellation, he argues that

> this book is absolutely new and unique. We can learn to understand it only on its own terms. To judge it according to an idea of genre drawn from custom and belief . . . is as if a child tried to clutch the stars and the moon in his hand and pack them in his satchel.
>
> (GM 275)

For the novel to be "new and unique" is constitutive of what it is to be a novel; it must exceed genre requirements – as emblems of traditional authority – as a condition for it to be a work of art. To fail in this regard would be for a work to be a mere imitation, a copy; the idea of being a mere imitation or copy can now be understood as itself a consequence of the emergent requirement for uniqueness and newness (the new as the guarantor of the unique). The absence of pre-established norms and standards entails that the very idea of what it is for something to be a novel, and by inference to be a work of art *überhaupt*, can only be given through the work itself. Hence the work must inscribe and

153

project its own account of what it is to be work. To judge such a work on the basis of genre considerations, say the ideals of the classical, would be to miss it entirely. It requires that it be understood in its own terms. Minimally, this is to say that a romantic work is one that "spares the critic his labor" since "it carries its own judgement within itself . . . not only does it judge itself, it also describes itself" (GM 275). A romantic work must be both itself and the idea of itself.

To claim that modern, romantic works implicitly, allegorically in the case of *Wilhelm Meister*, include an idea of themselves is equally to say that

> the novel is as much an historical philosophy of art as a true work of art, and that everything which the poet so lovingly presents as his true aim and end [the work itself] is ultimately only means [for the revelation of the philosophical idea of the work].
>
> (GM 274)[25]

If a work of art is to be new and unique, it must implicitly propose a new idea of what it is to be a work; to propose a new idea of a work of art is a philosophical task. Hence, a romantic work must be both a work and, however implicitly, a philosophy of itself. It is an historical philosophy of itself because the idea being proposed is to be historically novel, a progress beyond where literature (poesy, art) has been. Because the idea being proposed is the self-consciousness of its object, a laying down of the necessary conditions of possibility for the work, then the historical philosophy of the novel is a form of transcendental reflection. Because each romantic work inscribes its own conditions of possibility, then works are also "critiques" of art in the transcendental sense, and every work of literary criticism simultaneously an effort of philosophical criticism. Thus, the romantic work of art is both a work of art and the philosophical reflection of the conditions of possibility of the work. In joining art and transcendental reflection the concepts of literary criticism and poetic self-reflection necessarily and imperceptibly modulate into "critique" in the austere Kantian sense. The capsule demand for this entanglement and modulation is succinctly expressed in *Athenaeum* fragment 238.

> But just as we wouldn't think much of an uncritical transcendental philosophy that doesn't represent the producer along with the product and contain at the same time within the system of its transcendental thoughts a description of transcendental thinking, so too this sort of poetry should unite the transcendental raw materials and preliminaries of a theory of poetic activity – often met with in modern poets – with the artistic reflection and beautiful self-mirroring that is present in Pindar . . . and, among the moderns, in Goethe. In all its descriptions, this poetry should describe itself, and always be simultaneously poetry and the poetry of poetry.

"On Goethe's *Meister*" offers a prescient account of artistic modernism; not needing to wait upon Flaubert, James, Proust, Joyce or Mann, it unnervingly anticipates some of the burdens the novel would find itself required to undertake. But it also overburdens the novel, pressuring it in a direction in which it would cease being a work of art, in which the "beautiful self-mirroring" of Pindar or the lyric fragments of the Greeks would be eclipsed by the demands of transcendental reflection – just the eclipse of the idea of painting. If Schlegel goes awry in making these demands, he does so with reason; his error subtle, not crude. The precise conceptual difficulty Schlegel is attempting to solve, what he thinks a truly modern philosophy of art must explicate, is how it is possible to have a conception of works of art that shows how they can be normatively compelling without following any antecedent norms. This correctly poses the issue of the meaning of freedom in a post-Kantian frame in which three distinct items need to be triangulated: freedom, normativity without *a priori* backing, and phenomenal appearing, a work realizing the interlocking of freedom and normativity. Schlegel is clear that the notion of poetry is normative; a definition of poetry is not the establishment of a natural kind, but of an ideal to be realized (AF 114). But, with the end of classicism, the ideal cannot be timelessly stated. The rightly famous closing sentences of *Athenaeum* fragment 116 assert just this thought.

> The romantic kind of poetry is still in the state of becoming; that, in fact, is its real essence: that it should forever be becoming and never be perfected. It can be exhausted by no theory and only a divinatory criticism would dare try to characterize its ideal. It alone is infinite, just as it alone is free; and it recognizes as its first commandment that the will of the poet can tolerate no law above itself. The romantic kind of poetry is the only one that is more than a kind, that is, as it were, poetry itself: for in a certain sense all poetry is or should be romantic.

How treacherous these sentences can become, we shall come to. For the moment, let us assume that they simply state the requirement that romantic works realize an ideality for which there is no antecedent. How is this possible? Kant attempted to answer this dilemma by demonstrating how judgements of taste, that is judgements that do not rely upon a given conceptuality, are possible: actual judgements of taste reveal that the subjective conditions of judgement in general involve a non-demonstrable fitness between our powers of judgement and nature as a whole. Judgements of taste reveal a transcendentally inexplicable but necessary harmony between human powers for knowing and acting, and their natural surrounding. Schiller, more modestly but equally with an eye toward an expansion of the analysis that will make it fully appropriate to works of art, attempts to show generally how judgements of beauty consistently track a harmony between freedom and material instantiation: beauty is always a nonconceptual material appearance of meaningfulness (freedom) without gravity or mechanism. Since the puzzle of nature and freedom has already been pantheistically solved for Schlegel, these systematic solutions must be left behind.[26]

If there can be no general account of how judgements of taste or works of art are possible, no systematic account of the intelligibility of art and taste, then there can be no separate philosophy of art, no determination of the meaning of art apart from works themselves. Only works can reveal how works are normatively possible. From this it follows that authentic works of art satisfy what might be called a "transcendental function," that is, each authentic work of art, necessarily and minimally, exemplifies what it is for something to be a work of art. In this respect, there is indeed something "philosophical" about modern, autonomous works of art. But it is just here that Schlegel's first slippage occurs: while philosophy cannot legislate the conditions of possibility of art, and thus in order for a work to claim aesthetic approval (as beautiful or interesting or sublime) it must simultaneously offer that claiming as what art now demands, it does not follow that works can or need to directly or overtly provide an account of their own philosophical conditions of possibility. Schlegel, perhaps over-impressed by the self-consciousness and reflexivity of Goethe's *Meister*, conflates the legitimate insight that, with the coming-to-be of art as a fully autonomous domain, philosophy can no longer legislate for art, and hence that authentic art works themselves satisfy a transcendental function, with the untoward claim that what satisfies a transcendental function must be conceived as reflectively offering a transcendental account of its object, or at least the "the transcendental raw materials and preliminaries of a theory of poetic activity." Hence, Schlegel shifts from the at least plausible thought that works satisfy a transcendental function, each authentic work exemplifying the meaning of art in general, to the implausible claim that authentic works are both works and the philosophical accounting of themselves. Or, more directly, Schlegel moves from the legitimate thought that authentic modern works must be conceived as lodging a claim about what it is for an item to be a work, to the exorbitant thought that authentic modern works must explicitly provide a discursive account of their own conditions of possibility.[27]

Once philosophy can no longer extrinsically legislate, and the requirement for transcendental accounting (the representation of the producer along with product) accepted, then philosophy becomes poetry (freedom must freely configure, be a free self-representation of, itself and the revealing of itself), and all poetry must be a transcendental philosophy, a poetry of poetry. For Schlegel the demand that poetry absorb philosophy, that there be an utter unification of philosophy and poetry, emerges as a direct requirement of the project of triangulating freedom, normativity, and their reciprocal determination of one another in a work.[28] Because Schlegel is untouched by the disillusionment which, in Schiller, say, makes the duality of freedom and nature, form-drive and sense-drive, philosophy and art the aporetic condition permanently disrupting and fragmenting subjectivity, ruining it, he presumes there must be, at least formally,

an unconditional formulation of what would satisfy the triangulation requirement. Jena romanticism is modernism without disillusionment; this is both the
source of its continuing appeal and of its theoretical exorbitance. The mark of
that exorbitance is, again, the requirement that the romantic work be fully both
work and the philosophical, transcendental accounting of itself as the actualiza-
tion of freedom. Bearing up under the burden of the second limb of the
requirement comprehensibly comes to squeeze out and finally disqualify the first
limb. So what can appear as the utterly marginal shift involved in requiring that
the implicit transcendental function of modern works become explicit, tenden-
tially engenders the philosophical disenfranchisement of art. This is what
poetry without the idea of painting comes to.[29]

"On Incomprehensibility" or the end of the work

I interpret Schlegel's little essay "On Incomprehensibility" (1800),[30] in reality a
commentary on *Athenaeum* fragment 216 linking the French Revolution,
Fichte's philosophy, and Goethe's *Meister*, as a radicalization of that shift, as,
that is, the fullest articulation of the disenfranchising tendency. This essay was
the final item in the final issue of the *Athenaeum*; the essay is thus the journal's
summation, apologia, and farewell; the farewell, on my reading, is of a different
order than Schlegel conceives it. In the essay the *Athenaeum* generally, and the
Fragments from 1798 in particular, come to displace Goethe's *Meister* as the
exemplary romantic work, or, one might say, fragment and irony come to
displace work and reflection; I interpret this shift as the hermeneutic key for
comprehending the underlying intention of the idea of romantic poesy.
Schlegel's growing doubts about Goethe's novel could be understood as a consequence of coming to see it as more representative of Weimar classicism than
Jena romanticism, and hence of simply coming to doubt that it could bear the
weight of significance being attributed to it. While not wrong, the real doubt
about *Wilhelm Meister*, I think, is simply that it is *a work*.

The closing sentences of *Athenaeum* fragment 116 could be interpreted as
stipulating that with romanticism the meaning of art is given through works
and cannot be *a priori* legislated. But that would radically underdetermine the
effort of transcendental reflection Schlegel thinks an authentic work must
accomplish. Jena romanticism contends that each authentic work reflectively
articulates itself as a further determination of the idea of art, where the idea of
art is nothing less than the full exposition of the idea and actuality of the
meaning of human freedom. If the heart of romanticism is taken as the philosophical thought that the idea of art is given through each work, then no fully
self-sufficient work, no matter how self-conscious, can be adequate to the idea.
Any *determinate* work would be insufficient with respect to the idea that
romantic poetry "should be forever becoming." Hence, even exemplary works
could be taken as falsifying the Zarathustrian thesis that "the will of the poet
can tolerate no law above itself." So the slippage from implicit to explicit came

157

to be understood as disqualifying autonomous works as satisfying the romantic idea of art. Schlegel thus insists that the core impulse of fragment 216 is not given through the constellation formed by the troika of the French Revolution, Fichte and Goethe, but

> lies in the word *tendencies* . . . And so I now let irony go to the winds and declare point blank that in the dialectic of the *Fragments* the word means that everything now is only a tendency, that the age is the Age of Tendencies.

(OI 301)

The palpable collapse that occurs in the claim that since the romantic idea of art is necessarily indeterminate, then a determinate work is incompatible with it must be taken to be a consequence of the earlier conflation of works being required to satisfy a transcendental function with the requirement that they provide a transcendental accounting of themselves. Without the pressure from the requirement that works discursively account for their own conditions of possibility, fully uniting art and philosophy thereby, it is not obvious why determinate works must be insufficient to romanticism. Once, however, only works can be the reflective bearers of the idea of romanticism, with the idea declaring that romanticism is forever becoming, then a self-sufficient work would transparently belie the idea. For a work to fully exemplify and reflectively articulate the idea of poetry as infinite becoming it would have to cancel itself as work, bracket itself as work for the sake of the indeterminate idea, unwork its being as work, forfeit its status as material presence in favor of art's "not yet," be itself and always beyond itself. It would need to be a fragment without being a part of a whole, and rehearse an ironic displacement of whatever immanent claim it would make. So the romantic concepts of fragment and irony emerge as the form of work and reflection required by a transcendental poetry which will sustain the idea of art as forever becoming, where the forever becoming thesis encapsulates freedom's sublimity: its power to legislate, give the law to itself, and always be beyond whatever law it legislates.[31] As the dissolution of the autonomous work, fragment and irony are nothing but the systematic undoing of the claim of the idea of painting. The idea of painting is what romanticism emphatically disqualifies. In the midst of its presumptive pantheism, Jena romanticism cancels any synthesis, harmonization, riveting together of materiality and the social sign. On the contrary, and doubtless despite itself, romanticism becomes the thought of their incommensurability, an incommensurability that for it emerges from the demand for configuring the power of legislation, configuring sublime autonomy.

As in the defense of artistic modernism in "On Goethe's *Meister*," Schlegel's best thoughts and his worst ones seem to be the same notions seen from different angles. The high moment of "On Incomprehensibility," providing the metaphysical basis on which fragment and irony as forms rely, is his defense of the necessity for opacity and darkness, for the incomprehensible.

Yes, even man's most precious possession, his own inner happiness, depends in the last analysis, as anybody can easily verify, on some such point of strength that must be left in the dark, but that nonetheless shores up and supports the whole burden and would crumble the moment one subjected it to rational analysis. Verily, it would fare badly with you if, as you demand, the whole world were to ever become wholly comprehensible in earnest. And isn't this entire, unending world constructed by the understanding out of incomprehensibility and chaos?

(OI 305)

"Über die Unverständlichkeit," say, "On the Impossibility of Understanding," is in its own way a critique of pure reason; its defense of the incomprehensible just the contention that the limits of the understanding are equally its conditions of possibility. However, and *pace* Kant, it is not the case that we can *a priori* determine the limits of the understanding: our desire for understanding is boundless, and our power for rendering transparent knows no limit – since our unending, that is, transparent world is constructed from chaos (anticipating Nietzsche), then we can always render the world transparent, leaving the chaos behind – it is this leaving behind that requires correction. One cannot *know* the limits of reason, turning Hegel inside out, since to know the limit would be indeed to step beyond the limit. Hence, the limit of reason cannot be known, it can only, but equally must, be accepted, acknowledged, experienced. And because at one level the understanding is without limit (in its hubris, its metaphysical desire, its relentless power for making transparent), then the attempt to provide a limit, to inscribe it, by producing writing whose ironic or fragmentary nature blocks full understanding, will naturally be resisted. Some of the outrage with which the *Athenaeum* was met stemmed from its routine frustration of that desire and power. Hence, Schlegel is detecting beneath the acceptance of the finitude of reason, the requirement that reason be self-limiting, that might have been thought to be the most routine accompaniment of idealism, a resistance in practice. When actually faced with forms of writing that demand an acknowledgment of limits, when our actual attempts at comprehension are blocked and frustrated, we balk, angrily.

A true transcendental idealism must be aesthetic, poesy, because only aesthetic forms can appropriately exhibit the self-limitation of reason; only in them are comprehension and the incomprehensible entwined – "It is equally fatal for the mind to have a system and to have none. It will have to decide to combine the two" (AF 53). Hence, in reality, it is only the *Athenaeum* itself that could, and did, provide a critique of pure reason. It is no accident that Schlegel breaks off his defense and concludes the essay with a poem – the discursive claim for incomprehensibility displaced and affirmed by its poetic exhibition. At this level of generality, Schlegel's argument is delicate and compelling. But are fragment and irony as forms adequate to the task Schlegel assigns them? I have been

159

arguing that Schlegel's attempt to absorb philosophy into poesy, to create a transcendental poesy as the appropriate form of transcendental idealism, necessarily reverses into the philosophical disenfranchisement of art, precisely the opposite effect to what might have been anticipated. Standardly, as with Lessing and Schiller, the aesthetic is to taken to exceed the understanding in virtue of the predominance of sense over concept, hence, precisely because works are medium-bound; with the disenchantment of nature, whatever is medium-bound, occurs as semblance. Hence the notion of the aesthetic becomes an intertwining of sense and semblance. Now while Schlegel's various comments on fragment and irony do not all match up, it is at least noteworthy that the two most forceful defenses of Jena romanticism, Paul de Man's "The Concept of Irony" and Maurice Blanchot's "The Athenaeum," both read these notions in emphatically anti-aesthetic terms.[32] I will use de Man's essay to help think romantic irony, and Blanchot's as a guide in the delineation of the romantic fragment. That de Man and Blanchot identify their own thinking with what is accomplished in these concepts gives their accounts a particular urgency.

De Man's irony

De Man's analysis can be parsed into two steps.[33] In *Lyceum* fragment 42 Schlegel argues that Socratic philosophy is the true home of irony because in it irony occurs everywhere. At this level of analysis, irony is being compared to an open-ended, non-systematic dialectic with its recurring patterns of assertion and negation, (self-)creation and (self-)destruction (dialectic and romantic irony always have, at least, a Fichtean tinge in Schlegel). Poetry can rise to the level of philosophy because it allows irony to be everywhere and not only in restricted passages; in the poems (novels) in which this occurs

> there lives a real transcendental buffoonery. Their interior is permeated by the mood which surveys everything and rises infinitely above everything limited, even above the poet's own art, virtue, and genius; and their exterior form by the histrionic style of an ordinary good Italian *buffo*.

The *buffo* in commedia dell'arte is the aside to the audience that disrupts the narrative illusion of the play. In rhetorical theory the technical term for the interruption of a discourse by a shift in rhetorical register is *parabasis*. But, de Man contends,

> parabasis is not enough . . . Irony is not just interruption; it is (and this is the definition which he [Schlegel] gave of irony), he says, the "permanent parabasis," parabasis not just at one point but at all points, which is how he defines poetry: irony is everywhere, at all points the narrative can be interrupted.[34]

In those poems in which there lives a real transcendental buffoonery there is irony everywhere; in order for there to be irony everywhere, a permanent parabasis, there must be at each moment the illusion and the disruption of the illusion.

In order to begin thinking how it is conceivable that there be disruption everywhere – surely, the critic would object, disruption presupposes some homogeneity that gets disrupted, and so cannot be everywhere – de Man points us toward the little chapter of *Lucinde*, "A reflection," which on a first pass sounds like a bit of Fichtean philosophy, but which, scandalously, also can be read as, simultaneously, a reflection on some of the physical aspects of sexual intercourse. High philosophical conceptuality and base physical sexuality occupy the same linguistic space even if they are opposed semantically. Everywhere the base sexual interrupts the abstractly philosophical which would think itself forever independent from and beyond the crudely sexual. But this, however charming, is less than an illustration of permanent parabasis; it is, at least without some Freudian heavy lifting, just a metaphor for permanent disruption. Nonetheless, it is the right sort of metaphor since what it projects as disruption is a system of complete reciprocity between the ideality of meaning (philosophy) and the brute materiality of mechanism (sex), or so de Man urges. What Schlegel needs then is some account of language, of linguistic activity that would enable him to reveal, let's say, a stratum of nonsense (incomprehension/non-system) beneath each moment of sense (comprehension/system). And this points to the second part of de Man's analysis.

With our large Lessing ears, we might have anticipated this moment. From the outset, the universality of poesy relative to the plastic arts has turned on the arbitrariness of the linguistic sign, on language not being a (productively) resistant medium. The systematic downgrading of the plastic arts demanded by modern reflexivity, no poetry without a poetry of poetry, and the requirement that reflexivity be fully discursive, the becoming philosophy of art, are inconceivable without aesthetics generally, the philosophy of art as the philosophy of freedom, taking a linguistic turn. Equally, the possibility of aligning freedom and normativity, each poet and each human a lawgiver, has depended upon language possessing a moment of radical indeterminacy, of non-meaning,[35] which would thus make possible meaning-giving, the bestowal or creation of meaning. So the taking of a linguistic turn is necessary for the possibility of the transformation of philosophy into poesy; and within that linguistic turn it is necessary for there to be a metaphysically charged arbitrariness of the sign if poesy is to be the bearer of the appearing of human freedom in a manner compatible with poesy being universal (capable of addressing everything). While things do not turn out quite this neatly (the romantic ideology of poesy as imaging perfectionism, an infinite self-making, does not survive the steps taken to defend it), nonetheless whilst de Man and Blanchot run this moment somewhat differently, for both it is some version of the arbitrariness of the sign, its excess beyond rational control, that is the pivotal moment.

De Man opts for a passage from the "Speech on Mythology."[36] In it Schlegel is comparing mythology as "the artwork of nature" with the wit of romantic poesy, as in Shakespeare and Cervantes, which, like irony, is not limited to particular passages, but is to be found everywhere. Wit in this passage stands for what joins the unlike; so it is "this charming symmetry of contradictions, this wondrous, eternal exchange of enthusiasm and irony" – all this the analogon to traditional mythology. Let us call what mythology and romantic wit share here a holistic structure of aesthetic illusion, a joining of the different without system – or, what is the same, a system of tropes. Schlegel now claims that mythology and romantic wit so understood share a massive presupposition.

> Neither this wit nor a mythology can exist with something primal and inimitable [that seems to be the authentic language], which is absolutely indissoluble, which after all transformations still allows the original nature and the original force to shine through, where naive profundity allows the glimmer of the absurd and the crazy, or of the simpleminded and the stupid, to shine through. For this is the beginning of all poesy: the sublation of the course and the laws of reasonably thinking reason and our transportation again into the beautiful confusion of fantasy, the original chaos of human nature for which I have yet to know a more beautiful symbol than the colorful swarm of ancient gods.[37]

The meaning of this passage is far from unambiguous. From the fact that Schlegel immediately goes on to discuss Spinoza and ancient, non-Western mythologies, we might suspect that what is being thought in this "original chaos of human nature" is some sort of Dionysian pantheism. De Man suppresses this possibility. He wants the authentic language to be the one of "error, madness, and stupidity." This is authentic language, *reelle Sprache*, de Man asserts, because it "is a mere semiotic entity, open to the radical arbitrariness of any sign system and as such capable of circulation, but which as such is profoundly unreliable."[38]

In "On Incomprehensibility" Schlegel quotes Goethe's thesis "that words often understand themselves better than do those who use them" (OI 298). De Man thinks that words slipping by our control, their having meanings in themselves beyond and prior to whatever meanings we might assign to them, is the arbitrariness of the sign being gestured toward by Schlegel. But he infers from this something more radical: what slips past control must *a fortiori* be controlled from elsewhere. Call that elsewhere *mechanism*.

> There is a machine there, a text machine, an implacable determination and a total arbitrariness, *unbedingter Willkür*, he says [*Lyceum* fragment 42], which inhabits words on the level of the play of the signifier, which undoes any narrative consistency of lines, and which undoes the reflexive and the dialectical model, both of which are, as

you know, the basis of any narration. There is no narration without reflection, no narrative without dialectic, and what irony disrupts (according to Friedrich Schlegel) is precisely that dialectic and that reflexivity, the tropes.[39]

Responding to this requires delicacy, since what is being addressed is not the nature of language in general (that the determinacy of any linguistic meaning is a determination of an indeterminate base is not in question), nor that particular works might inscribe the appearance of meaning as possessed by its radical, material absence. What is at issue, rather, is the meaning of romantic works as bearers of the philosophical idea of art, hence the claim of such works. For de Man the ultimate referent for romantic irony as a permanent parabasis is that feature of language which is like a machine in that meanings come from it independently of our willing. This is a curious claim to make, since one would have thought that the idea of a "text machine" with "an implacable determination" would be the exact opposite of "total arbitrariness" – the rule of meaning is not the rule of what is intended nor one binding word to object, but the rule of mechanical law, say, which is hardly "arbitrary": it appears arbitrary from the perspective of intention, but if mechanically determined, then fully determinate, albeit determined elsewhere than from the will. Nor is it at all clear how this theory of irony would be compatible with any form of writing; on the contrary, by making the romantic notion of irony devolve into, rather than merely being related to, the authentic language of error, madness, and stupidity, de Man seems to make impossible a practice of ironic discourse – which would, of course, be an intentional/intended practice. Or, better, he makes ironic discourse, even if there could be some, unnecessary by making the two levels of meaning production, intentional and mechanical, coincide everywhere. But by coinciding everywhere the specificity of romantic works as works of art disappears. Only the philosophical thought of meaning and its absence remains.

Nonetheless, it is possible to see why de Man thought this satisfactory: if we allow that at the level of production, so to speak, that irony as text machine refers to a blind, quasi-causal mechanism, then at least the thought of non-meaning, the causal or quasi-causal mechanism, beneath (intentional) meaning emerges. And at least in that respect irony means "disruption, disillusion."[40] If disruption *were* related to another irruption of meaning, then the case for romanticism would have been at least possible. But for de Man the disruption runs in the opposite direction; not freedom but eternal mechanism is the result. But does not that result turn semblance into mere semblance, illusion pure and simple? One can see what de Man is after, namely, the revelation that beneath the illusion of emphatic meaning which the work of art provides there lies an unavoidable absence of meaning; by acknowledging this absence of meaning, romantic irony achieves an authentic, heroic and stoical, affirmation of the empty ground of each human construction of meaning. But to say that meaning is without ground or foundation is emphatically different from saying that beneath each appearing of meaning lies a system of mechanism as fierce as the laws determining atoms in a Newtonian universe.

Blanchot's fragment

In being more explicit about language's excessive semiotic potential, the potential for meaning beyond or outside intentional or representational meaning, the passage Blanchot lights upon from Novalis's *Monolog*, monologue or soliloquy, a text, Blanchot says, of "angelic penetration,"[41] fits the demands of the theory in a less reductive manner than does de Man's account.

> Speaking and writing is a crazy state of affairs really; true conversation is just a game with words. It is amazing, the absurd error people make imagining they are speaking for the sake of things; no one knows the essential thing about language, that it is concerned only with itself. That is why it is such a marvelous and fertile mystery – for if someone merely speaks for the sake of speaking, he utters the most splendid truths. But if he wants to talk about something definite, the whims of language make him say the most ridiculous stuff. . . . If it were only possible to make people understand that it is the same with language as it with mathematical formulae – they constitute a world in itself – their play is self-sufficient, they express nothing but their own marvelous nature, and that is the very reason why they are so expressive. . . . And though I believe that with these words I have delineated the nature and office of poetry . . . I know . . . what I have said is quite foolish because I wanted to say it, and that is no way for poetry to come about.[42]

Again, hardly an unambiguous passage. One way through it would make poetry that form of writing that, in letting words themselves speak, in permitting intransitive sense to emerge, construes language as itself a resistant medium.[43] That would push the passage toward modernism. However, that hypothesis needs instant revising if I now complete the sentence stating that words are so expressive because they express nothing but their own marvelous nature, because in being self-sufficient, Novalis continues,

> they are the mirror to the strange play of relationships among things. Only their freedom makes them members of nature, only in their free movements does the world-soul express itself and make of them a delicate measure and a ground-plan of things.

This would make pantheism, some enchanted conception of nature with man as a part, a condition of possibility for language having meaning before and in excess of its intentional/representational meaning; in letting language speak, poetry lets nature come to self-consciousness. Again, it is at least not obvious that these thoughts are not consistent with the "Speech on Mythology," and for all of which the title "magical idealism" is not a bad one. All this, romanticism's wholly un-disillusioned side, appears as almost the opposite of language as mechanism.

But there is a third interpretive possibility, the one required to make the romantic understanding of language fit with its notions of fragment and irony. Blanchot wants the excised version of this text, say only that portion of it that I originally quoted, to provide the key to romantic philosophy generally (rather than just Novalis). Without the background pantheist naturalism, the passage possesses an almost Saussaurean ambition; and this ambition, for Blanchot, expresses the "non-romantic essence of romanticism,"[44] acknowledging thereby romanticism's internal ambiguity and ambivalence, its hovering between opti-mistic utopian idealism and radical disillusionment. What these two moments share, what makes them both sides of romanticism, is that they both can be seen as having poesy express the finitude of human thought, its forever becoming, hence a poetic perfectionism. And for both formulations of romanti-cism there must be an aspect of language passed over by representational discourse. For Blanchot what this other side of language points to:

> that to write is to make (of) speech (a) work, but that this work is an unworking; that to speak poetically is to make possible a non-transitive speech whose task is not to say things (not to disappear into what it signifies), but to say (itself) in letting (itself) say, yet without taking itself as the new object of this language without object.[45]

Earlier we noted the puzzle of the incommensurability between the work as determinate object with poesy as project. Blanchot is wanting to hear in the thought of the poet as heeding language, and thus retreating from the ambition to represent the world, the coming-to-be of meaning, where this event or coming-to-be can only be revealed by dissolving the work as (representational) meaning. For Blanchot it would appear to be the case that adequate theoretical self-consciousness, that is adequate acknowledgement of the excess of the *possi-bility* of meaning over its actuality, requires the suppression of self-consciousness since the moment of self-consciousness would be a second-level determinacy, the determinate comprehension of the indeterminacy of meaning exemplified by the event of meaning. The fragment thus becomes, ideally, the indetermi-nate presentation of the indeterminacy of meaning, the coming-to-be of meaning without any attendant meaning.

With that thought in mind, Blanchot can now knit two claims: (i) It is no accident that romanticism is almost without works, that it ended so quickly and badly with suicide, loss, forgetting:

> this is because it is the work of the absence of (the) work; a poetry affirmed in the purity of the poetic act, an affirmation without duration,

a freedom without realization, a force that exalts in disappearing and that is in no way discredited if it leaves no trace, for this was its goal.[46]

(ii) The fragment *is* the ironizing of representational discourse, its unworking, not for the sake of suspending it, merely disrupting it (as de Man would have it), but for the sake of making the momentary, the becoming, absolute:

> the work's power to be and no longer to represent; to be everything, but without content or with a content that is almost indifferent, and thus at the same time affirming the absolute and the fragmentary; affirming totality, but in a form that, being all forms – that is, at the limit, being none at all – does not realize the whole, but signifies it by suspending it, even breaking it.[47]

We now have, in effect, four versions of romanticism: (a) romantic poesy as the expression proper to the poesy nature itself is – romantic pantheism; (b) romantic poesy as the only non-self-defeating expression of human freedom – transcendental poesy as the truth of transcendental idealism; (c) romantic irony as the permanent disruption of the illusions of philosophy and art; (d) the romantic fragment as the revelation of the finitude of meaning, the event of meaning prior to any stable, representational meanings.[48] The first, pantheistic reading, whilst almost certainly the most hermeneutically accurate, is equally the least philosophically interesting. I have argued that the second, and most acute version emerges not just by-the-way but essentially out of a radicalization of Lessing's privileging of poetry over the plastic arts, a privileging that Schlegel rightly hears as converging with the universality and productivity of human freedom: poesy as the only pure, which is to say, purely human art. But this is the version of Lessing's conception of poetry that dispenses with the idea of painting, the idea which, finally, is necessary in order for poems to be works of art. Without the ballast of the idea of painting, romantic poesy is literally unstable, tending toward, well, toward the very disappearance of the work that de Man and Blanchot, however differently, hear in romanticism – in the claims of irony and fragment – as its non-romantic essence.

In the context of Lessing's emergent modernism and Schiller's underwriting of that modernism, de Man's and Blanchot's excision of the idea of painting, their anti-aesthetic, looks terribly like a pure anti-aesthetic ideology. For Schiller the finitude of the work of art, its mortal being, depends on its being mere semblance, its posing of the materiality of meaning, of nature as meaningful and freedom as materially realized, as both necessary and impossible. Nothing supports the possibility in general of the materiality of meaning other than aesthetic meaning, the compellingness of works themselves. The finitude of meaning in its aesthetic appearing is its being bound to works that are necessarily and forever subject to denial, collapse, loss. Authentic finitude of meaning requires the possibility of the death of meaning; but there can be no death without works, items that can in their significance pass away; significant stone cracks, crumbles, becomes chips then dust; or, even more commonly, the claim of the work fades as semblance dissolves, the construction of meaning disrupting the meaning constructed. Hence, the distinctive character of Schiller's modernism was its lodging of human meaningfulness in the ether of aesthetic appearance.

De Man and Blanchot track romanticism's philosophical disenfranchisement of art by seeking a meaning, which for both is simultaneously the absence of meaning, beyond semblance. In the case of de Man this absence of meaning is bizarre; in elaborating Kant's conception of the sublime, in his most bracing formulation of his materialism, of the non-phenomenalizable conditions of the possibility of meaning, de Man states: "this vision is purely material, devoid of any semantic depth and reducible to the formal mathematization or geometriza-tion of pure optics."[49] Why did we need to go through the tortures of idealist aesthetics, through the infinitely demanding and complex reflections of *The Critique of Judgment*, Hegel's *Aesthetics*, or the *Athenaeum* at all if, at the end of the day, we are to end up with the dematerialized materiality of nature that was the very problem which made the turn toward aesthetics tempting in the first place? Did we need that detour to tell us that beneath meaning there lies the mechanism of nature? Why would one turn to philosophical aesthetics to uncover the mechanism behind meaning since it is *everywhere* before aesthetics ever raises a finger? This again is not to deny that modernist art has been centrally concerned, in *Lucinde*-like works, with the occurrence of an uprising of meaning out of material non-meaning (think: Pollock). In modernism, however, the insistence upon material non-meaning has been the means through which meaning and materiality might be soldered together: significant stone reveals mere stone as silent stone. Since significant stone is semblance, then only semblance holds in place the difference between silent and mere stone, enchanted and disenchanted nature.

Blanchot is more anxious and nuanced, wanting fiercely, in his own name and for romanticism, to avoid the philosophical reflexivity and surety which his writing nonetheless conveys: "for if poetry is simply a speech that claims to express the essence of speech and of poetry, one will, and scarcely more subtly, return to the use of transitive language."[50] The difficulty, of course, is that the aim of romantic discourse, as exemplified in the romantic fragment, is emphati-cally to express the essence of language, indeed the essence of human freedom, as the essence of poetry. Hence, even in the unworking of the romantic frag-ment, precisely in its not being a work, there emerges a reflexivity and essentialism that cannot be anything else but knowledge – without that emergence there is nothing to experience in the fragment. Eschewing aesthetic semblance, the romantic fragment becomes philosophical idea. Both de Man and Blanchot, in wanting to get to the non-meaning that is the condition of meaning, call it text machine, call it event, must displace, forever, the fragile aesthetic object and replace it with, however mediated and detoured, philosophical knowing, the knowing of non-knowledge. But this is metaphysics in the bad old sense, since it is a pure knowledge of the absence of meaning, dependent on no particular objects for its presence or absence. This is why it is an ideology of finitude: it is the knowledge of the finitude of meaning without finite beings, the unworking of works but without there being any works, no significant stone that might reveal silent stone. There is in all this something too knowing and comforting, as if the loss of meaning would be tolerable after all if we could so possess it, have it, so surely, authentically, stoically, and beautifully. A beautiful death after all.

Notes

1 Philippe Lacoue-Labarthe and Jean-Luc Nancy, *The Literary Absolute: The Theory of Literature in German Romanticism*, trans. Philip Barnard and Cheryl Lester, Albany NY, SUNY Press, 1988, pp. 30–1, get right the crisis of the subject, its loss of substance, but conspicuously fail to mention the crisis of nature.

2 For an elaboration of this thought see Robert Pippin, "Avoiding German Idealism: Kant, Hegel, the Reflective Judgment Problem," in his *Idealism as Modernism: Hegelian Variations*, Cambridge, Cambridge University Press, 1997; and my *The Fate of Art: Aesthetic Alienation from Kant to Derrida and Adorno*, Cambridge, Polity Press, 1994.

3 I am aware that it is just this comprehension of modernism that Duchamp meant to contest. On my reading, Duchamp conflated the reasonable thought that the claim of the medium was bound to the tradition of painting (which is finite, and hence mortal), with the general claim for art being medium-bound in my restrictive sense; alas, Duchamp's conflation was affirmed by the defenders of painterly modernism (above all, Greenberg), and the artists who wanted to contest modernism. It is the wider thesis that I do not think has yet had a general hearing. So, for example, on my reading, works normally viewed as postmodern, or, at least, anti-modernist, like those of Joseph Cornell and Louise Bourgeois, not to speak of much of minimalist art or the sculptures of Richard Serra, can be interpreted as unproblematically modernist. For this see my "Readymades, Monochromes, Etc.: Nominalism and the Paradox of Modernism" and "Freedom From Nature? Reflections on the End(s) of Art," both forthcoming in my *Against Voluptuous Bodies: Adorno's Late Modernism and the Idea of Painting*, Stanford, Stanford University Press, and, from a wildly different angle, Rosalind E. Krauss, "Reinventing the Medium," *Critical Inquiry* 25, Winter 1999, pp. 289–305. In this setting, I am taking the material binding of meaning through medium-specificity to form a taken-for-granted hypothesis. The excesses of Jena romanticism hence form a test of the thesis.

4 Against the background of the eighteenth-century crisis of reason, and in the tradition of "The Oldest Program for a System of German Idealism" wherein "*truth and goodness are brothers only in beauty*," I would hope the claim that aesthetic reason is distinguished from formal reason in making ideas sensible, hence in binding meaning and matter (medium), can be regarded as an uncontentious thesis about the meaning of aesthetic reason at this historical juncture. My interest here is not in the thesis itself, but in its dissolution at the hands of (a certain) romanticism; there are, to be sure, other romanticisms. As will become apparent, there is reason to think that this romantic dissolution of aesthetic reason amounts to a general repudiation of the aesthetic, and hence to an anti-aesthetic; if that is true, then it should serve as, at least, indirect support for my taken-for-granted hypothesis.

5 Gottfried Ephraim Lessing, *Laocoön: An Essay on the Limits of Painting and Poetry*, trans. A. W. Steele, chs 16–24 in J. M. Bernstein (ed.) *Classical and Romantic German Aesthetics*, Cambridge, Cambridge University Press, 2003.

6 Needless to say, I regard the doctrine of the arbitrariness of the sign as mistaken; I track its current critical espousal in my "Freedom From Nature? Reflections on the End(s) of Art." Here I am interested in the genealogy of that espousal that runs from Lessing through Schlegel's romanticism.

7 References to the *Athenaeum Fragments* (AF), *Lyceum Fragments* (LF), and *Ideas* (I) are to the fragment number in Friedrich Schlegel, *Philosophical Fragments*, trans. Peter Firchow, Minneapolis, University of Minnesota Press, 1991. Firchow entitles the *Lyceum Fragments* "Critical Fragments."

8 Lessing, *Laocoön*, ch. xiv, p. 79.

9 In Jochen Schulte-Sasse, Haynes Horne, Andreas Michel, Elizabeth Mittman, Assenka Oksiloff, Lisa C. Roetzel and Mary R. Strand (eds and trans) *Theory as Practice: A Critical Anthology of Early German Romantic Writings*, Minneapolis, University of Minnesota Press, 1997, p.180. Further references to this volume will be abbreviated: TP. While I do not know the origin of the romantic version of the idea of artistic creation imitating divine creation, Schlegel and Novalis would have had at least the version of it from Moritz's "On the Artistic Imitation of the Beautiful" (1788), a partial translation of which appears in J. M. Bernstein (ed.) *Classic and Romantic German Aesthetics*, pp. 131–44.

10 See T. J. Clark, *Farewell to An Idea: Episodes from a History of Modernism*, New Haven CT, Yale University Press, 1999, who makes the soldering together of the sociality of the sign and re-enchantment of nature the question of modernist painting.

11 Translated by Stuart Barnett, Albany NY, SUNY Press, 2001. Although written wholly independently, this essay contains a conception of the relation of ancient to modern that is quite similar to that found in Schiller's *On Naive and Sentimental Poetry*, published just months before Schlegel's essay, forcing him to write a preface taking into account Schiller's work. *On the Study of Greek Poetry* thus can be regarded as triangulating romanticism with Schiller's modernism and Lessing's defense of poetry.

12 *On the Study of Greek Poetry*, p. 32.

13 *Ibid.*, p. 42.

14 *Ibid.*, p. 59, italics mine.

15 *Ibid.*

16 *Ibid.* In making a severe distinction between pure and hybrid art, Schlegel is not making an obvious intellectual error. On the contrary, if nature, especially as it functions as a medium of art, is dead nature, then how can it be a source of vitality? From the perspective of scientific rationality, would not the ascription of vitality to dead nature be a form of animism? And hence is not Schlegel's consignment of the non-poetic arts to the domain of the hybrid just the acknowledgment of the authority of the self-determining subject? Would not the presumption of a source of meaning outside subjectivity be tantamount to conflating, through the efficacy of projection, self and world? The problem of art in modernity is indissoluble from the problem of animism; which is why that problem forms the inaugural gesture of Hegel's account of the death of art: only mind can be a source of intelligible vitality.

17 Famously, in chapter xvi of *Laocoön*, Lessing argues that the plastic arts depend upon natural signs (figures and colors) spatially coordinated with one another, whilst the linguistic arts depend upon articulated sounds in time. Hence objects, and objects alone, become the proper object of the plastic arts, while actions are the true subjects of poetry. Sound, in its original appearance here, is regarded as immaterial, or, at any rate, as not material in the way in which extended stuff is material.

169

18 *On the Study of Greek Poetry*, p. 60.

19 *Ibid.*

20 This, of course, is the premise of Kant's transcendental deduction.

21 I may be underestimating Schlegel. His argument could be taken to have the form: what was in the closed world of the Greeks the idea of a unitary action, a praxis, an action complete in itself and not done for some end beyond it, is only possible under conditions of modernity in the production of artistic works. (It is sometimes claimed that even Aristotle thought that the representation of praxis, hence the means through which any praxis might be perceived, was dependent upon poetic action.) Only art works can be for us self-sufficient actions hence only art works are a praxis in modernity. While an argument to this effect is kicking around in this period, and certainly possesses a surface attractiveness, it is highly contentious if for no other reason than it presumes a one-to-one correspondence between Aristotle's ethical conception of *praxis* and the "one action" requirement of his *Poetics*.

22 As will become evident, my attempt here is to unpack the whole of Jena romanticism from the lead given by fragment 216.

23 De Man, "The Concept of Irony," pp. 170–3, convincingly relates the dialectic of self-creation, self-destruction and self-limitation to the three moments in the transcendental constitution of actuality in Fichte's *Wissenschaftslehre*.

24 Passages marked GM refer to "On Goethe's *Meister*" in the version that appears in my *Classic and Romantic German Aesthetics*, pp. 269–87.

25 This is the development of the idea that the significant unity of a work of art lies not in what is represented but in the representing. Now that representing, the novel's "I think," its specific synthetic unity of apperception, is its idea of itself. But if its idea of itself is indeed its unique "I think," then in truth the novel must be for the sake of the revelation of it and not what is represented. Without further ado, the work is vanquished, so to speak, by the philosophical idea of itself.

26 Since I have already suggested that his conception of freedom presupposes the disenchantment of nature, whilst this run of thought presupposes the exact opposite, then I am ascribing to Schlegel a systematic ambivalence about the standing of nature – a thought that is anyway required for the comprehension of his shifting alliance with and departures from Novalis. As much as I dislike ascribing contradictory beliefs to a serious thinker, interpretive necessity demands it here.

27 Which is not to deny that, to the degree to which they must take up the burden of legislating for themselves what it is for a work to be a work, and thus art to be art, modern works possess an implicit self-consciousness of themselves. But this self-consciousness is purely formal, representing only the implied awareness of the predicament of art which is given by the sheer fact of a work's being a new and original work under modern conditions.

28 All this simply assumes that there cannot be a (transcendental) law of freedom; a law of freedom would make the law, so reason, higher than freedom itself. But this is not to support the opposite: freedom as arbitrariness or sheer spontaneity. The self-showing of freedom as freedom must be normatively authoritative. Hence the self-figuring of freedom as freedom here anticipates, fully and self-consciously, Nietzsche's critique of the categorical imperative.

29 Again, and problematically, in indifference toward the pantheism which remains a constant presence. One could say that pantheistic ideas run deep in Novalis, but are only casually embraced by Friedrich Schlegel, so casually that they offer no resistance to the idea of poesy that emerges between 1797 and 1800. Or perhaps, the right way to express the thought is to say that it is the pantheism that supports the lack of disillusionment which in its turn provides the condition for the exorbitant theoretical quest.

30 All references, designated OI, are to the translation of "On Incomprehensibility" that appears in *Classic and Romantic German Aesthetics*, pp. 297–307.

31 This Nietzschean-sounding principle is here, of course, a direct consequence of the embrace of Fichte's conception of freedom.

32 In addressing de Man and Blanchot I do not mean to imply that their account of Schlegel is somehow more obviously accurate than competing interpretations. Rather, their argumentation fulfills and focuses on what is obviously one line through Schlegel: romantic anti-aesthetics. The best competing analysis, which does pick up a discernible line of thought which connects Novalis and Schlegel, holding together romantic irony with the notion of "hovering," and so getting right the Fichtean moment in romanticism, is to be found in Peter Szondi, "Friedrich Schlegel and Romantic Irony, with Some Remarks on Tieck's Comedies," in his *On Textual Understanding and Other Essays*, trans. Harvey Mendelsohn, Minneapolis, University of Minnesota Press, 1986. Although sympathetic, Szondi's reading would fall foul of the Hegelian critique of romantic irony. It is, I think, the exposure of the idealist reading of irony to Hegelian critique that silently lies behind de Man's and Blanchot's efforts.

33 I am ignoring the opening argument relating the structure of romantic thought to Fichte's system mentioned in note 22 above. Roughly, de Man there construes the first moment of Fichtean self-positing as equivalent to, for Schlegel, an arbitrary act of naming, a performative exceeding cognitive control, which is equally the basis of the cognitions that follow.

34 "The Concept of Irony," pp. 178–9. The thesis that "Die Ironie ist eine permanente Parekbase" occurs in "Zur Philosophie" (1797), fragment 668. In fact, de Man is wanting this thesis to operate as a deconstruction of Fichte and thus of idealism in general, which is how he is construing Schlegel's philosophy. So in his own technical terms his thesis is that "irony is the permanent parabasis of the allegory of tropes" (*ibid.*, p. 179). This is less obscure than it sounds. De Man interprets the primitive acts of likening things to one another and distinguishing them from one another by means of which the simplest judgements are formed as having the structure of metaphor, the structure of tropes (p. 174). So, more broadly now, since Fichte aligns his dialectic of positing to the minimum conditions for judgement, then the structure of the whole Fichtean system is "tropological" (p. 176). The system of tropes, it is argued, covers over, via the narration the system performs (which is what the system of tropes is, a narrative), the original self-positing or performative. Rhetorically: the original catachresis (the universality of language to name anything as emerging from its power to misname any item) moves the system but exceeds it as performance exceeds cognition. What is novel with de Man is that presumptive rational transparency or system here comes not from reason, but from the system of tropes, precisely what we normally think of as disrupting the transparency of reason. Hence for de Man the literary as tropes and the transparency of reason are the same illusion; the illusion of philosophical system is an aesthetic illusion. What disrupts this illusion, aesthetic semblance, the ideology of the aesthetic, *and* the transparency of reason, is irony as permanent parabasis. So to say that irony is the permanent parabasis of the allegory of tropes translates into irony being the permanent disruption of philosophy and aesthetics.

35 This is an illegitimate inference since indeterminacy of meaning is not equivalent to non-meaning. The Wittgensteinian critique of the identification of a meaning with a rule, for example, turns on the demonstration that no rule can saturate a usage (because future usage could reveal a potential for meaning in a present usage indecipherable from the present), without that thought entailing skeptical collapse into non-meaning. How thoroughly the illegitimate inference governs de Man's account is worth registering and interrogating. Certainly, de Man nowhere entertains the

171

thought that linguistic indeterminacy is just the form of potentiality for meaning that is compatible with context coming to play a determining role, without that determination again entailing unconditional determinacy. This suggests that de Manian disillusionment turns heavily on the presumption of full determinacy; dogmatism and skepticism again perform their familiar dance in his thought.

36 TP, pp. 186–7.
37 The bracketed phrase is from a later version of the passage used by de Man.
38 "The Concept of Irony," p. 181.
39 *Ibid.*
40 *Ibid.*, p. 182.
41 "The Athenaeum," in his *The Infinite Conversation*, trans. Susan Hanson, Minneapolis, University of Minnesota Press, 1993, p. 356.
42 "Monologue," in J. M. Bernstein (ed.) *Classic and Romantic German Aesthetic*. See also TP, pp. 145–6.
43 Think of this as the recovery of the semiotic dimension of meaning – sound, rhythm, association, desire – within the discursive/symbolic/semantic construction of meaning. I take the semiotic/symbolic doublet from the writings of Julia Kristeva, say her *Black Sun: Depression and Melancholia*, trans. Leon S. Roudiez, New York, Columbia University Press, 1989.
44 "The Athenaeum," p. 357.
45 *Ibid.*
46 *Ibid.*, p. 353.
47 *Ibid.* It is worth noting that the thesis about the other side of language does not in fact entail the notion of fragmentary emptiness or that of the event of meaning beyond meaning proposed in (i) and (ii). Not every bracketing of representational meaning will yield the specific almost contentless event of meaning Blanchot is wanting here. Still, it is a marvelously illuminating false inference. The limpidity and brilliance of Blanchot's essay has not gone unnoticed; it has begotten, quite directly and immediately, two of the finest readings of Jena romanticism: Philippe Lacoue-Larbarthe and Jean-Luc Nancy, *The Literary Absolute: The Theory of Literature in German Romanticism, op. cit.*; Simon Critchley, *Very Little . . . Almost Nothing: Death, Philosophy, Literature*, London, Routledge, 1997, lecture 2, (a)–(c).
48 I construe Szondi's interpretation in "Friedrich Schlegel and Romantic Irony," *op. cit.*, as one expression of the second version, while the marvelously patient account of Ernst Behler, *German Romantic Literary Theory*, Cambridge, Cambridge University Press, 1993, would like some version of romanticism as anticipating literary post-modernism to be correct.
49 "Phenomenality and Materiality in Kant," in de Man, *Aesthetic Ideology, op. cit.*, p. 83. This same materiality is, finally, for de Man, "the prosaic materiality of the letter" (*ibid.*, p. 90), which I take to be synonymous with the text machine of the Schlegel essay.
50 "The Athenaeum," p. 357.

8

IRONY AND ROMANTIC
SUBJECTIVITY[1]

Fred Rush

It is still somewhat commonplace to chart the development of philosophical thought in Germany immediately following Kant as consisting in a series of sophisticated and highly complex systematic attempts to make more rigorously "scientific" Kant's own systematic philosophy.[2] Thus do Fichte, Schelling, and Hegel still command center stage in most historical considerations of the period. Yet, there existed a competing strand of thought that developed along-side the great philosophical systems of the day in constant reaction against prevailing reductionist tendencies. This counter-movement to German idealism, which developed in Jena as a philosophical *salon des refusés* during the height of Fichte's influence in the 1790s, has received comparatively little attention.[3] Its major philosophical representatives were Friedrich von Hardenberg (writing under the pseudonym Novalis)[4] and Friedrich Schlegel. Both Novalis and Schlegel were also literary minds of the highest order – Novalis, a lyrical poet and poetic novelist, whose *Heinrich von Ofterdingen* is widely considered a canonical work of German romanticism, and Schlegel, one of the most original and influential literary critics of his time. The literary preoccupations of the Jena school of early German romanticism are not inci-dental to their philosophical concerns. Two of the main distinguishing features of early romantic philosophy are directly related to the proximity of literary and philosophical concerns. The first of these is the idea that art has an important, if not preeminent, philosophical function. Second, and closely connected with the first idea, is the belief that the form of writing in which philosophy is done and disseminated is itself philosophically crucial.[5]

In order show what is distinctive, and distinctively Kantian, about early German romanticism's account of subjectivity, I first provide an overview of the central developments in German idealism to which it reacts. Second, I discuss Novalis's criticisms of Fichte and his own reformulation of the problem of subjectivity that provides the basis for the romantic concept of the "absolute" and the anti-foundationalism associated with it. The third section of the paper provides an "interlude" that is meant to give a slightly broader cultural context

FRED RUSH

for the technical, systematic philosophical analysis of the first two sections. I then turn to Schlegel in some detail, discussing the particular ways that he extends and modifies Novalis's work in terms of the central concept of irony. The last section deals with Hegel's reception of Jena romanticism, focusing on his treatment of Schlegel.

Kant, Reinhold, Fichte

The philosophical landscape of later eighteenth-century German philosophy was very diverse, inhabited at the same time by pre-Kantians, Kantians and post-Kantians. Simplifying somewhat, there were four lines of reaction to the critical philosophy: (1) an attempt to re-enfranchise Leibniz-Wolffian metaphysics, led by Eberhard and Mendelssohn; (2) Lockean claims that Kant had merely replicated Berkeley's incoherent empirical idealism; (3) counter-Enlightenment responses that either focused on claimed inconsistencies in key Kantian doctrines, i.e. the idea of a thing in itself (Jacobi, Salmon Maimon) or on Kant's inadequate account of the role of language in cognition (Hamann and Herder); and (4) thinkers who saw themselves as furthering the critical philosophy. This last group can be further sub-divided into philosophers (4a) who were intent on disseminating Kant's philosophy with utmost textual fidelity, and (4b) those who understood their task to be building upon and completing Kant's Copernican revolution. Fichte famously labeled these two camps respectively Kantians by "the letter" and by "the spirit."[6] In the first group was the loyal Beck, in the second the insurgent Fichte.[7]

I would like to begin discussing the philosophical views of the Jena romantics by turning to the thought of K. L. Reinhold, who began of the letter but quickly went over to the ranks of spirit. Particularly important for Jena romanticism is his criticism of Kant's theory of consciousness and attempt to improve on it.[8] This is linked with Reinhold's very influential claim that Kant's philosophy is not systematic enough by its own lights and generates Reinhold's own form of monistic philosophical foundationalism centered on the nature of subjectivity.[9] Reinhold was dissatisfied with Kant's failure to deduce the various faculties of mind from one common root.[10]Absent such a deduction, Reinhold thought, Kant merely assumes the discreteness of the faculties empirically, and has shown an aggregate subject, not a truly integrated one. The thesis that the faculties are fundamentally distinct in terms of their epistemic role is central to Kant's epistemology, as well as to his negative critique of both rationalism and the empiricism; nonetheless, Reinhold believes that defeating skepticism introduced by the critical philosophy itself requires a more rigorous idea of systematicity involving a reduction of Kantian faculties and the rules governing their exercise to one faculty with one self-certifying ground principle (*Grundsatz*) from which all other rules of thought can be deduced. Reinhold attempts to work out this monistic foundationalism in his so-called "philosophy of elements."

For Reinhold the concept of representation (*Vorstellung*) forms the content of the foundational principle whose adoption is required to ground consciousness and, thus, experience. According to the principle, consciousness necessarily involves a distinction by the subject between (1) itself, (2) its object and (3) representation, and (4) a relation of the representation to the subject and to the object. (1)–(3) say that the conscious subject distinguishes itself from the object of its consciousness and the representation of the object in virtue of which it is conscious of it. (4) says that, though distinguishing itself from both the object and the representation of it, the subject nevertheless must view the representation as belonging to itself *as subject* and as being *of the object*.[11]

Fichte sympathized with Reinhold's view that Kant's conception of the ground for subjectivity was not well founded, and shared many of the reasons Reinhold adduced on behalf of that claim. But he thought Reinhold's own principle of representation inadequate. This reaction is evident as early as 1792 in Fichte's positive review of a book by G. E. Schulze, writing under the pseudonym "Aenesidemus".[12] According to the standard view, the primary thrust of Schulze's criticism is that Reinhold's principle results in an infinite regress which robs it of its coherence and its claim to be fundamental. If representation requires the ascription of the representation to the subject, then the subject making the self-ascription would have to have an antecedent ability to recognize herself as the representing subject. But this self-awareness cannot be accounted for in terms of the conception of representation at hand, for that would require the subject to be an object for herself, requiring another subject in contrast to it, and so on.[13] Schulze's skeptical conclusion is that Kantianism as a theory of consciousness is doomed, a conclusion he reaches because he accepts Reinhold's characterization of the essential components of Kant's theory of knowledge: (1) that all consciousness is representational, and (2) all representation has the reflective and reflexive quality that Reinhold ascribes to it. Schulze thinks he has shown that the requirement that all consciousness be representational has a secret commitment to some non-representational base state in which the subject has immediate self-acquaintance, and he believes that Kant's epistemological views rule out the only possible candidate for such an item of acquaintance, a Humean impression. Fichte, however, believes there are resources within the critical philosophy to account for this sort of non-representational awareness.[14] Fichte attempts to halt the regress – and, in doing so, establish a unitary ground for object-consciousness – by arguing for an immediate, non-reflective, self-awareness by the subject (the "I") on what he takes to be Kantian grounds. Fichte's theories of self-positing, the *Tathandlung* and intellectual intuition, are all attempts to elucidate this sort of activity.[15]

This is not the place to try to detail Fichte's various ways of understanding this implicit pre-reflective awareness. Roughly, intellectual intuition is "pre-reflective" for Fichte in two senses. First, it is a transcendental requirement upon the possibility of reflection and logically prior to it. Second, it is an activity that

175

does not have a reflective structure, yet is one from which reflective states of mind issue. Of course the only way one has to *understand* the activity is reflectively – as soon as one attends explicitly to the activity, one must avail oneself of precisely the reflective, conceptual apparatus foreign to it. Simply put, one can never capture the immediacy and implicitness of the state as such by representing it *as* immediate and implicit. Foundational knowledge will be of a different sort – not propositional, not a skill – if it is knowledge at all.

Novalis, or feeling

The circle that gathered itself around the brothers Schlegel coalesced in the years 1796–8 in Jena, where Fichte had taken a chair in philosophy and was at the height of his popularity. From the outset, members of the Jena Circle found Fichte's attempts to further systematize Kant's critical philosophy along foundationalist lines misguided.[16] This negative reaction follows for essentially Kantian reasons, for the Circle thought Fichte's views on what can be expected from a well grounded philosophical system were insufficiently "critical." Kantian critique involves *inter alia* reason's self-limitation and recognition of the abiding nature of dialectical illusion.[17] This self-limitation dictates for Kant the form of systematicity that a properly critical philosophy can take. Such a system or form of philosophy will not achieve what might be perfect systematicity by either rationalist or Fichtean lights just because that sort of systematicity is not available to it once critique is in place.[18] Thus, the feature of Kant that exercised many post-Kantian idealists – that the system is not "complete" and requires merely regulative bridging principles to achieve what systematicity it has – is not for Novalis or Schlegel a disappointment. Over and against the massive wave of monistic foundational accounts of post-Kantian German idealism, the Jena writers are resolutely anti-foundationalist.[19]

Novalis was in the lead in pressing objections to Fichte's foundationalism, working out his analysis of and objections to Fichte's views in the 1795–6 notes known as the *Fichte-Studien*. Novalis agrees with Fichte that Reinhold was incorrect to hold that subjectivity is grounded in a reflective relation of representing subject to thing represented: the reason he cites for this is just the one Fichte forwards in the *Aenesidemus* review, namely that analytic to the concept of reflection is the problematic distinction between subject and object. He also agrees with Fichte that the basic form of subjective activity is immediate self-awareness. The problem with Fichte's view lies elsewhere: with the idea that the immediate self-relation of the subject has a cognitive status that permits it to serve as a deductive ground for knowledge. Novalis claims that Fichte impermissively accords the immediate self-relation of the "I" a status that is proper only to reflection. But, if the I's immediate self-awareness is not conceivable on the reflective model, then the I cannot be something of which we can even be implicitly conscious. For, we can only be conscious of what, tacitly or otherwise, can stand as *an object* for consciousness and this holds as well for the I. In short, if such acquaintance were immediate, as Fichte insists it is, it would have to be unconscious. Yet if it is unconscious, we can have no direct awareness of it, intellectual or otherwise.[20] One might experience such a ground at best indirectly, through feeling (Gefühl), to which Novalis assigns the epistemic status of "non-knowledge" (Nicht-Wissen) or "faith" (Glauben).[21] In thinking of access to the root of subjectivity as faith, Novalis attempts to capture both the fact that the root can never be known and that a coherent account of consciousness is forced to rely upon it and posit it as unknowable in principle. It is against this general epistemological background that one must understand the term that Novalis uses to refer to this ultimate ground, the "absolute" (das Unbedingte). Unbedingt means unconditioned, but Novalis is also exploiting what he takes to be the substantival root of the verb from which the adjective is derived, Ding ("thing"). Unbedingt therefore also means "un-thinged," i.e. what cannot be experienced with any determinacy.[22]

The point Novalis is making is essentially a Kantian one, i.e. that the primordial non-reflective state of subjectivity from which other forms of consciousness must be said to arise can never be an object. Philosophy is not going to be able to achieve much in the way of penetrating beyond reflection, since it is the reflective enterprise par excellence. Thus Novalis writes that philosophy, in deploying this all-important conception of feeling, can indicate the limit of reflection – philosophy is, in effect, the result of reflection's self-critique. Reflection, by critically assessing its inability to reconstruct the ground for its own possibility, realizes the limits of reflective thought. Novalis does not think that the stricture against the incursion of reflective thought into its own origin precludes everything we can say about the relation of the ground for subjectivity to our experience of that subjectivity. For instance, from the fact that one can only feel the I's immediate self-awareness, Novalis concludes that the I must have the status of a datum for consciousness and not, as Fichte argued, a factum. Further, Novalis argues that, since anything like feeling that is passive must be the effect of something active, the I must be active (he sometimes says "spontaneous").[23] But this is as far as philosophy can go and, crucially, it can go this far only by transcendental regression on the conditions required for the possibility of consciousness. The rest is left to art and, particularly, to poetry.

Interlude

The historical significance of early German romanticism is often put in terms of its reaction to Enlightenment's "disenchantment" of nature. Beginning roughly with Bacon and Galileo, human understanding of nature is increasingly dominated by the idea that our knowledge of its basic structure is possible without assuming that it is the product of a divine will. Non-naturalistic features of the world incrementally migrate into the structure of the cognitive subject so that, by Kant's time, one is left with a minimalist account of non-natural forces: the *idea* of a thing in itself, a thing as it is abstractly thought as being independent of the apparatus of experience. This naturalizing of nature is paired with a radical reconceptualization of ethical life with the idea of autonomous rationality at its center that makes no necessary appeal to religious experience.

But the story is radically incomplete as stated, for the divinity once attributed to nature – the impulse, one might say, to make such an attribution of divinity to the world – did not just disappear. Rather, it is transposed into the aesthetic sphere. Again, Kant is the summation of one phase in this displacement of enchantment and the beginning of another, that of "aesthetic theodicy."[24] It is striking that Kant incorporates those elements of what he calls "dogmatic metaphysics" that secured prior conceptions of nature as (partly) enchanted in regulative principles that govern viewing nature as purposive for various goals. One main category of experience that is governed solely by the implication of purposiveness is aesthetic; Kant analyzes beauty as a non-conceptual, purposive accord between the freedom of the imagination in sheer synthesis and objects of perception. Indeed, the a priori principle of the purposiveness of nature for judgment is the normative basis for a capacity for judgment that Kant holds bridges the "great gulf"[25] that exists between the sphere of theoretical reason, constrained by the causal principle, and the domain of the non-natural moral law.

The weight that Kant gives to natural beauty in his aesthetics marks him as an early case of the reenchantment of nature through art. But the crucial effects of the metaphysical turn to aesthetics are all present in his thought. The first of these is a reconceptualization of the philosophical status of feeling. Non-discursive representation or feeling becomes a point of unity between the two radically divergent aspects of the subject, phenomenal and noumenal. In the wake of the loss of significance that followed from the disenchantment of nature – it was not for nothing that Moses Mendelssohn called the author of the *Critique of Pure Reason* the "all-destroying Kant" – aesthetics and feeling give hope for a re-unification of the subject, for a basis for overcoming alienation from nature, and for the ideal of a human community in which inclination and reason harmonize. Schiller's *Briefe über die ästhetische Erziehung des Menschen* (1795) are perhaps the most famous expressions of the melancholy loss of and hope for reconciliation of nature and freedom that take their leave from art, although one might cite the final sections of Schelling's 1800 system or his 1802 Jena lectures on the philosophy of art to similar effect.

The second component of the introduction of aesthetics as the bearer of the enchantment of nature has to do with the manner in which art reflects that enchantment. Theories of the significance of art as a reaction to Enlightenment desacralization that take their cue from Hegel – I have in mind here Horkheimer and Adorno, Lukács, Charles Taylor – observe that nature is reenchanted via art in a compensatory way, in a way that both preserves the idea of divine nature and the melancholy of its retreat. There are many ways to approach this phenomenon, but the one that I would like to stress involves the material of art or of aesthetic experience more generally. Alienation from nature on the modern paradigm is expressed in the requirement that experience be mediated discursively. Concepts are rules for thinking things together in terms of their similarities, not in terms of their singularity. Concept use introduces our purposes into nature, for any deployment of a concept involves taking the world to be a particular way, if only defeasibly. The capacity to encounter things as singularities of which one can have knowledge is ruled out on this picture. Because they do not involve subsuming intuitions under concepts, aesthetic encounters with nature allow a much closer relationship between subjects and the material element present in things. In a line of thought beginning in Kant and continuing on through Schelling, Hegel, Heidegger, Benjamin and Adorno, art is seen as the unique sphere in which (1) nature (including human nature) can be encountered without the alienation expressed in antecedent conceptual categorization, and (2) the formal capacities definitive of human agency are still present (non-conceptually) in a general, non-determining way. It is this species of the content/form dichotomy that characterizes artistic activity and the structure of its products.[26]

Novalis deploys the concept of feeling at precisely this point, but not with the result that the alienation from nature is entirely overcome. There is a sense in which feeling is "knowledge" of a radically non-discursive sort for Novalis which constitutes a mode of "experience" that he thinks makes discursivity possible. Following through on this thought may require something like criteria of truth and falsity to apply to feeling, as well as the idea of a subject's more or less "proper attunement" with nature. Even though the absolute outruns any possible conception of it, non-discursive "fittingness" of feeling might still constrain interpretations or expressions of the absolute. It is fairly clear that Novalis assumes something like this general picture; no matter how individualistic points of view on the absolute might be, they will, if attuned enough to "natural subjectivity," share a great deal. It also seems that Novalis does not think that the impossibility of conceptually grasping the absolute undermines the objectivity of experience that it grounds. In fact, throughout the *Fichte-Studien* he experiments with showing how a method he calls *ordo inversus* provides an interpretation for the Kantian categories and forms of intuition consistent with the requirement that the absolute be posited as reflectively inaccessible. The results he obtains are not very impressive, but the fact that Novalis does not think that "correct" intuition so underdetermines conception that there are no possible universal constraints on discursive experience shows again that he is pursuing a transcendental program of a generally Kantian sort: Kantianism with a radicalized conception of the thing in itself.

Friedrich Schlegel, or irony

At the time that Novalis is deep into his study of Fichte's philosophy, Schlegel is completing a period of intensive classical research. As were Winckelmann,

Lessing and Schiller, Schlegel is concerned with understanding the relationship of ancient to modern art and literature.[27] His interest in this contrast is not academic or merely literary. Although they differ fundamentally on the issue of the appropriate response to modernity, Schlegel, like Schiller, diagnoses his contemporary scene as one of upheaval of a prior order that calls for reflection on what sort of new orientation is possible.

According to most eighteenth- and nineteenth-century German speculation on the nature of Greek culture, Attic art expresses an almost immediate unity between subject and community; its making and content reflect no essential division between what is and what should be. By contrast, modern art reflects the active and constitutive agency of artists who seek to create something original out of inherited forms, implicating distance between the ideal and actual and between individual and social existence. Modern art is inherently philosophical on this view because it must be reflective – it must seek to establish normative coherence in a situation in which the very idea of a definitive normative structure is deeply problematic. Schlegel works out his reflections on the role of art in experience against this general background and in terms of its demand for explicitly reflective art. Two ideas stand at the center of his analysis: irony and the nature and importance of what he calls "fragments."

Schlegel endorses Novalis's view that the ultimate ground of subjectivity is forever unavailable to thought, restricted as thought is to the deployment of concepts to manifolds of intuition. And he holds with Novalis that, in the train of philosophy's default, poetry can display, not the absolute, but its elusiveness. Poetry does this in virtue of its elliptical manner, indeterminate content and metaphoric structure – suggesting more than it could possibly be interpreted as saying. To the extent that a poetic work presents a specifiable content, it is only to, at the same time, indicate that the content is not an exhaustive expression of the absolute. Structured in this way, art indicates one's reflective inability to grasp final content in the very act of trying to do so, paralleling one's situation as a discursively bound being in relationship with a fundamental, unbounded nature that can never be known as such.[28] Expressing just this situation – one in which one forms and discovers oneself by striving to display the absolute – dominates Jena literary output. Novalis's *Heinrich von Ofterdingen,* whose title character embodies the structure of the work in his development toward ever more differentiated and esoteric experience, is exemplary.[29]

All art has the character of indeterminacy or "infinity" that reflects our inability to represent the absolute,[30] but not all art does so self-consciously and explicitly of course. Some art openly draws attention to its inherent incompleteness and some does not. Schlegel counts as ironic both implicit and explicit artistic expressions of the problematic relationship of finite beings to the absolute. Irony is not for Schlegel, in the first instance, a literary device or trope; it is a general, transcendentally mandated property of a work or a philosophical position.[31] Each work has *a* content, if but indeterminate, and expresses insights, feelings, beliefs, or philosophical propositions to which it is committed.

The work *affirms* the point of view expressed in it, and Schlegel treats this affirmation or commitment as one of two components of irony. But, Schlegel thinks, if one reflects with sufficient acumen, one will recognize that no single expression or group of expressions can plumb the ground for expressivity – there are other possible ways that the world may be like for others, expressive of points of view that are different from one's own, yet expressive of the absolute. In fact, there is any number of ways to express the absolute by representing the world as being a certain way. If one is conscious of this, one registers *within the work* the fact that, as a work having *a* point of view, the work is merely one of many attempts to express the absolute. Schlegel thinks, therefore, that a correct cognitive stance toward the absolute balances a critical *distance* from the work in the work with the affirmation of its expression, and this is the second element in irony. Irony thus involves an acute and circumspect awareness of a work as *perspectival*. Put another way, irony is the acknowledgement that works are "partial," in two senses of the word – one who shares the affirmation they contain is partial to them and one recognizes they are but partial representations of the world. Schlegel expresses the tension inherent in irony in terms of many schemata, but two stand out. Both borrow from Fichte. Perhaps the most famous characterization involves the idea that the ironist "oscillates" between or "hovers" over (*schwebt*) self-creation (*Selbstschöpfung*) and self-annihilation (*Selbstvernichtung*).[32] A slight variant identifies three elements, adding self-limitation (*Selbstbeschränkung*) as a median term.[33] Romantic poetry, and by extension romantic philosophy, is "infinite" because the oscillation is constant: there is no resolution of the tension in favor of either element.

When Schlegel writes that ironic poetry is "transcendental," "critical," or "poetry of poetry" he means to emphasize that it contains within it a statement or view *and* the grounds for the statement's or view's possibility,[34] which "excites a feeling of the insoluble antagonism between the conditioned and the absolute, between the impossibility and necessity of complete communication."[35] These are not claims limited to "poetry" in the usual sense of the word. Schlegel is willing to extend all of these "poetic" requirements to philosophy, for he expands his early credo that all poetry must be philosophical to include its converse: that all philosophy must be poetic. By the time of Schlegel's mature Jena writings, "poetry" is an umbrella term whose extension includes lyric and epic poetry, novels, painting, music, and philosophy. In fact, Schlegel states that what he seeks is a unification of poetry and philosophy[36] and that philosophy, and not poetry "is the true home of irony."[37]

It is possible and profitable to understand irony as a version of what has come to be known as "perspectivism," although Schlegel never uses that term. Sometimes Schlegel speaks of ways of viewing the world as varying with individual points of view, so that we may all be said to inhabit different perspectives on the world, indeed any one of us at different times may inhabit many such. This may seem to ratify the received opinion that romanticism extols first-person perspective above all else. And since what is apt to differentiate any two

181

person's perspectives in the standard case is often emotive content, another received view of romanticism is reinforced, i.e. that it harps on feeling at the expense of discursivity. But Schlegel also talks about ways of life that may be shared by people and as varying greatly between peoples, both synchronically and diachronically. And this brings up the interesting question of conceptual variance, and indeed variance in the base or core concepts that might be said to differentiate fairly comprehensive alternative ways of understanding the world.

What exactly does irony require in the way of "recognizing" other perspectives? Is it enough to recognize their possibility, and if so, what does "possible" mean in this context? Or does distancing in irony recommend or require "entertaining" or "entering into" other perspectives as ways to deepen the sense of the ineffability of the absolute? It may seem that it is sufficient for Schlegel that one has a rather formal recognition that one's own expression of the absolute cannot be definitive. One need not for this even think about other discrete, actual perspectives in any concrete way; one need only know that there are (must be) other possibilities. But there is good reason to interpret Schlegel otherwise, for he often exhorts his reader to be open to and investigate different expressions of the absolute. The romantic notion of *Symphilosophie* requires *this*, not just co-authoring texts. Of course exhortations are not requirements, but there is an argument to be made that entertaining other possible perspectives (and not just entertaining their possibility) is a precondition to ironic distancing. The thought would be that merely thinking abstractly about one's perspective as one amongst many possible perspectives is too insubstantial to motivate treating as "real" the alternatives that might loosen easy identification with the "home" perspective.[38] In turn, this would influence the level or force of affirmation in irony, since affirmation is tempered by distancing – which is just to say that the two elements in irony are dialectically related. Schlegel seems to think about interpretation rather like Schleiermacher, i.e. he believes that one can experience another point of view as it is experienced by those for whom it is native (Winckelmann's writings on classical art provide Schlegel with just this model of understanding a culture "from the inside out"). The experience of alternative perspectives could have a very strong subjective impact, assuming this view on interpretation – one that might provide real friction for the components in irony. The thoroughgoing ironist might even attempt to enter as many other ways of thinking as she can, thereby developing and adopting other points of view and, where possible, incorporating them into her own perspective (or not). The more perspectives one occupies, the more ways one has available to take the world and adumbrate the absolute.[39] Still, to entertain is not to endorse, and one would want to insist that one need not discount one's perspective against all comers. I can benefit from seeing things as Oblomov does and still get out of bed.

Here is where art, and in particular ironic art, reenters the discussion. Art is a means through which one can imaginatively enter into a point of view in a substantial way, yet one that stops short of actually living in terms of that point of view. An artwork presents the richness of the world from the perspective of the artist and its indeterminacy solicits intersubjective understanding and communal participation through critical interpretation. This criticism is supposed to be "poetic" as well.[40] That is, criticism is no more final and determinate than is poetry, at least in its best ironic form. This is so in two senses. First, criticism does not determine its critical object; it cannot achieve a definitive understanding of the work. Second, as an object for further criticism, criticism is indeterminate. This is why Schlegel adds the injunction that criticism be poetic to his earlier idea that poetry should be critical. The idea that perspectives solicit unending intervention by other perspectives is closely tied to the idea that perspectives are "partial," in both senses I mentioned above. A work, philosophical or otherwise, is never completed. The value of "going on" is in increasing the richness of the ways that one can try to understand it.

Schlegel thinks he has found a device uniquely suited to express the ineliminable tension in endorsing a view in the face of its perspectival nature, or, alternatively, between the closed and the open character of system: the fragment.[41] Schlegel uses the term "fragment" to denote both a particular genre of literary and philosophical writing and to designate a property that other types of writing have, i.e. essays, plays, novels, dialogues, lectures, even philosophical systems.[42] Although Schlegel was eager to praise contemporary writers like Tieck and Jean Paul for their fragmentary works in which effects such as *parabasis*[43] were put in the service of explicit irony, Schlegel also deemed the work of authors as diverse as Goethe, Diderot, Sterne, Cervantes, Leibniz and Plato as "fragmentary." Schlegel ascribes to fragments two opposing properties that track the two cognitive aspects of irony we discussed above. The first of these is that a fragment must be complete. In this vein, he writes that "[a] fragment, like a miniature work of art, must be wholly isolated from the surrounding world and complete in itself like a hedgehog [*Igel*]."[44] But a fragment is also a *fragment*, i.e. it is incomplete by design, overtly elliptical and suggesting various interpretations. A well-crafted fragment is supposed to offer a discrete opinion, view, or assertion, but at the same time it suggests, either through its internal ellipsis or its inclusion in a system or collection of like fragments, that there is much more to be said and that any determinate thought is yet highly provisional and even artificial. What I said earlier with respect to the role of imagination and interpretation in irony holds as well in the case of the romantic fragment: although no fragment will be made non-fragmentary by its interpretations, interpretative interactions with fragments fuse perspectives and create a community of thought.[45] In the best of all romantic worlds this process is continuing: the interpretations will themselves be art, and self-consciously fragmentary art at that. It is this convergence of fragment upon fragment that makes for an infinitely complex nesting of perspectives,[46] the idea of which is crucial to early romantic conceptions of community and state.

Novalis was not always as keen as was Schlegel to think of irony as primary, but there is a concept in Novalis that does similar work. Novalis writes that "the world must be romanticized"[47] and "romanticizing" is a procedure with two aspects. On the one hand, the commonplace or ordinary is made to be seen as extraordinary, even supernatural. This requires the poet to treat the given objects of the world as problematically so, by showing what they "are not" – i.e. by taking them out of the contexts in which they can appear to be normal. Novalis calls this part of the romanticizing procedure "potentializing," and says that it contrasts the ordinary with the "infinite." On the other hand, romanticizing the world also involves treating the infinite, mysterious, or extraordinary as ordinary. This is done in order to emphasize the "remote closeness" of the absolute. Combining the two aspects of the one operation, Novalis thinks that life is characterized by a tension between endorsing the way of life that we find ourselves in and endorsing it critically, i.e. in the face of the fecundity of the absolute.

Hegel, or sobriety

Hegel's unstinting opposition decided the philosophical fate of Jena romanticism as a historical matter. Because his reception of early German romanticism has had such great influence – many contemporary criticisms of philosophical romanticism are just versions of Hegel's arguments against it[48] – a consideration of his interpretation of romanticism is an important part of assessing its present significance. I shall concentrate on his criticisms of Schlegel and, in particular, of the romantic concept of irony.

Hegel's reaction to Schlegel is quite complex and separating out its various motifs a substantial task that I can only begin here. Even a cursory reading of Hegel cannot miss his animus against Schlegel, so a word about the tone of Hegel's critique is pertinent. Schlegel provoked strong reactions, and Hegel was hardly alone in viewing him as arrogant and condescending. Especially in his literary criticism, Schlegel's tone is often superior, dismissive, and his wit exercised at the expense of others. Beyond a general dislike for Schlegel's snide manner, his choice of target also upset Hegel's tame Weimar sensibility. Schiller, revered by Hegel, came under criticism by Schlegel as something of a "young fogey" (after an earlier period of intense admiration by Schlegel of Schiller), causing Schiller to respond in kind in *Xenien*. Some of Hegel's own mockery when discussing romantic irony can also be taken in this spirit; in places the usually staid and sententious Hegel attempts to turn the tables and write ironically in the person of the romantic ironist in order to undercut irony's seriousness as a philosophical position – in essence playing what Hegel takes to be Socratic irony off against its romantic counterpart. Hegel also appears to have been a bit of a misogynist and a prude; the rather liberal ideas of the Circle with regard to "open marriage" and the liberation of women set him on edge, as did Schlegel's mildly racy novel *Lucinde*.[49] Schlegel's conversion to Catholicism in 1808 was also highly problematic.[50] This latter point is not a matter of sheer personal bias, for Hegel believes that he has philosophical grounds for rating Protestantism superior to Roman Catholicism in terms of its conception of autonomy.

If personal animosity were the end of Hegel's negative reaction to the Jena romantics, his views would not merit any philosophical scrutiny. But Hegel has more properly philosophical reactions to Schlegel, which are part of a larger project of discrediting "subjective" idealism. The main focus of this critique is Fichte, and Hegel interprets the Jena romantics in general, and Schlegel in particular, as followers of Fichte. I have already indicated where both Schlegel and Novalis depart in significant ways from Fichte's early Jena program. The question then becomes: assuming for the purpose of argument that Hegel's interpretation of Fichte is sound, does Schlegel's own Fichte critique insulate him from Hegelian objection?

Generally the problem with subjective idealism according to Hegel is its alleged withdrawal into the self as the sole basis for normativity. Subjective self-activity alone cannot furnish real constraints upon thought or action; therefore, any theory that takes such activity to be exclusively foundational cannot provide an account of how and why a principle or pattern of action is truly binding on an agent. Any account of freedom on such a basis would be one merely of the freedom to act arbitrarily or capriciously (*willkürlich*).[51] Fichte's concept of the "check" (*Anstoß*) that acts as a constraint upon the I's activity is purely formal (indeed, it too is a posit of the I), and thus provides no real constraint on subjective action. Hegel believes that romantic irony is the logical extension of this empty self-reference. It is an "aestheticized" form of Fichte's philosophy that substitutes feeling for intellectual intuition as the founding state or activity and conceives of expression or realization of the self in the world in terms of an "art of life," where the relevant faculty is not reason seeking a systematic whole of laws, but rather rhapsodic imagination.[52] Although Schlegel is not mentioned by name, in the *Phenomenology of Spirit* Hegel labels just this lack of external constraint on the "mere play" of subjectivity and the resulting "God-like geniality" of the ironist who holds herself above any particular set of constraints "evil," and likens it to the defiant self-involvement of Lucifer.[53] Schlegel's ever-becoming poetical philosophy is nothing but a prescription for what Hegel calls "bad infinity" and the famous claim in *Athenäum Fragment* 116 that romantic poetry is "progressive" no more than an idle boast.[54]

There are two tendencies in Hegel's treatment of romantic irony that draw upon this general critique of subjective idealism. Mostly Hegel portrays the ironist as a knowing celebrant of the relativity and ultimate interchangeability of all alleged principles, not caring at all about offering a viable account of subjective constraint or normativity. This makes Schlegel out to be a self-conscious nihilist, and, in this vein, Hegel stresses over and over again the negative or critical element of irony almost as if it were the only component present: ironic distance is simply disdain. Now, in moments of high spirit Schlegel indeed does dwell on indeterminacy for indeterminacy's sake, but I hope to have shown that he does not *think* that he is offering a relativistic theory or one that begs for an account of normativity. Of course, he may be mistaken about that; perhaps what he believes to be an alternative to standard accounts of normative commitment is incoherent. But it is a vast oversimplification to present the structure of irony as Hegel often seems to, as if the only component Schlegel claims on its behalf were skeptical. The better tack from a Hegelian standpoint is to acknowledge that Schlegel wants to account positively for what binds one to a particular form of life, but then argue that he is unable to maintain the dialectical structure claimed for irony because it necessarily collapses into its "negative" pole – in other words, that romantic irony, unlike its Socratic counterpart, is not truly dialectical.[55] Ironic identification or commitment is so dependent upon ironic distance that it ceases to be "real" commitment: i.e. perhaps I can identify with X only to the extent that I can destroy it (or perhaps even *because* I can do so).

On the other hand, Hegel sometimes seems to lump Schlegel in with other romantics as a failed foundationalist, seizing upon the alleged absence of a rational account for commitment to assume for Schlegel an irrational way to fill in the gap. One way that romantics are typically thought to provide for the sought constraint is mystically, in terms of a foundational role for feeling. The controlling idea would be that (unalienated) human feeling is not so divergent as to create problems for ethics or science and holds out the prospect for converging in final reconciliation when inauthentic elements are filtered out. As do others, Hegel sometimes interprets romanticism as a type of non-discursive foundationalism that holds out the prospect of actually reaching the absolute by means of art.[56] From Hegel's point of view the problem with this sort of foundationalism is its intuitive character. At best, it owns up to what Fichte did not: i.e. that such immediacy is not "intellectual" at all. However one finally views Novalis along these lines, this sort of foundationalism is at odds with Schlegel's skeptical concept of ongoing critique and, with it, the idea that the absolute can be striven for but never achieved. Hegel did not, after all, have the benefit of Novalis's and Schlegel's mid-1790s notebooks that contain much of their anti-foundationalist assessment of Fichte.

Another way romanticism might be taken to be a foundational enterprise that is somewhat closer to Schlegel's thought involves not mysticism but mythology. Perhaps romanticism can make good on its claims for normativity if it can, largely through the experience of a common art, engender unity of life from establishing a new faith-inspiring religious base to replace decadent religious forms.[57] On the outer cusp of the period under consideration, Schlegel writes his *Gespräch über die Poesie* (1800), where he begins a consideration of the place of myth in philosophy that was to occupy him for the rest of his life. Of course the relation of myth to philosophy and of both to art is something that would have concerned Schlegel, given his early classicism. How these thoughts sit with the relentlessly critical nature of irony is a complicated issue. One possibility, and to my mind the most plausible interpretation of their relation, is that Schlegel calls for a new mythology not in order to install a cosmology nor in order to clothe older mythic or folk forms in superficial modern trappings. Rather, he wants a background of fairly implicit and shared experience that can nurture precisely the requirements of the modern sensibility famously described in *Fragment* 116. Part of these requirements will be viewing experience as lying on a continuum between identification and distance that typifies irony, along with the commitment to constant self-criticism. The resulting mythology, developed through ironic communal discovery, would not orient agents in terms of the non-reflective immediacy of faith, but rather would be a spur to further criticism.

I return to the claim that Schlegel is an unknowing nihilist and the related charge that romantic irony is not truly dialectical. Assessing this criticism of Schlegel requires becoming more precise about the sense in which subjectivity has priority for him. Schlegel's rejection of Fichte's foundationalism is supposed to involve a denial that the subject can entirely determine what stands opposed to it as an object. Reality for Schlegel then is not reducible to subjectivity; rather, the capacity of a subject to comprehend reality itself presupposes much on the part of reality that is not due to the constitutive role of the subject, or, even stronger, is incomprehensible. Put more in terms of the problematic concept of the self-positing I, Schlegel's claim is that the subject encounters itself with its most basic form of subjectivity already there for it, not as the result of a posit, empirical or otherwise. The problem concerning Fichtean escapism and sheer play in self-creation is not supposed to arise on this picture at all, and precisely for the epistemological reasons we have discussed concerning the mode of "givenness" proper to the romantic account of subjectivity. Schlegel's conception of irony tracks this "realism." The ability to detach (in part) from one's life involves at least an intimation that what transcends experience constrains experience in ways that cannot be exhaustively understood. In dialectical terms, subjects externalize themselves in the world, partly forming it, but likewise they "come back to themselves" from that world, internalizing it and coming to recognize limitation in virtue of that activity. Schlegel does not think that commitment is compromised by the recognition that it does not fully express the absolute – irony is a form of commitment, not its lack. Irony is just what it *is* to be a committed, finite being. One commits in the face of the knowledge that any finite mode of life cannot exhaust the absolute, one does not fail to commit because of it.

Still, one might respond that the sought constraint is ineffable and, because of that, its constraining nature is indeterminate, not accessible to reason and no better than Fichte's formalism. It is as if Kantian things in themselves and the relations between them were able to stand in the place of the laws of the understanding. This is, it seems to me, the crux of the matter. Although much has been done to recruit Schlegel into the ranks of postmodernists by interpreting his conception of the absolute to preclude laws, principles, or norms of general application, there is scant evidence in his writings that he holds such views. It is true that Schlegel emphasizes above all else the variation amongst practices, beliefs and concepts, and fashions his notion of the absolute to underline the inexhaustibility of the particular instantiations of life. But this does not entail in the least that there are not laws that abstractly unite life in general ways.[58] As is Hegel, Schlegel is wary of an overemphasis of the universal at the expense of the particular and especially the tendency to think of one's identity as consisting mostly or only in abstract universal terms. Schlegel takes over from Schiller (and others) a view of especially Kant's ethics where duty and inclination are adversaries and duty singled out as the significant component of character. Fichte's *Sittenlehre* is even more rigoristic in attempting to deduce very specific duties from abstract moral principles. Schlegel may be taken to offer a corrective to this formalism that takes for granted the universalistic component, but tempers its force by arguing for a dynamic interaction of it with the particulars of sentiment and culture that are its expressions. For Schlegel, identity has more to do with the unity of particularity and universality and, crucially, in the great underdetermination of the former by the latter. All general norms: (1) support any number of particular instantiations, some of which vary in the particulars to great degrees and (2) are subject to potential revision. A modest interpretation of Schlegel, which orients him in terms of his Kantian rather than Fichtean legacy, can charitably render the critical moment in irony not as a subjective free-for-all, but rather as a provocative way of insisting upon both (1) and (2). None of this implies skepticism about norms, unless one thinks that a norm must have the form of a strict law that holds true come what may. It does, however, involve a certain skeptical/critical willingness never to close the door on experience.

This extension of Kantian critique naturally connects up with Schlegel's concern to do justice to the availability of the particular *qua* particular by representing at a reflective level what is pre-reflective, without appealing to some form of immediate intuition. According to Schlegel this will not be an experience of pre-reflectivity as such – that would be impossible – but it will be a special sort of reflective experience that makes certain adjustments at the reflective level in order to, as best one can, acknowledge and discount for the distorting effects introduced by reflection. This "correction" will itself be reflective and thus will self-consciously and imperfectly represent the pre-reflective. The claim is not that reflection blocks some more truthful sort of experience that one can have once reflection is out of the way. It is rather an attempt to treat the category of immediacy integrally while holding that all one can do is experience reflectively. Irony is this corrective procedure. It reconstructs at the conceptual level what is below the level of concepts. It is concerned with what it means to *come to have* a concept or principle and is an attempt to represent the passage from indeterminacy to relative determinacy at a point in which the very idea of indeterminacy having a positive role is in danger of being lost. From the point of view of reflection the only way to represent its pre-reflective "past" is to emphasize the potential defeasibility of determinative understanding of the world in the face of a demand that the world be understood in one way rather than another. One of Schlegel's fundamental thoughts is that the coming to have a concept or rule can never be deemed complete and thus that pre-reflectivity will always potentially inform normative practice.[59]

Compare this treatment of the category of immediacy in Schlegel with the same in Hegel. Hegel also disdains simple immediacy, but this disdain takes the form in Hegel of discounting the relevance of immediacy that is not resolved to a higher-order account of reflection. To be sure, this resolution is not to reflective, representational awareness, but rather to what Hegel calls "the Concept," which is supposed to contain immediacy as one of its mediated elements. To Schlegel this appeal to a special sort of "speculative" thought, depending as it does upon Hegel's teleology, would be unconvincing (it is, in essence, not speculative enough for Schlegel). Hegelian dialectic preserves immediacy only by denying immediacy *as such* any ineliminable role in experience. Nowhere is Schlegel closer to Kant than in refusing to eliminate immediacy because of the impossibility of its reflective capture.

Concluding remarks

Schlegel explicitly presents his theory of irony as a form of historical dialectic; irony is a synthesis of antitheses in which the individual character of both constituents is preserved and, indeed, enhanced.[60] Schlegel's Jena *Lectures on Transcendental Philosophy* of 1800–1 develops in greatest detail his notion of dialectic. Hegel attended these lectures[61] and they were no doubt important for the development of his own account of dialectic. Indeed, some of his contemporaries angered him by suggesting (improbably) that he cribbed his own concept of dialectic directly from Schlegel.[62] In Hegelian dialectic the two elements held in tension in their contradiction are eventually shown to be contradictories only in virtue of an inadequate set of background assumptions about the relationship of subjects to objects in the world. Any dialectical conflict resolves into an initially indeterminate further theory that preserves the content of the prior tension in the superior terms of the successor theory. Romantic irony juxtaposes a definite content with the fact that it is not *definitive*, in this way obliquely indicating an unspecifiable total context forever beyond reach. While it is true that irony does not involve a contradiction involving the content of two claims, an ironic work does contrast the apparent completeness of a work or fragment with its "opposite," i.e. with its ultimate incompleteness. Ironic dialectic is historical, contextual and open-ended; Hegelian dialectic is historical, teleological and closed.

When one stresses the dialectical dimension of Schlegel's thought, one can see in early German romanticism an anticipation of an important post-Hegelian development – indeed one from within the ranks of Hegelianism – i.e. what Adorno came to call "negative dialectic." In recognizing that the fragments of modern life cannot be perfectly reassembled into a whole that coheres come what may, Schlegel rejects idealistic retrenchments designed to do just that. Considered in this light, Hegel's reaction to Jena romanticism may date his own views as a reaction to modern life so bent on rational sobriety that it misses the radical shift in modern self-understanding for which contingency and historicity are so crucial.

Notes

1 I thank Karl Ameriks, Richard Eldridge, Lydia Goehr, Gary Gutting, Pierre Keller, Pauline Kleingeld, Nikolas Kompridis, Stephen Watson, and Allen Wood for helpful and challenging comments and conversation.

 Citation to Novalis is to volume and page number in *Novalis Schriften*, eds R. Samuel, H.-J. Mähl and G. Schutz (Stuttgart: Kohlhammer, 1960–88) [= NS]. The *Fichte-Studien* [= FS] are also cited according to their paragraph number. Citation to Friedrich Schlegel is to page and volume number in *Kritische Friedrich Schlegel Ausgabe*, eds E. Behler, J.-J. Anstett, H. Eichner *et al.* (Paderborn: Schöningh, 1958B) [= KFSA]. The fragments are also cited according to their Minor numbers and the following abbreviations: AFr. = *Athenäum-Fragment*, LFr. = *Lyceum-Fragment*, I. = *Ideen*. Citation to the *Critique of Pure Reason* utilizes the customary A/B format to refer to its first and second editions. All other citations to Kant are to *Kants gesammelte Schriften*, ed. Königlich Preussischen Akademie der Wissenschaften (Berlin: de Gruyter, 1902–) [= AA]. Citation to Hegel is to *Werke*, eds E. Moldenhauer and K. M. Michel (Frankfurt a/M: Suhrkamp, 1970) [= HW].

2 Excellent in this vein is Robert Pippin, *Hegel's Idealism: The Satisfactions of Self-Consciousness* (Cambridge: Cambridge University Press, 1989) which charts the development of idealism with reference to Kant's theory of apperception without papering over the real differences among those in the Kant-Hegel line. For perhaps the most optimistic account of a direct and seamless passage from Kant to Hegel (except, of course, Hegel's own), see Richard Kroner, *Von Kant bis Hegel*, 2nd edn (Tübingen: Mohr, 1961).

3 Exceptional is the work of Manfred Frank, especially his *Unendliche Annäherung* (Frankfurt a/M: Suhrkamp, 1997); see also *Einführung in die frühromantische Ästhetik* (Frankfurt a/M: Suhrkamp, 1989). Dilthey's *Das Erlebnis und die Dichtung* (1905, repr. Göttingen: Vandenhoeck & Ruprecht, 1961) is still relevant and Benjamin's brilliant *Der Begriff der Kunstkritik in der deutschen Romantik*, Vol. I.1 in *Gesammelte Schriften*, eds R. Tiedemann and H. Schweppenhäuser (Frankfurt a/M: Suhrkamp, 1991) is much more than that. Fred Beiser, *The Fate of Reason: German Philosophy from Kant to Fichte* (Cambridge MA: Harvard University Press, 1987) provides a stimulating account of the immediate reaction to Kant, concentrating on figures important to the Jena school, primarily Jacobi, Reinhold and Herder.

4 The choice of pseudonym is interesting. A *novalis* is a species of *ager* under Roman and medieval civil law. The term can refer either to a field that is ready for cultivation, or one that has been fallow for a year.

5 This paper focuses on the thought of Novalis and Schlegel and is restricted to their conceptions of subjectivity, certainly the most important philosophical contribution of Jena romanticism. I shall not discuss the significance of Friedrich Hölderlin, whose views were developed with no substantial contact with the Jena philosophical scene (although he had met Novalis and Schlegel at least once at the home of their common friend Immanuel Niethammer, himself an important figure in the development of German idealism after Kant). For Hölderlin's views and their immediate intellectual context, see Dieter Henrich's magisterial *Der Grund im Bewußtsein: Untersuchungen zu Hölderlins Denken (1794–1795)* (Stuttgart: Klett-Cotta, 1992). Another limitation: I am only interested here in the views of Novalis and Schlegel prior and up to 1800, the period that they are most concerned to explicitly extend

what they understand to be the most important inheritance of Kant's critical thought. Novalis dies in 1801 and afterwards Schlegel's thought undergoes significant change, becoming philosophically, politically and religiously more conservative, as was the general trend in German romanticism.

6 "Ueber Geist und Buchstab in der Philosophie in einer Reihe von Briefen," in *Johann Gottlieb Fichtes sämmtliche Werke*, ed. I. H. Fichte (Berlin: Veit, 1845–6) VIII: 270–300.

7 Kant and his closest allies fought hard not only to secure transcendental idealism against rationalist counter-attack, but also to protect it from appropriation by more "friendly" forces who did not, in Kant's opinion at least, share his modest proposals concerning the rightful role of pure reason. The high-water mark of Kant's own aversion to this second line is his so-called "open letter" to Fichte, dated 7 August 1799 and first published in the *Intelligenzblatt der allgemeinen Litteratur* no. 109, 28 August 1799 (AA XII, 370–1).

8 Reinhold's response to Kant is much more complicated than I can indicate in this chapter. For one thing, he subscribed (as did almost all of the post-Kantian idealists) to Jacobi's famous claim that the notion of a thing in itself is incoherent. According to Jacobi, it is incoherent because it is, strictly speaking, unthinkable if one stays within the strictures of the critical philosophy. This is because things in themselves allegedly cannot be represented at all and thus are unintelligible. This view may rest on a mistake; one may maintain that Kant does think that the thing-in-itself can be represented, just not in a way that produces knowledge. On this view the categories, albeit unschematized, would condition such thought, i.e. a thing-in-itself is the idea of a thing with its sensible conditions abstracted. In short, one cannot know what things in themselves are because they cannot be objects for us. But we do know that they are, and perhaps something of what they are not – e.g. they are not spatiotemporal, are not bearers of only relational properties, etc. Versions of Jacobi's complaint still surface, most famously in Peter Strawson, *The Bounds of Sense* (London: Methuen, 1966), part IV. For a more recent vintage of the objection, under the Strawson influence, see John McDowell, *Mind and World* (Cambridge MA: Harvard University Press, 1994) and A. W. Moore, *Points of View* (Oxford: Oxford University Press, 1997), pp. 119–20.

9 The claim that the final form of the critical philosophy is not well grounded is a commonplace among post-Kantian idealists and takes many forms. In addition to the claim that the discreteness of the faculties is not proved, there were claimed problems with the unity of theoretical and practical reason (Fichte), the unity of empirical and rational subjectivity (Schiller), the unity of the categories as a system (Hegel) and others. The verso of these claims is the notion that Kant is still open to a variety of skeptical attacks. The most sophisticated treatment of this aspect of post-Kantian idealism is Paul Franks, *All or Nothing: Skepticism, Transcendental Arguments, and Systematicity in German Idealism* (Cambridge MA: Harvard University Press, 2005). For the importance of skepticism to Hegel, see the excellent Michael Forster, *Hegel and Scepticism* (Cambridge MA: Harvard University Press, 1992).

10 Although Kant never claimed to have discovered such a faculty, there are passages from his work that encouraged those searching for such a "common root." But it is important to note right at the outset how un-Kantian the idea that such a root could *ever* be discovered is. This is brought out by a closer consideration of the passage that is often cited for the proposition that Kant thought such a root in principle discoverable by us: section VII of the introduction to the first *Critique*, where Kant says that such a common root is "unknown to us" (*uns unbekannt*). A15/B29. While it is true that this formulation does not literally rule out the possibility of locating such a common root, as would be the case if he wrote that the root is "unknowable", it is a bad inference to reason that from something being unknown it is knowable. There might

be plenty of things unknown to us that remain so, and not because of any lack of trying. It is worth recalling the final form of the critical philosophy, in which Kant presents subjects as having "dual citizenship" in both intelligible and sensible worlds. Such bifurcation might certainly introduce tensions in life that are not reconcilable at some "deeper" level. On all available evidence, Kant believed this to be a true and complete analysis of the basic constitution of subjectivity and would have disagreed with the reasoning implicit in the "common root" objection to the Kantian program, i.e. that lack of this sort of unity of the subject shows a theory that ascribes it to the subject to be deficient. There is nothing implausible, and certainly nothing contradictory, about a theory whose final understanding of the nature of being a subject ascribes to that subject the sorts of *ultimately* discrete faculties that Kant's theory does.

11 *Beyträge zur Berichtigung bisheriger Mißverständnisse der Philosophen* (Jena: Mauke, 1790), I: p. 167: "in consciousness, the subject distinguishes the representation from the subject and the object, and relates it [the representation] to both."

12 *Aenesidemus, oder über die Fundamente der von dem Herrn Prof. Reinhold in Jena gelieferten Elementar-Philosophie* (Jena, 1792).

13 See Frederick Neuhouser, *Fichte's Theory of Subjectivity* (Cambridge: Cambridge University Press, 1990), pp. 69–70, 73 n. 9 for a clear statement of the standard view. Cf. Wayne Martin, *Idealism and Objectivity: Understanding Fichte's Jena Project* (Stanford: Stanford University Press, 1997), pp. 88–9. Dieter Henrich implicitly challenges this reconstruction of Reinhold's position (as well as his own earlier interpretation of it) in "Origins of the Theory of the Subject," in *Philosophical Interventions in the Unfinished Project of Enlightenment*, eds A. Honneth, T. McCarthy, C. Offe *et al.* (Cambridge MA: MIT Press, 1992), pp. 64–6 and n. 22. See also Franks, *All or Nothing* §4.4. I cannot go into the complex question of the correctness of the standard view here.

14 This is what Henrich calls Fichte's "original insight." See "Fichtes ursprüngliche Einsicht," in *Subjektivität und Metaphysik*, eds D. Henrich and H. Wagner (Frankfurt a/M: Klostermann, 1966), pp. 188–232.

15 The idea has some provenance in the first *Critique*, but not in Kant's idea of intellectual intuition. The direct counterpart to Fichte's conception of intellectual intuition in Kant is located in the account of the transcendental unity of apperception, where Kant discusses the question of non-representational, immediate states of awareness in his analysis of the sense in which one is aware of the "I think" when one is aware that the contents of thought belong to oneself. Kant famously holds that the "I think" is a representation, not of an introspectable self or soul, but of a logical unity of thought through synthesis (B132). But he also suggests that, in the activity of thinking as such, one is immediately aware of one's "existence" or of the activity as thinking, in short, of the spontaneity of thought (B157–58n).

16 In fact, at about the time the Circle was forming there was in place, thanks to August Wilhelm Rehberg and Niethammer, a similar reaction to Reinhold's foundationalism. See Frank, *Unendliche Annäherung*, Vorlesungen XIII–XV.

17 As Hans Vaihinger was the first to note, "critique of pure reason" must be understood as both a *genitivus subiectivus* and *obiectivus*: the critique is carried out by pure reason and the critique has pure reason as its object. *Commentar zu Kants Kritik der reinen Vernunft* (Stuttgart: Spemann, 1881) I, 117–20.

18 That Kant thought his views were presented in a perfectly systematic manner can be seen from his 1787 letter to Reinhold, in which he forwards the third *Critique* as the completion of the system (AA X, 513–15). From the Kantian perspective, the inference from presence of dualism to non-systematicity is a bad one. System for Kant preserves a *harmony* between the two contrasting aspects of our finite natures and does not require their unity.

19 Yet another feature of Kant's philosophy that involves issues of the form and task of philosophy that also was deemed wanting – his insistence that the proper form of philosophy is to give arguments for the necessity of the assumption of certain claims to explain the possibility of certain antecedently given "facts," i.e. experience – was amenable to the development of romanticism in Jena. Here Niethammer's interpretation of Kant is decisive. Niethammer argued, against the current of the time, that Kant need not prove that experience is possible. Rather, transcendental argumentation assumes experience to be actual and then argues regressively from that fact to the necessary conditions for its possibility. On this interpretation of Kant's project, the problem of radical skepticism drops away (at least in some of its more intractable forms). See Karl Ameriks, *Kant and the Fate of Autonomy* (New York: Cambridge University Press, 2000), pp. 64–6. Neither Novalis nor Schlegel finally accepted Niethammer's "common sense" philosophy, however, arguing instead that Fichte was right to demand proofs in this area. See, e.g., *Philosophische Lehrjahre* no. 25 [1796–7], KFSA XVIII, 21. The power of Niethammer's critique for the romantics lies in the simple fact that it cuts against systematic pretensions, a point that Ameriks stresses.

20 See FS I.16, NS II, 114 where Novalis writes that, at best, intellectual intuition can display the limit of reflection.

21 FS I.15–22, 32–43, NS II, 113–20, 126–33.

22 See especially *Blüthenstaub* 1, NS II, 413: "Wir suchen überall das Unbedingte, und finden immer nur Dinge."

23 FS I.15, 17, NS II, 113, 115.

24 For the concept of aesthetic theodicy, see Raymond Geuss, "Art and Theodicy" in his *Morality, Culture, and History: Essays in German Philosophy* (Cambridge and New York: Cambridge University Press, 1999), pp. 78–115.

25 AA 5:176–8; AA 20:246–7.

26 The best accounts of the development of this idea of which I am aware are J. M. Bernstein, *The Fate of Art: Aesthetic Alienation from Kant to Derrida and Adorno* (Cambridge: Polity Press, 1994) and Gregg Horowitz, *Sustaining Loss: Art and Mournful Life* (Stanford: Stanford University Press, 2001). For a detailed criticism of the idea that art should shoulder this metaphysical burden, see Jean-Marie Schaeffer, *L'art de l'âge moderne: l'esthetique et la philosophie de l'art du XVIIIe siècle à nos jours* (Paris: PUF, 1992).

27 I use the term "modern" in the sense that it was used in the late seventeenth- to early nineteenth-century debate on the relative values of "ancient" and "modern" art and culture.

28 Cf. I. 69, KFSA II, 263.

29 Whereas Goethe's *Meister* develops from the inchoate and diffuse dreams of youth to an acceptance of the possibilities offered him by the real world "as it is," Novalis's hero moves from a conventional everyday life to one that is suffused with possibilities of his own making.

30 Cf. I. 95, KFSA II, 265.

31 Schlegel treats Socratic dialectic as an important precursor to his views on irony. LFr. 26, 42, KFSA II, 149, 152. Clarifying the Socratic element in Schlegel's thought is a very important part of any full analysis of romantic irony, and in particular, its relation to Hegel and Kierkegaard. I cannot hope to do that here, but it is worth mentioning that influential deconstructive interpretations of Schlegel tend to ignore this and to stress instead the connection to the European rhetorical tradition. See, e.g., Paul de Man, "The Concept of Irony" in his *Aesthetic Ideology* (Minneapolis: University of Minnesota Press, 1996), pp. 163–84. This is not to say that Schlegel develops his conception of irony in utter isolation from the rhetorical tradition. In particular, he is very interested in Quintillian's *Institutio oratoria* which was hugely influential in fifteenth- to seventeenth-century thought, where it became the model

for acceptable Latin argument. But what is decisive for Schlegel is that Quintillian is not just a manual on stylistics, but provides a general pedagogical framework that promotes a vision of how life should be lived – one that presents itself rather explicitly as a turn away from Seneca and Lucan (i.e. Neronian decadence) and as a return to older models (i.e. Cicero). Schlegel is also very interested in Isocrates, whose *Panegyrikos* influenced both Cicero and Quintillian.

32 AFr. 51, KFSA II, 172; see also LFr. 37, 48, KFSA II, 151, 153; "Über Goethes Meister" KFSA II, 137.

33 LFr. 28, KFSA II, 149.

34 AFr. 22, 238, KFSA II, 169, 204.

35 LFr. 108, KFSA II, 160.

36 LFr. 115, KFSA II, 161.

37 LFr. 42, KFSA II, 152.

38 AFr. 121, KFSA II, 184–5.

39 Schlegel need not be committed to the idea that the ironic philosopher must proliferate all manner of life-styles, in order to become more whole by being more differentiated and transgressive. Cf. Bataille's notion of transgression and Foucault's advocacy of it. Michel Foucault, "A Preface to Transgression," in *Language, Counter-memory, and Practice*, eds D. Bouchard and S. Simon (Ithaca NY: Cornell University Press, 1977), pp. 29–52.

40 LFr. 61, 115, 117, KFSA II, 154, 161–2; AFr. 249, 304, 439, KFSA II, 207, 216–17, 253; cf. AFr. 116, KFSA II, 182–3.

41 Schlegel develops his conception of the fragment partially in terms of prior literary models, ancient and modern, perhaps the most notable being the eighteenth-century French aphorist Chamfort. See Ernst Behler, *German Romantic Literary Theory* (Cambridge: Cambridge University Press, 1992), pp. 151–2. Charles Rosen argues for a direct and general musical influence on the Jena school's account in *The Romantic Generation* (Cambridge MA: Harvard University Press, 1995), ch. 2.

42 In an often quoted fragment, Schlegel states that "it is equally deadly for the spirit to have a system and to have none. It will have to decide to combine the two." AFr. 53, KFSA II, 173; cf. Novalis, FS VII.648, NS II, 288–9. Benjamin emphasizes that Jena romanticism does not forsake all ideas of systematicity, only ones inconsistent with the idea of a fragment. *Der Begriff der Kunstkritik in der deutschen Romantik*, in *Gesammelte Schriften* I.1, 40–53. The issue of the systematicity of Jena romanticism is very important, but I cannot address it here.

43 *Parabasis* is a convention in Old Comedy in which the chorus steps forward and addresses the audience in the poet's name. A more modern example would be Tieck's *Der gestiefelte Kater* (1797) where the audience members are supposed to become characters in the play. Perhaps the high-point of the use of this device within romanticism is found in Clemens Brentano's novel *Godwi* (1801), where the characters finish the book for the narrator, who has died.

44 AFr. 206, KFSA II, 197. This might remind one of Leibniz's dictum that monads have no windows. Comparison of the fragment to the monad is interesting and one that Schlegel averts to fairly often. See, e.g., *Philosophische Lehrjahre* [1798] KFSA XVIII, 42–53.

45 I take it that this is one of the main points in Schlegel insisting on "incomprehensibility" (*Unverständlichkeit*) from fragments and essays. "Über die Unverständlichkeit," KFSA II, 363–71. Schlegel means for the reader to be aware of the Kantian notion of *Verstand* as the faculty of deploying concepts in order to determine manifolds of intuition. A fragment is not subject to conceptual determination and does not have, therefore, a comprehensive rendering.

46 LFr. 103, KFSA II, 159; AFr. 77, 112, 125, 342, KFSA II, 176, 181, 185–6, 226.

47 FS I.37, NS II, 384.

48 See, e.g., György Lukács, *Die Zerstörung der Verfunft* (Neuwied: Luchterhand, 1962); Isaiah Berlin, *The Roots of Romanticism* (Princeton: Princeton University Press, 1999). Hegel-like criticism persists today even among those open to reassessing the contemporary significance of romanticism, for instance the excellent Richard Eldridge, *Leading a Human Life: Wittgenstein, Intentionality and Romanticism* (Chicago: University of Chicago Press, 1997), pp. 82–5. Kierkegaard's influential treatment of Schlegel is also very indebted to Hegel.

49 For an example of Schlegel's views, see AFr. 34, KFSA II, 170. For Hegel's, see *Grundlinien der Philosophie des Rechts* §164 Zusatz, HW 7:317.

50 Letter to Niethammer, 7 May 1809 in *Briefe von und an Hegel*, ed. J. Hoffmeister (Hamburg: Meiner, 1952) I, 283; *Philosophie des Rechts* §141 Zusatz, HW 7:290.

51 "Vorrede," *Phänomenologie* HW 3: 15–16; *ibid.*, pp. 70–1; see also "Vorrede zu Hinrichs Religionsphilosophie," HW 11: 61; *Vorlesungen über die Geschichte der Philosophie*, HW 20: 415–16.

52 HW 13: 93–4.

53 HW 3: 563.

54 KFSA II, 182. For a discussion of the progressive element in irony, see Peter Szondi, "Friedrich Schlegel und die romantische Ironie mit einer Beilage über Tiecks Komödie," in *Schriften* (Frankfurt a/M: Suhrkamp, 1978) II, 21–2.

55 "Rezension von Solgers nachgelassene Schriften und Briefwechsel," HW 11: 234, 255. Hegel distinguishes here sharply between Schlegel's views on irony and Socratic dialectic. See also *Philosophie des Rechts* §140(f) and Zusatz, HW 7:277–9, 284–6. Schlegel claims a rather direct influence from Socratic *elenchos*. See *supra* note 31.

56 See, e.g., HW 13: 93–8; see also *ibid.*, pp. 348–9. Hegel's own aesthetic theory of course reverses the romantic emphasis on art as the foremost access to the absolute. Although he accords art some role as a vehicle for "truth," he holds that it was only the most adequate expression of truth at a relatively underdeveloped stage in human self-consciousness, i.e. in Attic Greece. It may be something of a dig at romanticism that Hegel denominates any art that is outstripped by the truth that it attempts to present "romantic."

57 This of course is not an aim limited to romanticism – there is a fairly continuous strain in German intellectual history from Herder to Heidegger that rings changes upon this idea. Hegel stands in this continuum as well, arguing a very close relationship between art and religion in the formation of character (e.g. the idea of *Kunstreligion* that he takes over from Schleiermacher).

58 I am especially indebted to discussions with Karl Ameriks and Manfred Frank on this issue.

59 A fully satisfactory account of Schlegel on this issue would include a lengthy technical analysis of how he thinks universals and particulars dialectically co-determine.

60 I. 74, KFSA II, 263; see also AFr. 121, KFSA II, 184–5.

61 See "Über den Vortrag der Philosophie auf Universitäten," HW 4: 420–1.

62 This allegation continued throughout nineteenth-century Hegel reception, provoking defenders like Karl Rosenkranz to issue pointed rebuttals. *Hegels Leben* (Berlin, 1844, repr. Darmstadt: Wissenschaftliche Buchgesellschaft, 1963), p. 223. Hegel does admit vaguely that his conception of dialectic bears a resemblance to Schlegel's. See HW 20: 415.

9

NOVALIS' OTHER WAY OUT

Jane Kneller

> Doch das Paradies ist verriegelt und der Cherub hinter uns; wir müssen die Reise um die Welt machen, und sehen, ob es vielleicht von hinten irgendwo wieder offen ist.
> (Paradise is barred and the cherub behind us; we must travel around the world, and see if maybe somewhere it is open again from the back.)[1]
>
> (Kleist, "Über das Marionetten Theater")

Kleist summed up the mix of awe and profound disappointment that many intellectuals in the 1780s and 1790s must have felt in the wake of Kant's philosophy. For although in it human cognitive activity takes on new constitutive powers that define the boundaries of the real, the cost of shifting this constitutive power to human subjectivity was high: loss of access to a world beyond appearances. In spite of Kant's claim to have made room for faith in his philosophy, knowledge of the world of things "in themselves" was barred, so it seemed, once and for all. In his fictional essay "On the Marionette Theater," Kleist frames the philosophical problem of knowledge as a problem within the context of performance art. His narrator interviews a renowned dancer who aims to move with absolute grace across the floor, freely and without alienation, but recognizes that the impossibility of achieving his goal is rooted in self-consciousness. The great dancer tells Kleist's narrator that the artist should look to the marionette as a model of unselfconscious expression of absolute, unalienated movement.

The dancer's remarks are a metaphor for human striving after that which is beyond the pale of possible human experience: absolute knowledge and perfect self-expression. Kleist's essay captures the problem that seemed almost without exception to plague philosophers in the immediate wake of Kant's relativization of knowledge to the human capacity to know. Kleist is not typically classified as a romantic, but his call for a back-door strategy to solve the problem of knowledge and self-expression is characteristic of much of early German romanticism, and describes the major project of this movement's most fascinating figure, Friedrich von Hardenberg, known as Novalis. Kant's philosophy was a fact of life for Novalis and the philosophers and poets of the famous Jena Circle. Indeed, the "Copernican" paradigm in philosophy was so well entrenched that in his encyclopedic "Allgemeine Brouillon" Novalis could speak of the Copernican turn as established fact:

> Here Kant played the role of Copernicus and explained the empirical I along with its outer world as a planet, and placed the moral law or the moral I at the center of the system – and Fichte has become the Newton – the second Copernicus – the inventor of the laws of the system of the inner world.
>
> (3:335)[2]

Novalis was as convinced as was Kant that the new philosophy of the subject had dissolved past errors in philosophy once and for all. Along with most of the intellectuals of his circle, Novalis abandoned the vaulting structures of Leibnizian and Wolffian rationalism for shelter in the Kantian alternative account of what the human mind can know. Kant himself recognized that human beings would forever be tempted to strive after the absolute, or "unconditioned," but in the end his tendency was to be rather sanguine about the fact that everyday cognition, science, and even ethics, would have to do without final metaphysical answers. At the same time this great purveyor of rationalist humanism betrayed a fondness, even sympathy for metaphysical fantasizing that has been almost wholly ignored by commentators on his work.[3]

In the last section of this paper I will return to Kant to examine the place that metaphysical speculation retains in his system, and thus to argue for a continuity between his system and early German romanticism. To suggest that romanticism takes its cue from Kant is likely to raise philosophical hackles. It has become a cliché in many anglophone philosophical circles that German idealism and its pyrotechnical metaphysics jettisoned Kantian limits on knowledge. Early German romanticism is typically cast in this same unflattering role, with the additional offense of "irrationalism and mysticism" added to the indictment. In fact, however, many if not all of the early German romantics associated with the Jena Circle renounced metaphysical knowledge claims and speculative thinking in harsher terms than did Kant himself.[4] No one better exemplifies this strict adherence to the Copernican turn than does Novalis, whose philosophical efforts culminate in the glorification of aesthetics and the practice of art as the embodiment of human freedom. This chapter will begin, then, with a look at the surprisingly modest metaphysical underpinnings of this great romantic poet and philosopher. In so doing I hope to exonerate Novalis, and by extension the early German romantic circle, of charges of metaphysical excess and irrationalism. In the second part of the chapter I look at the consequences of Novalis's views for an account of the nature of ordinary cognition.

Novalis's Kantianism

In 1795–6 Novalis undertook a serious study of Fichte's *Science of Knowledge* (*Wissenschaftslehre*) after having met Fichte, along with Hölderlin, in the home of a mutual friend in Jena. The set of notes on Fichte which comprised the bulk of a large handwritten manuscript written by Novalis has been called "the most significant philosophical work of early romanticism."[5] In it, Novalis comes to grips with the early philosophy of this thinker who had claimed ascendancy to Kant's throne in German philosophy. There is no doubt that Fichte's philosophy was of great importance to Novalis, yet what emerges in the *Fichte Studies* is not a student's reworking of the master's ideas, but rather a persistent criticism of the fundamental assumption of Fichte's major work. Whereas Fichte had argued that the inner world of the self may be accessed initially via an intellectual intuition of self-activity, in his *Fichte Studies* Novalis repeatedly insists that no immediate knowledge of the self as it is in itself is possible. He argues that self-observation is a kind of "eavesdropping on the self" in order to learn about it, but by "learning," he says,

> we mean absolutely nothing but intuiting an object and impressing it along with its characteristics upon ourselves. It [the self] would thus become an object again. No, philosophy cannot be self-observation, because it would not then be what we are after [i.e. it would not be immediately known as subject – JK]. It is perhaps self-feeling. What then is feeling?. . . . It can only be observed in reflection – the spirit of feeling is then gone. The producer can be inferred from the product in accordance with the schema of reflection.
>
> (2:113–14, #15)

Novalis goes on to argue that since feeling cannot represent itself, and reflection can only represent feeling in thought, our intuition of our Self is never of a thing as it is "in itself" but is necessarily always mediated or "inferred," a synthetic product of feeling and reflection (2:114, #16). Novalis may have honored Fichte with the title of the "second Copernicus," but this did not prevent his rejecting the Fichtean central assumption of the inner world of the self, namely that the "absolute" self can be known. Not only does Novalis reject claims of access to the "absolute I," his "positive" account of the self resembles Kant's notion of the noumenal, or thing in itself, as a limiting notion. As von Molnár points out, Novalis typically refers to the concept of the "I" as a regulative one:[6]

> I – has, perhaps, like all ideas of reason merely regulative, classificatory use – Nothing at all in relation to reality.
>
> (2:258, #502)

Referring to Fichte's notion of a *Tathandlung*, the originary intuitive act of positing of the self, Novalis says,

Every state, every fact-act [*Tathandlung*] presupposes an other ... all quest for a First [genus] is nonsense – it is a *regulative idea*.

(2:254, #472)

Novalis's reaction to Fichte places limitations on the power and reach of the intellect that are essentially Kantian in spirit. Especially as a student of the natural sciences, Novalis was critical of metaphysical speculation, insisting that although a "tendency to seek the universal" [*Universaltendenz*] is essential to the scholar,

One must never, like a phantast, seek the undetermined – a child of fantasy – an ideal. One proceeds from determinate task to determinate task. An unknown lover of course has a magical charm. Striving for the unknown, the undetermined, is extremely dangerous and disadvantageous. Revelation must not be forced.

(3:601, #291)

Given these strong views on the unknowability of the self as it is in itself, it is not surprising that Novalis's intense study of Fichte led him back again to a study of Kant. The very short collection of notes and commentary now collected under the title of *Kant Studien* (1797) was found together with a group of notes on the Dutch philosopher Hemsterhuis.[7] Probably his renewed interest in Kant's views on the natural sciences was piqued by Hemsterhuis' frequent reference to the "Metaphysical Foundations of the Natural Sciences" in Hemsterhuis' "Metaphysics of Nature," but given his abrupt turn away from Fichtean idealism it is likely that he turned to Kant's works to support his developing views on the limits of philosophizing about metaphysical matters.[8]

However, a set of very brief notes in this collection suggests that it could also have been another Kantian text, and a far more obscure one, that may have provided Novalis with impetus for the further development of his philosophy as well as his artistic enterprise. Amidst the notes on Kant's philosophy were also found notes on Kant's reply to Samuel Thomas Sömmerring, a well known medical doctor and physiologist from Frankfurt. Sömmerring's book "Über das Organ der Seele" raised the question of the "seat of the soul [*der Sitz der Seele*]," or the location of the mind in the body. The book was published with a short appendix written by Kant and sent to Sömmerring specifically for the book.[9]

If I am supposed to make the place of my soul, that is, of my absolute self, intuitable somewhere in space, then I must perceive myself through that very same [spatial intuition] through which I also perceive the matter right around me.... Now the soul can only perceive via *inner sense*, but the body (whether internal or outer) can only perceive through *outer sense*; hence it can determine absolutely no place for itself, because in order to do this it would make itself the object of its own outer intuition and would have to transpose [*versetzen*] itself outside itself – which is a contradiction. So the desired solution of the problem of the seat of the soul which is demanded of metaphysics leads into an impossible dimension . . . and one can, with Terence, call to those who would undertake it: "You wouldn't succeed any more than if you were to try to be rationally insane." ["Nihilo plus agas, quam si des opera ut cum ratione insanias."]

(Kant, letter to Sömmerring, 1796)

To Sömmerring's question Kant replies that the spatial location [*der Ort*] of the soul, where "soul" is understood as "my absolute self" would have to be perceived in the same way we perceive matter around us, namely through outer sense (this includes our physical "insides" as well). But the absolute self can only perceive itself through inner sense, nonspatially, and therefore cannot determine a spatial place for itself. For the soul to make itself the object of its own outer intuition would mean that it would have to transpose [*versetzen*] its nonspatial being "outside" itself in space – and that is a contradiction, Kant says. The demand that metaphysics solve the problem of the seat of consciousness leads it into an impossible dimension, Kant continues, and he admonishes would-be metaphysical speculators with a quotation from Terence, the context of which involves advice to a spurned lover to give up on the idea of convincing through reason the heartless object of his desire.

The question of the "seat" of consciousness raised by Sömmerring, as well as an apparent dissatisfaction with Kant's deflationary response, might well explain Novalis's strong emphasis on the centrality of feeling to self-knowledge. Although Novalis makes no independent comment in his notes on the Sömmerring passage, later in his notes on the first *Critique* the question of the "seat" of consciousness is addressed obliquely:

The concept *of sense*. According to Kant, pure mathematics and pure natural science refer to the form of outer sensibility – What science refers to the form of inner sensibility? Is there yet *extra-sensible* knowledge? Is there still another way open for getting outside oneself and to get to others, or to be affected by them?

(II:46)

This getting "outside ourselves" is in all probability a reference to Kant's claim in the reply to Sömmerring, that the self cannot without contradiction be said to set itself outside itself. Later, in his well known work *Pollen* [*Blütenstaub*], Novalis picks up this thought in the following fragment:

The seat of the soul is there, where the inner world and the outer world touch [*sich berühren*]. Where they permeate – it is in every point of the permeating.

(Novalis, II: 418, #20)

The "inner world" is the world that Fichte tries to elucidate by recourse to intellectual intuition of an original act of self-consciousness, an account that, as we saw, Novalis rejected on Kantian grounds.[10] At the same time, Novalis is unhappy with Kant's refusal to countenance any possibility for "externalizing" the inner world of the self. What Novalis seems to suggest here is a third option involving the redefining of self-consciousness as the interface between the inner world of self-feeling and the outer world of objective self-consciousness. This redefinition, he suggests, might also involve a way of reaching others and in turn being affected by them.

Novalis's insistence on the centrality of feeling to self-consciousness and hence to philosophy in general was very likely due in part to the influence of Hemsterhuis' philosophy. The latter's emphasis on desire, feeling, and the importance of poesy in understanding the sciences must have appealed greatly to the poet.[11] A strong commitment to the importance of feeling to knowledge certainly helps explain the following exasperated comment in the midst of Novalis's *Kant Studies*:

> The whole Kantian method – the whole Kantian way of philosophizing is one-sided. And it could with some justice be called *Scholasticism*.
>
> (II:392 #50)

In another fragmentary note just prior to his pondering the possibility of another way of getting "outside ourselves," Novalis suggests that the practice of philosophy itself, and practical reason, must move into a new, aesthetic dimension:

> Philosophizing is just scientizing [*wissenschaften*], thinking through thought, knowing knowledge – treating the *sciences* scientifically and *poetically*. Should the *practical* and the poetic be one – and the latter simply signifies absolute practice made specific?
>
> (II:390, #45)

Now, whatever it would it mean to find another way, an extra-sensible knowledge, for Novalis, it cannot involve abandoning the real world or embracing some noumenal thing in itself as known:

> Everything absolute must be ostracized from the world. In the world one must live with the world.[12]

Underlying all Novalis's comments and criticisms, his underlying metaphysical assumption remains Kantian: the unknowability of the thing-in-itself is no longer up for debate. In fact, he makes the rather brash claim that Kant's belaboring of the issue can appear too obvious, "superfluous and wearisome" to thinkers of his own time if they did not keep in mind the historical context within which Kant worked.[13] So when Novalis speaks of discovering an extra-sensible knowledge, he is by no means taking issue with Kant's circumscription of cognitive experience. For Novalis, finding a way to get "outside" ourselves is not a matter of conflating the spheres of the cognitive and moral self that Kant had so carefully separated.[14] The wisdom of that path is already apparent to the young philosopher-poet as he finishes the *Fichte Studies* and works on Kant and Hemsterhuis. Novalis saw that getting outside ourselves requires making concrete and tangible *in art* our inner world based on self-feeling that is impossible to capture reflectively. Novalis's "other way" of locating the seat of consciousness in the world is through its embodiment in art.

Thus what Novalis finds lacking in Kant is not metaphysical, but *imaginative* commitment.[15] The transposition of the self that Novalis seeks and fails to find in Kant's one-sided approach is, for Novalis, an imaginative transformation. Novalis's impatience with Kant appears to stem from his view that Kant fails to see the possibility of poeticizing the world, or as he would soon come to say – of "romanticizing" it. By "romanticizing" the world Novalis means something quite specific: to romanticize is to make what is ordinary and mundane extraordinary and mysterious, and conversely, to make what is unknown and mysterious ordinary.

> The world must be romanticized. In this way one rediscovers the original meaning. romanticizing is nothing but a qualitative raising to a higher power [*Potenzirung*]. The lower self becomes identified with a better self. Just as we ourselves are such a qualitative exponential series. This operation is still quite unknown. Insofar as I give the commonplace a higher meaning, the ordinary a mysterious countenance, the known the dignity of the unknown, the finite an appearance of infinity, I romanticize it. The operation is precisely the opposite for the higher, unknown, mystical and infinite – these are logarithmized by this connection – they become common expressions. Romantic philosophy. Lingua romana. Alternating elevation and lowering.[16]

"The world must be romanticized." This activity was, for Novalis, something Kant failed to theorize in his "one-sided" attempt to explain human knowledge in terms of pure reason. Novalis intended not to reject Kant's system but to complement and complete it, and his notion of romanticizing was a key step in that program. In this sense, Novalis saw himself as opposing Kant, who could certainly come off as a dour old scholastic in the mind of a twenty-four year old poet, by wanting to give free reign to the imagination as a vehicle for externalizing and hence realizing what could only be felt. Imagination, Novalis believed, would produce poetry that would be literally the embodiment and external vehicle for taking the self where it needed to be – outside itself and into the world. Therein lay Novalis's philosophical solution to Kleist's Kant-induced dilemma: the key to the back door to paradise would be aesthetic.

Novalis's other way

I have argued that Novalis's position in no way betrays Kant's Copernican revolution and does not embrace a metaphysical noumenon. Novalis is not an idealist in this sense. Yet the view that art is a supersession of philosophy appears to lend credence to another common criticism of romanticism, namely that it embraces irrationalism and mysticism. This too is an unfair characterization of Novalis's own views. To see why, it is important to begin with Novalis's characterization of the nature of philosophy itself.

Given Novalis's views on the regulative nature of the "I" and his renunciation of an absolute in any but a negative sense, one might expect him to read Kant's letter to Sömmerring with approval. However, as we just saw, the "seat of the soul" discussion appears to have sent him in another direction, one that marks a departure from Kant's views on self-knowledge. Novalis's philosophical account of self-knowledge depends crucially on the view that our "inner" sense of ourself – self-*feeling* – is absolute and immediate, but that our knowledge of it, being reflective, is never absolute and immediate. For Novalis the intellectual intuition that Fichte postulated as the basis of knowledge is replaced by what could be called "reflected self-feeling." Novalis argues that thinking about our self-feeling does not give us direct access to this immediate self-experience, but it does gesture in the right direction, *reminding* us of it in an image: "Consciousness is an image of being within being" (#2). As Manfred Frank puts it, for Novalis, reflected self-feeling becomes the "orientation towards, or better, the longing for, the absolute."[17] In the *Fichte Studies* this longing is taken by Novalis to be the very heart of philosophy, or rather philosophizing – the "unique kind of thinking" that is the activity of doing philosophy:

> What do I do when I philosophize? I reflect upon a ground. The ground of philosophizing is thus a striving after the thought of a ground.... All philosophizing must therefore end in an absolute ground. Now if this were not given, if this concept contained an impossibility – then the drive to philosophize would be an unending activity.... Unending free activity in us arises through the free renunciation of the absolute – the only possible absolute that can be given us and that we can only find through our inability to attain and know an absolute. This absolute that is given to us can only be known negatively, insofar as we act and find that what we seek cannot be attained through action.
>
> (#566)

Novalis's view of the activity of philosophy is that it involves a conscious recognition that it "absolutely" cannot attain its goal. But he also suggests that human consciousness cannot ultimately live with this paradoxical situation. Toward the very end of the *Fichte Studies* he calls for a free creative response to the limitations philosophy recognizes in reason:

Objects must not do violence to us – They must not hem us in, not determine [*bestimmen*] beyond the *borders*. . . . We must seek to create an inner world that is an actual pendant to the outer world – that insofar as it is in direct opposition to [the outer world] at every point, constantly increases our freedom. . . . All determinations proceed outward from us – we create a world out of ourselves. . . . The more we determine, the more we lay out what is in us – the freer – more substantial – we become – we set aside, as it were, more and more that which is inessential and approach the thoroughly pure, simple essence of our I. Our creative power gets as much free play as it has world *under it*. But since our *nature*, or the fullness of our being, is unending, we can never reach this goal *in time* – But since we are also in a sphere outside time, we must reach it there in every moment, or better, if we want, in this sphere we are able to be pure simple substance. Here is morality and peace of mind, because an endless striving after what hovers ever out of reach before us seems unbearable.

(#647)

These musings recall Kant's view that the human being has a higher vocation, a "standpoint" in an intellectual realm where it is possible at any time to transport oneself.[18] But whereas Kant says that we can only *think* ourselves into this world, Novalis argues for the power of imagination to create a "sphere outside time." Moreover, he claims that it is in this imaginative world that we first "approach . . . the pure simple essence of our 'I.' " The passage is cryptic, leaving the reader to speculate further on the nature of this world. But Novalis's notes seem to suggest a kind of moral oppositional consciousness – a utopian vision – a world of what ought to be as opposed to what is. It is unreal and unattainable, but we nevertheless can dwell in it because we are its imaginative architects. It is a sphere to be accessed "in every moment" precisely because it is outside time and place, in our imagination.

Two points need to be made about this matter of "world-making" in Novalis. First, it is not a mystical or transcendent account. Novalis is quite clear that the "inner" imaginative world is a "pendant" to the outer. It is oppositional and for that very reason dependent upon the world of objects, as any part depends on its counterpart. There is thus nothing ineffable about it. In *Pollen* he writes:

It is the most arbitrary prejudice that it is denied to human beings to be able to be outside themselves, to have consciousness beyond the senses. Humans may at any moment be supersensible beings. Without this ability they could not be citizens of the world, they would be animals. Of course the composure and self-discovery in this state is very difficult since it is so perpetually, so necessarily, bound up in the alternation of our other states. The more we are able to become conscious of this state, the livelier, more powerful and enjoyable is the conviction that arises from it; the belief in genuine spiritual revelation.

(II:421,#22)

Novalis goes on to describe this "appearance" as a kind of emergent experience rooted in ordinary life:

> It is not a sight, a sound or feeling; it is all three together, more than all three: a sensation of immediate certainty, an insight into my truest, most characteristic life . . . the appearance [*Erscheinung*] strikes us particularly at the sight of many human forms and faces, especially in a glimpse of some eyes, some demeanors, some movements, or at the hearing of certain words, the reading of certain passages, certain perspectives on life, the world and fate. Very many coincidences, many events in nature, especially times of the year and day, deliver such experiences to us. Certain voices are particularly well-suited to producing such revelations. Most of them [revelations] are momentary, a few last awhile, a very few endure.

Novalis then says that different people will have different experiences of "revelation" depending on their propensities toward sensibility or understanding, and he also allows that this ability to "get outside oneself" is capable of becoming pathological when a person's senses and understanding are out of balance. Romanticism's detractors may or may not agree that this is a case of being "outside" oneself, but it is what Novalis means by the phrase, and it is a far cry from an irrationalist mystic's description of consciousness.

This leads to a second observation about Novalis's doctrine of imaginative world-making. It is an account of at least one important aspect of ordinary human cognition. Very typically his work, along with that of other romantics, is characterized as obsessed by the notion of individual genius. Novalis speaks as if he is characterizing ordinary human consciousness, the objection might proceed, but if self-discovery of what he called the "pure, simple I" depends so heavily on imagination, can this account be true for ordinary people? Or is it a description of the elite domain of artistic consciousness?

There is no doubt that in this section of the *Fichte Studies* Novalis was working out the rudiments of a theory of artistic process for himself. But in this connection it is important to keep in mind his subsequent views on artistic genius and talent, since they are far more liberal than is generally attributed to romanticism. In his *Mixed Remarks*, for instance, he advances the view that genius is a universal human faculty. He argues that genius is the ability to treat imagined objects as real and that it should be distinguished from the talent for presentation and precise observation that is necessary for the development of genius. He then quite explicitly states:

Without geniality, none of us would exist at all. Genius is necessary for everything. What is usually meant by genius however, is the genius of genius.[19]

This is unequivocal. For Novalis, as for Fichte and Kant as well, imagination is a universal, necessary condition of human cognitive experience. It is precisely the naturalness of the capacity that he finds significant for self-knowledge. Revelation itself is natural, and "must not be forced." It is this capacity for momentary, everyday transcendence as in revery and day-dreaming that defines the human: a being to be found "there, where the inner world and the outer world touch."

Kant's Romanticism

Novalis's theory of the self aestheticizes and materializes Kant's account of human beings as at any point in time members of an intellectual realm. The one-sidedness that Novalis finds in Kant seems to be the latter's inability to recognize the transformative and transpositional power of the human imagination for turning feeling and inner experience into something concrete and external. Yet Novalis's diagnosis of Kant's one-sidedness is perhaps too hasty. There is much in Kant's work, especially tied to his aesthetic theory, that suggests real sympathy for the sort of position Novalis eventually develops. Frederick Beiser has argued that Kant "divorced" himself from metaphysics after 1765, whereupon he directed his philosophical energies more to practical concerns.[20] The *locus classicus* of Kant's self-avowed conversion to the primacy of the practical is a statement made in his "Remarks on the 'Observations on the Feeling of the Beautiful and the Sublime'":

> I am myself by inclination a seeker after truth. I feel a consuming thirst for knowledge and a restless desire to advance in it, as well as a satisfaction in every step I take. There was a time when I thought that this alone could constitute the honor of mankind, and I despised the common man who knows nothing. Rousseau set me right. This pretended superiority vanished and I learned to respect humanity. I should consider myself far more useless than the common laborer if I did not believe that one consideration alone gives worth to all others, namely, to establish the rights of man.[21]

Beiser sees the concern expressed by Kant that his philosophizing be "useful" as a concern shared generally by later Enlighteners in Germany:

> The *Aufklärung* was a practical movement insofar as its purpose was not to discover the first principles of reason – most *Aufklärer* believed that this task had already been achieved by thinkers such as Leibniz,

Wolff, and Kant – but to bring them into daily life. In short, its aim was to surmount the gap between reason and life, theory and practice, speculation and action.... Most thinkers of the late eighteenth century saw themselves as *Aufklärer*, not only older figures such as Kant, Herder, and Wieland, but also younger ones such as Schlegel, Hölderlin, and Novalis.[22]

This turn to the practical explains, according to Beiser, why Kant comes to manifest a "complete skepticism toward metaphysics." It is so deep, he says, that in *Dreams of a Spirit-Seer*, "he likens metaphysics to the dreams of the visionary or spirit-seer,"[23] and he also claims that for Kant

> Both metaphysicians and spirit seers live in a private fantasy world and chase after illusory abstractions ... the aim of [Kant's] skepticism [about metaphysics] is to expose the vanity of speculation, so that we direct our efforts toward finding what is truly useful for human life.[24]

In giving preference to practical over theoretical reason, Beiser suggests, the honeymoon with metaphysics is over for Kant. Still, Beiser correctly maintains that the supposed divorce was never fully carried out, and that "the flames of the old love affair burnt to the bitter end" of Kant's life.[25] Beiser finds the old flame burning most strongly in Kant's hypostatizing in the second *Critique* of the conditions under which human beings could hope to bring about a just world – the highest good, that is, in the postulates of metaphysical notions of God and immortality. This return to metaphysics constitutes a "deep betrayal" of the radical spirit of his republican politics, and represents an inconsistency in his philosophy, Beiser says.[26]

Although Beiser is surely correct to point to Kant's disillusionment with metaphysics in 1765 and even before, he overstates the situation in labeling Kant's position one of "complete skepticism" about the value of metaphysics. While it is true that Kant castigates metaphysics for being *schwärmerisch*, and prone to fanaticism, it is important to remember that Kant was not himself immune to "enthusiasm," nor was he ashamed to admit that fact. The oft-cited passage from the "Remarks" is certainly indicative of Kant's own susceptibility to *Schwärmerei*, both for knowledge and morality: he confesses to a "consuming thirst for knowledge and a restless desire to advance it" that only gave way after reading Rousseau to an even more consuming desire "to establish the rights of man." Even more important, from time to time throughout his career Kant actually embraced metaphysical *Schwärmerei* in the service of morality and eventually even found a limited place for this enthusiasm in the critical system. Thus Kant's critical philosophy by no means forecloses the early romantic option of seeking a back door to paradise.

There are a number of places where Kant discusses *Schwärmerei* or enthusiasm and admits that it has, or at least is capable of having, a positive moral value. In his "Reflections on Anthropology," Kant defines the "fantast" as one who takes his own fictions for reality, and he identifies two kinds: the "fantast of sensation" and "of concepts." The former are "dreamers" who mistake their own feelings for actual perceptions, i.e. they take what is merely in their thoughts to be perceived through the bodily senses (lovers and melancholics are examples he gives).[27] Fantasts of concepts are visionaries, or "enthusiasts" who "realize" i.e. take to be real, the idea of the Good. Fantasts of both sorts confuse imagination with reality, but it is for the latter that Kant has the most sympathy. Kant claims that Rousseau and Plato were just such enthusiasts of reason.[28]

In the essay entitled "An Old Question Raised Again: Is the Human Race Constantly Progressing?" written in 1794 and published in 1798 as the second section of "Streit der Fakultäten," Kant writes that

> There must be some experience in the human race which, as an event, points to the disposition and capacity of the human race to be the cause of its own advance toward the better, and . . . toward the human race as being the author of this advance.[29]

Kant uses the question of moral progress to take the opportunity to express his own support for the goals, if not the means, of the French Revolution. Yet the "event" that indicates the human capacity for moral progress is not the revolution, but rather "the mode of thinking [Denkungsart] of the spectators." That is, the event that indicates human ability to be the "author" of a more moral world is the publicly expressed, unselfish (uneigennützig) feeling of sympathy and excitement for those who participate in struggles to end human oppression. The glimmer of hope that history holds out to those seeking reason to believe in moral progress is the spectators' "wishful participation that borders on enthusiasm," an enthusiasm that Kant identifies as a "passionate participation in the good."[30] Or, in other words, these spectators' moral passion is aroused by the vision of their moral and political ideals being realized.

As we saw, Kant's reference to enthusiasm is a reference to a particular use of imagination in which ideas are taken to be real. Kant certainly worried that this enthusiasm could be simply a kind of madness, and he by no means glorified the state. The point here is simply to note his ambivalence. In the same passage from the "Old Question" Kant makes a point that he repeatedly made in his lectures on anthropology: "Genuine enthusiasm always moves only toward what is ideal and, indeed, to what is purely moral, such as the concept of right."[31] In his anthropology lectures[32] during the 1770s, Kant told his students that "An enthusiast is always a noble Fantast, *full of life and strength*, and so, in addition, inclined to virtue. Indeed, much that is good disappears from the land where they are purged."[33] Kant is of course not arguing that we all incorporate enthusiastic tendencies into our moral development. He is simply responding to the view that all madness is evil and must be rooted out. During periods of crisis such as the one he knew so well, Kant was no doubt well aware how easily politically radical views could be dismissed and "treated" as a kind of insanity. Spectators to the revolution, whose sympathetic fervor "borders" on enthusiasm, are a mild and even socially useful case of the disease because they approach the state of mind of the "noble fantast" in their ability to visualize and desire the ideal.

In this respect they also resemble the metaphysicians maligned by Kant in "Dreams of a Spirit-Seer." Kant associates Rousseau with this sort of enthusiasm, yet it was Rousseau who awakened him from his dogmatic metaphysical slumbers and caused him to divorce himself from "elitist" metaphysical speculation in favor of the practical! Kant's fondness for Rousseau, and his more tolerant views on moral visionaries in general, may have prompted him in the end to find a systematic place for this sort of "fantastic" thinking in his philosophy. One place where it appears that Kant may be doing precisely that is in the third *Critique* at section 17 ("On the Ideal of Beauty"). Kant here describes a kind of judging that involves the connecting of intuitive presentations with a moral idea, producing a concrete presentation of what is merely a rational idea. In the exhibition of this idea of reason, imagination makes the realization of that idea *subjectively* possible – "imaginable." For instance, perfect human virtue is an unattainable ideal. But "a very strong imagination" can give this intellectual idea a flesh and blood quality that it did not have before, bringing it down to earth, as it were, and enabling a vision of that which moral reason requires human beings to strive for.[34] Interestingly enough, Kant hints that this will not be found in all people:

> in order for this connection to be made visible, as it were, in bodily expression (as an effect of what is inward), pure ideas of reason must be united with a very strong imagination in someone who seeks so much as to judge, let alone exhibit it.[35]

The similarities in this section of the third *Critique* to Kant's account of the "pathological" state of the fantast of reason are clear: the person judging according to an ideal of beauty is seeing genuine reality in his/her idea. And yet here Kant is in no way suggesting that taking ideas for reality is deranged. It is simply a way of putting aesthetic judgment to moral use, although presumably only a few will have the requisite powers of imagination to produce this ideal. Here at last, Kant's abandoned metaphysical longings seem to have found a new home in aesthetic feeling.

Of course, in Kant's account of taste, the pleasure taken in the beautiful object is not bound up with an interest, that is, with the desire for the existence of the object. This is what it means to say that we take a disinterested pleasure in the beautiful. "But," Kant says, "it does not follow from this that, after the judgment has been made as a pure aesthetic one, an interest cannot be connected with it."[36] Kant then allows two possibilities: one "empirical" and the other "intellectual," and it is the intellectual interest arising from disinterested pleasure that appears to be a repackaged version of Kant's old desire for meta-physics. Since reason has an interest, as Kant puts it, in the "objective reality" of its moral ideas, it cannot be a matter of complete indifference to us, when contemplating the beautiful, that nature here "shows a trace or gives a hint that it contains some basis or other for us to assume" an orderliness that may be conducive to, or at least not out of sync with, our moral desires.[37]

Kant is suggesting that in the process of making an aesthetic reflective judg-ment about the beauty of an object, we may come to care for the nature of which it is but a part. We may come to value the whole of the natural world for its own sake. A condition of this disinterested love of the world may be the fact that we, as moral beings, are charged with the task of bringing moral order into the natural world – a demand on human nature that hardly seems possible. Thus we are intellectually interested in finding that nature outside us, in what appears to be the rational orderliness and purposiveness of her beauty, may be suited to the nature "within."

At this point we may return to Novalis. For the feeling of pleasure that we take in the "hint" of a rational order outside ourselves is precisely that longing for the absolute that Novalis argued human beings can attain through art. Kant retains a place for metaphysics and the enthusiasm it breeds by reintroducing it into his theory of aesthetic reflection. Here it is no longer "banished altogether" but is nevertheless contained: it may project visions and fantasies in its judgments about beauty and in the course of artistic creativity. It may even take a kind of moral interest in these aesthetic constructions. But they can never be more than regula-tive longings. The person who comes to love the whole of nature based on disinterested contemplation bears a close resemblance to the "noble fantast" and finds her place alongside Plato's philosopher gazing out of the cave, or with Rousseau, surveying the natural goodness of humanity in the state of nature, or even standing with Kant, gazing in awe at the starry heavens above. In Kant's terms, all these persons take an intellectual interest in the beautiful, And, what is most interesting for our purposes, they are also "romanticizing" in Novalis's sense of the term. The desire to recognize inner human states in the outer world, to make the unknown known, is precisely the way Kant defines the fantast. Kant had already discerned Novalis's recipe for romanticizing the world.

That the desire for metaphysical speculation is inevitable and unavoidable is, of course, a recurring theme in the first *Critique*. Reason seeks the uncondi-tioned by its very nature. For Kant, as for Novalis, the danger is believing that one has found it. Both Novalis and Kant advocate a certain tough-minded resis-tance to the urge to take flight in fantasy and to forget the actual world. But as we saw, Kant's attitude toward fanaticism is not uniformly negative, and in a footnote in the *First Introduction to the Critique of Judgment* ("On the Aesthetic Power of Judgment") Kant makes the following surprising admission:

> In fact man can desire something most fervently and persistently even
> though he is convinced that he cannot achieve it, or that it is perhaps

even [something] absolutely impossible . . . and it is indeed an important article for morality to warn us emphatically against such empty and fanciful desires, which are often nourished by novels and sometimes also by mystical presentations, similar to novels, of superhuman perfections and fanatical bliss. But some empty desires and longings . . . do have their effect on the mind. . . . It is indeed a not unimportant problem for anthropology to investigate why it is that nature has given us the predisposition to such fruitless expenditure of our forces as [we see in] empty wishes and longings (which certainly play a large role in human life). It seems to me that here, as in all else, nature has made wise provisions. For if we had to assure ourselves that we can in fact produce the object, before the presentation of it could determine us to apply our forces, our forces would presumably remain largely unused. For usually we do not come to know what forces we have except by trying them out. So nature has provided for the connection between the determination of our forces and the presentation of the object [to be there] even before we know what ability we have, and it is often precisely this effort, which to that very mind seemed at first an empty wish, that produces that ability in the first place. Now wisdom is obligated to set limits to that instinct, but wisdom will never succeed in eradicating it, or [rather] it will never even demand its eradication.[38]

So a "a predisposition" to "empty desires and longings" that appear to be a "fruitless expenditure of our forces" could in fact be an enabling mechanism – part of nature's plan for advancing human capacities unbeknownst to them. In the end, Kant seems to have finally settled on the view that the *desire* for metaphysics is useful, and may, indeed *ought* to be, embraced by Enlightenment.

Conclusion

Kant, like Novalis, firmly believed that longing and striving for the absolute, the unconditioned, was an essential characteristic of human reason that neither could nor should be entirely resisted. Both also agreed that knowledge of the absolute could never be attained, and that claims to have done so were necessarily in error. The difference between Kant and Novalis was thus not a difference over the value of unattainable rational ideals or the need to avoid transcendent delusions. What really separates the two is Kant's willingness to simply accept the limitations of human reason and hence of philosophy. Novalis took this resignation to be a kind of "scholasticism" – a "one-sided" approach that assigned philosophy to the domain of reason alone. His innovation, and that of his cohort in Jena, was to redefine philosophy itself as an "unending, free activity" that at its limits may become an aesthetic, creative endeavor.

JANE KNELLER

Notes

1 *Heinrich von Kleist: Werke in einem Band*, Munich, Karl Hanser Verlag, 1966, 802–7.
2 All references to Novalis's works are to *Novalis Schriften: Die Werke Friedrich von Hardenbergs*, edited by Paul Kluckhohn and Richard Samuel, Stuttgart, Verlag W. Kohlhammer. The second and third volumes, edited by Samuel together with Hans-Joachim Mähl and Gerhard Schulz, contain Novalis's philosophical writings, published in1981 and 1983 respectively.
3 Although Kant was not always comfortable with this attitude. Kant throughout his life was fascinated by apparently "supernatural" phenomena. Cf. Hartmut and Gernot Böhme's *Das Andere der Vernunft*, Frankfurt, Suhrkamp, 1996.
4 In this essay I deal only with Novalis and his circle of early German romantics. The later romantics, especially those associated with Heidelberg, but even including Schlegel and Tieck in their later period, are not under discussion here.
5 Manfred Frank, in *Einführung in die Frühromantische Ästhetik*, Frankfurt, Suhrkamp,1989, p. 248. Novalis's work, which included the so-called *Fichte Studies* and *Kant Studies*, comprised about 500 pages of handwritten notes that were left unpublished until 1901, when Ernst Heilborn brought out a substantial selection of the notes. The entire set, however, remained unpublished and was lost to scholarship for thirty years between 1930 and 1960, when it resurfaced at an auction in New York.
6 Geza von Molnár argues for this point in *Novalis's 'Fichte Studies': The Foundations of His Aesthetics*, The Hague, Mouton Press, 1970, pp. 41–2.
7 Hemsterhuis lived from 1721 to 1790. See Hans-Joachim Mähl's introduction to the Kant and Eschenmeyer Studies, *Novalis Schriften* 2:334. According to Mähl, based on the handwriting and the type and format of the paper, these were probably written during or immediately following his work on Hemsterhuis, and within a year after finishing the *Fichte Studies* in 1796.
8 *Ibid.*, p. 332. The fact that his focus of study seems to have been primarily the preface and introduction to the first *Critique* as well as the *Metaphysical Foundations of Natural Science* also supports this view.
9 See the letter to Sömmerring dated 10 August 1795. *Kants gesammelte Schriften*, Prussian Academy edn, XII.3:30–5.
10 Although Novalis appeared to believe that some sort of phenomenology, a science of inner sense, is possible. As we saw, he also took Fichte to be the "Newton" of this science. See *Allgemeine Brouillon*, *Novalis Schriften*, 3:335 (#460).
11 Cf. Hans-Joachim Mähl's introduction, II: 314ff.
12 This is taken from the *Fragmentblatt* found along with the Kant notes (*Schriften*, II:395, #55) It follows a remarkable passage in which Novalis suggests, presumably in opposition to Fichte's notion of an originary self-postulation or *Tathandlung*, that "the true philosophical act is suicide . . . only this act corresponds to all the conditions and characteristics of the transcendental act." I.e. we can't bring ourselves into being, but we can take ourselves out.
13 *Kant-Studien* #49, 2:392.
14 See FS #649: "we are also in a sphere outside time" – Novalis retains Kant's view that to be human means to be able to "transport" oneself into a realm of intellect.
15 See my "The Failure of Kant's Imagination," in *What is Enlightenment?: Eighteenth-century Answers and Twentieth-century Questions*, James Schmidt (ed.), Berkeley, University of California Press, 1997, pp. 453–70, for a discussion of the role imagination did and could have played in Kant's overall theory.
16 2:545, #105.
17 Cf. Frank, *Einführung*, p. 253.
18 E.g. in the *Groundwork of the Metaphysics of Morals*, IV:452ff.
19 *Novalis Schriften* II, p. 420, #22.

20 Frederick Beiser, *Enlightenment, Revolution, and Romanticism*, Cambridge MA, Harvard University Press, 1992; and in his "Kant's Intellectual Development: 1746–1781" in the *Cambridge Companion to Kant*, Paul Guyer (ed.), Cambridge, Cambridge University Press, 1992, pp. 26–61.

21 *Kants Schriften*, XX:8–16.

22 F. Beiser, *Enlightenment, Revolution and Romanticism*, p. 9.

23 F. Beiser, "Kant's Intellectual Development," *Cambridge Companion to Kant*, p. 45.

24 In "The Politics of Kant's Critical Philosophy," *Enlightenment, Revolution and Romanticism*, *op. cit.*, p. 28.

25 F. Beiser, "Kant's Intellectual Development," p. 57.

26 F. Beiser, *Enlightenment, Revolution and Romanticism*, p. 55.

27 *Kants Schriften*, 15.1:210, #488; and 217,#499.

28 *Ibid.*, 15.1:210, #488. See also the lecture notes. For example, the Pillau notes: 25:2.2:764, 767.

29 The essay, although complete in its own right, was included as the second part of the 1798 publication entitled *Streit der Fakultäten*. The translation here is from *Kant on History*, edited by Lewis White Beck (New York, Macmillan, 1986) pp. 137–54. The citation is from p. 142 (AK VII:84–5).

30 *Ibid.*, VII: 85, 86.

31 *Ibid.*, VII:86.

32 Based on the notes taken by a student, Theodor Friederich Brauer, dated 1779, taken from transcripts now available at the Philips-Universität Marburg. I would like to thank Werner Stark for assistance in the use of these materials, and for helpful information about the historical context in which they were written. Although these sources are from student transcriptions of Kant's lectures, and are therefore not the final word on any disputed question in Kant interpretation, nothing that I rely on here is out of character for Kant, but rather corroborates views he expressed elsewhere on enthusiasm. I have relied only on passages from Brauer that also appear in notes taken down by other students during that time.

33 Brauer, ms. p. 88.

34 Kant, *Critique of Judgment*, trans. Werner Pluhar, Minneapolis, Hackett, 1987, V:231ff. All translations here are from Pluhar. Page references are to the Academy Edition pagination indicated in his text.

    The potential value of imagination's capacity to enliven morality is especially apparent in the case of Kant's doctrine of the Highest Good, that is, of a moral world in which virtue and happiness are commensurate, or at least in which human beings make every effort to maximize the correspondence of happiness to virtue. In the *Critique of Practical Reason*, Kant argues that the moral law requires that human beings strive to bring about such a moral world on earth, but that in order for this command to be legitimate, it must be possible for human beings to believe that such a command could be fulfilled, i.e. they must have some rational hope that the end commanded is possible. As is well known, at this point Kant argues that human beings have no reason to suppose that they *can* bring about a perfectly moral world in which happiness coincides with virtue, and so they must postulate the existence of God (and the immortality of the soul) to ground their hope, and to make action in accordance with the moral law rational. This is the place, according to Beiser, where we see Kant bringing metaphysics in the service of the practical.

35 *Critique of Judgment*, V:235.

36 *Critique of Judgment*, VII:296.

37 *Ibid.*, VII:300.

38 *First Introduction to the Critique of Judgment*, Ak 11:230–1, n. 50. Published in Pluhar translation of the *Critique of Judgment*, pp. 383–441.

Part IV

THE LIVING FORCE OF THINGS

10

THE PARADOX OF ROMANTIC METAPHYSICS

Frederick Beiser

A strange wedding plan

By the late 1790s, some of the leading romantic thinkers in Germany had already sketched the basic outlines of their new metaphysics, the *Weltanschauung* that would later become so characteristic of the romantic school. From 1795 to 1797 Hölderlin, Novalis and Friedrich Schlegel drafted the rudiments of this metaphysics in various fragments; Schelling later gave it more systematic formulation in his 1800 *System des transcendentalen Idealismus* and 1801 *Darstellung meines Systems*. In the formulation of this doctrine there are some important differences between these thinkers; but there are also some striking similarities, some common characteristics. Just one of these characteristics will be our special concern here.

This was the attempt of romantic metaphysics to synthesize idealism and realism, and more specifically the idealism of Fichte and the realism of Spinoza.[1] *Prima facie* this characteristic is puzzling and problematic. Without doubt, Fichte and Spinoza were the most influential philosophers upon the romantic generation. But they were also, in fundamental respects, completely incompatible: Fichte's idealism, indeterminism and dualism clash with Spinoza's realism, determinism and monism. Though perfectly aware of these incompatibilities, the romantics still wanted to join them. Nothing less than marriage would do because, in their view, each had captured but one half of the truth. Just like ideal wedding partners, Fichte and Spinoza were perfect complements in an indissoluble whole.

The first reaction anyone is likely to have about this project is that it is a quixotic absurdity, another romantic *Schnappside* which, fortunately, never came to fruition. Fichte's idealism and Spinoza's realism are so contradictory, so fundamentally opposed in both purpose and content, that it seems any attempt to unite them is doomed to failure. One might as well try to square the circle. Surely, it does not bode well that Kant and Fichte themselves ruled out any thought of a liasion with Spinoza. Explicitly and emphatically, they conceived their idealism as the *antithesis* of Spinoza's realism and naturalism.[2] The only remedy against his fatalism, they warned, lay with their transcendental idealism.

Such suspicions pose questions. How did the romantics attempt to unite Fichte and Spinoza? And could such a synthesis be coherent? Any attempt to understand the romantic *Weltanschauung* must, I believe, eventually come to terms with these questions. All too often romantic metaphysics is understood as a poetic form of Fichte's idealism or of Spinoza's naturalism, as if it were one or the other. But these common interpretations are too one-sided, missing what is the most striking characteristic of romantic metaphysics: its attempt to wed Fichte and Spinoza. If this marriage is not understood, the most characteristic feature of romantic metaphysics remains a cipher, a paradox.

Dated though it might seem, there is still something of abiding interest in the romantic project of synthesizing Fichte and Spinoza. Nowadays philosophers often write of the bankruptcy of the Cartesian tradition, whose epistemology ends in a complete subjectivism, the limitation of knowledge to the circle of consciousness; they see the antidote to such subjectivism in a naturalistic or a Heideggerian ontology, which makes the self either part of nature or part of history. But such a remedy is problematic, not least because it does not answer the skeptical problems that motivated Cartesian epistemology in the first place: How do we *know* that there is a nature or history beyond consciousness? We are then left with a dilemma: either skeptical epistemology or dogmatic ontology. It is one of the most intriguing aspects of romantic metaphysics that it attempted to escape these extremes. The young romantics knew this dilemma all too well: it was present for them in the choice between Kantian criticism or Spinozian dogmatism. The point of their synthesis of Fichte and Spinoza was to surmount this dilemma, avoiding the extremes of both subjectivism and dogmatism, and combining the virtues of a critical epistemology with a naturalistic ontology.

What follows is an attempt to unravel the paradox of romantic metaphysics, to explain their attempt to surmount this apparently eternal dilemma. Romantic metaphysics is perfectly comprehensible and coherent, I will argue, once we place it in the context of its underlying organic concept of nature. It was this concept that allowed the romantics to join Fichte's idealism with Spinoza's naturalism, Fichte's belief in the primacy of the self and Spinoza's faith in the priority of nature.

Of course, there is nothing new in stressing the importance of the organic concept for romanticism. For generations, scholars have emphasized its crucial role, seeing it as a central characteristic of the romantic *Weltanschauung*.[3] It must be said, however, that this traditional view does not agree with the most recent trend of *Romantikforschung*, which has questioned the old emphasis on the organic concept, and which has stressed instead the lack of completeness and closure in romantic thought.[4] We shall soon see, though, that this organic concept is indispensable in unraveling the paradox of romantic metaphysics, and more specifically in understanding its apparently quixotic attempt to wed idealism and realism. This will help to vindicate the older scholarly tradition and to restore the rightful place of the organic in romantic thinking.

Profile of a mismatch

Before we explain the romantic project, it is necessary to have a more concrete idea of the challenge facing them. What, more precisely, were the incompatibilities between Fichte and Spinoza?

There are several basic issues dividing Fichte and Spinoza. First, they are at odds concerning the reality of the external world or nature. Fichte's philosophy is *idealistic*: it denies the reality of the thing-in-itself, that is, anything that exists independent of our awareness of it; and it maintains that everything exists for some actual or possible consciousness. In contrast, Spinoza's philosopy is *realistic*: it affirms the reality of the whole of nature, which exists independent of, and prior to, awareness of it. Rather than existing only for some subject, subjectivity is simply a mode, appearance, or part of nature as a whole. Second, Fichte and Spinoza clash concerning the scope of natural explanation. Fichte's philosophy is *anti-naturalistic*: it limits the realm of nature to experience, and it postulates a realm of reason and freedom beyond experience. Spinoza's philosophy, however, is *radically naturalistic*: it places everything within nature, so that nothing escapes its laws. Following from this second difference, Fichte affirms, and Spinoza denies, the reality of human freedom in one very important sense: the power of choice, the capacity to do otherwise independent of external causes. For Spinoza, human volition and action are parts of nature, and so occur of necessity according to its laws; for Fichte, however, human volition and action transcend nature, so that it is possible for them to be otherwise.

The conflict between Fichte and Spinoza appears at its most extreme when we consider the third issue dividing them: their opposing visions of ultimate reality or the absolute. Fichte makes the ego his absolute, proposing to explain all of nature as its product; Spinoza makes nature his absolute, attempting to explain the ego as its product. We cannot combine Fichte and Spinoza, then, any more than affirm the existence of two absolutes, two infinite realities. We cannot both "make the self everything and the world nothing *and* the world everything and the self nothing."[5]

Our suspicions about the romantic synthesis only grow when we ponder what they saw in Fichte and Spinoza. What attracted the romantics to Fichte was his radical concept of human freedom, according to which the self posits itself, making itself what it is. It was this concept of the self-positing that rationalized the French Revolution, the right of the self to remake laws and institutions according to the demands of reason. As supporters of the Revolution in France, the young romantics could only embrace the concept behind it. What the romantics admired in Spinoza was his synthesis of religion and science. Spinoza's pantheism seemed to resolve all the traditional conflicts between reason and faith. It had made a religion out of science by divinizing nature, and a science out of religion by naturalizing the divine. But it is precisely in these respects that Fichte and Spinoza seem utterly irreconcilable. If nature is divine, then it is infinite, and everything should fall under its laws; hence there cannot be any transcendental realm of freedom above and beyond nature. Rather than creating itself, the self will simply realize of necessity the essence given to it by the natural order of things.

Given all these incompatibilities, it seems there can be no hope for a marriage of Fichte and Spinoza. We cannot wed them anymore than we can pair idealists and realists, dualists and monists, indeterminists and determinists. If marriages between opposites sometimes succeed, that is only because of some deeper underlying affinity. But here we find none. Why attempt to wed enemies?

Subject-object identity

Ironically, it was Fichte who first inspired the matchmaking efforts of the romantics. Despite all his bluster against Spinoza, Fichte virtually forced the romantics to embrace his nemesis as his necessary complement. This was the inevitable result of one of the fundamental principles of the *Wissenschaftslehre*, the principle that Fichte sometimes called *subject-object* identity, the thesis that the subjective and objective, the ideal and real, are ultimately the same. Taking their cue from this principle, the romantics used it to rationalize their move beyond Fichte. They took the subjective or ideal pole to represent Fichte's idealism, the objective or real pole to stand for Spinoza's realism.

Why did the romantics feel compelled to interpret Fichte's principle in such an anti-Fichtean manner? The answer lies in the inherent difficulties of Fichte's own interpretation of this principle. In the Jena *Wissenschaftslehre* Fichte interpreted subject-object identity essentially in terms of self-knowledge. Since knower and known are the same in self-knowledge, it has the required identity of subject and object, ideal and real. Fichte believed that this fact alone should entitle self-knowledge to be the paradigm of all knowledge. Since all knowledge presupposes some identity of knower and known, and since such identity is demonstrable in self-knowledge, self-knowledge should be the basis for all knowledge. If we can somehow show that all knowledge is a form of self-knowledge – even if subconscious self-knowledge – then we will provide a foundation for it.[6]

The inspiration behind Fichte's principle was nothing less than the guiding idea behind Kant's "new method of thought": that we know a priori only what we create.[7] Kant had claimed that the innate activity of the mind is transparent to itself, so that whatever it creates it knows.[8] Since the self embodies or reveals its activity in its objects, its knowledge of them amounts to a form of self-knowledge, so that self-knowledge is the paradigm of all knowledge. This paradigm of knowledge plays a basic – if not entirely explicit – role in the Transcendental Deduction of the first *Kritik* in the form of the unity of apperception, the "I think" or self-awareness that accompanies all representations. Such self-awareness amounts to the self's awareness of its own creativity, whose products are the various forms of a priori synthesis, namely the categories of understanding and forms of space and time of sensibility.

In fundamental respects the romantics adopted Fichte's principle of subject-object identity. They agreed with Fichte that the principle of subject-object identity amounts to some form of self-knowledge, and that self-knowledge should be the basis of all knowledge. But they took issue with him regarding his *one-sided* subjectivist reading of this principle. Fichte's reading of this principle is subjectivist, in their view, insofar as it locates subject-object identity in the self-awareness of the transcendental subject, in the *Ich denke* of the unity of apperception or the *Ich bin Ich* of the *Wissenschaftslehre*. For Fichte, subject-object identity essentially consists in transcendental self-knowledge, the subject's awareness of its spontaneous activity. He insisted that such identity must be *immanent*, lying within the realm of possible consciousness; to place it outside this realm, as Spinoza had, was *transcendent*, nothing less than hypostasis, "the fallacy of pure reason."[9]

The romantics made two fundamental objections against Fichte's subjectivist interpretation of the principle of subject-object identity. First, the very concepts of the subjective and objective make sense only in contrast to one another; they have their specific meaning only within the realm of experience; but the principle is supposed to be transcendental, explaining the very possibility of experience, and so cannot be within experience; in that case, however, it cannot be either subjective or objective.[10] Second, such a reading makes it impossible for the principle to perform its function of explaining the possibility of knowledge. If it is a constitutive or theoretical principle, such as "I am" or "I think," then it cannot derive the dualism between the subject and object in experience, let alone the content of empirical knowledge. If, however, it is a regulative or practical principle, which expresses nothing more than the striving of the ego to control nature, then we are caught in a dilemma. Insofar as the ego dominates nature, the object is nothing more than a product of its activity, a mere noumenon; but insofar as it does not dominate nature, the object is an unknowable = X. We therefore have to choose between self-knowledge or a thing-in-itself. Toward the close of the 1794 *Wissenschaftslehre* Fichte admitted that this dilemma was unavoidable for any finite knower. For the young Schelling and Hegel, this was tantamount to an admission of failure.[11]

The essence of the romantics' critique of Fichte's principle is that it does no justice to the reality of experience, the existence of the external world. Fichte's principle of subject-object identity is subjectivist because it does not accommodate the experience of the objective world. *Prima facie* this objection seems unfair because Fichte intended his transcendental idealism to be a form of *empirical realism*, which explains the reality of things in space independent of the conscious subject. It was indeed the very purpose of the *Wissenschaftslehre* to explain the feeling of necessity accompanying our representations, the fact that they appear to come and go independent of our will and imagination. But the romantics were very well aware of Fichte's intentions; their point against him is twofold: first, empirical realism is insufficient; and second, Fichte does not even guarantee that. Empirical realism is insufficient because although it allows objects to exist independent of the empirical self, it does not permit them to exist independent of the transcendental self, who is the lawgiver of nature. The romantics wanted to go further than Fichte in giving an independent reality to nature; they demanded a "higher realism," which would give reality to nature independent of the self, whether empirical or transcendental.[12] This higher realism was both a ground for, and result of, their sympathy for Spinoza. Second, Fichte could not establish even his empirical realism because he admitted that the first principle of the *Wissenschaftslehre*, "the ego posits itself absolutely," cannot derive the reality of the non-ego, which is opposed to itself. All the immensely subtle and sophisticated reasoning of the first part of the 1794 *Grundlage der gesammten Wissenschaftslehre* finally came to the conclusion that the self-positing ego cannot limit itself by positing a non-ego opposed to itself. The failure of Fichte's deduction program in the 1794 *Grundlage* was crucial in convincing the romantics to go beyond the limits of his own subjectivist principles.

The organic concept of nature

It was the need to explain the reality of the external world, to do justice to the sheer otherness of the non-ego, that eventually forced the romantics to abandon the one-sidedness of Fichte's idealism and to complement it with the "higher realism" of Spinoza. Somehow, they would have to find an interpretation of the principle of subject-object identity that would accomodate our experience of an external world. This was an inherently paradoxical undertaking, since the principle of subject-object identity postulates the identity of subject and object, but ordinary experience seems to show that they are distinct from one another. Somehow, there would have to be an identity of subject-object identity and subject-object non-identity. But merely to formulate the desideratum one seems to contradict oneself. Another way of formulating this desideratum – no less paradoxical – is to claim that there must be some unity of Fichte's idealism and Spinoza's realism.

For the romantics, the path out of this impasse lay with their organic conception of nature. This conception was developed in greatest detail and rigor by Schelling, first in his 1799 *Von der Weltseele* and then in his 1798 *Entwurf eines Systems der Naturphilosophie*. But the same idea also appears in the notebooks of Friedrich Schlegel, Novalis and Hölderlin.

The fundamental concept behind the romantic concept of nature is that of a natural purpose (*Naturzweck*). Kant had defined this concept very specifically in section 65 of the *Kritik der Urteilskraft*, a crucial text for Schelling and the romantics. Something is a natural purpose, Kant wrote, only if it satisfies two essential conditions. First, it must have *organic unity*, where each part is insepable from the whole, and where the idea of the whole determines the place of each part. Second, it must be *self*-generating and *self*-organizing, so that all parts are reciprocally the cause and effect of one another, having no outside cause. Kant argues that this second condition is the specific characteristic of a natural purpose as opposed to a work of art. Both works of art and natural purposes have in common that they are produced according to some idea of the whole; but only a natural purpose is *self*-productive. Its design and structure arise from within according to some internal principle; they do not arise from outside, as in a work of art.

The organic concept of nature arose from generalizing or extending Kant's idea of a natural purpose, so that it held for nature as a whole. The organic concept means that nature as a whole is one vast natural purpose, each of whose parts are also such purposes, so that nature is an organism of organisms. This concept postulates a single living force throughout all of nature, so that all the different species of minerals, plants and animals, and even all the different kinds of matter, are simply so many different degrees of its organization and development. All of nature then forms one huge hierarchy, which consists in the various stages of organization and development of living force. Living force first manifests itself in the most simple forms of matter; it then passes through the more complex minerals, vegetables, and animals; and finally it ends with the most sophisticated forms of life, such as the self-consciousness of the transcendental philosopher and the creativity of artistic genius itself. Such self-consciousness is nothing less than the highest organization and development of all the powers of nature. This means that the artist's or philosopher's awareness of nature is also nature coming to its *self-awareness* through them.

The most important implication of the organic concept of nature is that there is no distinction of kind, but only one of degree, between the mental and physical. The mind and body are no longer heterogeneous substances, but they are only different levels of organization and development of the single living force throughout nature. The mental is simply the highest degree of organization and development of the living forces active in matter; and matter is merely the lowest degree of organization and development of the living forces present in the mind. We can therefore regard mind as highly organized and developed matter, matter as less organized and developed mind. As Schelling put the point: "Nature should be visible spirit, and spirit invisible nature" (II 56).

The rationale for organicism

No doubt, Schelling's organic concept of nature is daring and imaginative, and it has duly been condemned by positivists and neo-Kantians for careless and excessive speculation. But such judgments fail to consider the context of

Naturphilosophie, and more specifically the crisis of physics and physiology at the close of the eighteenth century. While Schelling could not – and did not – claim final experimental proof for his concept, he did believe it to be warranted by the latest scientific results of his day. More importantly, however, Schelling developed his concept in the first place because he saw it as the only solution to the persistent problems facing physiology and physics. The main argument for the organic concept was more conceptual than empirical: it alone seemed to resolve the crises inherent in eighteenth-century natural science.

Schelling proposed his concept first and foremost as a solution to an apparently inescapable dilemma which had troubled physiology since the early seventeenth century: dualism versus mechanistic materialism. These extremes seemed to be the only possibilities if one adopted the Cartesian concept of matter and its paradigm of mechanical explanation. According to that concept, the essence of matter consists in extension, and it is inherently inert, moving only if it is moved by some external force. According to that paradigm, we explain all events as due to the impact of one body upon another, where we measure impact in terms of how much a body must change its place within a given amount of time. If we adopt this concept and paradigm, then we have to choose between two unwelcome alternatives: either we place life outside nature – and so become dualists – or we reduce it down to matter in motion – and so become mechanists. But both alternatives are unsatisfactory. While the mechanist upholds the principles of naturalism, he seems to ignore the characteristic qualities of life; and whereas the dualist recognizes such qualities, he transports them into a mysterious *sui generis* realm where they cannot be explained according to the methods of science.

It was the purpose of Schelling's organic concept to provide some middle path between the horns of this dilemma.[13] Schelling agreed with the dualist that mechanism could not explain the *sui generis* characteristics of life; but he also sympathized with the efforts of the materialist to explain life according to natural laws. The organic concept of nature alone, he believed, could avoid the problems of both dualism and materialism by providing a *naturalistic yet non-reductivistic* account of life and the mind. Since an organism is not reducible to a mechanism, it does not reduce life down to a machine; but since it also acts according to natural laws, there is no violation of the principles of naturalism. Hence the organic concept calls into question the common premise behind dualism and materialism: that all natural explanation is mechanical. Rather than accounting for natural events by external causes acting upon them, it explains them by their necessary place in a systematic whole. The paradigm of explanation is now holistic rather than analytical or atomistic.

Schelling's organic concept was dictated not only by a crisis in physiology, but also by one in physics. In the late eighteenth century the main challenge to physics came essentially from the fact that the mechanical paradigm, which had dominated physics ever since Descartes, no longer seemed to account for matter itself. The source of the problem lay with Newton's law of gravity. No one could doubt Newton's law, which had been confirmed time and again by observation and experiment; yet it postulated a force of attraction between bodies which seemed to operate through empty space. Hence arose the question of "action at a distance." This was a serious problem for the mechanical physics, which insisted that one body acts upon one another only through impact, by one body striking another. Stubbornly but desperately, some physicists attempted to explain gravitational attraction by postulating subtle media or fluids between bodies; but experiments failed to detect their presence.[14]

The research on electricity, magnetism and chemistry at the close of the eighteenth century seemed to ring the death knell for mechanism. The problem of explaining action at a distance became even more critical because the latest findings in electricity, magnetism and chemistry seemed to suggest that matter itself consisted in forces of attraction and repulsion; the forces Newton postulated for the macrocosm now seemed to hold for the microcosm itself. The essence of matter no longer seemed to be inert extension but dynamic force. But if this were so, then not only life but matter resisted mechanical explanation. Such, at any rate, was the main conclusion of Schelling's first work on *Naturphilosophie*, his 1797 *Ideen zu einer Philosophie der Natur*.

We are now in a much better position to understand the general intellectual forces driving Schelling toward his organic concept of nature. If it is necessary to extend the naturalistic world view, so that mind and life were part of nature; and if, furthermore, there could not be a mechanical explanation of matter, let alone life and mind; then the only step forward lay in extending the organic paradigm so that it held for all of nature itself. The great promise of the organic paradigm is that, after the collapse of mechanism, it guaranteed the principle of the unity of nature, a single form of explanation for both life and matter. The *lex continui* was finally upheld. Mind and matter, the organic and inorganic, were no longer divided but simply different manifestations of living force.

The great ancestor of this organic concept of nature was that old *Erzfeind* of Cartesianism: Leibniz. It was not the exoteric Leibniz of the pre-established harmony, who made the mental and physical distinct realms; but the esoteric Leibniz of the monadology, who made matter only an appearance of vital force. It was no accident that Herder and Schelling, self-consciously and explicitly, revived Leibniz.[15] Ironically, the arch dogmatist, so recently interned by Kant, had now been resurrected. Leibniz's hour had finally come; despite that baroque peruke, he had become a darling of the romantic age.

Revitalized Spinozism

Of course, that other sweetheart was "the sacred Spinoza," to whom Schlegel, Novalis, Schelling, Hölderlin and Schleiermacher would all pay tribute. It was in the aether of Spinoza's substance that one had to learn to philosophize, Hegel later said, summarizing the conviction of an entire generation.[16] It would be a serious mistake, however, to see romantic metaphysics as little more than a revivification of Spinoza. For the romantics profoundly re-interpreted Spinoza, and indeed in ways that would have made Benedictus turn in his grave. It was only by re-interpreting Spinoza, of course, that they could integrate his naturalism and realism with the idealism of Kant and Fichte.

The romantics were especially attracted to two aspects of Spinoza's system. First, his monism, his belief that there is a single universe, of which the mental and the physical are only different attributes. Spinoza's monism was the antithesis to the dualistic legacy of the Cartesian tradition, which had created so many problems in physiology. Second, his pantheism, his identification of the divine with nature. The romantics rejected the all-too-common interpretation of Spinoza as an atheist, which simply confused *natura naturans* with *natura naturata*. Rather than an atheist, Spinoza was *"der Gott betrunkener Mensch"* because he saw everything as a mode of the divine. This identification of the divine with nature seemed to be the only way to keep religion alive in an age of science. The old theism had collapsed to the forces of Biblical criticism; and deism had faltered in the face of Humean and Kantian criticism. Only Spinoza's pantheism was not vulnerable to rational criticism or scientific advance. The slogan *deus sive natura* seemed to make a science out of religion by naturalizing the divine, and a religion out of science by divinizing the natural.

Despite the attractions of Spinozism, the romantics believed it suffered from insuperable problems. The central drawback to Spinoza's system is that it was still limited by the antiquated dogmas of Cartesian physics. Spinoza not only accepted the Cartesian concept of matter as extension, but he also endorsed the mechanical paradigm of explanation. But in these respects Spinoza had shown himself to be a child of his time. If Spinoza's system were to stay alive, it would have to be reinterpreted according to all the latest advances in electricity, magnetism and chemistry. For the romantics, this could mean only one thing: reinterpreting Spinozism according to their new organic paradigm of explanation.

Such an organic interpretation involved several profound changes in Spinoza's system. First, it introduced a notion of development into his frozen, rigid universe. Spinoza's substance was now nothing less than living force, *die Urkraft aller Kräfte*. Such a substance was no longer static and eternal, but active and temporal, undergoing development from the inchoate to the organized, from the indeterminate to the determinate, from the potential into the actual. Although Spinoza himself understood substance in terms of force,[17] he never understood force in organic terms along the lines of Leibniz's *vis viva*. Furthermore, his force never acted in time but eternally since substance related to its modes purely logically.

Second, the organic interpretation injects an element of teleology into Spinoza's system. If the divine substance is an organism, then it too is a natural purpose, whose aim is to realize its potentiality throughout nature. Notoriously, Spinoza banished teleology from his system on the grounds that it is anthropomorphic and anthropocentric, implying that nature were designed by God for human ends. But the romantics believed that Spinoza's rejection of teleology was far too hasty. They too rejected the old physio-theology of the past, which understood nature as if it were only an instrument created by God to serve man. But this was an "external teleology," which sees purpose as imposed upon things; it is not an "internal teleology," which sees purpose as inherent in a thing, as the very idea or concept of the whole. An internal teleology has no necessary reference to human ends, because it assumes that the purpose of a thing derives from its own inherent concept or essence.

Third, the organic interpretation also involves the idea of a pyramid or hierarchy in nature, the idea of "the great chain of being." Spinoza had placed all modes on the same footing; a rock, a vegetable, or a human being are equal manifestations of the infinite, which is completely present in all things. The romantics' organic concept meant, however, a return to the old hierarchic concept of nature. If the universe is a living force, then, like all such forces, it develops in degrees and stages, through levels of increasing organization. For the romantics, the highest degree of organization and development of the living forces of nature is nothing less than the creativity of the artist itself. What the artist creates is what the divine creates through him, so that his work of art reveals the divine itself. This apotheosis of art, which is so characteristic of *Frühromantik*, seems absurdly extravagent; but it follows immediately and inevitably from three straightforward premises: (1) that human activity is one part of nature, and indeed its highest organization and development; (2) that art is the most creative, and therefore the highest, form of human activity; and (3) that in the organism of nature the whole is in each of its parts, so that each part reflects the whole universe from its point of view. It follows from (1) to (3) that the activity of the artist reflects or embodies the whole universe; it is the entire universe as it acts through the artist.

Fourth, the organic interpretation also meant a new account of Spinoza's attributes, his doctrine that the mental and physical are simply different attributes of a single indivisible substance. Indisputably, this doctrine is one of the most difficult to understand in Spinoza's system. How we interpret it depends upon whether an attribute is something purely subjective – simply the way in which the intellect explains or understands substance – or whether it is something objective – a property of the divine which follows of necessity from its nature. But however we understand Spinoza's doctrine, and however close our interpretation brings him to the romantics, there is still one respect in which the romantics *reinterpret* it. Namely, they understand Spinoza's attributes in organic terms as different degrees of organization and development of living force. The mental and the physical are not simply different properties or perspectives on substance but different degrees of organization and development of living force.

It is fair to say that, by organicizing Spinoza's universe, the romantics reinterpreted it along Leibnizian lines. Their reinterpretation of Spinoza was essentially a synthesis of Spinoza and Leibniz. The romantics fused Leibniz's *vis viva* with Spinoza's single infinite substance, creating a vitalistic pantheism or pantheistic vitalism. If they accepted Spinoza's monism, they rejected his mechanism; if they rejected Leibniz's pluralism, they accepted his vitalism, his organic concept of nature implicit within his dynamics. It was with this remarkable fusion of Leibniz and Spinoza – the two greatest dogmatic metaphysicians of the seventeenth century – that the romantics would attempt to solve the *aporiae* of the post-Kantian age.

The happy nuptial bonds of idealism and realism

It is in terms of this revived Spinozism that we must interpret the romantics' attempt to fuse idealism and realism. The wedding of Leibniz and Spinoza was the basis for the marriage of Fichte and Spinoza. A vitalistic monism, or monistic vitalism, seemed to be the best way to preserve the truths, and to negate the errors, of Fichte's idealism and Spinoza's realism.

The romantics' attempt to fuse idealism and realism has to be understood first and foremost as an attempt to revive Spinoza's doctrine of attributes. According to that doctrine, we can view the entire universe, the single infinite substance, under the attribute of thought or extension. The mental and the physical are no longer distinct substances but simply different attributes – either properties or perspectives (or both) – of one and the same thing. Since the mental and physical are no longer heterogeneous things, there is no longer a problem of explaining the interaction between them. The single infinite substance – the entire universe – remains undivided since one can explain everything under the attribute of either thought or extension.

On at least one interpretation of Spinoza's difficult doctrine, it seems to give equal weight to the claims of idealism and realism. If we interpret everything under the attribute of thought, we proceed idealistically, as if everything that exists is mental or ideal; and if we explain everything under the attribute of extension, we account for everything materialistically or realistically, as if everything that exists is only an appearance or manifestation of matter. Whatever the merits of such an interpretation, the romantics endorse it, taking it as their cue for the synthesis of idealism and realism. They now reintepret Fichte's principle of subject-object identity along Spinozian lines. The identity of subject and object is not located in the self-knowledge of the transcendental subject but in the single infinite substance, which remains one and the same whether interpreted subjectively (idealistically) or objectively (realistically).

Of course, the romantics give an organic twist to Spinoza's doctrine, so that the synthesis of idealism and realism must be understood in organic terms. We can interpret the entire universe in idealistic terms insofar as we see everything from top to bottom, viewing matter as nothing more than the lowest degree of organization and development of the living forces in the mind. We can also understand it in realistic terms insofar as we see everything from bottom to top, viewing mind as nothing more than the organization and development of the living powers already potential and inherent in matter. If nature is nothing more than visible mind, and if mind is nothing more than invisible nature, then both idealism and realism have been correct. The point is not to privilege one form or explanation over the other; both are independent and equally valid perspectives on a single reality, living force.

It would be naive to think that this synthesis of idealism and realism accommodates both viewpoints without remainder, as if all their claims could be accepted. If their insights are to be preserved, their illusions are to be negated. It was an insight of idealism to think that nature can be understood in teleological terms, to assume that everything can be explained in terms of self-consciousness or subjectivity. Self-consciousness is indeed nothing less the purpose of nature, the highest organization and development of all its powers. But the idealists went astray, the romantics believe, in confusing the *teleological* with the *ontological*; in other words, if self-consciousness and subjectivity is the *purpose* of all of nature, it does not follow that everything *exists* only in some self-consciousness or subject. If subjectivity is the purpose of things, that does not mean that only subjectivity exists. Fichte's principle that everything is for the ego is correct, then, but that should not mean that everything *exists* in the ego, but only that nature achieves its final purpose in the ego. The idealists failed to observe an old but fundamental point of Aristotle: what is first in the order of explanation is not necessarily first in order of being. Although the mind is the purpose of nature – although everything comes into existence for its sake – it does not follow that the mind creates all of nature.

Regarding the realistic perspective, it is correct in thinking that there is a nature that exists independent of subjectivity, in assuming that nature exists apart from and prior to human awareness of it. If subjectivity is first in order of explanation, objectivity is first in the order of being. It is indeed correct that human self-consciousness is only the manifestation and development of the powers that are implicit, inchoate and potential within matter. The realist goes astray, however, in thinking that nature is a thing-in-itself that is indifferent to the human, subjective, or ideal. If human self-consciousness is the highest organization and development of all the organic powers of nature, nature only becomes fully actualized and determinate through it. If, for some reason, there were no such self-consciousness, nature would not fully realize itself. It would indeed continue to exist; but only in some potential, inchoate and indeterminate form. It would be like the sapling that never becomes the mighty oak.

It will be readily seen that the romantics' accommodation of idealism within their organicized Spinozism grants it an essentially teleological significance. The romantics want the universe to be no longer indifferent to the self; and they avoid this harsh implication of Spinozism by again recrowning the self as the culmination of creation. It might well be objected that this was simply a relapse into anthropomorphism and anthropocentrism, the very vices that Spinoza had once descried in teleology. It is important to see, however, that this is a new kind of anthropomorphism and anthropocentrism, one never within

229

the purview of Spinoza. As we have already seen, the romantics claim that the target of Spinoza's polemic was the *external teleology* of the old physico-theology, which saw everything existing only for man, as only a means to his ends. This was the teleology that explained the existence of cork trees from man's need for stoppers for wine bottles. The romantics' anthropomorphism and anthropocentrism grew out of an internal teleology, however, according to which everything in nature is an end in itself. It was in following the inherent laws of *its* development, the romantics claimed, that a natural purpose prepared the ground for the formation of human self-consciousness.

It is noteworthy in this context that the romantics' organic concept of nature implies that everything is reciprocally both means and ends. Depending on our standpoint, we can see each part of an organism as an instrument for the development of the whole, and the whole as an instrument for the development of each part. This means that it is possible to say both that man develops for the sake of nature as well as nature develops for the sake of man. If the romantics so often stress one implication rather than the other – the more anthropomorphic or anthropocentric aspect – that is only because they are so concerned to blunt the bitter edge of Spinoza's indifferent substance, its complete independence from all human concerns. For the romantics, such a belief was only one more troublesome legacy of the mechanical physics, whose demise could now be foreseen thanks to the organic concept of nature.

Revamping and revitalizing epistemology

In fundamental respects the romantics' organic concept of nature broke with the Cartesian epistemological tradition, which had analyzed knowledge according to some of the fundamental assumptions of its mechanical physics. One of these assumptions is that the subject and object of knowledge, like all substances in nature, interact with one another only through efficient causality. The subject and object are both substances, self-sufficient and independent entities, which are connected with one another only through relations of cause and effect. Either the subject is the cause of the object, as in idealism, or the object the cause of the subject, as in realism, or both are cause and effect of one another, as in some combination of realism and idealism. Whatever is the case, there is only a causal interaction between the subject and object which leaves the identity of both terms unchanged. Another assumption was Cartesian dualism. Since mechanism could not explain *res cogitans*, it placed it in a *sui generis* realm beyond the order of nature, which consisted entirely in the *res extensa*. This dualism meant that knowledge of the external world would have to consist in two very different terms: a mental representation and an extended object. This correspondence was usually understood as a kind of resemblance or isomorphism.

Of course, these assumptions created insuperable difficulties in explaining the possibility of knowledge. If the representation belongs in the mental realm, and if its object belongs in the physical realm, then how is there any correspondence between them? How is it possible to attribute a resemblance between such heterogeneous entities? The second assumption of the Cartesian model undermines the first, since the first assumes that the correspondence is effected through causal interaction; but the second makes it impossible to conceive of cause-effect relations between the mental and the physical. While the mechanical model presupposes that one object acts upon another through impact, where impact is measured by the amount of change of place in a given time, the mental-physical dualism means that the *res cogitans* occupies no space, so that it is impossible to conceive how a physical cause has a mental effect. Although the mechanical model works fine between extended objects in the natural world, it does not apply to objects that are not extended, such as the thinking substance that is the locus of knowledge. Hence the net result of the Cartesian conception of nature is that knowledge becomes an utter mystery. It is impossible to explain in what the resemblance between representation and its object consists, and indeed how it comes into being.

If we replace the mechanical model of nature with the organic, these mysteries of traditional epistemology disappear. First, there is no dualism between the mental and the physical since both are degrees of organization and development of living force. Hence there is no problem in explaining the correspondence between heterogeneous entities. The subject's representation of the object does not stand in a different world from the object but is only the higher degree of organization and development of the living powers within the objective world. Second, there are not only accidental causal relations between the subject and object but closer ties of identity where each realizes its nature only in and through the other. According to the organic model, everything in nature is part of an organic whole, where each part is inseparable from the whole, and where the whole is inseparable from each of its parts. No part has a self-sufficient or independent nature where it retains its identity apart from everything else; rather, each part reflects the identity of the whole. Like all parts of an organic whole, the subject and object are internally related to one another in this manner. The subject's awareness of an object develops and realizes the powers of the object, so that its awareness of the object is nothing less than the *self*-realization of the object. Since artistic creativity and philosophical contemplation is the highest organization and development of all the powers of nature, the artist's and philosopher's awareness of nature is nothing less than the *self*-awareness of nature through the artist and philosopher.

The organic concept of nature essentially involves a completely different model of the connection between the mental and physical from that prevailing in the Cartesian tradition. The connection is no longer simply causal, where each term retains its identity independent of the interaction; rather, it is teleological in the sense that each term realizes its nature only through the other. Each term becomes what it is only through the other, so that it becomes organized, actualized and determinate only through the other, so that without the other it remains inchoate, potential and indeterminate. As long as the analysis of knowledge remains stuck with the causal model it becomes impossible to explain the possibility of knowledge, because the activity of the subject upon the object, or of the object upon the subject, will affect the representation of the object, so that it gives us knowledge only of how the subject affects the object or the object affects the subject, but no knowledge of the object in itself apart from and prior to the interaction.[18] Hence the inevitable result of the mechanical model of interaction was the idea of an unknowable thing-in-itself.

On the basis of this new organic model of nature, the romantics believed that they had finally overcome the traditional antithesis between idealism and realism. They held that idealism and realism are one-sided perspectives, which are both true and false: they are true about one aspect of the whole but they are false about the whole itself. If nature is an organic whole, it is not possible to say with idealism that is completely *inside* consciousness nor with realism that it is entirely *outside* consciousness. Rather, it is both and neither.[19] The organic whole is inside consciousness because consciousness is the highest organization and development of *all* its living powers; the philosopher's and artist's awareness of nature is all of nature coming to its self-awareness through them, so that all of nature culminates within artistic creativity and philosophical contemplation. The organic whole is also outside consciousness, because human consciousness is only one part of nature, which exists apart from and prior to us. Without humanity nature does not realize its purpose; it remains inchoate, unorganized and indeterminate; but it does not follow that it does not exist. From this perspective, then, the idea of a thing-in-itself proves to be an absurdity. While it is true that nature exists apart from our awareness of it, it is false that nature has a complete and self-sufficient nature apart from the awareness of it; that idea would be simply an artificial abstraction from the idea of an organic whole.

The question of freedom

The question remains: How did the romantics square their new metaphysics with their belief in freedom? There seems to be an irreconcilable conflict between that belief and their pantheism, which holds that everything happens of necessity according to the laws of nature. The fact that these laws are teleological as well as mechanical ultimately makes little difference. In this respect, their pantheism seems identical with that of Spinoza; but Spinoza was notorious for his fatalism as well as his atheism. How, then, did the romantics avoid the charge of fatalism? This was a problem that deeply troubled Friedrich Schlegel, Schelling, and Novalis, who dealt with it in their lectures, notebooks and drafts from the late 1790s to the early 1800s.[20]

The romantics' organic concept of nature made it impossible for them to accept Kant's and Fichte's solution to the problem of freedom. Central to that concept is its firm belief in the unity of nature, in the oneness of the subjective and objective, the ideal and real. Kant's and Fichte's solution to the problem of freedom presupposed, however, a dualism between these realms. To save freedom, Kant and Fichte postulated a noumenal realm above and beyond the phenomenal realm of nature; while the noumenal realm complies with moral laws imposed by reason, the phenomenal realm is governed by strict necessity according to the laws of nature. The romantics rejected such a solution essentially because of its dualistic implications. They also questioned the underlying basis for the dualism: that the realm of nature is governed strictly by mechanical laws. If nature does not follow only mechanical laws, the whole question of freedom and necessity had to be rethought.

True to their anti-dualism, the romantics placed the self within nature, insisting that it is one mode of the single infinite substance, one part of the universal organism. They are no less naturalistic than Spinoza: they too affirm that everything is within nature, and that everything in nature conforms to law. Contrary to one popular image of romanticism, they do not allow for caprice, arbitrariness or chance in nature. Rather, they maintain that everything that happens in nature happens of necessity, such that it could not have been otherwise. The romantics also do not question that everything that happens must occur according to mechanical laws, so that for every event there will be some prior causes determining it into action. Where they differ from Spinoza is not in exempting events from mechanical necessity but in bringing mechanical necessity itself under higher organic laws. It is not that there are special organic laws, which are somehow beyond the jurisdiction of mechanism; rather, it is that mechanism is subordinate to organicism. The mechanical is simply a limited cause of the teleological, deriving from a partial perspective which considers only the parts in their immediate relations to one another, but not in their relation to the whole. Mechanism considers what happens for determinate events under certain initial conditions; but it does not ask for the whys and wherefores of these initial conditions in the first place; instead, it allows the series of causes to regress *ad infinitum*.

Because of their commitment to monism and naturalism, the romantics could not allow freedom in the radical sense intended by Kant and Fichte. They question the possibility of freedom in two senses championed by Kant and Fichte. First, Kant's concept of freedom as *spontaneity*, according to which the self initiates a causal series without determination by some prior cause. Second, Fichte's concept of *self-positing*, according to which the self makes itself what it is, having no essence given to it by nature. Since both concepts exclude determination by natural causes, they presuppose the noumenal-phenomenal dualism, which the romantics reject.[21]

Given their naturalism and monism, and given their rejection of transcendental freedom, it would seem that the romantics have no place for freedom. In what sense were they ready to admit freedom at all? Their own agenda is to reconcile freedom and necessity, to show that true freedom and necessity are not opposed but ultimately only one. They see this unity first and foremost in the divine nature itself, which is free in Spinoza's sense: it acts from the necessity of

233

its own nature alone. It is striking that while Schlegel and Schelling refuse to attribute freedom to any part of nature, they are happy to attribute it to the whole of nature, the infinite divine substance itself.[22] This substance is free in the sense that it is *causi sui*, both self-causing and self-making. Since it includes everything, there is nothing outside it, so that there are no external causes to compel it into action. For anything less than the whole, however, there will always be other parts outside it that determine it into action according to the laws of necessity. It is noteworthy, however, that even Spinoza's infinite substance is not free in the sense of Kantian spontaneity or Fichtean self-positing; for both concepts assume that the self can act otherwise, that it can choose a different series of causes or have a different nature. For Spinoza, the divine nature cannot be or act otherwise without contradicting itself.

Although Schlegel and Schelling attribute *absolute* freedom only to nature as a whole, they still attempt to dodge the implication of fatalism. While they deny the self is free as a part of nature, they affirm that it is free in its unity with nature as a whole. They make a distinction between two perspectives or standpoints: the self considered in its relations to other things, which is the self as individual, as one finite thing opposed to others; the self considered in itself, apart from these relations, which is the universal self, the self as identical with everything else. If the individual self falls under the sway of necessity, the universal self shares in the divine freedom. Its identity is not limited to one part of the whole, where everything is determined by external causes; but it extends to the whole of all things, which acts with freedom, according to the necessity of its own nature alone. True freedom then arises from sharing or participating in divine necessity, in seeing that in all my actions the divine acts through me. This was the freedom of Spinoza's intellectual love of God, the freedom that reconciled the self to necessity when it recognized its identity with the whole universe.

While there was always this Spinozist dimension to the romantic reconciliation of freedom and necessity, it would be wrong to limit it to this dimension alone. Its unique and characteristic element came from their organic concept of nature. This concept gave a greater place for freedom than Spinoza's system chiefly because it made humanity the *telos* of nature itself. "Man is free," Friedrich Schlegel wrote, "because he is the highest expression of nature."[23] If the self is the highest organization and development of all the powers of nature, then nature ceases to be some external power outside the self, an external cause that compels him into action. Rather, nature becomes part of the self because its intrinsic ends are achieved only through it. If the self is the highest expression of nature, then nature contracts to the limits of the self as the self expands to the whole of nature. The reciprocity of means and ends means not only that the self is a means for the ends of nature but also that nature is only a means for the self. All of nature then becomes the organic body of the self. Once the self finally grasps its identity with nature, it then regards determination by nature as another form of *self*-determination.

If the romantics had succeeded in salvaging some sense of freedom in their organic universe, it also must be said that it was no longer the radical sense of freedom with which many of them began. They had to abandon the sense of freedom as spontaneity and self-positing. In Fichte's dramatic choice between criticism and dogmatism they had taken the plunge with dogmatism, affirming a universal necessity. There was indeed a remarkable change in the romantic ethos as the days of revolutionary ardor began to grow old. The parole was no longer to change the world according to the demands of reason but to perceive the reason already within nature and society, reconciling oneself with its necessity.[24] In moral and political respects the romantic marriage of Fichte and Spinoza, of idealism and realism, was lopsided, to the disadvantage of Fichte's titanic striving and to the advantage of Spinoza's beatific stoicism. Like all marriages between incompatible partners, someone had to lose something. It was the price to be paid for an otherwise very remarkable alliance.

Notes

1 Evidence that the romantics had such a project is evident from their notebooks and fragments. On Schelling, see his *Briefe über Dogmatismus und Kriticizismus*, Werke I, 326–35. Schelling's later absolute idealism, as expressed in the *System des transcendentalen Idealismus* and *Darstellung meines Systems*, can be regarded as attempts to synthesize Fichte's idealism and Spinoza's realism. On Novalis, see, for example, *Allgemeine Brouillon*, #75, 634, 820; HKA III, 252, 382, 429; and *Fragmente und Studien* #611; HKA III, 671. On Friedrich Schlegel, see, for example, *Philosophische Lehrjahre*, KA XVIII, 31, 38, 43, 80. On Hölderlin, see the preface to the penultimate version of *Hyperion*, GSA III/1, 236; the preface to *Fragment von Hyperion*, III/1, 163; and the final version of *Hyperion*, III/1, 38. The attempt to join Fichte and Spinoza was one of the fundamental aims of Hölderlin's early novel. This project was probably a subject of discussion between Hölderlin and Schelling around 1796–7. See Schelling's *Briefe über Dogmatismus und Kriticizismus*, Werke I, 284–90. In the penultimate letter of the *Briefe* Schelling sketches his own idea of a synthesis of idealism and realism, which later came to fruition in his *Identitätssystem*. See *Werke* I, 326–30. It is impossible to determine who among the romantics was the original creator of this project, since they conceive it partly independently, partly jointly through conversation, around the same time, especially in the formative years 1796-98.
2 See Fichte, *Grundlage der gesammten Wissenschaftslehre*, Werke I, 101; and Kant, *Kritik der praktischen Vernunft*, AA V, 101–2.
3 See, for example, Alois Stockman, *Die deutsche Romantik*, Freiburg, Herder, 1921, pp. 13–17; Oskar Walzel, "Wesenfragen deutscher Romantik," *Jahrbuch des Freien deutschen Hochstifts* 29 (1929), 253–76; Adolf Grimme, *Vom Wesen der Romantik*, Braunschweig, Westermann, 1947, p. 13; René Wellek, "The Concept of Romanticism in Literary History" and "Romanticism Re-examined," in *Concepts of Criticism*, ed. Stephen G. Nichols, New Haven, Yale University Press, 1963, pp. 165, 220; Morse Peckham, "Toward A Theory of Romanticism," in *Proceedings of the Modern Language Association* 66 (1951), 5–23; and Lawrence Ryan, "Romanticism," in *Periods of German Literature*, J. M. Ritchie (ed.), London, Oswald Wolff, 1966, pp. 123–43.
4 See, for example, Paul de Man, "The Rhetoric of Temporality," in *Blindness and Insight*, 2nd edn, Minneapolis, University of Minnesota Press, 1983, pp. 187–228,

FREDERICK BEISER

esp. 220–8; and Alice Kuzniar, *Delayed Endings: Nonclosure in Novalis and Hölderlin*, Athens GA, University of Georgia Press, 1987, pp. 1–71.

5 This was the formulation of Hölderlin in the preface to the penultimate version of *Hyperion*, GSA III/1, 236.

6 This was Schelling's reasoning in his early Fichtean work *Abhandlungen zur Erläuterung des Idealismus der Wissenschaftslehre*, *Werke* I, 365–6.

7 See Kant, *Kritik der reinen Vernunft*, Vorrede, B xviii.

8 *Ibid.*, B xiii, Axx, Axiv.

9 Fichte, *Grundlage der gesamten Wissenschaftslehre*, *Werke* I, 101.

10 This criticism is most explicit in Hölderlin's famous fragment "Urtheil und Seyn," GSA IV/1, 216–17. Hölderlin was not alone in making it, however. The same point was made by Schelling, *Briefe über Dogmatismus und Kriticizismus*, *Werke* I, 329; and *Vom Ich als Princip der Philosophie*, *Werke* I, 180–1. See too Novalis, *Fichte Studien*, HKA II, 107; #5–7.

11 This second criticism is most apparent in early Hegel and Schelling. See their *Fernere Darstellung aus dem System der Philosophie*, in Schelling, *Werke* IV, 356–61; and their "Ueber das Verhältniß der Naturphilosophie zur Philosophie überhaupt," in Schelling, *Werke* V, 108–15.

12 For Schlegel, see, for example, *Philosophische Lehrjahr*, KA XVIII, 31 (#134), 38 (#209), 80 (606). On Novalis, see *Allgemeine Brouillon*, HKA III, 382–4 (#634), 252 (#69), 382 (#633), 429 (#820); and *Fragmente und Studien*, HKA III, 671 (#611).

13 See Schelling, *Von der Weltseele*, *Werke* II, 496–505; and his *Erster Entwurf eines Systems der Naturphilosophie*, *Werke* III, 74–8.

14 On these experiments, see Thomas Hankins, *Science and Enlightenment*, Cambridge, Cambridge University Press, 1992, pp. 46–80.

15 See Herder, *Gott, Einige Gespräche*, *Werke* XVI, 458–64; and Schelling, *Ideen zu einer Philosophie der Natur*, *Werke* II, 20.

16 Hegel, *Geschichte der Philosophie*, *Werkausgabe* XX, 165.

17 See *Ethica*, part I, prop. xxxiv.

18 On this reasoning, see Schelling, *System der gesammten Philosophie*, *Werke* VI, 138–40, §1.

19 See Schelling, *System der gesammten Philosophie*, *Werke* VI, 141–5, §4; and Schelling and Hegel, *Fernere Darstellungen aus dem System der Philosophie*, *Werke* VI, 356–61; and Novalis, *Allgemeine Broullion*, HKA III, 382–4 (#634), 252 (#69), 382 (#633), 429 (#820).

20 See Schelling, *System der gesammten Philosophie*, *Werke* VI, 538–70, §§302–17; Schlegel, *Transcendentalphilosophie* KA XII, 50, 52, 57, 72, 74, 86; and Novalis, *Die Lehrling zu Sais*, HKA I, 77, *Fichte-Studien*, HKA II, 154, 202, 270, and *Allgemeine Broullion*, HKA III 271 (#172), 381–2 (#633–4), 404 (#713).

21 The generalization about the romantics' identification of reason with nature is especially evident in the case of Friedrich Schlegel and Schelling; but it is also apparent in the case of Schleiermacher, who in his *Reden über die Religion* identified religion with the standpoint according to which all human actions occur of necessity. See KGA 1/2, 212: "die Religion athmet da, wo die Freiheit selbst wieder Natur geworden ist." In his early 1790–2 manuscript *Über die Freiheit*, KGA 1/1, 217–356, Schleiermacher had already defended determinism and had attacked the Kantian conception of freedom for dividing the self from nature.

22 Schlegel, *Transcendentalphilosophie*, KA XII, 57, 72, 74; and Schelling, *System der gesammten Philosophie*, *Werke* VI, 541–8, §305.

23 Schlegel, *Transcendentalphilosophie*, KA XII, 72.

24 See Schleiermacher, *Über die Religion*, KGA II/1, 232

236

Citations and abbreviations

AA   Kant, Immanuel, *Gesammelte Schriften*, Akademie Ausgabe, Wilhelm Dilthey (ed.), Berlin, de Gruyter, 1902f. All references to the *Kritik der reinen Vernunft* are to the first and second editions, cited as A and B respectively.

HKA   Hardenberg, Friedrich von, *Novalis Schriften, Kritische Ausgabe*, Richard Samuel, Hans Joachim Mähl and Gerhard Schulz (eds), Stuttgart, Kohlhammer, 1960–88.

GSA   Hölderlin, Friedrich, *Sämtliche Werke, Grosse Stuttgarter Ausgabe*, Friedrich Beissner (ed.), Stuttgart, Kohlhammer, 1961.

KA   Schlegel, Friedrich, *Kritische Friedrich Schlegel Ausgabe*, Ernst Behler, Jean Jacques Anstett and Hans Eichner (eds), Munich and Paderborn, Schöningh, 1958f.

KGA   Schleiermacher, Friedrich Daniel, *Kritische Gesamtausgabe*, Hans-Joachim Birkner, Gerhard Ebeling, Hermann Fischer and Günter Meckenstock (eds), Berlin, de Gruyter, 1984f.

All references to Schelling are to *Sämtliche Werke*, K. F. A. Schelling (ed.) Stuttgart, Cotta, 1856–61. All references to Fichte are to *Fichtes Werke*, I. Fichte (ed.), Berlin, Veit, 1845–6. All references to Herder are to *Sämtliche Werke*, B. Suphan (ed.), Berlin, Wiedmann, 1881–1913. All references to Hegel are to *Werke in zwanzig Bänden, Werkausgabe*, E. Moldenhauer and K. Michel (eds), Frankfurt, Suhrkamp, 1969.

11

BROKEN SYMMETRIES

The romantic search for a moral cosmology

Albert Borgmann

In memory of Will Griffis (1942–2001)

"Two things fill the mind with ever new and increasing admiration and reverence, the more often and steadily our reflection attends to them," Kant said
famously in the conclusion to the *Critique of Practical Reason* (1788), "the starry
heavens above me and the moral law within me."[1] Ever since, cosmology has
been unavailable as a backdrop for daily life and for scholarship in the humanities. Kant's dictum did not, of course, signal the end of cosmology simply, not
even for Kant. The cosmos, after all, continued to fill his mind "with ever new
and increasing admiration and reverence." But beginning with Copernicus,
cosmology had been developing into a chiefly scientific discipline and has
remained such to this day. What has become attenuated is the moral force of
cosmology that would inform our sense of what it is to be human and our awareness of the place we occupy in the universe. As a consequence, perhaps,
philosophers have for the most part lost interest in cosmology or, more accurately, have surrendered it entirely to the sciences. Cosmology failed to rate an
entry in the 1995 Cambridge *Dictionary of Philosophy*.[2] In the 1998 *Routledge
Encyclopedia of Philosophy*, Ernan McMullin distinguishes between cosmology as
world view, cosmology as a brand of metaphysics, and cosmology as a scientific
enterprise, devoted to "the construction of plausible universe models."[3] The first
two kinds of cosmology are mentioned only to be dismissed.

When I speak of the search for a moral cosmology, I take "moral" in the wide
sense of Hume and Dewey to include not only modern ethical norms like rights,
pleasure, and tolerance, but also supererogatory norms like heroism, generosity,
and diligence, and what are now considered nonmoral norms such as virtuosity,
vigor, or grace. "Moral" in this broad sense refers to all the excellences that
characterize the culture of a particular time and place. Thus a moral cosmology
would give us an all-encompassing sense of orientation and the good life.

Mythic cosmology was surely moral in this sense. For the ancient Greeks as
much as for the Blackfeet in Montana the world was a spiritual plenum,

resonating with the voices of divinities, both with those of plants, animals, streams, and mountains and with the voices of the sun, the moon, the planets, and the stars. It was a world that humans responded to in a spirit of piety. To be pious was to be attentive to the commands of gods and spirits and, in the end, to be favored with grace and good fortune. Virgil's Aeneas, *pius Aeneas*, is an exemplar of such piety.

Thales may have been the first to be moved by curiosity rather than piety. Not that everyone was pious prior to Thales. Blasphemers were not, but blasphemy is the tribute impiety pays to divinity. Nor were people before Thales lacking in curiosity. Hunters and peasants had to be curious to survive, and geometers had, by Thales's time, shown disciplined and ingenious curiosity. But Thales was the first to be moved by cosmic curiosity, he was the first to think that laws rather than gods ruled the universe. To be sure, in Ionian hylozoism, the laws of condensation and rarefaction were rudimentary and closely tied to the stuff they governed.

In Aristotle's physics, there are more distinct laws of motion. But they too are linked to the divine order of the universe. We can see here a magnificent, if unsustainable as it turned out, balance between the moral resonance and the physical lawfulness of the cosmos. What was almost seamlessly one in mythic cosmology had become a unified and artful structure of three elements – metaphysics, cosmology, and ethics. This is the conventional way of stating the threefold structure. A more accurate statement, and one I will adopt in what follows, is to think of a primarily twofold structure, namely, of cosmology and ethics or morality, and to think of cosmology as having two parts, a theory of the *nature and character* of reality (ontology) and a theory of the entire *structure and order* of reality (astronomy). Strictly speaking, we could divide the moral component too, namely, into a part comprising the moral norms *qua* rules of conduct (ethics) and into another part stating the moral norms as divine commands (theology). However, I will simply and synonymously speak of morality and ethics and take it to be understood that in the premodern and early modern periods morality had a divine extension.

To sum up the conceptual framework of this essay in terms of McMullin's distinctions, I think of modern cosmology as consisting of metaphysics (the second sense of cosmology; what I call ontology) and of the construction of cosmological models (the third sense; what I call astronomy); the concern I share with the romantics is whether this two-part cosmology can be shown or can be extended to have moral significance (McMullin's first sense of cosmology; what I call a moral cosmology). To complete the framework, we may need to think of a moral cosmology as a relation of two terms. Assuming we discover moral significance in the cosmos, we can say that a moral cosmology is (1) the moral force of the cosmos (2) for a given cultural situation. Without some consideration of the second term, a moral cosmology might be entirely idle. What moral force the cosmos has depends in important part on whether cultural conditions are receptive to cosmic significance or not. I will use the notion of scientific lawfulness as a thread to follow the long and complicated developments that led from Aristotle's moral cosmology to the search of the romantics and beyond.

To begin, then, with Aristotle and to speak informally, things in Aristotelian ontology had a certain character. They were fiery, heavy, or ethereal, and they moved in characteristic ways – fiery things tended upward, heavy things tended downward, and ethereal things, the planets and stars, moved in perfect circles with perfect uniformity. In Galileo's kinematics, things begin to lose their character. Light things tend to fall no differently from heavy things. Cognitive interest shifted from the character of things to the uniform laws that govern their behavior. This shift reached a first point of resolution and rest in Newton's laws of motion that resolved Galileo's laws of terrestrial with Kepler's laws of heavenly motion into one encompassing theory. Things that once had a color and personality of their own were now reduced to point masses and mere instances of the laws that covered them.

This ontological development converged with changes in astronomy that began with Copernicus. The naive geocentric vision of the world has an engaging solidity and intuitive plausibility. But it could only be sustained, in view of careful astronomical observations, at the price of the extravagantly complex Ptolemaic astronomy. Copernicus exchanged terrestrial solidity and astronomic complexity for cosmic simplicity and intuitive implausibility. Here again Newton's *Principia* is the endpoint of a development, the rigorous explication of the structure of astronomy through physical lawfulness.

In an ontology where things have lost their commanding presence, the moral eloquence of reality had to fall silent as well. A natural-law-physics leaves no room for a natural-law-ethics. Morality withdrew from ontology and became a matter of pragmatic prudence in Descartes; it entirely detached itself from reality in Hume's is-ought distinction; and it was finally set over against knowledge and reality in Kant's ethics of practical reason, an opposition reflected in the Kantian dictum quoted at the start of this essay.

The world of Newtonian mechanics seemed deeply inhospitable to the romantics. In fact, opposition to the mechanical universe is a defining trait of romanticism and, at any rate, one of two I will concentrate on. More narrowly still, I will focus on German romanticism, and most particularly on Schelling and two of his predecessors, Kant and Goethe. All three felt acutely that something crucial had been lost or, at least, was unaccounted for in a world described as matter in motion.

The romantics responded primarily to the new theoretical ontology, to physics, and their response can be read as a critique of atomist and mechanist science. But we must not forget that "mechanical" is also, by etymology and semantics, the adjective that belongs to the noun "machine." It is one of the great ironies in the history of ideas that in the treatises, essays, novels, and dramas of what was between 1770 and 1830 perhaps the greatest flowering of German letters, the seminal development that in time entirely transformed terrestrial reality and by now has eclipsed if not destroyed the world of letters went almost unnoticed – the rise of machinery and technology in the Industrial Revolution.

Almost, but not entirely. Goethe in *Wilhelm Meisters Wanderjahre* has Susanne, who presides over a pre-industrial spinning and weaving business, say:

> The overpowering rise of machinery pains and frightens me; it is rolling along like a thunderstorm, slowly, slowly; but it has taken its direction, it will come and strike.[4]

The romantics generally were not unaware of the industrial and commercial transformation of reality.[5] They felt estranged from this powerful development, and their estrangement, more as a background condition than a focal concern, lent additional urgency to the search for a moral cosmology.

One other factor needs to be considered to situate the romantic response to the mechanical universe. The romantics were not the advocates of a universally realized need. Not everyone felt a grievous loss in the face of rising modernism. There was always one party or another that was confident of rational explanation without remainder and of beneficial reconstruction from the ground up. All that was needed was supposedly available – building materials (atoms) and rational designs (scientific and technological theories). The constituencies and banners of this movement have shifted and changed over time, but it is if anything more vigorous and self-confident now than it was some 200 years ago.

Before Susanne revealed her anxiety about machinery, her interlocutor noticed "a certain melancholy, an expression of concern" about her, and upon concluding her diagnosis, Susanne can only see a choice between two unlovely alternatives – joining the rush to machinery or emigration to America.[6] A similar despair clings sometimes to the notion of romanticism. When in social criticism and theory a position is called romantic, the appellation is often thought to be tantamount to a refutation – romanticism is hopeless and regressive if not reactionary. For German romanticism, this burden has been made worse by the truly reactionary, and worse than that, use the Nazis have made of romantic themes.[7]

Yet it remains that no one has been able to answer the romantic complaint that there is more to the world than a mechanical universe and a mercenary world and that we cannot be fully human beings until the missing regions of reality have been recovered by an appropriate ontology and appropriated by vigorous practices. To be sure, the mechanical universe has yielded to astrophysics and the Philistine society to the affluent society; but the fundamental cosmological predicament is much the same today as it was at the turn from the eighteenth to the nineteenth century.

The romantics, ancient and recent, are not alone, of course, in their critique of science and culture. There is a second defining trait of romanticism as I understand it. The critical competitors of romanticism are exclusively progressive and forward-looking, and so they tend to aggravate and radicalize crucial features of modernism rather than reform them. Marxism has rightly criticized inequality and oppression, but it has uncritically embraced and has hoped to universalize technological affluence as such. Today, social constructivism has implicitly adopted Marxist liberation and emancipation, but it unthinkingly champions a fundamentalist anthropocentrism.

Romantics, as I understand them, hold that you cannot truly look forward without looking back. What needs regard are the great continuities of culture and nature. It is against the cultural and natural background that the real liabilities and possibilities of the present come into view. These peremptory theses need substance and detail, of course, and I will now try to furnish these by turning to Kant, Goethe, and Schelling and using the lawfulness of nature as the pivot of my investigation.

Cosmology was an early and prominent concern of Kant's. His first ambitious work, published anonymously in 1755 and immediately the victim of his publisher's bankruptcy, is the *Universal History and Theory of the Heavens or Essay on the Constitution and Mechanical Origin of the Entire Cosmic Edifice, Carried Out According to Newtonian Principles.*[8] As the full title shows, Kant's treatise is remarkable for its whole-hearted embrace of Newton's mechanical lawfulness. In historical context, however, it is equally notable for the moral inferences Kant drew from his cosmology.

Though Newton famously explicated the structure of the solar system through his laws of motion, he was unwilling to attempt an explanation of how that structure had come into being. Newton regarded the astronomic conditions that instantiate the laws of motion as God-given data. Kant employed Newton's mechanics to propose an explanation of how the universe evolved from an original chaos of atoms in infinite space. Though many of his explanations turned out to be wrong, Kant delineated a crucial trend in the devolution of moral cosmology.

To illustrate the issue, consider the question why the sun and its planets constitute a stable system. Newton thought that "[t]his most elegant system of the sun, planets, and comets could not have arisen without the design and dominion of an intelligent and powerful being."[9] Kant attempted an explanation in terms of attractive and repulsive forces that led by coagulation and according to differences in density to planets orbiting at appropriate distances to the sun and in the same plane with the sun.[10] This explanation is wrong in many details though it does agree in spirit with current theory.[11]

Regardless of these errors, the moral point at issue is of general significance. In Newton's astronomy, there is a definite local indication of divine action, an internal element, or more accurately, a fragment of moral cosmology since, even if Newton were correct, the sharply defined and localized divine presence within cosmology would do next to nothing in teaching us what place we occupy in the world and how that placement tells us who we are and what we are to do. At any rate, a scientific explanation of planetary stability dissolves God's presence within cosmology.

There is a quaint piece of internal or local ethics in Kant's cosmology. It derives from his thesis that warm climates make people think and act slowly and cold ones quickly and wisely. Hence the intelligent creatures on Jupiter likely possess more wisdom than the slow and dim-witted inhabitants of Venus.[12] Humans are so placed in the solar system that they occupy the perilous middle position "where the temptations of sensuous stimulations possess a powerful capacity of seduction against the supremacy of the spirit and where the spirit nevertheless cannot deny the ability whereby it can resist those temptations."[13]

The prevailing moral import of Kant's early cosmology is, however, universal or systematic. The moral significance of the cosmos is not to be found in a particular location or feature of the universe but rather in its entire order or structure. It is, moreover, of a theological cast. Commenting on the incomprehensible infinity of the cosmos, Kant said: "The wisdom, the goodness, the power that have revealed themselves are infinite and to the same extent fruitful and active; the design of their revelation must therefore, likewise be infinite and without limits."[14] Kant attempted to build a bridge between his internal and his systematic ethics by arguing that humans must aspire to the spiritual dimensions humans owe to their distance from the origin and center of the universe if they are to grasp the systematic import of cosmic morality.[15]

Kant's systematic moral cosmology evidently has more practical force than Newton's local moral cosmology. If Kant is right, we know ourselves to be placed in a world that reflects and witnesses to a wise, beneficent, and powerful God. Newton's cosmic morality, though practically bland, is more definitely and, if Newton had been right, indisputably evident in astronomy. Thus the best is divided between two worlds – Newton's indisputable and Kant's inspiring divine presence; and so being divided each is fatally weakened – Newton's by vacuity and Kant's by its tenuous attachment to astronomy as the later Kant was the most vigorous to argue.

In the *Critique of Pure Reason* (1781) Kant denied that the universe exhibits any empirically demonstrable evidence of divine origin or design. Any attempt to pronounce conclusively on the ultimate constitution of reality, i.e. on ontology, or on the all-encompassing structure of the universe, astronomy, leads to antinomies – to every apparently sound claim there is an equally persuasive counter claim. Such fundamental or universal assertions, Kant argued, assume what we cannot have, knowledge of reality in itself and by itself.[16] In particular, proofs for the existence of God are based on inconclusive evidence at best and must in any case illicitly slide (via the "ontological proof") from something that can be thought to something that supposedly exists in fact.[17]

All this suggests that in the aftermath of the first *Critique* not only moral cosmologies are ruled out as far as Kant is concerned, but any cosmology that presents a definite ontology and astronomy. What is left is cosmological research without cosmological conclusions. In the discussion of the antinomies, Kant's sympathies lie with the skeptical and empirical side. He applauds its insistence on an ever open horizon of inquiry when it comes to the composition and origin of the world (though he rejects the skeptical denial of undetermined freedom and of the hypothetical or regulative use of metaphysical notions).[18]

More to the point, the *Critique of Pure Reason* severed Kantian ontology both from cosmology and morality, and, as it turned out, this jejune theory of reality left Kant himself unsure and dissatisfied. The burr under the saddle turns up when we look more closely at the connection between Kantian and Newtonian ontology. In the conventional view, Kant attempted to justify Newtonian physics by deriving it from synthetic a priori principles. I agree, however, with Gordon Brittan that Kant argued for more and less than the common interpretation has it – less in arguing, though not without inconsistencies, that Newton's physics is merely one among indefinitely many "really possible" kinds of physics; more in that he gives Newtonian physics a realist rather than an instrumentalist or phenomenalist reading.[19] It is Kant's realism that makes him search for a substantial ontology. Kant thought that Newton's laws of motion gave the best available account that actually conformed to the strictures of real possibility. He disagreed, however, with Newton's cosmological extension of mechanical lawfulness, namely, with Newton's claim that the universe is enclosed in absolute space and composed of impenetrable atoms in empty space.[20]

Kant had originally conceived of the first *Critique* as an enterprise of clearing the ground whereon to erect a metaphysics that avoided the airy arrogance of the rationalists and the studied ignorance of the skeptics and instead had application to experience. He proceeded to do just this for the natural sciences in the *Metaphysical Foundations of Natural Science* of 1786.[21] What was conceived as an enterprise of secure and orderly construction came to reveal a problem Kant was finally unable to solve. It lay in the implicit question whether the account of a mechanical universe adequately reflected the force of reality. Divine power had been reduced to a postulate of non-empirical ethics, and the ordinary force of things remained philosophically unaccounted for since it appeared only as the unpredictable content of the a priori conceptual forms or categories.

Matter, force, and dynamics are some of the headings under which the romantic search for a moral cosmology proceeded from then on. In Kant's particular case, the search was for the substantial something that would fill and animate the structure of mechanical lawfulness on a footing of rigor and demonstrability equal to that of the categories of understanding.

Newtonians thought of matter as consisting of impenetrable atoms in empty space and of the density, elasticity, and cohesion of molar objects as derivable from configurations and mechanical forces of atoms. Kant called this the mathematical-mechanical explanation. It was unacceptable to him for the obvious and ostensible reason that the notion of impenetrability was empirically inconceivable. But a deeper reason, I would like to suggest, was the failure of the mechanical-mathematical explanation to capture the living force of things. He proposed therefore as an alternative the metaphysical-dynamical hypothesis.[22]

Invoking the notion of the living or internal force (*vis viva vel interna*) puts Kant's problem in a tradition that reaches down to one of his earliest writings where he had engaged a still earlier tradition – the dispute between, on the one side, the Cartesians and Newtonians who championed external or dead forces (*vires externae vel mortuae*) and, on the other, the Leibnizians who sided with the living force. In his *Thoughts of the True Estimation of Living Forces* of 1747 Kant had proposed a sweetly reasonable both-and solution.[23] But now, in the *Metaphysical Foundations of Natural Science*, he found himself in a dilemma. Giving, on the one side, scientific standing to truly living forces, forces that resided and originated from within contingent material things, amounted to hylozoism, and this, Kant said, would be "the death of all natural philosophy."[24] Lawful scientific description requires that we explain phenomena with "mathematical evidence."[25] On the other side, Kant's preferred metaphysical-dynamical approach, had a primarily negative function – to remove the supposedly dogmatic assumptions of atomism.[26] In so saving the metaphysical-dynamical hypothesis, Kant once again left the living and commanding presence of reality philosophically unaccounted for.

While Kant is commonly thought to have tied his philosophy too closely to Newtonian physics, thus supposedly sentencing it to death, Goethe, in the conventional view, responded to Newtonian science with uncomprehending hostility. His *Farbenlehre* (doctrine of colors) is taken to illustrate his position best. Goethe could not get himself to accept Newton's demonstration that white light is the compound of the colors of the spectrum. Colors, Goethe claimed, were things that white light did and suffered. So strong was his opposition that Goethe pronounced his "refutation" of "the error of the Newtonian doctrine" to be his epochal contribution to humanity.[27] The same attitude appears where Goethe talked directly about astronomy. Cosmology has an important place in Goethe's most important work, at the beginning of *Faust*. In the "Prologue in Heaven," the archangels behold and praise the universe, but it is, alas, a geocentric and more particularly Pythagorean world, albeit with the inconsistency of the earth revolving rapidly about its axis.[28] Immediate and thoughtful observation was Goethe's forte; the rigorous mathematical approach to nature was foreign to him as he explained to Eckermann:

> In the natural sciences I have tried my hand in pretty much all areas; however my concerns were always and only directed toward those subjects that surrounded me here on earth and that could be immediately perceived by the senses; which is the reason why I have never been concerned with astronomy since here the senses are not sufficient, but rather one needs to resort to instruments, computations, and mechanics which require a life of their own and were of no concern to me.[29]

When it comes to the structure of the universe at large, then, Goethe agreed with Kant that the rise of Newtonian mechanics had emptied the cosmos of moral force and interest. Goethe knew the solar system and its planets well enough, but it was their immediate splendor rather than their lawful structure that engaged his admiration.[30]

Goethe was, however, deeply fascinated by a phenomenon of modern ontology that at the time was widely investigated and discussed under the headings of chemistry, electricity, and magnetism. This was a period of excitement and frustration, excitement about the rapid succession of discoveries, frustration about the scientists' inability to explain and connect the discoveries in one lawful theory. Kant, in fact, thought that chemistry would forever remain a collection of empirical observations that defied mathematical methods and did not deserve to be called an "actual science."[31]

The phenomenon of elective affinity or attraction, so called, was as fascinating to the imagination as it was recalcitrant to explanation.[32] To put it schematically, a certain chemical compound of two elements, say AB, when mixed with a third element, say C, reacts in such a way that A lets go of B and then combines with C to yield AC. Thus A and C have an elective affinity with each other that A and C do not have with B.

A still more fascinating case is crosswise elective affinity. Goethe has the Captain in the eponymous novel *Elective Affinities* give an example:

> Think of an A that is intimately bound to a B and cannot be separated from it by many different means and not even through some violence; think of a C that is likewise related to a D; now bring those two pairs into contact: A will throw itself on D and C on B, and you could not tell which first deserted the one and which first connected itself again with the other.[33]

To call this "elective affinity" is to explain nothing, as Schelling was to stress repeatedly.[34] Nothing, of course, was farther from Goethe's mind than the explication of elective attraction in terms of a rigorous theory. What he tried to find and explain in this striking item of the new scientific ontology was its moral force. In an advertisement that Goethe wrote for his novel he said of himself:

> It seems that his continued work in physics made the author choose this strange title. He may have noticed that often in natural science ethical similes are used to bring something nearer that is remote form the region of human knowledge, and so, presumably, he may have wanted to trace the parlance of a chemical simile back to its spiritual origin, all the more so since there is after all just one nature.[35]

Goethe, then, seemed to think of his novel as a literary attempt to reunite the spiritual and the material, the moral and the physical. In the event, both Kant and Goethe were wrong about chemistry. *Pace* Kant, it became a rigorous quantitative science; *pace* Goethe, the elective affinity of elements need not and cannot be reduced to a spiritual origin but is explained in terms of the electropositive or electronegative structure of their electron shells.

A great work of art allows for endless interpretation. Goethe himself directs us to what is at least one important theme in the *Elective Affinities* – the force of contingency and presence. In his advertisement, he abruptly turned from the themes of science and coherence to the unpredictable and uncontrollable force of contingency. The quotation above continues as follows:

> since there is after all just one nature and even the realm of serene rational freedom is irresistibly pervaded by traces of turbid, passionate necessity that can only be erased fully by a higher hand and perhaps not even in this life.[36]

The necessity that concerns Goethe is not the formal necessity of logic or the nomic necessity of science but that of contingency.

The *Elective Affinities* takes place on a baronial estate, and the efforts of the four protagonists, of the men in particular, are directed toward gaining a lucid and explicit grasp of the estate and to giving it a more commodious and pleasing shape. They turn to chemistry because Charlotte, Baron Eduard's wife, is worried about the lead glaze on their pottery and verdigris on their copper containers.[37] When Eduard, Charlotte, and the Captain (later promoted to Major) apply the chemical puzzle of crosswise affinity to themselves, they obviously identify the first pair, AB with Charlotte and Eduard, and the second, CD, with the Captain and with Charlotte's yet to arrive niece, Ottilie. But when it comes to the separations and affinities, Eduard assumes the harmless and amusing association of the two men and the two women. Their pleasant and constructive life, however, is upset by unforeseen and wrenching events. Charlotte and the Captain are drawn to each other, Eduard and Ottilie fall hopelessly in love, Charlotte and Eduard have an unexpected offspring, Ottilie causes the infant boy to drown, and when finally the way to pairwise dividing and crosswise uniting seems open, Ottilie renounces her happiness.

While contingency heightens presence, lawfulness diminishes it, theoretically by reducing full-bodied things to instances of scientific laws and practically by furnishing the explanations that make technological control and the reduction of the contingencies of hunger, cold, illness, and untimely death possible. Contingencies come in many sizes and shapes. The large and captivating incidents and accidents present themselves with commanding force. Once present, there was no preventing them through planning, and there is no escaping them now through a technological fix. If the event is positive, we are willing to accept it as sheer good fortune or just deserts. If it is negative, we tend to react with uncomprehending anger and the indignant protest: "I don't need that." Goethe's contemporaries too were brought up short by the darkness of contingency. The "serene rational freedom" of the Enlightenment had already become the ruling cultural assumption.[38]

If scientific explanation and rational planning are to no avail in the face of outrageous fortune, what attitude is appropriate? It is exemplified by Charlotte, who from the start has respect for contingency and shows fortitude in the face of misery. When the Captain suggests that the notion of *elective* affinity implies preference and a choice, Charlotte replies:

> Forgive me as I forgive the scientist; but I would not at all think of a choice here, much rather of natural necessity, and not even of that, for in the end it is perhaps just a matter of opportunity; opportunity makes relationships, just as it makes thieves.[39]

So far, however, Charlotte's attitude seems to point forward more to the existentialist self-assertion in the face of absurdity than to the romantic recovery of continuity with nature and tradition. The treatment of nature in the *Elective Affinities* is a warning rather than an exemplar. The hills, creeks, ponds, rocks, and trees of the baronial estate are endlessly subjected to planning and improvement without grace and repose ever settling on it all. The recovery of tradition is tellingly triggered by an "incident" (*Vorfall*) concerning a dispute about an endowment for the cemetery near the castle.[40] The incident calls attention to the church inside the cemetery and finally leads to the discovery of a chapel, attached to the side of the church.

Though Goethe in his later years had many a mordant thing to say about the romantics, he, along with Herder, Hamann, and others, was one of the pioneers in the rediscovery and appreciation of the tradition that had been outshone by the Enlightenment.[41] Church and chapel are evidently in the gothic style that had seemed barbarous and negligible to Enlightenment tastes. Charlotte, Ottilie, and a young architect now set about to restore and embellish the church and particularly the chapel.

One's heritage is a contingency too. You do not get to choose it from a catalogue. Goethe stresses the point: "This church had been standing there for several centuries in the German style and art, erected in substantial proportions and happily adorned."[42] The concern of the three is to make that heritage present again – a formidable task. In the conversation about the disputed cemetery endowment, Charlotte reminds her listeners of "how hard it is to honor the present properly."[43] Goethe described the convergence of past and present that occurred in the church by saying that the church "grew, so to speak, toward the past."[44] Goethe further described the past that comes to be present in the ancient drawings that the architect shows Charlotte and Ottilie and that serve as models for the figures that the architect and Ottilie are to paint on the vaults of the chapel. Of the archaic character of these drawings Goethe says: "how engaging did the viewers find it! From all of these figures, purest presence was shining forth."[45]

The chapel becomes the place of rest and grace. Ottilie and Eduard were buried there. The novel ends with these sentences:

> Thus the lovers are resting next to one another. Peace dwells over their place; serene, familiar images of angels are looking down on them, and what a pleasant moment it will be when some time in the future they will awake together.[46]

When joining Goethe's novel with present knowledge, we see the chemical and human elections and affinities separate from one another. The former are now scientifically and lawfully intelligible, the latter, by contrast rather than in springing from a common root, are all the more commanding in their contingency and presence. Commanding presence is a large and varied theme in Goethe's writings and is often in tension with the theme of restless striving – a tension not always resolved though it is decided in favor of restful presence in the *Elective Affinities*. Presence and immediacy can be found at three different levels in the novel. Immediate presence in the broadest sense is simply part of Goethe's genius as a writer (and perhaps his limit as a philosopher and scientist as well). What Goethe always does is show rather than tell, and especially so in the *Elective Affinities*, as Benno von Wiese has noted: "everything is presence, image, and figure; nothing is merely thought."[47]

Within this widest region of presence, a stronger sort of presence belongs to those archetypal entities that in an exemplary way unite the universal and the particular. Carl Friedrich von Weizsäcker accuractely observed that the exemplar (*Gestalt*) rather than the law (*Gesetz*) is at the center of Goethe's conception of science.[48] Some scholars see in it a scientific ontology in its own right.[49] Weizsäcker thinks it hearkens back to a Platonic ontology of ideal forms.[50] Both of these claims seem mistaken to me.

As for Goethe's putative Platonism, it would conflict with Goethe's delight in the concrete presence of things. Spinoza was the early philosophical influence on Goethe, and from him he took the notion that tangible reality is entirely the presence of the spiritual. To this Goethe added his own profound pleasure in shaping reality. It is what he practiced as the master of his household, as director of the Weimar theater, and as a minister of the Duchy of Saxe-Weimar-Eisenach, and it is what the old Faust looks back to with satisfaction.[51]

Though Aristotle was a minor figure in Goethe's pantheon, the fourfold Aristotelian causality serves best to explicate Goethe's view of how humans should shape reality. The transformation of the baronial estate was an exemplar of Aristotelian craft with Eduard's friend, the Captain, to be the efficient cause of the fusion of the material and formal causes. As Eduard explains to Charlotte:

> Country folk have the right knowledge; however, the information they provide is confused and not candid. The experts from the city and the

academies are, to be sure, clear and consistent, but they lack immediate insight into things. My friend promises to furnish both.[52]

Alas, no final cause of rightful and persuasive authority was available to Goethe,
nor was the hierarchy of being that would lend Aristotelian forms their place in
a cosmic order, nor, finally, did Spinoza's plenitude and perfection of God or
nature have the kind of forceful presence that would constitute a background
(inconsistent, to be sure, from Spinoza's point of view) for the ordering of reality.

"Goethean science" has been captured by outsiders and cranks. Though
Goethe himself has abundantly aided and abetted his scientific acolytes, he has
left few traces in serious contemporary science. More to the point here, the world
of Aristotelian exemplars and Spinozist necessity is overwhelmed in the *Elective
Affinities* by a yet more formidable presence, implacable at first and finally
consoling. Goethe's ontology is, of course, for the most part implicit in his
literary works of art. In the *Elective Affinities* it is richly presented and morally
eloquent and yet imperiled by doubts and deficiencies. The most elaborate
account of the good life in the *Elective Affinities* is the description of the calm
before the catastrophes and the respite between the catastrophes and the final
denouement. It is a highly educated life, musical, enterprising, and companion-
able, enacted in a prosperous, graceful, and engaging setting. But it is a brittle
world, finally shattered by contingency; and though rest and grace prevail in the
end, the final word is a promise with little hope of durability and prospect of
detailed realization.

The rigorous ontology of Newtonian physics was for Goethe an incomprehensible iron cage. The distant rumble of the rising Industrial Revolution that
was to reshape terrestrial reality from the ground up Goethe observed with helpless anxiety. And the deeply engrained if benign paternalism of the *Elective
Affinities* was insensible to the democratic impulses that were about to reform
social reality. Goethe's enduring bequest, however, is the appreciation of the
splendor and presence of reality.

Schelling recognized that Kantian lawfulness and Goethean presence had to
be reconciled with one another. While still in his teens, he studied Kant at the
Tübinger Stift, the famous college where the spiritual and administrative elite
of the Duchy of Württemberg was trained and where, as it happened, many a
poet and philosopher was educated as well. Schelling also took courses at the
Stift in mathematics and in theoretical and experimental physics. After the
conclusion of his studies and a year of teaching as private tutor, Schelling went
to the University of Leipzig where he attended lectures in physics, chemistry,
and medicine.[53] Thus, unlike Goethe and much like Kant, Schelling took the
physical sciences seriously. He was well read in the scientific literature of his
day, and he was determined to take on the task of coming to philosophical
terms with rigorous quantitative science.

Like Goethe and unlike Kant, Schelling was taken with the datum of all
data, with the unsurpassable givenness of nature.[54] This awakening to natural

reality was an original and surprising event in young Schelling's life. His philo-sophical curiosity and self-confidence had been stimulated by a meeting with Fichte in 1794 while Schelling was still a student at the Tübinger Stift. But rather than follow Fichte in tracing all there is to the sole and original given-ness of the ego, Schelling pleaded for the equally primordial datum of nature.[55] The results of this remarkable turn of thought were Schelling's *Ideas for a Philosophy of Nature* of 1797 (when Schelling was twenty-two) and of *On the World Soul*, published the following year.[56] Goethe recognized a soul mate in Schelling – sometime between 1798 and 1802 he responded with his poem "World Soul."[57] They met in 1798; the result was a life-long friendship.

What Schelling had in common with both Kant and Goethe was the surrender of astronomical cosmology to physics. To Schelling too, the large-scale structure of the universe, a few comments aside, seemed morally barren. He also shared with Kant and Goethe the particular point of departure in the search for a moral cosmology: the critique and the transcendence of the atomist and mechanical Newtonian ontology. There were differences of emphasis, to be sure. Schelling was much more pointed than Kant in his criticisms of Newtonian science, and contrary to Goethe, Schelling was concerned primarily with Newton's physics rather than Newton's optics.[58] Schelling is notorious for his variable and impressionist approaches to philosophy.[59] Thus, unsurprisingly, he did not work out a resolution of the Kantian-Goethean conflict in his seminal books, but rather furnished a variety of instructive explorations. Here again the notion of physical lawfulness provides a thread we can follow in tracing Schelling's search for a moral cosmology.

One way of recovering a moral cosmology that Schelling pursued was to limit the scope and significance of the scientific theories that threatened to reveal a merely mechanical universe. It is a path that has remained dear to humanists and social scientists. They counter the claim that physics gives us a uniquely penetrating and accurate account of reality with the claim that scientific theories are in the first instance not about reality at all, but are merely convenient fictions or instruments for the prediction and control of the reality we are all familiar with. Schelling gave a clear statement of what has come to be called scientific instrumentalism in his *Ideas for a Philosophy of Nature*:

> It is precisely this that in large part constitutes the task of a philosoph-ical theory of nature, viz., to determine the admissibility as well as the limits of those fictions in physics that are simply necessary for further progress of investigation and observation and that impede scientific progress only if we intend to employ them beyond their limit.[60]

There is evidently a Kantian impetus in Schelling's realization that the physical lawfulness of reality needs to be acknowledged somehow; and, *pace* Goethe, he agreed with Kant that this lawfulness has a mathematical structure. In fact he went beyond Kant in holding out for the inclusion of chemistry among the properly scientific theories:

> For, if a theory of nature is a *science of nature* only to the extent that mathematics can be employed in it, then a system of chemistry that admittedly rests on false presuppositions, but is in a position, on the strength of those presuppositions, to render this experimental doctrine mathematically, is preferable to one that may have the merit of resting on true principles, but, those principles notwithstanding, must give up on scientific precision (on the mathematical construction of the respective phenomena).[61]

Yet unlike Kant, Schelling holds that what today we call theoretical objects fail to *explain* phenomena. Speaking of "magnetic matter" as a theoretical object, Schelling says: "To assume the latter is fine as long as it is only taken as a (*scientific*) *fiction* that is used as a basis for *experiments* and *observations* (as a *heuristic device*), but not for *explanations* and *hypotheses* (as a *principle*)."[62]

What fell outside the scope of the fictional objects and laws of physics, according to Schelling, were the phenomena of force and organism.[63] To mark out a realm of agency and life was to recover the contours of a moral cosmology. Schelling knew of course that force was prominent in Newtonian physics as universal attraction and as the product of mass and acceleration in the second law of motion.[64] Regarding the force of attraction, Schelling, following Kant, tried to show its inadequacy by arguing that attraction without repulsion is unintelligible. In this line of attack he felt much encouraged by Newton's own misgivings about a force that acted instantaneously at a distance.[65] In the general scholium to the *Principia*, Newton acknowledged that he had "not yet assigned a cause to gravity," and, having summarized the effects of gravity in the solar system, he conceded that he had "not as yet been able to deduce from phenomena the reason for these properties of gravity." Yet he pronounced himself satisfied "that gravity really exists and acts according to the laws that we have set forth and is sufficient to explain all the motions of the heavenly bodies and of our sea."[66]

Schelling, however, denied that, absent a causal account, it is legitimate to claim that an explanation has been forthcoming:

> If therefore Newton was really doubtful, as he says in several places (disregarding others where he explicitly claims the opposite) what "the actual cause of attraction" is supposed to be, whether it is not perhaps actuated by an impulse or in some other way, unknown to us, then the use he made of that principle in the construction of a world system, was in fact mere semblance of a use; or rather the force of attraction itself was for him a scientific fiction that he used merely to reduce the phenomenon as such to laws without thereby intending to explain it.[67]

What Schelling found missing in Newtonian mechanics were "spontaneously moving forces."[68] At times he hoped to locate them in those fields where mechanics had so far failed to provide coherent and comprehensive explanations, namely in chemistry and electricity.[69] Most remarkably, Schelling thought that chemistry as a science would reveal how living matter sought "to step out of its equilibrium and to surrender to the free play of forces."[70] The marks of life and agency for Schelling were freedom and contingency while mechanics was the science of necessity.[71] What remained unexplained was how chemistry as the mathematical discipline that Schelling was looking forward to would consist with chemistry as the science of contingency. Analogously it was unclear how the recognition of repulsion as the supposedly necessary complement to attraction would be compatible with and perhaps complementary to attraction and gravity. Just as Kant finally had to all but emasculate his favored metaphysical–dynamical hypothesis and salute the philosophically flawed mathematical–mechanical version, so Schelling damned the repulsive force with faint praise and conceded explanatory power to the attractive force of gravity:

> Hence we cannot use the repulsive force in its application any further than to make basically comprehensible how a material world is possible. As soon, however, as we try to explain how a certain system of the world is possible, the repulsive force does not take us even one step ahead.
>
> The structure of the heavens and the motions of the heavenly bodies we can explain only and solely by virtue of the laws of universal attraction.[72]

Still, concern with force remained one of the hallmarks of Schelling's philosophy of nature, and on occasion he called his approach "dynamical philosophy" to distinguish it from the mechanical philosophy of the Newtonians.[73]

The *Ideas for a Philosophy of Nature* of 1797 was concerned with physics, chemistry, magnetism and electricity. The study of organic nature was projected for a later work.[74] Although Schelling denied that his *On the World Soul* of 1798 was the sequel to the *Ideas*, it clearly centers on the notion of organism.[75] In fact the full title of the book reads: *On the World Soul: A Hypothesis of Higher Physics Toward the Explanation of General Organism.* Schelling was searching for the seat and origin of force and life and at one point placed it in the infinite spaces of the universe. He declared that "in these regions actually lies the source of those inexhaustible forces that in individual matter spread in all directions and that compel and sustain movement and life on the solid cosmic bodies."[76] This, he adds, is where we find the "fullness of force that, being generated ever afresh in the depths of the universe, pours forth in individual streams from the center toward the periphery of the world system."[77]

There was, no doubt, a grand vision of a moral cosmology in these declarations. But it confronted Schelling with two problems – (1) how to make this vision of a life-giving cosmos articulate and fruitful for everyday life; and (2) how to square this vision with the part of contemporary cosmology that had assumed hegemony as Newtonian physics. Schelling's answer to the second question was indirect and was given some ten years later. The answer to the first question was characteristic of the openness and insight of young Schelling. He stated the problem as a dilemma. Speaking of the failed efforts of "most natural scientists" to appreciate "the meaning of the problem of the origin of organized bodies," he said:

> If some of them posit a special *life force* that, as a magic power, suspends all effects of natural laws in a living being, they thereby suspend *a priori* any possibility of explaining organization physically.
>
> If, to the contrary, others explain the origin of all organization on the basis of *dead chemical forces*, they thereby suspend any freedom of nature in formation and organization.[78]

In a formulation, reminiscent of Kant's effort to reconcile the freedom of imagination with the lawfulness of understanding, Schelling sketched the path between the horns of the dilemma as follows: "Nature, in its blind lawfulness, must be free, and conversely must be lawful in its full freedom; in this union alone lies the concept of organization."[79] He hoped that this union could be accomplished through the notion of a "formative drive." But in the end he realized that the formative drive had no more explanatory power than the repulsive force. For purposes of explaining the union of freedom and lawfulness, he realized, the formative drive is no more than "a barrier for investigative reason or the cushion of an obscure quality on which to get reason to rest."[80] The bulk of *On the World Soul*, as well as that of *Ideas*, is devoted, however, not to such revealing overviews, but rather to detailed discussions of contemporary scientific problems and to attempts at aiding their solutions through theoretical considerations. Some of Schelling's extended conjectures strike us as bizarre today.[81] Yet Schelling was willing to submit to the discipline of experience and often called for experiments that would decide the fate of his conjectures.[82]

Schelling's two early books won him Goethe's admiration and friendship and, as a consequence, a professorial appointment and regular contact with Goethe in Jena.[83] How this interchange influenced the intellectual careers of the young philosopher and the mature poet is controversial and difficult to adjudicate. In his Jena years, at any rate, Schelling's comments on the natural sciences became more impatient and peremptory.[84] A dialectical monism of mind and matter began to eclipse and cover up the dilemma Schelling had uncovered in the *World Soul*. Eventually, art (and later religion) took the place of nature as the great datum philosophy had to acknowledge and understand. In the introduction to his lecture *Philosophy of Art*, delivered in the winter semester of 1802–3, Schelling marked his change of focus as follows:

If we feel irresistibly driven to behold the inner essence of nature and to uncover that fruitful source that, with eternal uniformity and lawfulness, pours out of itself so many grand phenomena, how much more must it be of interest to us to penetrate the organism of art wherein, out of absolute freedom, supreme unity and lawfulness constitute themselves which allow us to recognize the wonders of our own spirit much more immediately than nature.[85]

Evidently, the reconciliation of freedom and lawfulness remained Schelling's concern, but he now thought that its actuality could be detected both in nature and in art. In his *Further Presentations from the System of Philosophy*, also of 1802, Schelling specified the difference and consonance of these reconciliations and claimed cosmic significance for the reconciliation of the reconciliations.

The universe, taken as an absolute, is articulated as the most perfect organic being and as the most perfect work of art – for reason, which recognizes it in the absolute, it is so *qua* absolute truth, for imagination, which represents it, it is so *qua* absolute beauty. Each of these simply expresses the same unity from different sides, and both coincide in the absolute point of indifference in whose recognition lies at once the beginning and the goal of all knowledge.[86]

This passage suggests a complementary relationship between imagination and reason and, by extrapolation, of art and science. Robert J. Richards, in a most insightful and helpful essay, has argued that "the aesthetic-epistemic principle of the complementarity of the poetic and scientific conceptions of nature" was "a fundamental organizing conception in the philosophy of the early Romantics."[87] Complementarity, he further urges, is also the resolution Schelling helped to achieve of the tension between Kant and Goethe and between lawfulness and freedom. Although I have developed these tensions in ways that differ from Richards's argument, I accept and am indebted to his principal claim – complementarity is the resolution to, as I put it above, the dilemma of lawfulness and contingency. I would like to offer, however, a modification or extension of Richards's complementarity that bears significantly on the search for a moral cosmology.

There are two connected features of complementarity as Richards understands it that need clarification. Richards finds his notion of complementarity both in Schelling at the beginning of the nineteenth century and in Helmholtz at the close of the century. Schelling, Richards says, "theoretically demonstrated that scientific understanding and artistic intuition did not play out in opposition to one another, as Goethe once thought, but that they reflected complementary modes of penetrating to nature's underlying laws."[88] Helmholtz's conception of complementarity, drawn from Goethean sources, Richards summarizes thus: "Both aesthetic intuition and scientific comprehension drove down to the type, to the underlying force that gave form to the surface of things."[89]

The first problem lies in the putative point of convergence of science and art. The first quotation from Richards suggests that science and art converge on "underlying laws." These are elsewhere characterized by Goethe as "an unknown law-like something" and as the "secret laws of nature," and by Richards (following Schiller) as "ineffable rules," (following Schelling) as "inarticulable laws," and as "nature's concealed laws."[90]

Taken at face value, these laws are the notorious wheels that turn without turning anything else. There can be no substantive disagreements about them because they are unavailable for appeal or proof. They cannot link causes and effects because we do not know their causal structure. They cannot be the laws that concern the natural sciences because those laws are known and articulate, and where they are not, science does not rest until they are discovered and spelled out.

Hence there can be no convergence of art and science. There can be, again taking the parlance of laws at face value, a kind of complementarity, and here we come to the second problem of Richards's complementarity. It might be called *alternative complementarity*, the sort that is familiar from the Copenhagen interpretation of quantum theory where our inability to comprehend the particle model and the wave model of, say, the electron in one single model has led to the decision to baptize the problem "complementarity" and be done with it.

If alternative complementarity is the final word, the romantic search for a coherent and morally promising cosmology is no closer to its goal than was Schelling before he met Goethe. There is, however, a second kind of complementarity, the more usual sort actually, the one we may call *interdependent complementarity*. Two things are complementary in that sense if they are distinct but cannot be thought or exist apart from one another. A simple example is the relation of matter and form. That we should not perhaps take *law* as Richards, following Goethe, Schiller and Schelling, uses it at face value, i.e. in the sense of an explicit and informative assertion that carries nomic necessity and a universal quantifier, appears from Richards's summary of Helmholtz's view where it is the "type" and the "underlying force," and not necessarily a law, that art and science converge on.[91] Goethe too uses law in the sense of "exemplar" and in the wider sense of cultural or artistic constraint.[92]

The interdependent complement of a law of nature is the instance that constrains the law to yield the description and explanation of a state of affairs or an event. Newton's laws of motion merely outline a possible space. They describe an actual world when we insert the values of, for example, the solar system in place of the variables for mass, acceleration, distance, etc. Among the greatest of instantiations are works of art. They are the most eminent complements to laws. They are instances of high contingency – unpredictable and unprocurable and, in that sense, free. So are the nuisances of life and the results of throwing dice. But these are part of the low contingency of everyday reality. Works of art rise above and lend orientation to the plains of normalcy.[93]

Between these landmarks and the laws of science are intermediate instantiations, regularities that possess neither the universal necessity of laws nor the commanding presence of art works. Among them are the natural kinds of everyday life, the species of biology, and the genres of literature. Goethe's preoccupation with regularities was a distraction, it seems to me, and led him into a hopeless competition with scientific lawfulness. His great accomplishment was the disclosure of presence. The solution to Schelling's problem is the interdependent complementarity of Kantian lawfulness and Goethean presence. Before I suggest how this romantic bequest can bear moral fruit today, I have to remark briefly on how Kant, Goethe and Schelling instruct us as regards the second term of a moral cosmology – the cultural receptivity, or the lack of it, for cosmic significance.

Kant was most attuned to the emancipatory aspirations of his age though he did not escape the ethnic and masculine prejudices of the times. His hope for an era of equality, dignity and self-determination (the three aspects of the moral law) was tempered by his dark view of human goodness, and it was largely untouched by the rising Industrial Revolution.[94] Goethe contemplated the rise of machines with dismay and put little store by the ability of the bourgeoisie to deal intelligently with the challenges of the age. In the "Prologue in Heaven" he has Mephisto explain why there was little hope that people might join in the cosmic contemplation of the archangels. Mephisto likens humanity to a grasshopper

that ever flies and, flying, leaps
and in the grass still sings its same old song;
if only it would always lie there in the grass!
It sticks its nose in every nuisance.[95]

Schelling generally paid little attention to everyday culture and people, and in a lecture where he did so, in his "On the Essence of German Science" of 1807, he justified this neglect by claiming that the deplorable state of German culture was beyond philosophical illumination and redemption.[96] More important, among the causes of this calamity he mentioned "mechanism," an implicit extension of the mechanical ontology of Newton to the cultural and political sphere. "Complete mechanization of all talents, all history and institutions," Schelling said, "is here the highest goal." Not that the state achieves wholeness in this way, but the reason for this failure is always sought in the imperfection of mechanism; new wheels are installed that need still other wheels for their regulation, and so on ad infinitum; what remains ever equally distant is the mechanical *perpetuum mobile* whose invention is reserved entirely for the organic art of nature and humanity.

The romantic bequest for today's task of finding a moral cosmology tells us that we need to discover the moral force of the complementarity of lawfulness and contingency for a technological society. First of all, then we have to follow Kant and Schelling in taking contemporary scientific cosmology seriously. It presents great obstacles and opportunities. The obstacles lie in the astoundingly unsettled state of contemporary astrophysics. First, more than 90 percent of the universe is unaccounted for. We know of these missing parts only because of their gravitational force (dark matter) or their accelerating force in driving the expansion of the universe (dark energy). Second, the two theoretical pillars of contemporary physics, quantum theory and relativity theory, are inconsistent with one another. And third, there is at least a possibility that ours is not *the* universe but only a phase or a part of a multiverse, a system of many, perhaps infinitely many and perhaps fundamentally different, universes.[97]

But new vistas and opportunities have opened up as well. Hubble's discovery of the expanding universe in the late 1920s led by way of retrospection to the discovery of the big bang, and this in turn reunited astronomy and physics to give us astrophysics. There is, moreover, a solid majority view in astrophysics that we should proceed on the assumption that there is just one universe, ours; and there is a somewhat less solid majority view that a unified theory, a "final theory," of relativity theory and quantum theory will be reached and that string theory is currently the most promising contender.

There are now the beginnings of moral cosmologies that depart from some outline of the final theory. There is Frank Tipler's provocative *The Physics of Immortality*.[98] Eric Chaisson disavows any moral or teleological intentions, and yet exhibits an enthusiasm that is hard to identify.[99] Brian Swimme and Thomas Berry have told a creditable story of the cosmos that begins broadly and then zeroes in on our planet and our environmental obligations.[100] The most magnificent moral cosmology is Robert Pack's *Before It Vanishes*, a cycle of thirty-one poems that ponder and respond to Heinz R. Pagels's *The Cosmic Code*.[101] It unites scientific lawfulness with the poetic presence of nature and culture. Philosophers need to catch up with Pack, and just to gesture in the direction of that task let me point out how astrophysics allows us to trace a remarkable path from lawfulness to contingency and to the threshold of a moral cosmology.

The notion of force that so occupied Schelling has divided into four kinds in the twentieth century, and the task since has been to discover their original unity and the history of their unfolding. At the beginning of the process stands the symmetry of the cosmos. The early universe was the most symmetrical possible. In mathematics and physics, symmetry is a principle of invariance that connects with what we ordinarily mean by symmetry, but then also greatly exceeds the ordinary sense of symmetry. It makes common sense to say that a daisy has a greater symmetry than a lady's slipper. The latter looks the same from left and right. The daisy however, looks the same no matter how you turn it on its vertical axis. A sphere is more symmetrical yet because, unlike a daisy, it looks the same however you turn it on any of its infinitely many axes. These are spatial symmetries, but there are also symmetries of time, illustrated, for example, by laws that hold today as well as tomorrow and in fact at any time whatever. There are more recondite symmetries, and altogether there is a half-dozen of them.[102]

In the early universe there was no distinction between gravity, electromagnetism, the strong force, and the weak force. As the temperature fell, this perfect symmetry was broken. First the gravitational force crystallized out from the other three, then the strong force, and finally the weak and electromagnetic forces separated from one another. They govern, as far as we know, today's entire universe. But there is also a local breaking of symmetries. The geology of Earth is notably asymmetrical so that, when something natural approaches symmetry, it becomes noteworthy for that reason, a mountain peak that approximates the rotational symmetry of a pyramid (like Haystack Butte in Montana) or the bilateral symmetry of a stone arch (like the Eye of the Needle above the Missouri in Montana, now destroyed). Many conifers and flower heads are instances of rotational symmetry. The full moon and the ripples of a stone thrown in a calm pond are fleeting examples of perfectly round symmetry. Most remarkable is the bilateral symmetry of most animals, and it grows in force from fish to lions and finally to humans, who in their erect posture display bilateral symmetry most fully. This is the least kind of symmetry. It is entailed by all others and entails no other. Hence when it comes to symmetry, the Earth, its inhabitants, and humans particularly, occupy a singular position.

Part of a cosmic symmetry is the homogeneity and isotropy of the universe. It is homogeneous in that it looks the same from every location and isotropic in that it looks the same in all directions. This is so for the universe at large. At the scale of galaxies there are differences of shape and distance. The solar system is still less homogeneous and isotropic. Every human being, finally, embodies a strongly oriented space with the significantly different up-and-down, front-and-back, and left-and-right orientation that is reflected in the hundreds of metaphors we use all the time.[103] Likewise the natural and cultural space humans inhabit is oriented around landmarks.

The breaking of symmetries leads us from lawfulness to contingency, from causal links to unforethinkable presence. We owe technology the instruments that have enabled us to discover the ontology of nuclear physics through accelerators and to discover the astronomy of space and time through terrestrial and satellite telescopes. But technology as a culture has also made us unaware of the starry heavens through light pollution, and unconcerned about science and ethics through the distractions of consumption. To cure these maladies we need to learn again the depth and presence of nature and culture from poets like Goethe and Pack.

Notes

1 Immanuel Kant, *Kritik der praktischen Vernunft*, Akademie-Ausgabe, Berlin, Georg Reimer, 1913, vol. 5, p. 161. All translations from the German are mine.
2 *The Cambridge Dictionary of Philosophy*, Robert Audi (ed.), Cambridge, Cambridge University Press, 1995.

3 Ernan McMullin, "Cosmology," *Routledge Enclyclopedia of Philosophy*, Edward Craig (ed.), London, Routledge, 1998, vol. 2, pp. 677–81.
4 Johann Wolfgang von Goethe, *Wilhelm Meisters Wanderjahre*, Hamburger Ausgabe, Munich, Beck, 1973, vol. 8, p. 429.
5 See Clemens Brentano's mordant "Der Philister" ("The Philistine") in *Clemens Brentano: Werke*, Friedhelm Kemp (ed.), Munich, Hanser, 1963, vol. 2, pp. 959–1016; and Frederick Beiser, *Enlightenment, Revolution, and Romanticism*, Cambridge MA, Harvard University Press, 1992, pp. 232–6.
6 Goethe, *Wilhelm Meister*, pp. 429, 430.
7 Beiser, *Enlightenment, Revolution, and Romanticism*, pp. 225–7.
8 Immanuel Kant, *Allgemeine Naturgeschichte und Theory des Himmels oder Versuch von der Verfassung und dem mechanischen Ursprunge des ganzen Weltgebäudes, nach Newtonischen Grundsätzen abgehandelt*, Akademie-Ausgabe, Berlin, Georg Reimer, 1910, vol. 1, pp. 215–368.
9 Isaac Newton, *The Principia*, trans. I. Bernard Cohen and Ann Whitman, Berkeley, University of California Press, 1999, p. 940.
10 Kant, *Allegmeine Naturgeschichte*, pp. 269–83.
11 Penny Fannia, "From Stardust Shroud, an Astral Child," http://www.theage.com.au/cgibin/print_article.pl?path=/news/2001/02/22/FFXCVT0WFJC.HTML (2 July 2001).
12 Kant, *Allgemeine Naturgeschichte*, pp. 361 and 358.
13 *Ibid.*, p. 366.
14 *Ibid.*
15 *Ibid.*, pp. 329–31.
16 Immanuel Kant, *Kritik der reinen Vernunft*, 2nd edn, Akademie-Ausgabe, Berlin, Georg Reimer, 1911, vol. 3, pp. 281–382 (A 405–567, B 432–595).
17 *Ibid.*, pp. 383–461 (A 567–704, B 595–732).
18 *Ibid.*, pp. 360–81 (A528–65, B 556–93).
19 Gordon G. Brittan Jr, *Kant's Theory of Science*, Princeton, Princeton University Press, 1978. We can think of *real possibility* as an ontological space intermediate between logical possibility and actuality. Brittan sketches Kant's really possible world as one "whose limits and general form are given by the Categories, a world having a particular spatial-temporal-causal form that contains enduring centers of attractive and repulsive forces" (p. 21).
20 Immanuel Kant, *Metaphysische Anfangsgründe der Naturwissenschaft*, Akademie-Ausgabe, Berlin, Georg Reimer, 1911, vol. 4, pp. 481–2, 523–4.
21 *Ibid.*
22 Kant, *Metaphysische Anfangsgründe*, pp. 523–4.
23 Brittan, *Kant's Theory of Science*, p. 160.
24 Kant, *Metaphysische Anfangsgründe*, p. 544.
25 *Ibid.*, p. 525. In part, however, the dispute about *vis viva* was not about whether but about how to quantify or mathematize it and about whether the resulting equation agreed with experiment.
26 *Ibid.*, pp. 524–5.
27 *Goethes Gespräche mit Eckermann*, Franz Deibel (ed.), n.p., Insel-Verlag, 1949, p. 124.
28 Johann Wolfgang von Goethe, *Faust*, Hamburger Ausgabe, Hamburg, Christian Wegner, 1966, vol. 3, pp. 16 (lines 243–70).
29 *Gespräche mit Eckermann*, p. 278. See also Goethe's "Erfahrung und Wissenschaft," Hamburger Ausgabe, Hamburg, Christian Wegner, 1971, vol. 13, pp. 23–5.
30 *Gespräche mit Eckermann*, p. 396.
31 Kant, *Metaphysische Anfangsgründe*, p. 471. See also pp. 468–9.

32 An account of Goethe's long-standing interest in elective affinity can be found in Benno von Wiese's notes to *Die Wahlverwandtschaften*, Hamburger Ausgabe, Hamburg, Christian Wegner, 1968, vol. 6, pp. 680–4.
33 Goethe, *Wahlverwandtschaften*, p. 276.
34 Friedrich Wilhelm Joseph von Schelling, *Ideen zu einer Philosophie der Natur*, *Schellings Werke*, Manfred Schröter (ed.), Munich, Beck, 1956, pp. 82, 170; *Von der Weltseele*, 2nd edn, Hamburg, Friedrich Perthes, 1806, p. 67.
35 Goethe, *Wahlverwandtschaften*, p. 632.
36 *Ibid.*
37 *Ibid.*, p. 268.
38 See notes to *Wahlverwandtschaften*, pp. 627–53.
39 *Ibid.*, p. 274.
40 *Ibid.*, pp. 360, 365.
41 *Goethes Gespräche mit Eckermann*, pp. 460, 466–7, 698.
42 Goethe, *Wahlverwandtschaften*, p. 366.
43 *Ibid.*, p. 365.
44 *Ibid.*, p. 367.
45 *Ibid.*
46 *Ibid.*, p. 490.
47 *Ibid.*, p. 653.
48 Carl Friedrich von Weizsäcker, "Nachwort," Hamburger Ausgabe, Hamburg, Christian Wegner, 1971, pp. 540–2.
49 Frederick Amrine and Francis J. Zucker, "Postscript: Goethe's Science: An Alternative *to* Modern Science or *within* It – or No Alternative at All?" in *Goethe's Science*, Amrine Zucker and Harvey Wheeler (eds), Dordrecht, Reidel, 1987, pp. 373–88.
50 Weizsäcker, "*Nachwort*," pp. 542–5.
51 Nicholas Boyle, *Goethe*, vol. 2, Oxford, Clarendon Press, 2000, pp. 92–3, 202–6.
52 Goethe, *Wahlverwandschaften*, p. 245.
53 Hans Jörg Sandkühler, *Friedrich Wilhelm Joseph Schelling*, Stuttgart, Metzler, 1970, pp. 63–7.
54 Schelling, "Ueber den wahren Begriff der Naturphilosophie" (1801), in *Ausgewählte Schriften*, Manfred Frank (ed.), Frankfurt, Suhrkamp, 1985, vol. 2, pp. 1–35.
55 Joseph L. Esposito, *Schelling's Idealism and Philosophy of Nature*, Lewisburg, Bucknell University Press, 1977, pp. 31–46.
56 See note 34 above.
57 Goethe, "Weltseele," Hamburger Ausgabe, Hamburg, Christian Wegner, 1966, vol. 1, pp. 248–9.
58 Schelling, *Ideen*, pp. 197–200.
59 Esposito, *Schelling's Idealism*, pp. 9–10.
60 *Schelling, Ideen*, p. 107.
61 *Ibid.*, pp. 269–70.
62 *Ibid.*, p. 168. Schelling is not consistent on explanation. Sometimes he claims it for philosophy; at other times he surrenders it to science. See *Weltseele*, p. 11.
63 Esposito, *Schelling's Idealism*, pp. 68–77.
64 *Ibid.*, pp. 68–77.
65 Schelling, *Ideen*, pp. 234–46.
66 Newton, *Principia*, p. 943. See also Bernard Cohen's comments to *The Principia, ibid.*, pp. 274–80.
67 Schelling, *Ideen*, p. 198.
68 *Ibid.*, p. 62.
69 On chemistry, see *ibid.*, p. 259; on electicity, *ibid.*, pp. 144–6.

70 *Ibid.*, p. 193.

71 *Ibid.*, pp. 193–4. See also p. 259.

72 *Ibid.*, p. 243.

73 *Ibid.*; *Weltseele*, pp. 11 and 46. Strictly speaking dynamics is a branch of mechanics (as are kinematics and statics). Perhaps in deference to this, Schelling in *Ideen*, p. 259, calls mechanical dynamics "general dynamics" and the dynamics of contingency "special dynamics."

74 Schelling, *Ideen*, pp. 349–50.

75 Schelling, *Weltseele*, p. XII.

76 *Ibid.*, p. 134.

77 *Ibid.*, p. 135.

78 *Ibid.*

79 *Ibid.*, p. 234. Kant, *Kritik der Urteilskraft*, Akademie-Ausgabe, Berlin, Georg Reimer, 1911, vol. 6, pp. 68–9.

80 Schelling, *Weltseele*, p. 235.

81 See his theories of light and of heat and heating, *ibid.*, pp. 29–42, 43–80.

82 Schelling, *Ideen*, pp. 121, 123, 139, 148, 153, 298, 304, 320; *Weltseele*, op. cit., pp. 95, 121.

83 Boyle, *Goethe*, pp. 593–4.

84 See Schelling's additions to the second editions of *Ideen* and *Weltseele* (included in the editions referred to in note 34 above).

85 Schelling, "Philosophie der Kunst," Manfred Frank (ed.), *Ausgewählte Schriften*, 6 vols, vol. 2, Frankfurt, Suhrkamp, 1985, pp. 185–6.

86 Schelling, "Fernere Darstellungen aus dem System der Philosophie," Frank, *Ausgewählte Schriften*, p. 167.

87 Robert J. Richards, "Nature is the Poetry of the Mind, or How Schelling Solved Goethe's Kantian Problems," forthcoming in *The Kantian Legacy in Nineteenth-century Science*, Michael Friedman and Alfred Nordmann (eds), Cambridge MA, MIT Press, 2006, p. 3 (this and the following page references refer to the electronic version that is available at http://home.uchicago.edu/vrjr6/articles/Schelling-Goethe.doc, 31 July 2003).

88 Richards, *Nature is the poetry of the mind*, pp. 26–7.

89 *Ibid.*, p. 3.

90 *Ibid.*, pp. 10, 27, 9, 23, 27.

91 *Ibid.*, p. 27.

92 Goethe, "Wissenschaft und Erfahrung," p. 12, and his poem "Natur und Kunst," Hamburger Ausgabe, Hamburg: Christian Wegner, 1966, vol. 1, p. 245.

93 For more on high contingency, see my *Holding On to Reality*, Chicago, University of Chicago Press, 1999, pp. 105–13.

94 Kant, *Grundlegung der Metaphysik der Sitten*, Akademie-Ausgabe, Berlin, Georg Reimer, 1911, vol. 4, pp. 406–45.

95 Goethe, *Faust*, p. 17 (lines 289–92).

96 Schelling, "Ueber das Wesen deutscher Wissenschaft," *Ausgewählte Schriften*, Manfred Frank (ed.), Frankfurt, Suhrkamp, 1985, vol. 4, pp. 11–28.

97 Max Tegmark, "Parallel Universes," *Scientific American*, May 2003, pp. 40–51.

98 Frank J. Tipler, *The Physics of Immortality*, New York, Anchor Books, 1995.

99 Eric J. Chaisson, *Cosmic Evolution*, Cambridge MA, Harvard University Press, 2001.

100 Brian Swimme and Thomas Berry, *The Universe Story*, New York, HarperSanFrancisco, 1994.

101 Robert Pack, *Before It Vanishes*, Boston MA, Godine, 1989.

102 Brian Greene, *The Elegant Universe*, New York, Norton, 1999, pp. 124–6, 167–70.

103 George Lakoff and Mark Johnson, *Metaphors We Live By*, Chicago, University of Chicago Press, 1980.

Part V

RETURNING THE EVERYDAY

12

FURTHER REFLECTIONS ON HEIDEGGER, TECHNOLOGY, AND THE EVERYDAY

Hubert L. Dreyfus and Charles Spinosa

The danger of technology

In writing about technology, Heidegger formulates his goal as gaining a free relation to technology – a way of living with technology that does not allow it to "warp, confuse, and lay waste our nature."[1] According to Heidegger our nature is to be world disclosers. That is, by means of our equipment and coordinated practices we human beings open coherent, distinct contexts or worlds in which we perceive, feel, act, and think. The Heidegger of *Being and Time* called a world an understanding of being and argued that such an understanding of being is what makes it possible for us to encounter people and things as kinds of beings.[2] He considered his discovery of the ontological difference – the difference between the understanding of being and the beings that can show up given an understanding of being – his single great contribution to Western thought.

Middle Heidegger (roughly from the 1930s to 1950) adds that there have been a series of total understandings of being in the West. He distinguished roughly six epochs in our changing understanding of being. Technology stands at the end of this series of epochs. First, things, people, and gods were understood on the model of nature as physis, i.e. as springing forth on their own. Then, things, people, and so forth were dealt with as needing to be helped to come forth, so what made encountering anything possible was understood as poeisis, or nurturing. Poeisis was followed by an understanding of things as finished works (res) that stood on their own. Understanding everything as res led to the understanding of all beings as creatures produced by a creator God. This religious world gave way to the modern one in which everything was organized as objects to stand over against and satisfy the desires of autonomous and stable subjects. In 1950, Heidegger declared that we were entering a new and especially dangerous epoch in the history of being which he called the technological understanding of being.

Yet Heidegger does not oppose technology. He hopes to reveal the essence of technology in a way that "in no way confines us to a stultified compulsion to push on blindly with technology or, what comes to the same thing, to rebel helplessly against it."[3] Indeed, he promises that "when we once open ourselves expressly to the essence of technology, we find ourselves unexpectedly taken into a freeing claim."[4]

We will need to explain "opening," "essence," and "freeing" before we can understand Heidegger here. To begin with, when he asks about the "essence" of technology we must understand that his question cannot be answered by defining our concept of technology, but rather by describing our practices. Heidegger notes that technology can be correctly defined as "a means and a human activity," and so it is as old as civilization. But if we ask about the essence of technology (the technological understanding of being, the style of our technological practices), we find that modern technology is "something completely different and ... new."[5] What, then, is the essence of technology, the technological life-style, which we can call technicity? And how does opening ourselves to technicity give us a free relation to technology – our technological devices?

Again, Heidegger makes clear that he is not announcing one more reactionary rebellion against technology, although many take him to be doing just that. Nor is he doing what modern thinkers would like to do: proposing a way to get technology under control so that it can serve our rationally chosen ends. We repeat this point because Heidegger has not always been clear about what distinguishes his approach from other contemporary accounts. Consequently, those who seek to make sense of Heidegger in terms of current anti-technological banalities can find support in his texts. Moreover, when he does finally arrive at a clear formulation of his own original view, it is so strange that interpreters tend to attend only to the steps he takes in getting to his view rather than the view itself.

At first Heidegger attacked consumerism, as do many:

> The circularity of consumption for the sake of consumption is the sole procedure which distinctively characterizes the history of a world which has become an unworld.[6]

Next, like many current critics of technology, in his mid-career Heidegger was under the impression that the danger of technology was that man was dominating everything and exploiting all beings for his own satisfaction. As if man were a subject in control, and the objectification of everything were the problem. He says in 1940:

> Western history has now begun to enter into the completion of that period we call the modern, and which is defined by the fact that man becomes the measure and the center of beings. Man is what lies at the

bottom of all beings; that is, in modern terms, at the bottom of all objectification.[7]

Even as late as 1955, in an address to the Black Forest peasants, he points out:

> The world now appears as an object open to the attacks of calculative thought.... Nature becomes a gigantic gasoline station, an energy source for modern technology and industry.[8]

In this address he also laments the appearance of television antennas on the peasants' dwellings, and gives his own version of an attack on the leveling power of the media and the need to return to the local.

> All that with which modern techniques of communication stimulate, assail, and drive man – all that is already much closer to man today than his fields around his farmstead, closer than the sky over the earth, closer than the change from night to day, closer than the conventions and customs of his village, than the tradition of his native world.[9]

Such quotations are eminently understandable and make Heidegger seem a nostalgic romantic who resists consumerism, the exploitation of the earth, and mass media in the name of the world of the simple peasants who are close to nature and live in a closed traditional world. No doubt Heidegger had some sympathy for such views but he works out a position that goes well beyond them.

As his thinking develops, he comes to the surprising and provocative conclusion that focusing on loss and destruction, as late romantics do, is itself a technological reaction to technology. It is fully inside the technological style of life.

> All attempts to reckon existing reality ... in terms of decline and loss ... are merely technological behavior.[10]

Seeing our situation as posing a problem that must be solved by appropriate action is also part of the technological understanding of instrumentality. The more we feel threatened by technology the more we seek to master it, to turn it into a resource for our purposes:

> [T]he instrumental conception of technology conditions every attempt to bring man into the right relation to technology.... The will to mastery becomes all the more urgent the more technology threatens to slip from human control.[11]

Heidegger is adamant that no attempt to arrest technology will work. "No single man, no group of men," he tells us, "no commission of prominent statesmen, scientists, and technicians, no conference of leaders of commerce and industry, can brake or direct the progress of history in the atomic age."[12]

Heidegger's view is both darker and more hopeful that commentators normally suppose. He thinks there is a more dangerous situation facing modern man than the technological destruction of nature and civilization, yet this is a situation about which something can be done – at least indirectly. Heidegger's concern is the distortion of human nature and subsequent loss of meaning that results from technicity, that is, the technological style of life; not the destruction caused by specific technologies. Consequently, he distinguishes the current problems caused by technology – the media, ecological destruction, nuclear waste, etc. – from the devastation that would result should technicity prevail and technology solve our environmental and other problems.

> What threatens man in his very nature is . . . that man, by the peaceful release, transformation, storage, and channeling of the energies of physical nature, could render the human condition . . . tolerable for everybody and happy in all respects.[13]

Not that Heidegger is against simply being happy, rather, for him "the greatest danger" is that

> the approaching tide of technological revolution in the atomic age could so captivate, bewitch, dazzle, and beguile man that calculative thinking may someday come to be accepted and practiced as the only way of thinking.[14]

The real danger, then, is not the destruction of nature or culture nor a self-indulgent consumerism, but a new totalizing style of practices that would restrict our openness to people and things by driving out all other styles of practice that enable us to be receptive to reality. This threat is not a problem for which we must find a solution, but an ontological condition that requires a transformation of our understanding of being. For that, we need to understand technicity as our current mode of revealing things and people.

To this end, Heidegger describes the hydroelectric power station on the Rhine as a paradigm technological device. He says:

> The revealing that rules throughout modern technicity has the character of a setting-upon, in the sense of a challenging-forth. That challenging happens in that the energy concealed in nature is unlocked, what is unlocked is transformed, what is transformed is stored up, what is stored up is, in turn, distributed, and what is distributed is switched about *ever anew*.[15]

And he concludes:

Everywhere everything is ordered to stand by, to be immediately at hand, indeed to stand there just so that it may be on call for a further ordering. Whatever is ordered about in this way has its own standing. We call it the standing-reserve (*Bestand*), i.e., resources.[16]

But we can see now that electricity is not a perfect example of technological stuff because it is not endlessly transformable. Rather, it ends up finally turned into light, heat, or motion to satisfy our desires. As soon as he sees that information is truly endlessly transformable, Heidegger switches to the computer manipulation of information as his paradigm.[17] He observes that nature has become "a system of information."[18]

With the endless transformability of information as his paradigm, Heidegger came finally to see that technicity could treat people and things as resources to be enhanced without setting desiring and controlling subjects over against objectified things. He notes that a modern airliner understood in its technological essence, is not a tool; it is not an object at all, but just a flexible and efficient cog in the transportation system.[19] Passengers are presumably not modern autonomous subjects who use the transportation system to satisfy their desires either, but resources recruited by the tourist industry to fill the planes. Likewise, the tourist industry is itself a resource for the aeronautics and entertainment industries, and so on with no primary, central, or anchoring institution or fact. We are standing reserve as much as any of the technological stuff around us. Heidegger concludes: "Whatever stands by in the sense of standing-reserve no longer stands over against us as object."[20] And he adds:

> The subject-object relation thus reaches, for the first time, its pure "relational," i.e., ordering, character in which both the subject and the object are sucked up as standing-reserves.[21]

The essence of modern technology Heidegger concludes, is to seek to order everything so as to achieve more and more flexibility and efficiency: "[E]xpediting is always itself directed from the beginning . . . towards driving on to the maximum yield at the minimum expense."[22] That is, our only goal is optimal ordering for its own sake.

Now, half a century after Heidegger wrote "The Question Concerning Technology," the new understanding of being as technicity is becoming evident. A concrete example of this change and of an old-fashioned subject's resistance to it can be seen in a *New York Times* article entitled: "An Era When Fluidity Has Replaced Maturity" (20 March 1995). The author, Michiko Kakutani, laments that "for many people . . . shape-shifting and metamorphosis seem to have replaced the conventional process of maturation." She then quotes a psychiatrist, Robert Jay Lifton, who notes in his book *The Protean Self* that "We are becoming fluid and many-sided. Without quite realizing it, we have been evolving a sense of self appropriate to the restlessness and flux of our time."[23] Kakutani then comments:

> Certainly signs of the flux and restlessness Mr. Lifton describes can be found everywhere one looks. On a superficial cultural level, we are surrounded by images of shape-shifting and reinvention, from sci-fi creatures who "morph" from form to form, to children's toys [she has in mind Transformers that can be transformed from robots into vehicles and back]; from Madonna's ever expanding gallery of ready-to-wear personas, to New Age mystics who claim they can "channel" other people or remember "previous" lives.[24]

From the perspective of those who share the technological life-style, goals like serving God, society, our fellow men, or even ourselves, no longer make sense. Human beings, on this view, become a resource to be used – but more importantly, to be enhanced – like any other, to be all they can be. Heidegger says:

> Man, who no longer conceals his character of being the most important raw material, is also drawn into this process.[25]

In the film *2001: A Space Odyssey*, the robot, HAL, when asked if he is happy on the mission, says: "I'm using all my capacities to the maximum. What more could a rational entity want?" This is a brilliant expression of what anyone would say who is in touch with our current understanding of being. We all want to get the most out of our possibilities. We pursue the development of our potential simply for the sake of further growth. We have no specific goals.

We thus become part of a system that no one directs but which moves towards the total mobilization and enhancement of all beings, even us. This is why Heidegger observes that the perfectly ordered society that succeeds in providing for the welfare of all is not the solution of our problems but the culmination of the devastation produced by technicity.

Heidegger also sees that "it would be foolish to attack technology blindly. It would be shortsighted to condemn it as the work of the devil. We depend on technical devices; they even challenge us to ever greater advances."[26] Instead, Heidegger suggests that there is a way we can keep our technological devices and yet remain true to ourselves as world disclosers, as receivers of understandings of being:

> We can affirm the unavoidable use of technical devices, and also deny them the right to dominate us, and so to warp, confuse, and lay waste our nature.[27]

To understand how this might be possible, we can use Japan as an example. In contemporary Japan, traditional, non-technological practices and life-styles exist alongside the most advanced high-tech production and consumption. The TV set and the household gods share the same shelf – the Styrofoam cup co-exists with the porcelain teacup. Each draws from the Japanese its own authentic style of care, not at all like our arch, hyper-aesthetic adornment in retro objects whether cars, drinks, movies, or behaviors. We thus see that, the Japanese can enjoy technological devices without taking over the technological understanding of being.

For us to be able to make a similar dissociation, Heidegger holds, we must rethink the history of being in the West. Then we will see that, although a technological understanding of being is our destiny, it is not our fate. That is, although our understanding of things and ourselves as resources to be ordered, enhanced, and used efficiently has been building up since Plato, we are not stuck with that understanding. Although technicity governs the way everything that matters shows up for us today, we can hope for a transformation of our opti-mizing style of life.

Only those who mistakenly think of Heidegger as opposing technology will be surprised at his next point. Once we see that technology is our latest under-standing of being, we will be grateful for it. This clearing is the cause of our distress, yet, if it were not given to us to encounter things and ourselves as resources, nothing would show up as anything at all, and no possibilities for action would make sense. And once we manifest in our dealings with people and things, not just understand conceptually, that we receive our technological understanding of being, we will have stepped out of technicity. For we then see that what is most important in our lives, namely our practical understanding of ourselves and everything else, is not subject to efficient ordering and enhance-ment. This transformation in our sense of reality is precisely what Heideggerian thinking seeks to bring about. Heidegger seeks to make us see that our practices are needed as the place where an understanding of being can establish itself. At first, Heidegger writes as though we acknowledge technicity as an under-standing of being by taking up a reverential relation to the way our practices come to be coordinated by a tacit style. The change is a matter of developing a sensitivity to the way understandings of being are not created or mastered by us. They are received by us.

> [M]odern man must first and above all find his way back into the full breadth of the space proper to his essence. That essential space of man's essential being receives the dimension that unites it to some-thing beyond itself . . . that is the way in which the safekeeping of being itself is given to belong to the essence of man as the one who is needed and used by being.[28]

According to Heidegger, unlike the slow process of cleaning up the environ-ment, which is, of course, necessary, this transformation in our understanding of being, this radical change of life-style, must take place in a sudden gestalt switch.

The turning of the danger comes to pass suddenly. In this turning, the clearing belonging to the essence of being suddenly clears itself and lights up.[29]

The danger – namely, that we have a restricted and totalizing understanding of being – when grasped as the danger, becomes that which saves us.

The selfsame danger is, when it is as the danger, the saving power.[30]

This remarkable claim gives rise to two opposed ways of understanding Heidegger's positive response to technology. Both interpretations agree that once one recognizes technicity for what it is – an historical understanding of being – one gains a free relation to it. We neither push forward technological efficiency as our sole goal nor always resist it. If we are free of the technological imperative we can, in each case, discuss the pros and cons. As Heidegger puts it:

We let technical devices enter our daily life, and at the same time leave them outside, . . . as things which are nothing absolute but remain dependent upon something higher. I would call this comportment toward technology which expresses "yes" and at the same time 'no," by an old word, releasement towards things.[31]

One natural way of understanding this proposal holds that once we get in the right relation to technology, namely recognize it as a clearing, a way of opening up a world, it is revealed as just as good as any other clearing.[32] Efficiency – getting the most out of ourselves and everything else, "being all you can be" – is fine, as long as we see that efficiency for its own sake is not the only end for man, dictated by reality itself, but is just our current understanding.

Heidegger seems to support this acceptance of the givenness of the technological understanding of being as a way of living with technology when he says:

That which shows itself and at the same time withdraws [i.e. our understanding of being] is the essential trait of what we call the mystery. I call the comportment which enables us to keep open to the meaning hidden in technology, openness to the mystery.[33]

But then Heidegger touches on a positive proposal, which he slips in unexplained at the end of "The Question Concerning Technology."

Through this we are not yet saved. But we are thereupon summoned to hope in the growing light of the saving power. How can this happen? Here and now and in humble things, that we may foster the saving power in its increase.[34]

So acceptance of the mystery of the gift of an understanding of being cannot be Heidegger's whole story about how to overcome technological nihilism, for he immediately adds:

> Releasement toward things and openness to the mystery belong together. They grant us the possibility of dwelling in the world in a totally different way. They promise us a new ground and foundation upon which we can stand and endure in the world of technology without being imperiled by it.[35]

Indeed:

> Releasement toward things and openness to the mystery give us a vision of a new rootedness which someday might even be fit to recapture the old and now rapidly disappearing rootedness in a changed form.[36]

So preserving our sense of ourselves as receivers of understandings of being is not enough. Only:

> That which shows itself and at the same time withdraws [i.e., our understanding of being] is the essential trait of what we call the mystery. I call the comportment which enables us to keep open to the meaning hidden in technology, *openness to the mystery*.[37]

What, then, is Heidegger proposing? He is suggesting we need to discover and cultivate humble everyday practices such as playing with our children, gardening or backpacking in the wilderness, practices that remain marginal precisely because they resist optimization. These practices can, of course, also be engaged in for the sake of mental improvement, health, and networking. Indeed, the greatest danger is that even the marginal practices will be mobilized as resources. What is not efficient and optimizing is seen as either trivial or as needing technological help so as to be more efficient. We must therefore protect these endangered species of practices. But just protecting non-technological practices, even if we could succeed, would still not give us what we need. We need to overcome the hegemony of our restricted modern clearing, by being drawn by our ways of dealing with humble things, into the various differentiated understandings of being that are still marginally available in our culture.

The saving power of the everyday

In "The Thing" (1949) and "Building Dwelling Thinking" (1951), Heidegger explores the positive aspect of the variety of practices that enable us to be world disclosers. In these essays, he turns to the local gatherings that set up local worlds. As in *Being and Time*, a world involves equipment, roles, and attunement to what matters. Such local worlds occur around some everyday thing whose origin usually lies in another understanding of being. Such things temporarily bring into their own both the thing itself and those involved in the shared activity concerning the use of the thing.

For Heidegger, the gathering of people around things like a jug of wine or a family meal resists the totalizing and dispersing effects of the efficient ordering demanded by the technicity. Heidegger calls this event a thing thinging and the tendency in the practices to bring things and people into their own, appropriation. Albert Borgmann has usefully called the practices that support this local gathering focal practices.[38] Typical Heideggerian examples of things that focus such local gathering are a wine jug and an old stone bridge. Such things gather Black Forest peasant practices, but, as Borgmann has seen, the family meal acts as a focal thing when it draws on the culinary and social skills of family members to create a world that solicits fathers, mothers, husbands, wives, children, familiar warmth, good humor, and loyalty to come to the fore in their excellence, or in, as Heidegger would say, their ownmost.

Heidegger describes such focal practices in general terms by saying that when things thing, they bring together earth and sky, divinities and mortals. When he speaks this way, his thinking draws on Hölderlin's difficult poetry; yet, what Heidegger means has its own coherence so long as we keep the phenomenon of a thing thinging before us. Heidegger, thinking of the taken-for-granted practices that ground situations and make them matter to us, calls them earth. In the example of the family meal, the grounding practices would be the traditional practices that produce, sustain, and develop the nuclear family. Historians who work on the origins of today's nuclear family in the seventeenth century, detail them for us. Among others, they consist of such practices as freedom to choose marriage partners, companionate marriage (as opposed to patriarchical marriage), architecture that withdraws a nuclear family from kin, affectionate relations with children, treating children as a class whose innocence is to be preserved, and moving sensuality from extramarital relations into marriage.[39] It is essential to the way these earthy practices operate that they make family gathering matter. That is why they tend to be affective practices. For families, such practices as the shared family meal, companionship between husbands and wives, love of children, and worry over their children's education are not simply retro options for the family to indulge in or not. They are the basis upon which all manifest options appear. To ground mattering, such practices must remain in the background. (When, for instance, we live as nuclear families, we just take it for granted that parents love children; we have no sensitivity to the steely emotional distance from infants and children who are not worth much affection because they are likely to die soon.) Thus, Heidegger conceives of the earth as being fruitful by virtue of being withdrawn and hidden.

By sky, Heidegger means the manifest stable possibilities for action that arise in focal situations.[40] When a focal situation is happening, one feels that certain actions are appropriate. At dinner, actions such as reminiscences, warm conversation, as well as questions to draw people out, are solicited. But, political arguments, impromptu combat, private jokes, and brooding silence are discouraged.

In describing the cultural paradigms that provide unified understandings of being, Heidegger was content with the categories of earth and world which map roughly on the thing's earth and sky. But when Heidegger thinks of focal practices, he also thinks in terms of divinities. When a focal event such as a family meal is working to the point where it has its particular integrity, one feels extraordinarily in tune with all that is happening, a special graceful ease takes over, and events seem to unfold of their own momentum – all combining to make the moment all the more centered and more a gift. A reverential sentiment arises; one feels grateful for receiving all that is brought out by this particular occasion. Such sentiments are frequently manifested in practices such as toasting or in wishing others could be joining in such a moment. The older practice for expressing this sentiment was, of course, saying grace. We sense that we did not and could not make the occasion a center of focal meaning by our own effort but rather that the special attunement required for such an occasion to work has to be granted to us, and that is what Heidegger wants to capture in his claim that when a thing things, the divinities must be present. How the power of the divinities will be understood will depend on the understanding of being of the culture, but the phenomenon Heidegger describes crosses cultures and understandings of being.

The fourth element of what Heidegger calls the fourfold is the mortals. By using this term, Heidegger is describing us as disclosers, and he thinks that death primarily reveals our disclosive way of being to us. When he speaks of death, he does not mean demise or a medically defined death. He means an attribute of the way human practices work that causes mortals (later Heidegger's word for people who are inside a focal practice) to understand that they have no fixed identity and so must be ready to relinquish their current identity in order to assume the identity that their practices next call them into attunement with.[41] But their current identity, like their role at a family dinner, is not experienced as arbitrary and to be played with, but as their identity that will be theirs as long as that local world lasts.

So far, we have described the phenomenon of a thing thinging in its most glamorized form. We experience the family coming together as an integrated whole at a particular moment around a particular event. Heidegger calls this heightened version of a thing thinging, a thing "shining forth."[42] But if we focus exclusively on the glamorized version, we can easily miss two other essential features of things that Heidegger attends to in "Building Dwelling Thinking." The first is that things thing even when we do not respond to them with full attention. For instance, when we walk off a crowded street into a cathedral, our whole demeanor changes even if we are not alert to it. We relax in its cool darkness that solicits meditativeness. Our sense of what is loud and soft changes, and we quiet our conversation. In general, we manifest and become centered in whatever reverential practices remain in our post-Christian way of life. Heidegger claims that things like bridges and town squares establish location and thereby thing even in ways more privative than our cathedral example. He seems to mean that so long as people who regularly encounter such things are socialized to respond to them appropriately, their practices are organized around the things, and the thing's solicitations are taken into account even when we do not notice.

Heidegger uses various sorts of bridges as examples of things thinging but not shining. His list of bridges includes a bridge from almost every major epoch in his history of the Western understandings of being. Heidegger's account could begin with the physis bridge – say some rocks or a fallen tree – which just flashes up to reward those who are alert to the offerings of nature. But he, in fact, begins his list with a bridge from the age of poiesis: "the river bridge near the country town [that] brings wagon and horse teams to the surrounding villages."[43] Then there is the bridge from high medieval times when being was understood as createdness. It "leads from the precincts of the castle to the cathedral square." Oddly enough there is no bridge from the subject/object days, but Borgmann has leapt into the breach with magnificent accounts of the heroic effort involved in constructing railroad bridges across huge gorges, and poets, starting with Walt Whitman, have seen in the massive iron structure of the Brooklyn bridge an emblem of the imposing power and optimism of America.[44] Such a modern bridge is solid and reliable but it is rigid and locks into place the locations it connects.

In reading Heidegger's list of bridges from various epochs, each of which things inconspicuously "in its own way," no one seems to have noticed the last bridge in the series. After a few kitschy remarks on the humble old stone bridge, Heidegger continues: "The highway bridge is tied into the network of long-distance traffic, paced as calculated for maximum yield."[45] Clearly Heidegger is thinking of the postmodern autobahn interchange, in the middle of nowhere, connecting many highways so as to provide easy access to as many destinations as possible. Surely, one might think, Heidegger's point is that such a technological artifact could not possibly thing. Yet Heidegger continues:

> Ever differently the bridge escorts the lingering and hastening ways of men to and fro. . . . The bridge gathers, as a passage that crosses, before the divinities – whether we explicitly think of, and visibly give thanks for, their presence, as in the figure of the saint of the bridge, or whether that divine presence is hidden or even pushed aside.[46]

Heidegger is here following out his sense that different things thing with different modes of revealing, that is, that each "gathers to itself in its own way earth and sky, divinities and mortals."[47] Figuring out what Heidegger might mean here is not a question of arcane Heidegger exegesis but an opportunity to

276

return to the difficult question we raised at the beginning: How can we relate ourselves to technology in a positive way while resisting its devastation of our essence as world disclosers?

We can begin to understand how Heidegger thinks we can respond to technological things without becoming a collection of disaggregated skills, if we ask how the interchange bridge could gather the fourfold. What is manifest as the sky are multiple possibilities. The interchange connects anywhere to anywhere else – strictly speaking it does not even connect two banks. All that is left of earth is the mattering of a thrill at the vastness of our possibilities, at being all we can be. What about the divinities? Heidegger has to admit that they have been pushed aside. As one speeds around a cloverleaf one has no pre-modern sense of having received a gift. Neither is there a modern sense, such as one might experience on a solid, iron railroad bridge, that human beings have here achieved a monumental triumph. All one is left with is a sense of flexibility and excitement. One senses how easy it would be to go anywhere. If one is in tune with technological flexibility, one feels lucky to be open to so many possibilities.

We can see that for Heidegger the interchange bridge is certainly not the best kind of bridge but it does have its style, and one can be sensitive to it in the way it solicits. One can speed around it with an appreciation of the endless possibilities of the freeway.

But what of the danger? Technology silently, secretly transforms us into resources. How can we be anything but resources for the automotive or petroleum industries? Would not getting in tune with the technological bridge turn us into a resource with no stable identity and no world that we are disclosing? How could we still have some sense of having an identity and of contributing to disclosing? This is where Heidegger's stress on our being mortals becomes essential. To understand oneself as mortal means to understand one's identity and world as fragile and temporary and requiring one's active engagement. In the case of the highway bridge, it means that, even while getting in tune with being a flexible resource, one does not understand oneself as being a resource all the time and everywhere. One does not always feel pressured, for instance, to optimize one's possibilities by refusing to get stuck on back roads and taking only interstates. Rather, as one speeds along the overpass, one senses one's mortality, namely that one has other skills for bringing out other sorts of things, and therefore one is never wholly a resource. Thus, because one has in readiness other skills for dealing with other styles of things thinging, one can relate to the highway bridge not just as a transparent device but as a specific way of bringing technological ordering out in its ownmost. But that is to say that the highway bridge can be affirmed as a possible kind of focal thing that calls to us as mortals, only if there are other focal things around that preserve other styles in which things can thing. We can experience ourselves as mortals on the highway bridge only if we are sufficiently attentive to other kinds of things thinging that we are ready to respond appropriately to them.

If we take the case of some everyday thing like a writing implement, we can more clearly see both the positive role that can be played by technological things as well as the special danger they present. Like bridges the style of writing implements reflects their place in the history of being. The fountain pen solicits us to write to someone for whom the personality of our handwriting will make a difference. When involved in the practices that make the fountain pen seem important, we care about such matters as life plans, stable identities, character, views of the world, and so on. We are subjects dealing with other subjects. A typewriter, however, will serve us better if we are recording business matters or writing factual reports simply to convey information. A word processor hooked up to the internet with its great flexibility solicits us to select from a huge number of options in order to produce technical or scholarly papers that enter a network of conversations. Using a word processor one cannot help but feel lucky that one does not have to worry about erasing, retyping, literally cutting and pasting to move text around, and mailing the final product.

We have just described what may seem to be a paradox. We have said that even a technological thing can gather earth, sky, mortals and divinities, which are supposed to be the aspects of practices that gather people, equipment and activities into local worlds, with roles, habitual practices and a style that provide disclosers with a sense of integrity or centeredness. But technological things notoriously do not gather. They disperse us as resources into a bunch of disaggregated skills with a style of flexible adaptation. So how could such prac-tices gather into a local world? There is only one answer here. Neither the technological equipment nor the technological roles gather in the first instance, but the skills for treating ourselves and the world as a disaggregated set of possi-bilities are what are gathered, so that we have a consistent openness that enables everything to appear crisply as a possibility for efficient action. In the context of our capacity to experience other local worlds, we feel awe for the vastness of our technological options. In the light of the local technological world, we see that in our general technological style of being everything is given to as possibilities. That is, everything is gathered as options. We are thus opened to the mystery of the givenness of a clearing in which things show up as optimal.

Here the dangerous seduction of technological devices becomes obvious. Because the word processor makes writing easy for desiring subjects, and this ease in writing solicits us to enter conversations rather than produce finished works, the word processor attached to the internet solicits us to substitute it for pens and typewriters, thereby eliminating the equipment and the skills that were appropriate for modern subject/object practices. It takes a real commit-ment to focal practices based on stable subjects and objects to go on writing personal letters with a fountain pen and to insist that papers written on the word processor must reach an elegant finish. If the tendency to rely completely on the flexibility of technological devices is not resisted, we will be left with only one kind of writing implement promoting one style of practice, namely those of endless transformation and enhancement. Then, indeed, as Heidegger says, we will have become resources ourselves.

Heidegger sees technology as disaggregating our identities into a contin-gently built-up collection of skills; technological things solicit certain skills without requiring that we take ourselves as having one kind of identity or another. This absence may make our mode of being as world disclosers invisible to us. This absence of worlds and disclosing would be what Heidegger calls the greatest danger. But this absence could also allow us to become sensitive to the various identities we have when we are engaged in disclosing the different worlds focused by different kinds of things. Then, as such disclosers, we could even respond to technological things as revealing one kind of local world and become sensitive to our openness to the mystery of worlds arriving. Hence, Heidegger's view of technology allows him to find a positive relation to it, but only so long as we maintain skills for disclosing other kinds of local worlds.[48]

Heidegger's thought until 1955, when he wrote "The Question Concerning Technology," was that preserving the saving power of humble everyday things was compatible with awaiting a single God.[49] But in his final reflections, Heidegger came to think that there was an essential antagonism between a unified understanding of being setting up one total world and local worlds. Of course, he always realized that there would be an antagonism between the style set up by a cultural paradigm and the everyday focal things that could only be brought out in their ownness in a style different from the dominant cultural style. Such things would inevitably be dispersed to the margins of the culture. There, they would "shine" in contrast to the dominant style but would have to resist being considered irrelevant or even wicked. But he later realized that, if there were a single understanding of being, even those things that come into their own in the dominant cultural style would be inhibited as things. Already in his "The Thing" essay Heidegger goes out of his way to distinguish the orig-inal meaning of "thing" in German from the gathering that concerns him. In German a thing is originally a gathering to discuss a matter of concern to the community. When a thing things, however, it is self-contained. It forms its own community.[50]

Given the way local worlds establish their own internal coherence that resists any imposition from outside, there is bound to be a tension between the glorious cultural paradigm that establishes an understanding of being for a whole culture and the inconspicuous everyday things. The shining of one would wash out the shining of the others. The tendency toward one unified world would impede the gathering of local worlds. Given this tension, in a late seminar Heidegger abandoned what he had considered up to then his crucial contribution to philosophy, the notion of a single world with a single style and its correlated notion of the ontological difference between the understanding of being and beings. He remarks that "from the perspective of appropriation [which we gloss as the tendency in the practices to bring things out in their ownmost] it becomes necessary to free thinking from the ontological difference." He continues, "From the perspective of appropriation, [letting-presence] shows itself as the relation of *world and thing*, a relation which could in a way be understood as the relation of being and beings. But then its peculiar quality would be lost."[51]

What presumably would be lost would be the self-enclosed and differentiated character of local worlds focused by everyday things thinging. The notion of being as the stage for beings washes out local worlds. It follows that, as mortal disclosers of worlds in the plural, the only comprehensiveness we can hope to achieve is our openness to dwelling in many worlds and the capacity to move among them. Only such a capacity allows us to accept Heidegger's criticism of technicity and, at the same time, share Heidegger's genuinely positive free relationship to technological things.

Notes

1 Martin Heidegger, *Discourse on Thinking*, trans. John M. Anderson and E. Hans Freund, New York, Harper and Row, 1966, p. 54.
2 Martin Heidegger, *Being and Time*, trans. J. Macquarie and E. Robinson, New York, Harper Collins, 1962.
3 Martin Heidegger, "The Question Concerning Technology," in *The Question Concerning Technology and Other Essays*, trans. W. Lovitt, New York, Harper Torchbooks, 1977, pp. 25–6.
4 *Ibid.*, p. 26.
5 *Ibid.*, p. 5.
6 Martin Heidegger, "Overcoming Metaphysics," in *The End of Philosophy*, trans. Joan Stambaugh, New York, Harper and Row, 1973, p. 107.
7 Martin Heidegger, *Nietzsche*, vol. 4, New York, Harper and Row, 1982, p. 28.
8 Heidegger, *Discourse on Thinking*, p. 50.
9 *Ibid.*
10 "The Question Concerning Technology," p. 48.
11 *Ibid.*, p. 5.
12 *Discourse on Thinking*, p. 52.
13 Martin Heidegger, *Poetry, Language, Thought*, trans. A. Hofstadter, New York, Harper and Row, 1971, p. 116.
14 Heidegger, *Discourse on Thinking*, p. 56.
15 Heidegger, "The Question Concerning Technology," p. 16, (our emphasis).
16 *Ibid.*, p. 17.
17 See Martin Heidegger, "On the Way to Language" (1959), trans. Peter D. Hertz, in *On the Way to Language*, New York, Harper and Row, 1971, p. 132. See also *Discourse on Thinking*, p. 46.
18 Heidegger, "The Question Concerning Technology," p. 23.
19 *Ibid.*, p. 17.
20 *Ibid.*
21 Heidegger, "Science and Reflection," in *The Question Concerning Technology and Other Essays*, p. 173.
22 *Ibid.*, p. 15.
23 Robert Jay Lifton as quoted by Michiko Kakutani, "When Fluidity Replaces Maturity," *New York Times*, 20 March 1995, C11.
24 Michiko Kakutani, "When Fluidity Replaces Maturity."
25 *The End of Philosophy*, p. 104.

26 *Discourse on Thinking*, p. 53.
27 *Ibid.*, p. 54.
28 "The Question Concerning Technology," p. 39.
29 *Ibid.*, p. 44.
30 *Ibid.*, p. 39.
31 *Discourse on Thinking*, p. 54.
32 See Richard Rorty, "Heidegger, Contingency and Pragmatism," in H. L. Dreyfus and H. Hall (eds), *Heidegger: A Critical Reader*, Oxford, Blackwell, 1992.
33 *Discourse on Thinking*, p. 55.
34 "The Question Concerning Technology," p. 33.
35 Heidegger, *Discourse on Thinking*, 1, p. 55.
36 *Ibid.*
37 *Ibid.*, p. 56 (our italics).
38 Albert Borgmann, *Technology and the Character of Contemporary Life*, Chicago, University of Chicago Press, 1984, pp. 196–210.
39 Lawrence Stone, *The Family, Sex, and Marriage*, New York, Harper and Row, 1979, pp. 149–50.
40 Martin Heidegger, "Building Dwelling Thinking," in *Poetry Language Thought*, p. 149.
41 Martin Heidegger, "The Thing," in *Poetry Language Thought*, pp. 178–9.
42 *Ibid.*, p. 182.
43 "Building Dwelling Thinking," pp. 152.
44 Albert Borgmann, *Crossing the Postmodern Divide*, Chicago: University of Chicago Press, 1992, pp. 27–34.
45 "Building Dwelling Thinking," p.152.
46 *Ibid.*, pp. 152–3.
47 *Ibid.*, p. 153.
48 Martin Heidegger, "The Turning," in *The Question Concerning Technology and Other Essays*, p. 43, where Heidegger claims that our turning away from technology will, at least initially, be a matter of turning to multiple worlds where things thing.
49 "The Question Concerning Technology," p. 33–5.
50 To put this in terms of meals, we can remember that in Virginia Woolf's *To the Lighthouse* arguments about politics brought in from outside almost ruin Mrs Ramsey's dinner party, which only works when the participants become so absorbed in the food that they stop debating external political concerns and get in tune with the actual occasion. The same thing happens in the film *Babette's Feast*. The members of an ascetic religious community go into the feast resolved to be true to their dead founder's principles and not to enjoy the food. Bickering and silence ensues until the wine and food makes them forget their founder's concerns and attunes them to the past and present relationships that are in accord with the gathering.
51 Martin Heidegger, "Summary of a Seminar on the Lecture 'Time and Being,'" in *On Time and Being*, trans. Joan Stambaugh, New York, Harper Torchbooks, 1972, p. 37 (our italics).

13

BEGINNING IN WONDER

Placing the origin of thinking

Jeff Malpas

> And the end of all our exploring
> Will be to arrive where we started
> And know the place for the first time.
>
> (T. S. Eliot, *Four Quartets* ["Little Gidding"])

The origin of philosophy

"It is through wonder [*thaumazein*]," says Aristotle, "that men now begin and originally began to philosophize";[1] and as Plato tells us, through the mouth of Socrates, "wonder is the feeling of a philosopher, and philosophy begins in wonder."[2] These sayings are well known, and they are also representative of an important thread that runs through much of the Western philosophical tradition,[3] and yet, in contemporary philosophy at least, they are not much reflected upon.

For the most part, it seems, such sayings are taken to indicate that philosophy has its starting point, understood in terms of its motivational or psychological impetus, in puzzlement or curiosity at some feature or features of the world. Yet while puzzlement and curiosity are undoubtedly an important part of philosophical experience, to say that it is wonder in the sense of puzzlement and curiosity alone that stand as the origin of philosophy seems inadequate both to the character of philosophy itself and to the character of wonder. If philosophy is to be more than a mere game, but an activity into which one is drawn because of the demanding nature of the issues it addresses – because of the way one is inevitably given over to caring about those issues – then mere puzzlement seems not to be a good description of that out of which philosophy first arises. If wonder is itself something that can capture us, that can enthrall and enrapture, as it surely can, then wonder must be more than puzzlement, more than curiosity.

The way that Plato and Aristotle themselves talk of the phenomenon of wonder seems to confirm that it is, indeed, not just puzzlement or curiosity that is at issue here. "He was not a bad genealogist who said that Iris [the rainbow/

messenger of heaven] is the child of Thaumas [wonder]" says Plato's Socrates,[4] while Aristotle goes on, in the *Metaphysics*, to say that "even the lover of myth [*philomythos*] is in a sense a lover of Wisdom [*philosophos*], for the myth is composed of wonders."[5] It is surely not wonder in the sense of puzzlement alone that the myth evokes; nor does curiosity seem a likely relative of the rainbow. Moreover, talk of wonder as that in which philosophy has its beginning is unlikely to mean, in the Platonic and Aristotelian context, merely that which serves as the psychological impetus towards the activity of philosophizing. For the Greeks especially, the idea of beginning or origin is not just the idea of a temporal starting-point, but also of that which determines the very nature of the thing whose origin or beginning it is. Aristotle explicitly connects these ideas when he tells us that "the nature of a thing is a beginning."[6] The Greek word *arche* (αρχη) captures just this idea of beginning or origin as also determining "cause" or first principle.

Talk of wonder as the beginning or origin of philosophy does not imply that philosophy is primarily about wonder or that there is a need for a "philosophy of wonder" as somehow the true and proper basis of philosophy, nor does it mean that philosophy can only ever be properly carried on while in a state of wonderment or that puzzlement and curiosity have no role to play in philosophical activity. Talk of wonder as the beginning of philosophy should rather be taken to indicate something about the character of philosophy as such, and so about its nature and limit, about that to which it is a response and so that to which it must be adequate. Inasmuch as wonder is taken to be "the feeling of the philosopher," so wonder must be that which is determinative of philosophy and philosophical activity, that which is its proper "measure," and to which it must, in some sense, always return. But what then is wonder, such that it may be the origin of philosophy? And what is philosophy, if wonder is its origin?

Appearance and encounter

Wonder can take a number of forms. We may wonder *at* things, but we can also wonder *about* them. In this latter sense our wondering takes the form of a questioning that may itself be a response to an initial astonishment, puzzlement or curiosity – to wonder about things may thus mean no more than to puzzle over them, to think about them or to seek some explanation for them. The sense of wonder at issue in Plato and Aristotle, however, is no mere wondering about, but rather the wonder that is indeed a response to things and to the world – the sort of wonder that is experienced, for instance, in the sight of the rainbow as it shines through a wet, cloudy, but suddenly sunlit sky.

Although they may well be associated with it, and so should not be viewed as irrelevant here, mere puzzlement and curiosity are indeed quite distinct from this sort of wonder. A clear demonstration of this distinction is given by the fact that we may be struck by wonder at some phenomenon in spite of being satisfied with our understanding and explanation of it. A rainbow, for instance, can inspire wonder in a way that is quite unaffected by the knowledge that it is produced by the refraction of sunlight through droplets of water in the atmosphere. This is important to note, since Aristotle, for one, clearly does not ignore the role wonder may play in giving rise to a search for explanations of just this sort, and yet wonder also seems to involve more than just this.

The point is not that wonder has no connection with this sort of "desire to know" (or with the puzzlement that may be associated with it), but rather that the satisfaction of such a desire does not exhaust the original wonder from which it may have arisen. Wonder proper should perhaps be viewed, then, as standing apart, not only from mere puzzlement or curiosity, but also from certain forms of astonishment or amazement, since the latter, while they can be used in ways that make them near synonyms with wonder, often carry a stronger suggestion of a temporary baulking of the ability to explain, understand or predict. Wonder is, in fact, consistent with both ignorance *and* understanding (this is something, as we shall see below, crucial to the character of wonder as such); it involves a way of seeing the world, and the things in it, that is independent of what one may know or what one can explain, even though, it may also have an important role in making knowledge or explanation possible.

Plato, as we have seen, associates wonder with the rainbow (Iris, "the messenger of heaven").[7] And the association seems particularly apt, since the experience of wonder goes hand-in-hand with the experience of things as suddenly illuminated or lit up – with the experience of things as shining forth into the world around them. Emmanuel Levinas comments on this by connecting the experience of wonder directly with the experience of light:

> The contact with light, the act of opening one's eyes, the lighting up of bare sensation, are apparently outside any relationship, and do not take form like answers to questions. Light illuminates and is naturally understood; it is comprehension itself. But within this natural correlation between us and the world, in a sort of doubling back, a question arises, a being surprised by this illumination. The wonder which Plato put at the origin of philosophy is an astonishment before the natural and the intelligible. It is the very intelligibility of light that is astonishing; light is doubled up with a sight. The astonishment does not arise out of comparison with some order more natural than nature, but simply before intelligibility itself. Its strangeness is, we might say, due to its very reality, to the very fact there is existence.[8]

There is a long philosophical tradition – one as old as philosophy itself – that associates light with intelligibility, and there is certainly something powerful, at least to those of us who are sighted, about the use of visual metaphors and images in this context.[9] But Levinas' point here would probably be almost as well served by reference to any other medium or mode of experience – think of the sudden *presencing* of things in a particular taste, a touch, a sound, a movement. What is at issue here is not only wonder at light and sight, but wonder as a response to the often sudden and striking *encounter* with things – whether it be light refracted through droplets of water in the sky, the explosion of taste in a mouthful of wine, the heady scent of blossoms on the still night, the experience of the open-ness of space and the capacities of the body in the exhilaration of a dance, or the complex interplay of elements in a piece of music. In each case, it is the encounter – and the character of that encounter as a revealing, an opening up, of things and of the world – that seems to lie at the heart of the experience of wonder.

Wonder is thus not so much a response to any particular appearance or set of appearances, although it always requires some such appearance as its focus and its immediate cause, as it is the response that is evoked in us by the very recognition of appearance as such (whether or not that recognition is well or clearly articulated). And if that recognition, and the wonder that accompanies it, is most often evoked by the beautiful, the tremendous, the elegant or the sublime, then this is perhaps because of the way in which these forms of appearance call attention, most immediately and directly, to their own appearing, to the fact of their being encountered. One is brought to a halt by the appearance, and forced to attend to it, not because it shows something else (as it may indicate some use, purpose or cause), nor because of anything that explains how it is (the processes or conditions that give rise to it), but merely by the fact *that* it is. The wondrousness of the rainbow thus resides in the very fact of its being; the wonder we experience in the face of someone we love lies in the simple fact of their existence and our encounter with them.

The encounter with the extraordinary that often gives rise to wonder – the encounter with the wondrous in its most strikingly immediate forms such as the sublime or the beautiful – brings suddenly to our attention the very fact of encounter. Yet in bringing such encounter to the fore, what is brought forward is not itself something that is extraordinary or unusual, but rather something that is itself "ordinary" and everyday. All of our activity, all of our existence, is constituted in terms of such encounter, although for the most part it is given little notice, and such encounter makes up the very fabric of our lives. In every act we touch something, respond to it, move in relation to it, and our lives are constituted by such encounter and response as if those lives were made up of the reciprocating movements between interconnected threads in a dense and intricate web. Inasmuch as the wonder that arises in the experience of the extraordinary brings such encounter into view, and so brings into view something that may be viewed as the most ordinary and ubiquitous of phenomena – such that it may seem trivial and unilluminating to draw attention to it – so it also shows such an encounter to be itself extraordinary and even strange.

One might say that while wonder is often immediately evoked by that which is self-evidently remarkable or extraordinary, that which is most remarkable, and which is present in every experience of wonder *as* remarkable, is nothing other than the simple fact of encounter, of intelligibility, of being. But in that case, wonder needs nothing "special" to bring it about. Thus Heidegger says of the "thinking of being" which he takes to be fundamental to philosophy that it

> does not require a solemn approach and the pretension of arcane erudition, nor the display of rare and exceptional states as in mystical raptures, reveries and swoonings. All that is needed is simple wakefulness in the presence of any random unobtrusive being, an awakening that all of a sudden sees that the being "is."[10]

Thus, while wonder may often be evoked by the self-evidently extraordinary, it may also arise out of the simple, sudden, immediate awareness of the existence of some thing; out of the recognition of the questionability, the strangeness, the wondrousness of things, and of our encounter with them, as it occurs in the most common and ordinary of ways. Indeed, this is surely wonder at its most basic; the wonder of which Blake seems implicitly to speak in *Auguries of Innocence*: "To see a World in a grain of sand, / And a Heaven in a wild flower, / Hold infinity in the palm of your hand, / And Eternity in an hour."[11] The experience of wonder might thus be understood as encompassing all those modes of encounter in which the ordinary is made remarkable, in which the extraordinary spills over into the mundane, in which the familiar becomes strange.

Often, of course, it is precisely the transformation in experience that comes with wonder (and to which Blake's lines give voice) – whether through the ordinary or the extraordinary – that has been the aim of poetry and art. "In the poetry of the poet," says Heidegger, "and in the thinking of the thinker, there is always so much world-space to spare that each and every thing – a tree, a mountain, a house, the call of a bird – completely loses its indifference and familiarity."[12] Yet if philosophy has its origins in the wonder that art and poetry may be seen as aiming to evoke, it surely does not aim at bringing such a state about. Philosophy may have its origins in the experience of the transformation of the world – its lighting up – that comes with wonder, but it is a *response to* that transformation, not its *cause*. Of course, poetry and art can also be seen as responsive, but they nevertheless have a mimetic quality that philosophy lacks – a mimetic quality that means that while poetry and art are responsive, they are also themselves "affective." Thus the artistic or poetic moment can be seen as "re-presenting" the moment of encounter or appearance in a way that makes it available to us in a renewed (or sometimes "new") form and thereby providing us with something that is itself the occasion for wonder.[13] Philosophy, for the most part, lacks any such "mimetic" character, but instead responds to that which appears, and to the moment of appearance, by way of exploration and articulation of that appearance and the moment, the region, the world, within which it occurs.[14] It is easy, nevertheless, to mistake philosophy for poetry, or *vice versa*, just because of the way in which each stands in an essential relation to the event of appearance and encounter, and so to wonder and the wondrous. It is also easy to reject or trivialize the origin of philosophy in wonder precisely out of a desire to prevent just such a confusion – although to do so is to commit no less an error.

Inasmuch as wonder arises out of the event of encounter as that event is brought strikingly to awareness – thereby showing the ordinary as *extra*ordinary, the familiar as strange – so wonder also constitutes a sudden awareness of our own existence, not as something separate or apart from the encounter nor from that which is encountered, but as already given over to it. The experience of the wondrous is an experience in which we find ourselves already moved, already affected, already opened up to what is before us. It requires no effort on our part, no decision or act. The experience of wonder is an experience of our being already given over to the world and the things in it. In this sense the experience of wonder is indeed, as Levinas says of the experience of light, "apparently outside of any relationship." Just as the experience of opening one's eyes is an experience of the immediate coming to visual presence of things – not the experience of the establishing of some relation, but of things being, simply, "there" – so the experience of wonder is the experience of ourselves as already in the sway of wonder, of ourselves as already "there" along with the wondrous.

In wonder, we encounter things in a way that is prior to encounter as any sort of *relating* to things; the encounter that wonder brings into view is just our being already *with* things, already given over to them and them to us. Thus Levinas talks of the "natural correlation between us and the world" – although such talk of correlation, no matter how "natural," undoubtedly suggests a sense of "co-relation" that must fail to capture what is really at issue. If there is a "natural correlation" between us and the world, it is a correlation that consists in nothing more than the fact of our already being "in" the world. In the experience of wonder it is thus our being already "in" that comes to the fore – our being already "there" in the very same place as the things themselves. In our wonder at the rainbow, we find ourselves already in the world and in no need of finding some way to relate to it, to come into coordination with it, to make contact with it. The world is there, and us with it and a part of it, just as we are there with the rainbow, and so with sky and cloud, wind and rain, earth and rock, animal and plant, friend and stranger. In wonder, even in the wondrousness of some single thing, the world is itself brought to appearance and with it our own prior belonging to that world. In this respect, while in wonder things are indeed "made strange," we do not thereby find ourselves "out of place." The "making strange" that occurs in wonder is a making strange of our very belonging inasmuch as that belonging is itself brought to light.

The experience of wonder that I have so far been describing is closely akin to the experience that Hans-Georg Gadamer describes as present in the experience of art[15] – and that he also finds elaborated in Heidegger's famous essay on "The Origin of the Work of Art."[16] Wonder is something that overtakes us, in which we are caught up, and in which we are given over to the wondrous; similarly, the artwork is not some "thing" that stands over against us, but rather something that "happens" to us and into which we are drawn. In the artwork,

JEFF MALPAS

moreover, we find a form of self-revealing on the part of the work itself that opens up a space in which we encounter something that goes beyond the work – a self-revealing that illuminates the world in which the work stands, as well as our own standing before that work and in that world. The artwork thus always exceeds anything that either the artist or the audience might intend in the work and so always bring with it a certain startlement or surprise:

> The work of art that says something confronts us itself. That is, it expresses something in such a way that what is said is like a discovery, a disclosure of something previously concealed. The element of surprise is based on this. "So true, so filled with being" (So wahr, so seiend) is not something one knows in any other way. Everything familiar is eclipsed.[17]

Gadamer takes the working of art, in this respect, to be exemplary of the experience of understanding and so of the very experience of encounter or appearance. Indeed, at the end of *Truth and Method*, Gadamer uses the concept of the beautiful – understood as "radiance," as that which self-evidently "shines forth"[18] – to explore the character of self-evidence that belongs to that which is intelligible or encounterable. Like beauty, understanding or encounter is an event in which something appears in and of itself, an event in which one finds oneself already caught up, an event that can surprise and surpass.

Gadamer says of beauty that it has the mode of being of *light*, but just as Levinas' use of light in illustrating the character of wonder need not be taken to indicate something that is exclusive to the visual alone, neither should Gadamer's comments be taken to indicate that the beautiful is only to be found within the domain of sight. In both cases, the image or metaphor of light is itself used to reveal something about the wondrous and the beautiful, which we can now see to be themselves closely related, namely, the way in which both are tied to the "self-presencing" of things in appearance or in encounter. The beautiful, then, in the sense Gadamer employs it, is that which is self-evidently apparent; wonder is that in which we find ourselves caught up in our response to such self-evident appearance.

Inasmuch as we find ourselves, in the experience of wonder, already caught up in response, and so, indeed, as already belonging to the world, so we find ourselves already caught up in care for and concern about that world. Wonder is thus a symptom of our prior commitment and involvement, since, although wonder may be possible only when we have the freedom of a certain degree of contemplation (Aristotle emphasizes the way in which philosophy arises only when we have some release from the constant demands of simple survival), it is out of our commitment and involvement that the "desire to know" itself arises. Moreover, as the desire to know drives philosophical activity, so philosophy is itself driven by our being already given over to the world in this way – it is, as I noted in the introduction, because we are already taken up by the issues with which philosophy deals that philosophy is more than a mere game, more than a simple "distraction." Yet inasmuch as the "desire to know," along with philosophy itself, arises out of our prior commitment and involvement in the world, then so we may say that this desire, and philosophical activity as such, only has content and significance insofar as that content and significance is supplied by the concrete circumstances of our involvement, of our being there, of our prior belonging to the world.

Recognition of this point can help to clarify the way in which wonder can be a response to the very fact of encounter or appearance, and so to our prior belonging, and yet it is nevertheless always directed towards some particular appearance, some particular feature or aspect of the world. It is not the world in general that preoccupies us, but the world in its specificity; and, similarly, it is not the world in general that immediately evokes wonder, but some part or aspect of the world. It is, however, through the part – through the particular thing or event – that the whole is brought to light; it is through the particular encounter or appearance that the fact of encounter or appearance as such is brought into view. In wonder, then, there is not merely the doubling up of light with sight, as Levinas puts it, but also the doubling up which is analogous to this, namely, the doubling up of the thing that appears with the appearing itself – what Heidegger refers to as "the twofoldness of what is present and of presence."[19] Properly then, it is this double "appearance" – of that which appears along with the appearing – that is the stimulus to wonder as well as its focus.

Strangeness and questionability

In the terms Levinas uses in the passage quoted above, and that are also echoed in Gadamer's discussion of the beautiful, wonder arises out of a response to the event of "intelligibility" – the event of our encounter with things, the event of experience – in which that event is itself brought to the centre of attention. Wonder is a response to existence, to being, that is brought about by the recognition of existence in the sheer fact of something's existing. Yet if the experience of wonder is a response to intelligibility, existence, encounter, and an experience of the very fact of encounter, then it also involves, as Levinas points out, and as Gadamer may also be taken to confirm, a certain surprise, a questioning, in the face of such encounter. Thus wonder halts us, and, like the stars Hamlet describes as brought to a standstill by the grief of Laertes at the death of Ophelia, we are "wonder-wounded."[20] In this respect, the experience of wonder, and the encounter with the wondrous, represents a sudden disabling, an intrusion into our normal activities and a disruption of those activities. The experience of wonder thus takes us out of our ordinary involvement with things and makes what is ordinarily unquestioned, questionable, makes what ordinarily seems familiar, strange.

It is precisely this aspect of wonder, this "making strange," that makes it natural to connect wonder, even if the connection is also misleading, with the experience of puzzlement. But the questionability and strangeness at issue here cannot be dispelled by any solution, since what is at issue – what is rendered strange – is the very fact of appearance and of encounter. Of course, this experience of things "made strange" may also give rise to philosophical (and even scientific) activity: in the face of our prior involvement, and so our prior care and concern, the strangeness and questionability of things constitutes a source of discomfort that we ordinarily seek to resolve or dispel through the search for answers and explanations. Yet while such activity may result in an explanation of that which is the immediate cause and focus for wonder (the rainbow, for instance), and so for the strangeness and questionability that accompanies it, such explanation does not touch that which is the underlying source of wonder, namely, appearance or encounter as such. Indeed, the fact that the surprise and questionability that seem so closely associated with wonder may be present, even when the phenomenon at issue is apparently well understood, can itself be most readily explained by pointing to the distinction between a particular phenomenon (say, the rainbow) and its phenomenal character as such (its appearing or being encountered). To elucidate the former is not to elucidate the latter.

Here, once more, we find the "doubling up" that we saw above, but now the doubling of that which appears with the appearing is matched by a doubling of two modes of strangeness that correspond to these. The strangeness of that which appears leads on to explanation, or may already be satisfied by an existing explanation, but the strangeness of the appearing is amenable to no such resolution. In this respect, wonder may give rise to puzzlement, and puzzlement to explanation, and yet the wonder, and the underlying strangeness, may nevertheless remain. Of course, for just this reason, the strangeness that is present in wonder need not always be doubled: when we encounter what is ordinary and familiar – what is understood and already explicable – as remarkable, strange and wondrous, then the "doubling" of that which appears with the appearing, of that which is encountered with the encounter, is matched, not by two modes of strangeness, but rather by the coupling of the remarkable and the *ordinary*, of the strange and the *familiar*, of that which is outside of any explanation and that which is *explicable*.

There is no way in which one can get behind the simple fact of appearance or encounter, the simple "given-ness" of things,[21] in order to find something more basic from the standpoint of which such encounter, such given-ness, might itself be investigated. That is not to say that we do not often try to do just this (indeed, a large part of philosophy is made up of just such attempts), but rather that to try to do so is already to have misunderstood the basic situation in which we find ourselves. In the experience of wonder what is brought strikingly to awareness is the event of appearing and encounter through a particular instance of such appearing or encounter. As such, what is also made evident is our own prior belonging to the world, our being "always already" *there*, and yet, in being made evident in this way, our "being-there" is also rendered strange.

We may well be able to describe and explain aspects of our concrete situation, both in general and in particular, and yet we can neither describe or explain that situation in its entirety (since there is always more that could be said and more that could be asked) and nor can we even begin to explain the fact of our situatedness as such (since we can never stand outside or apart from such situatedness).[22] Our "being there," the very fact of our situatedness, cannot properly be made the object of any explanation, and yet it is just such situatedness or belonging – our already "being-there" alongside things, in the encounter with things – that lies at the heart of the experience of wonder and that provides the impetus to explanation with which wonder is also associated.

Plato's association of wonder with the rainbow, and Levinas' treatment of wonder as like the experience of light, both suggest a conception of wonder as associated with visibility and *transparency*. Yet inasmuch as wonder is also associated with the inexplicable fact of our situatedness, so it is bound up, not merely with transparency, but also with a certain failure of transparency, with a certain *opacity*. In wonder, our "being there" is suddenly "lit up," and yet in being illuminated, it is also shown as essentially dark – while we can "see into" the intricacies of the world and our situation in it, that there is a world, and that we are already given over to it, is absolutely impenetrable. Our "being there," our situatedness, on the basis of which the transparency of encounter and of appearance is possible, cannot itself be made transparent, and thus, inasmuch as light is "doubled up" with sight, as that which appears is "doubled up" with the appearing, so also is transparency "doubled up" with opacity.

That there is such opacity here does not indicate, however, some "blindness" on our part, some defect in our intellectual "vision," for there simply is nothing here that can be an object of such vision. The opacity at issue thus represents the proper bound that limits the capacity for explanation and for questioning; inasmuch as it is tied to the situatedness on the basis of which any encounter or appearance, and so any explanation or question, is possible, so it can also be said to limit and to make possible transparency itself. In Gadamer and Heidegger, of course, the interplay between transparency and opacity that here appears as a fundamental element in wonder also appears, as a fundamental ontological structure (albeit in somewhat different form), in terms of the interplay of concealing and unconcealing that is the event of truth.[23] For Gadamer and Heidegger, this "event" is constitutive of the open-ness of the world on the basis of which any particular statement can be true or false or any particular thing can be present or absent. Thus, just as opacity can be said to underlie transparency, so, in the terms Gadamer and Heidegger employ, concealment can be said to underlie open-ness or unconcealment.

The impossibility of arriving at any complete "transparency" in respect of our situatedness, our "being-there," may be seen as identical with the difficulty that accompanies the attempt to make sense of subjectivity within a pure objective or "naturalistic" framework – a difficulty (though it is not always seen as such) that is associated with various forms of reductionism, materialism and perhaps also with the so-called "problem of consciousness." It would be presumptuous, however, to suppose that this means that it is *subjectivity* that is the problem here – at least so long as one thinks of subjectivity in terms of some inner "mental" realm of "thought," idea or consciousness. It is not that subjectivity brings a lack of transparency with it, but rather that such subjectivity is itself always situated, already given over to the world, and it is just this situatedness that gives rise to a lack of transparency. To be situated is always to stand in such a way that one is oriented towards some things and not others, it is to find some aspects of the world salient and others not, it is to find oneself literally "there." It is "being there," in this sense, that is the central element in subjectivity, and subjectivity does not underlie or explain such "being there."

Just as light illuminates, and yet, in illuminating, is not itself illuminated, so our situatedness, our "being-there," opens up the world, and us to it, and yet is itself hidden and closed off. In this respect, we may say that it is our situatedness that enables and yet also restricts our capacity for explanation; and similarly it is wonder, as a response to the sudden and striking awareness of our situatedness, that stimulates the desire for explanation, and yet also brings explanation to a halt. In wonder, then, explanation finds its origin and its absolute limit, and, consequently, part of the experience of wonder is finding oneself in the somewhat paradoxical situation of being confronted by that which seems both to demand explanation and yet also resists, and indeed stands prior to, such explanation – we are thus led to question while having no capacity to answer. As Levinas says of the question of being (which is one way in which the questionability at issue in the experience of wonder may be expressed):

> The questioning of Being is an experience of Being in its strangeness.
> It is then a way of taking up Being. That is why the question about
> Being – What is Being? – has never been answered. There is no answer
> to Being.[24]

If there is no answer here, then it may be mistaken to suppose that there is really a question. Perhaps what Levinas should be taken to be pointing towards is just the way in which what is at issue is an experience of strangeness – the strangeness of our prior belonging. The strangeness at issue is rather like the strangeness that arises when, as a child, one asks oneself how it is that one is *oneself*, that one belongs just *here*? Such questions are only questions in a somewhat peculiar and perhaps attenuated sense, since not only do they have no possible answers, but it is not clear what form answers could take nor is it obvious that answers (at least not to those questions) are actually what is required.

Focusing, not on being, but on the world and reason, Merleau-Ponty writes:

> The world and reason are not problematical. We may say, if we wish,
> that they are mysterious, but their mystery defines them: there can be

no question of dispelling it by some "solution," it is on the hither side of all solutions.[25]

The distinction Merleau-Ponty makes here between the "problematical" and what we may choose to call the "mysterious" (a distinction that echoes Gabriel Marcel's famous contrast between the "problematic" and the "mysterious"[26]) has a particular relevance to the discussion of wonder and the nature of the questioning that may arise in the face of wonder. For what wonder reveals, namely, our prior belonging to the world, is something that we may choose to call mysterious and marvelous, and yet, although it may give rise to questioning and surprise, is not itself something that can ever properly be put into question. The encounter with things and with the world is thus not rendered "uncertain" by the experience of wonder. On the contrary, wonder is the response to the immediacy and reality of encounter, of intelligibility, of existence. It returns us to the world (a world that we never properly leave), rather than taking us away from the world or the world from us. Consequently, although wonder involves a certain experience of strangeness, it does not involve estrangement from the world, but rather, constitutes a recognition of our prior belonging to the world – what appears as strange is just that prior belonging. It is just such belonging that leads us on to question and to explain, that makes such questioning and explanation significant, that makes it *matter*.

The return of philosophy

If the origin of a thing is what determines it, then the beginning of a thing is both its limit and also its end. The beginning of philosophy in wonder is thus significant, not because it tells us how it is that philosophy happens to come about, but rather because it tells us something about what philosophy is, about what it is not, about that at which it is directed, about that which constitutes its proper concern. Of course, in talking about "philosophy" here, we are not talking about everything that may possibly fall under this label. "Philosophy" names an institutional entity that is, in part, defined simply by a certain set of socio-cultural circumstances, and that may also change with those circumstances; "philosophy" also names a range of problems, activities, and concerns that may vary from one thinker, one time, one place to another. The word "philosophy" is thus employed here with all of this in mind, and yet in a way that nevertheless holds to the idea that "philosophy" does name something distinctive that is roughly continuous from the Greeks through to the present and that, whatever the various expressions and incarnations it may go through, remains centrally bound up with the experience of wonder found in Plato and Aristotle. But what more, then, can be said about philosophy, if it does indeed have its origin, and so also its end and limit, in the kind of wonder that has been explored and elaborated upon above?

Inasmuch as it begins in wonder, then philosophy has its origin in a response to the original event of encounter in which we find ourselves already given over to the world and to the things in it. In the experience of the wondrous we are brought face-to-face with that event in a particularly striking way. The experience of wonder, while it is on the one hand an experience of the accessibility and transparency of the world – in wonder we are brought to awareness of the self-evident appearing of things through some particular instance of such self-evident appearance – is also an experience of the strangeness of that accessibility and transparency. The experience of transparency always remains opaque and the more striking is our awareness of it, the more opaque does it seem. The experience of wonder is thus an experience of the way in which, to revert to Levinas' metaphor, the lighting up of things, their intelligibility, brings with it an essential and impenetrable darkness. It is not the darkness that arises through lack of light, but the darkness that arises as a consequence of light – like the darkness that stands behind the lit object itself, the darkness that stands behind the source of light.

Yet although philosophy arises out of the experience of this transparency and opacity as they occur together, it seems as if it has often tended to lose sight of this interplay and so of the real nature of the experience of wonder in which it begins. Thus contemporary philosophy, insofar as it reflects on the matter at all, does indeed tend to interpret its wondrous origin as indicating an origin in puzzlement, questioning and curiosity, rather than in the wonder that has been at issue in the discussion above. Yet such puzzlement, questioning and curiosity is not characterized by an experience of transparency as it is also bound to opacity, but rather of an opacity that increasingly gives way to transparency – puzzlement thus gives way to solution, questioning gives rise to answers, curiosity leads on to knowledge. Even if complete transparency is never actually achieved, still it is such complete transparency that is the paradigm. Moreover, when opacity does come to the fore in much contemporary philosophical discussion, it typically does so in a way that rules out the possibility of transparency – in a way that is, indeed, often intended to cast doubt on such transparency. Thus contemporary skepticism and relativism, which might be taken to arise out of a recognition of the inevitability of opacity and the impossibility of complete transparency, do not give recognition to the interplay and reciprocity between opacity and transparency, but instead remain fixated on a contrast between opacity and transparency understood as mutually exclusive alternatives – a contrast that seems only to be resolved on the side of opacity.

To construe matters in this way, however, is not merely to find oneself already cut off from the experience of wonder, but also as alienated from the world – indeed, in this respect, the very desire for transparency seems to lead to a loss in the capacity to see how transparency can ever be possible. Philosophy may thus begin in wonder, but inasmuch as the demand for explanation constitutes a demand for illumination and transparency, so it can also come to constitute a blindness to the interdependence between transparency and opacity, and so also a blindness to the prior belonging to the world that first drives the demand for explanation as such. In this respect, philosophy begins in wonder, but it often ends in alienation – alienation from self, from others, and from ordinary things, as well as the extraordinary. Such alienation is not just a matter of the experience of philosophical difficulty in understanding or explaining how there can be knowledge of the external world or of other minds or of one's own "mental states," but also of how philosophical activity can connect up with the fundamental and everyday experiences of human life, with the things that drive us, that affect us, that matter to us.

Historically, it was a desire to return philosophical thinking to the problems of "life" – understood not in terms of some category of *Lebensphilosophie*, but of life as that which takes us up, that makes demands on us, in which we already find ourselves immersed – that drove the work of the young Heidegger and that also led to Gadamer's own engagement with him in the 1920s.[27] It was in this light that Heidegger appropriated the phenomenology of Edmund Husserl, using it, not as a means to develop philosophy as a more rigorous "science," but instead as providing a path back to our original, "hermeneutic" situatedness, to our original encounter with things, to our original being "there." Heidegger's thought was always directed towards such a "turning back" to that situatedness, a turning back to the original happening of being and of truth. In this respect, Heidegger can be viewed as attempting to return to that which is also evident to us in the experience of wonder. Indeed, Heidegger himself says of wonder that it:

> displaces man into and before beings as such. . . . Wonder is the basic disposition that primordially disposes man into the beginning of thinking, because, before all else, it displaces man into that essence whereby he then finds himself caught up in the midst of beings as such and as a whole and finds himself caught up in them.[28]

In returning to recognize the origin of philosophy in wonder, we can see the significance of and motivation behind the sort of philosophical "revolution" that Heidegger attempted. Moreover, in returning to recognize the origin of philosophy in wonder, it also becomes possible to see how the philosophical preoccupation with transparency, and so with opacity as its alternative, first arises, as well as to recognize its deeply problematic character. Transparency is a misguided ideal, and opacity is not so much a barrier to understanding as it is, in part, its enabling condition.

Wonder is not the primary focus of philosophical inquiry or reflection, and yet there can be nothing more fundamental to philosophy than the event of encounter and appearance, and, with it, the interplay of opacity and trans- parency, that comes to the fore in the experience of wonder. It is this that is properly the end of philosophy in the sense of being that to which philosophy must finally address itself. Inasmuch as this event is not something that can itself be rendered transparent – inasmuch as it remains irreducibly opaque – then here philosophy comes up against its own proper bound and limit.

Moreover, while the experience of wonder may be unusual, and the event of encounter or appearance may itself be experienced, in the throes of wonder, as itself extraordinary and remarkable, still in being brought to awareness of such encounter or experience, we are brought to awareness of something that is indeed the most mundane, the most ordinary, the most ubiquitous of "happenings." In this respect, philosophy does not begin in something out of the ordinary, but in the bringing to awareness of the most ordinary; it does not find its limit in something that transcends our everyday experience, but in the very "being there" of that experience; it does not find its "end" in a space or time beyond, but only in this place – the place in which it already finds itself, which it never properly leaves, and in which there is always something further to explore. Wonder is thus a returning, sometimes with the abruptness of a sudden shock, to the world to which we always, already belong – it is in that return that philosophy begins and to which it must always itself go back.

Notes

1 Aristotle, *Metaphysics*, 982b11–12.
2 Plato, *Theatatus*, 155d.
3 R. W. Hepburn provides some indication of the extent to which the importance of wonder has been acknowleged throughout the western philosophical tradition in his "Wonder," in *"Wonder" and Other Essays*, Edinburgh, University of Edinburgh Press, 1984, pp. 131–54.
4 Plato, *Theatatus*, 155d.
5 Aristotle, *Metaphysics*, 982b19–20.
6 *Metaphysics*, 1013a20.
7 Iris can refer to the goddess or to the rainbow or to both. Whereas the other messenger of the gods, Hermes, had his winged helmet and sandals to enable him to move between heaven and earth, Iris used the rainbow as her bridge between the two realms. Iris had the dubious distinction of being the messenger who brought discord, whereas Hermes brought peace.
8 Emmanuel Levinas, *Existence and Existents*, trans. A. Lingis, The Hague, Martinus Nijhoff, 1978, p. 22.
9 See Hans-Georg Gadamer's discussion of light and radiance in connection with beauty and intelligibility in *Truth and Method*, trans. Joel Weinsheimer and Donald G. Marshall, New York, Crossroad, 1989, 2nd rev. edn., pp. 480–7. Gadamer's treatment of this issue will be mentioned briefly below.
10 Martin Heidegger, *Parmenides*, trans. André Scuwer and Richard Rojcewicz, Bloomington, Indiana University Press, 1992, p. 149.
11 "Poems from the Pickering MS," in *Blake: Complete Writings*, Geoffrey Keynes (ed.), London, Oxford University Press, 1966, p. 431. The ideas of eternity and infinity invoked by Blake may be taken to suggest a notion of transcendence that is sometimes taken to be an element of the experience of wonder, as well as of other phenomena, and that is itself worthy of investigation in its own right. See especially R. W. Hepburn, "Time Transcendence and Some Related Phenomena in the Arts," in Hepburn, *"Wonder" and Other Essays*, pp. 108–30. Gadamer takes a certain "time-transcendence" or, better, the transcendence of "ordinary" time and the emergence of, as he puts it, "fulfilled" or "autonomous" time, particularly as it is associated with the festival, as an important element in the experience of art, see "The Relevance of

the Beautiful," in *The Relevance of the Beautiful and Other Essays*, trans. Robert Bernasconi, Cambridge, Cambridge University Press, 1986, pp. 41–5.

12 Martin Heidegger, *An Introduction to Metaphysics*, trans. Gregory Fried and Richard Polt, New Haven, Yale University Press, 2000, p. 28.

13 Notice that this form of "mimesis" is not mere "imitation," but *realization*. See Gadamer's discussion of mimesis in *Truth and Method*, pp. 110–21.

14 David Rothenberg writes of the difference between philosophy and poetry that:

> It is not that one seeks to explain, while the other evokes. It is that the former must ask and ask, and keep on asking, until our very sense of perplexity becomes exact, complete, not solvable, but a place to contemplate and inhabit through *wonder*, a positive word, a state of grace, an excited way of loving the world.

(David Rothenberg, "Melt the Snowflake at Once! Toward a History of Wonder," in Edward F. Mooney (ed.), *Wilderness and the Heart*, Athens GA, University of Georgia Press, 1999, p. 20

15 Gadamer, *Truth and Method*, pp. 101–69.

16 See Hans-Georg Gadamer, "The Truth of the Work of Art," in *Philosophical Hermeneutics*, trans. and ed. David E. Linge, Berkeley, University of California Press, 1976, pp. 213–28; and Heidegger, "The Origin of the Work of Art," in *Off the Beaten Track*, trans. Julian Young and Kenneth Haynes, Cambridge, Cambridge University Press, 2002, pp. 1–56.

17 Gadamer, "Aesthetics and Hermeneutics," in *Philosophical Hermeneutics*, p. 101.

18 In German, the word *scheinen*, meaning to shine as well as to appear, is itself related to the word *schön*, meaning beautiful.

19 Martin Heidegger, "Cézanne," in *Denkerfahrungen 1910–1976*, Frankfurt, Klostermann, 1983, p. 163.

20 See *Hamlet*, Act V, Scene 1:

> What is he, whose grief
> Bears such an emphasis, whose phrase of sorrow
> Conjures the wand'ring stars, and makes them stand
> Like wonder-wounded hearers?

Shakespeare's conjoining of "wonder" and "wound" may be taken to reflect a deeper etymological connection. As Howard Parsons speculates:

> Wonder, from the old English *wundor*, might be cognate with the German *Wunde* or *wound*. It would thus suggest a breach in the membrane of awareness, a sudden opening in a man's system of established and expected meanings, a blow as if one were struck or stunned. To be wonderstruck is to be wounded by the sword of the strange event, to be stabbed awake by the striking.

(Howard L. Parsons, "A Philosophy of Wonder," *Philosophy and Phenomenological Research* 30, 1969–70, p. 85)

21 Note that the "given-ness" at issue here, namely, our prior belonging to the world, is not the same "given-ness" as is at issue in Sellars' famous "myth of the given" – see Wilfrid Sellars, *Empiricism and the Philosophy of Mind*, Cambridge MA, Harvard University Press, 1997. The latter consists in the idea that there must be some level of immediacy (sense-data, "experiences," facts, etc.) that provides the non-inferential basis for knowledge, and as such the "myth of the given" remains a response within an essentially epistemological framework according to which our prior belonging is already, in some sense or other, in question.

22 It is important to note that our inability to escape from our situatedness does not mean an inability to escape from the particular details of our situation, but only an inability to escape from, and so to make an object of explanation, the fact of situat-edness as such. A failure to appreciate this point often leads to the acceptance of relativist or historicist positions. Similarly, the fact that our being in the world always takes on a particular character and orientation does not make it any less a mode of being in the world or any less a mode of involvement in the world. To be in the world is to be involved with things in certain determinate ways.

23 See, for instance, Gadamer, "The Truth of the Work of Art," especially pp. 225–8. It is important to note that neither Gadamer nor Heidegger need be seen to be rejecting the mundane sense of truth according to which truth is a matter of the correctness of statements. Instead, they point towards a more basic sense of "truth" (assuming that we wish to use the term in this way) as the original event of concealing/revealing.

24 Emmanuel Levinas, *Existence and Existents*, p. 22.

25 Maurice Merleau-Ponty, *Phenomenology of Perception*, trans. Colin Smith, London, Routledge and Kegan Paul, 1962, p. xx.

26 See Gabriel Marcel, *Being and Having*, trans. Katherine Farrer, Boston MA, Beacon Press, 1951, p. 100: "A problem is something met with which bars my passage. It is before me in its entirety. A mystery, on the other hand, is something in which I find myself caught up, and whose essence is therefore not to be met before me in its entirety."

27 See, for instance, Hans-Georg Gadamer, "Reflections on My Philosophical Journey," in Lewis Edwin Hahn (ed.) *The Philosophy of Hans-Georg Gadamer*, Library of Living Philosophers vol. XXIV, Chicago, Open Court, 1997, pp. 8–9.

28 Martin Heidegger, *Basic Questions of Philosophy. Selected Problems of "Logic"*, trans. Richard Rojcewicz and André Schwer, Bloomington, Indiana University Press, 1994, p. 147.

INDEX

303